Michigan and the Cleveland Era

MICHIGAN and the CLEVELAND ERA

Sketches of UNIVERSITY OF MICHIGAN Staff Members and Alumni Who Served the CLEVELAND ADMINISTRATIONS 1885-89, 1893-97

Edited by EARL D. BABST and LEWIS G. VANDER VELDE

ANN ARBOR · THE UNIVERSITY OF MICHIGAN PRESS

1948

PRINTED IN THE U.S.A. BY
AMERICAN BOOK–STRATFORD PRESS, INC., NEW YORK

To the people of the State of Michigan for their unfailing support of the University of Michigan

For the whole earth is the sepulchre of famous men, and their story is not graven only on stone over their native earth but lives far away, without visible symbol, woven into the stuff of other men's lives.

PERICLES (490–429 B.C.)

The founders of a state soon pass away; but in their aims and purposes, and to some extent in their personal characteristics, they build themselves into the structure they create, and give to it a character and individuality of its own. Ages afterwards it may be found that the germinal thoughts which took root under their planting are still growing and expanding, and that the ideas with which they quickened the early polity are dominant in the life of the mature commonwealth, though possibly those who act upon and give effect to them may have lost the recollection of their origin.

THOMAS M. COOLEY (1824–1898 A.D.)

Religion, Morality, and Knowledge, being necessary to good Government and the Happiness of Mankind, Schools and the means of Education shall forever be encouraged.

ORDINANCE OF 1787

Foreword

AMONG the institutions created by man to promote his welfare as a social being, none is more difficult to understand or to describe than is a large university. The characteristics of this educational agency that are most apparent to the casual observer fail to provide the true measure of its importance. Numerous buildings, large numbers of students, many faculty members, a plethora of curricular offerings, and even impressive programs of research and large endowments do not in themselves indicate the success of a university in attaining its fundamental objectives. As a matter of fact, large size often distracts attention from essential activities. Further confusion is caused by the frequent changes in methods logically to be expected in any institution which endeavors to profit by experience and to keep abreast of the ever-growing educational needs of society.

In the last analysis, the fundamental objective of a university is to train men and women to be useful members of an integrated society. This purpose is frequently ignored because of two human tendencies. Many individuals find it easy, somewhere in the course of their preparation for life, to drift into the attitude of mind that their training is first of all to provide advantages for themselves. Again, in this era the large and increasing body of accumulated knowledge encourages others to extreme specialization and compartmentalization of learning, with a corresponding loss of interest in service to mankind.

Certainly, in the American way of life no individual should avoid his responsibilities as a citizen. Hence, one important measure of the success of a university is to be found in the performances of its alumni as public servants. It is with this point of view that this book has been prepared.

The volume does not purport to be a history. It is an account by alumni of the public service given by a group of their fellows in one period of our country's history.

Alexander G. Ruthven

Contents

Michigan and the Cleveland Era

Published under the auspices of the Michigan Historical Collections of the University of Michigan

Grover Cleveland

1837	*Born in Caldwell, New Jersey*
1851	*Worked as clerk in a grocery store in Fayetteville, New York*
1853–54	*Taught in the Institution for the Blind, New York City*
1854	*Moved to Buffalo, New York*
1859	*Admitted to the bar of New York*
1863	*Appointed assistant district attorney, Erie County, New York*
1870	*Elected sheriff of Erie County, New York*
1881	*Elected mayor of Buffalo, New York*
1882	*Elected governor of New York by a majority of more than 192,000*
1884	*Elected President of the United States on the Democratic ticket*
1886	*Married in the White House to Frances Folsom*
1888	*Renominated for the presidency, but defeated by Benjamin Harrison in the election*
1889	*Resumed the practice of law in New York City*
1892	*Re-entered public life with the delivery of an address on George Washington at the University of Michigan*
	Nominated for the presidency, defeating Benjamin Harrison
1893	*Opened World's Columbian Exposition*
1895	*Reasserted the validity of the Monroe Doctrine in his Venezuelan message to Congress*
1897	*On the completion of his second term as President, moved to Princeton, New Jersey*
1905	*Became chairman of the Board of Trustees and directed the reorganization of the Equitable Life Assurance Association, New York*
1907	*Elected president of the Association of Life Insurance Presidents*
1908	*Died in Princeton, New Jersey*

Grover Cleveland

Introduction

MARCH 4, 1885, the day Grover Cleveland became President of the United States, marked a turning point in American history. The inauguration of Cleveland broke the succession of military heroes who had held the presidency since the Civil War; it marked the substitution of presidential dominance for the Congressional dominance which had prevailed for twenty years; most significantly, perhaps, it brought a far more complete change in governmental personnel than had occurred since the inauguration of Lincoln. A new era—the Cleveland Era—had begun.

In this new era University of Michigan men were destined to play a prominent part. Though less than forty years had elapsed since its first degrees had been awarded, the University was one of the largest universities in the land; its great presidents, Henry Philip Tappan and James Burrill Angell, its widely spread alumni body, its pioneering ventures in education, the large number of nationally known scholars on its faculty, and the great success of its Medical and Law Departments had given it unique distinction.

President Cleveland was keenly aware of the unique distinction of the University. As a practicing lawyer in Buffalo, he had come into frequent contact with University of Michigan men; furthermore, he had as one of his chief advisers an alumnus of the University who bore an unswerving loyalty to his alma mater and to its interests. This was Don M. Dickinson, LL.B. 1867, prominent Detroit lawyer.

Dickinson, though not yet forty, had already achieved a national reputation as a political leader. At twenty-five, in the campaign of 1872, he had been a member of the Michigan

Democratic Central Committee; at twenty-nine, its chairman. By 1884 he had become a member of the Democratic National Committee. It was inevitable that his political and civic activities should have early brought him into contact with the Buffalo lawyer, nine years his senior, who had come to be looked upon as the most promising leader of the Democratic party. A staunch friendship developed between the two men, which they maintained loyally. It was to Dickinson, indeed, that the incoming President turned chiefly for advice as to appointments. A shrewd judge of character and ability, Dickinson was adept at proposing for appointment men well qualified not only to hold office but also to advise as to the filling of other offices.

Through the confidence of President Cleveland in the University of Michigan and through the knowledge and acquaintance of Dickinson with its staff and alumni, the University was called upon to make important contributions to the Cleveland Era. Many years later, long after his retirement from public life, Mr. Cleveland in personal reminiscence referred to these contacts in these significant words, "When I was in office and in need of help I usually turned to the University of Michigan." It is with the careers of the men he turned to that the sketches in this volume are concerned.

In University Hall at Ann Arbor Mr. Cleveland made one of the most important and strategic public addresses of his entire career. He had served a first term as President and had been defeated in 1888 by Benjamin Harrison for a second term, largely through the maneuvers of David B. Hill of New York. After this defeat, his plans with respect to re-entering public life had remained undisclosed, until Hill's friends unexpectedly issued a call for a Democratic convention to be held at Albany on February 22, 1892. How Cleveland's followers met this challenge is described by his secretary-biographer, George F. Parker:

> About the time that the Convention call was issued, Mr. Cleveland accepted a long-standing invitation, newly pressed upon him by his friend and former Postmaster-General, Don M. Dickinson, to address

the students of the University of Michigan on Washington's birthday, at the very moment when the Convention of his own State would be nominally condemning him. . . . I had never seen him enter with so keen a relish and enjoyment upon any task as upon this one. A reader who will seek out in his collected works the address on "Sentiment in Our National Life" will discover that, in this, the longest of his occasional addresses, there is a fervor, an eloquence, an enthusiasm, an interest in his subject, and, at the same time, a pathos, seldom manifested in his utterances. . . . When, on the following day the reprint of this address, and its accompanying descriptions and incidents, and the like reports of the Albany Convention appeared, side by side, it did not need any great prescience to see which was to be the more influential in creating sentiment.

The address provided the opportunity to contrast and to point up his leadership as the champion of honest and bossless government. The appearance of Mr. Cleveland in Ann Arbor was an event of tremendous interest, not only to the city, but to the whole state of Michigan, and soon to the entire country. Its current importance was attested not only by the fact that the *Detroit Free Press*, of February 23, 1892, devoted a page to the occasion, but also by its colorful description of the event. Considerably condensed, the account reads in part as follows:

ANN ARBOR, February 22.—The 22nd of February, in the year of grace 1892, will long be looked back to by the residents of the Athens of the west, as the admirers of this classic city are wont to designate it, as one of the most memorable occasions in its history. The day has been devoted exclusively to receiving and cheering the honored guest whose presence here has long been sought, and it is very doubtful if ex-President Cleveland in all his experience—and he has been the subject of more popular ovations than any American citizen of his time—was ever more enthusiastically, not to say vociferously received by a community of admirers than he has been here to-day. . . .

As early as 8 o'clock the local military companies were out and bestirring themselves, and at 8:45 marched to the Michigan Central depot and escorted the Ypsilanti Light Guards from there to the armory. . . . The early trains brought throngs of people from neighboring cities and towns, while the good country folk from the rural districts adjacent hereto came in to help swell the crowd in every conceivable kind of conveyance. Many people came over from Ypsilanti on the motor line, and special trains on the Michigan Central and Toledo & Ann Arbor Railroads transferred from the various towns along their lines a goodly share of the adult population of each. By 11 o'clock there were fully 5,000 strangers in the city, and by 3 o'clock in the afternoon that number was almost doubled. . . .

At 10:30 the students assembled at their various department headquarters, the first division being composed of the Ypsilanti Light Guards and the law students to the number of 600. Following the laws came the students of the literary, regular medical, pharmacy, dental and homeopathic departments, the classes of each department being separately organized. The total number of students in line was about 1,500, but by the time the first division, under command of Maj. Harrison Soule, treasurer of the university, arrived at the depot, all the students who were not in line were on hand to help welcome Mr. Cleveland. Even the co-eds were at the depot, safely placed in the most advantageous positions, so that they could see and hear all that occurred. The second division was formed at the court house. It consisted of the band, the Ann Arbor Light Infantry, and the Mayor, aldermen and members of the several official boards of the city in six carriages. The Michigan Central depot here is surrounded by terraces on two sides and a bridge on the third, and every available spot on terraces and bridge was filled with men, women and children all anxious to catch a glimpse of Mr. Cleveland the moment he emerged from the depot. Long before the train bearing Mr. Cleveland and party arrived the platform was jammed with human beings and it became necessary for the military company to clear the platform and post guards whose instructions were to keep it clear.

The special train which conveyed Mr. Cleveland and party to Ann Arbor from Detroit consisted of the private car of Supt. Miller, of the Michigan Central, and an ordinary coach, and left the Central depot in Detroit at 10 o'clock sharp standard time. The following students of the law school, acting as a special reception committee, went to Detroit and accompanied Mr. Cleveland to Ann Arbor: A. C. McKenzie, H. D. Jewell, H. A. Reese, J. A. Harmon, F. T. Hard, S. E. McMahon, P. J. Cosgrove, A. C. Gormley, J. W. McCaughey and H. A. Smith. A few minutes before 10 o'clock ex-President Cleveland, Richard Watson Gilder, Wilson Shannon Bissell, ex-Gov. James E. Campbell, of Ohio, and ex-Postmaster-General Dickinson arrived at the depot from Mr. Dickinson's house and proceeded directly to the train in waiting,

Mr. Cleveland being assigned to the comfortable and commodious observatory in the rear end of the car. The invited guests were soon aboard the train and the journey to Ann Arbor was begun on schedule time. The following is a list of the gentlemen who accompanied the ex-President from Detroit: Richard Watson Gilder, editor of the Century Magazine; Wilson Shannon Bissell, of Buffalo; ex-Gov. James E. Campbell, of Ohio; ex-Postmaster-General Don M. Dickinson; ex-Gov. Josiah W. Begole, of Flint; Chief Justic Allen B. Morse, of Ionia; ex-Chief Justice J. W. Champlin, of Grand Rapids; Mayor E. F. Uhl, of Grand Rapids; Mayor George W. Weadock, of Saginaw; Secretary of State R. R. Blacker, of Manistee; Gen. J. G. Parkhurst, of Coldwater; Hon. Peter White, of Marquette; W. L. Webber, of Saginaw; Judge A. C. Baldwin, of Pontiac; John D. Norton, of Pontiac; Ferris S. Fitch, Superintendent of Public Instruction, of Pontiac; Lieut.-Gov. John Strong, of South Rockwood; John Weadock, City Attorney of Bay City; Hon. John Power, of Escanaba; D. O. Watson, of Coopersville; R. A. Montgomery, of Lansing; Judge J. C. Shields, of Alpena; John H. Fedewa, of St. Johns; E. O. Lamphere, Register of Deeds of Clinton Co., St. Johns; Claude Meeker, of Columbus, O.; F. A. Dean, of Charlotte; L. E. Rowley, of Lansing, Deputy Secretary of State; and Richard Storrs Willis, Ashley Pond, William A. Moore, William E. Quinby, Levi L. Barbour, Alfred Russell, Levi T. Griffin, C. Sheehy, John J. Enright, Alfred J. Murphy, C. A. Kent, S. L. Smith and E. G. Stevenson, of Detroit. There were also seven representatives of the press on the train. . . .

As the train pulled into Ann Arbor it was evident that the ex-President was expected, for the tooting of fish horns and the shouting of college cries, made a discordant chorus that roused the slumbering echoes. The moment the train stopped and Mr. Cleveland stepped from his car, ex-Postmaster-General Dickinson at his side, there went soaring up into the blue vault of Heaven and tearing around the sullen masses of vapor that hung like a pall between sky and earth, a mighty Titanic shout of welcome that fairly rent asunder the warm and humid atmosphere. After Mr. Cleveland had advanced a few steps, and doffing his hat smilingly bowed his acknowledgments for the enthusiastic greeting accorded him, Mayor Wm. G. Doty, of Ann Arbor, who was surrounded on three sides by the other officers of the city government, stepped forward and handed to Mr. Cleveland a black leather case which contained a solid silver casket holding a series of engrossed resolutions passed by the City Council extending to Mr. Cleveland the freedom of the city, and electing him to honorary citizenship in the municipality. In making the presentation Mayor Doty said:

Mr. Cleveland—Pursuant to a resolution of the honorable the Common Council, of the City of Ann Arbor, the executive and the legislative branches of the municipal government have assembled here to-day for the purpose of extending to you the freedom and the honorary citizenship of the city whose precincts you are now about to enter.

It is very pleasing to us, Mr. Cleveland, that it is our happy fortune upon this hallowed day to welcome to our city and to our citizenship one who has so worthily and so honorably worn the mantle of the immortal Washington. To us and to our posterity the 22d day of February will be ever memorable, not only as the natal day of the first of American Presidents, but also as the natal day of the first American President born into our civic family.

And now permit me, sir, on behalf of the Common Council of the City of Ann Arbor, in behalf of the free American citizens for whom the council speaks, in behalf of our great university—the city's ornament and pride—to confer upon you the highest honor in our power to bestow.

Receive this little casket and with it the freedom of our city with all its appurtenant rights and privileges, even the assurance of the continued and abiding confidence and love of your fellow-citizens of Ann Arbor.

Mr. Cleveland, who had stood with uncovered head during Mayor Doty's remarks, received the beautiful token from the Mayor's hands, and in so doing responded as follows:

Mr. Mayor and Fellow-citizens:

I thank you very much for the complimentary allusions you have made to the high offices that I have held, and I beg to assure you that the incumbency of none of them has afforded me more pleasure than did the position of Mayor of the city where I lived so long. Ever since that time I have taken a deep interest in municipal affairs, which makes me appreciate all the more highly the reception you have given me here to-day. I regard this city as one containing not only one of the greatest universities in the country, but one known throughout the world as a great seat of learning. I beg to assure you that this beautiful offering will be treasured as one of the most valued souvenirs I have ever received.

The casket presented to Mr. Cleveland is a veritable work of art. It is of solid silver, seven by four inches and two inches deep. Engraved on the casket is this inscription:

To the Honorable Grover Cleveland, ex-President of the United States, with freedom and the favoring citizenship of the City of Ann Arbor, February 22, 1892.

Attest:

William G. Doty,
Mayor.

Mortimer E. Cooley,
President of City Council.

William J. Miller,
City Clerk.

A copy of the city seal was engraved in an appropriate place on one corner of the casket.

After the reception Mr. Cleveland was escorted through the depot by President Angell and ushered into a carriage where he was joined by Don M. Dickinson, President Angell and Prof. J. C. Knowlton, dean of the law faculty. The carriage occupied by these gentlemen was drawn by four white horses, and carriage and horses were alike decorated with the university colors—blue and maize. The other members of the ex-President's party were placed in carriages in the following order, each with an escort from the law school: Second carriage, ex-Gov. Campbell, of Ohio; ex-Chief Justice Champlin, W. S. Bissell, of Buffalo, and A. C. McKenzie. Third carriage, R. W. Gilder, ex-Gov. Begole, Prof. Thompson and F. T. Hard. Fourth carriage, Lieut-Gov. Strong, Chief Justice Morse, William E. Quinby and J. A. Harmon. Fifth carriage, Gen. Parkhurst, Hon. Peter White, Prof. Conely and H. P. Jewell. Sixth carriage, Mayor Weadock, of Saginaw; Wm. A. Moore, Prof. Abbott and H. A. Pease. Seventh carriage—Alfred Russell, Judge Baldwin, Hon. John Powers and P. J. Cosgrove. Eighth carriage—Secretary of State Blacker, Mayor Uhl, of Grand Rapids; Wm. L. Webber and A. C. Gormley. Ninth carriage—Ashley Pond, C. A. Kent, John D. Norton and J. W. McCaughey. Tenth carriage—Deputy Secretary of State Rowley, Levi L. Barbour, S. L. Smith and S. E. McMahon.

After all the guests were seated in the carriages placed at their disposal, the procession took up the line of march, volleys of cheers and college cries greeting the head of the procession as it passed slowly along the streets. . . .

Arrived at President Angell's house, Mr. Cleveland and party alighted from their carriages and became Mr. Angell's guests at lunch, which was a purely informal affair. The moment Mr. Cleveland and accompanying friends disappeared behind the portals of President Angell's house, the students, townspeople and strangers made a dash for the hotels and restaurants and boarding houses of the city and lucky indeed was he who was fortunate enough to find a place where he could sit down and eat his dinner. . . .

Soon after 2 o'clock in the afternoon the law students, on whose invitation ex-President Cleveland visited Ann Arbor, to the number of 600, were admitted to University Hall, where the address was delivered, and arranged themselves in the down-stairs seats north of the center aisle. . . . Before 3 o'clock the hall was literally jammed full of human beings, there probably being at least four thousand souls crowded into the space that would comfortably seat about three thousand. Pending the arrival of the orator of the day the army of young collegians in the hall amused themselves by shouting: "Michigan, Michigan, rah, rah, rah, U. of M. hurrah, hurrah," "R-u-t-h Cleveland," "H-o-w d-o y-o-u d-o Mr. Cleveland" and "Who was George Washington? First in war, first in peace and first in the hearts of his c-o-u-n-t-r-y-m-e-n." Then to vary the monotony incident to such startling vocal pyrotechnics, a score of rubber overshoes were tossed back and forth in the hall to the imminent danger of the fashionable head-gear worn by the ladies present.

At 2 o'clock ex-President Cleveland, President Angell, ex-Postmaster-General Dickinson and about sixty other prominent citizens, including the faculty of the law school, appeared on the platform and a deafening series of cheers that almost raised the roof off the hall where such a multitude of young graduates have received their diplomas from the University of Michigan, went up in one long drawn-out shout of welcome. As soon as quiet and good order were restored the courtly and accomplished President Angell stepped forward and said:

Ladies and Gentlemen—I think that our illustrious visitor is already convinced of the heartiness of his welcome. I will assure him, though, in your names, that it is as hearty as it is vociferous, and human ability can go no farther. I have never wished as here to-day that this hall covered one-quarter of the campus, but even then I am convinced it would be crowded to its uttermost limits by the men and women and children anxious to hear our distinguished visitor. We all owe the law department a debt of gratitude for its annual observance of Washington's birthday, and in times past it has brought a number of famous visitors to us, but none more so than he who is to address us to-day—one whom all of us, regardless of party convictions or belief, delight to honor and respect for his incorruptible integrity, high administrative ability, lofty ideas of civic virtue, and the splendid and invincible courage with which he adheres to what he believes to be right. I have the honor and the pleasure of presenting to you this afternoon ex-President Cleveland, of New York City.

Mr. Cleveland was greeted with long continued applause as he arose from his chair and stepped forward to the reading desk, from which he read his address, and after a brief survey of eager faces before him he began his address as follows, in a remarkably clear, strong and well modulated voice:

SENTIMENT IN OUR NATIONAL LIFE

MR. PRESIDENT, LADIES AND GENTLEMEN:

Among the few holidays which the rush and hurry of American life concede to us, surely no one of a secular character is so suggestive and impressive as the day we celebrate on this occasion. We not only commemorate the birth of the greatest American who ever lived, but we recall, as inseparably connected with his career, all the events and incidents which led up to the establishment of free institutions in this land of ours, and culminated in the erection of our wondrous nation.

The University of Michigan, therefore, most appropriately honors herself and does a fitting public service by especially providing for such an observance of the day as is calculated to turn to the contemplation of patriotic duty the thoughts of the young men whom she is soon to send out to take places in the ranks of American citizenship.

I hope it may not be out of place for me to express the gratification it affords me as a member of the legal profession, to know that the conduct of these exercises has been committed to the classes of the Law Department of the University. There seems to me to be a propriety in this, for I have always thought the influences surrounding the practice and study of the law should especially induce a patriotic feeling. The business of the profession is related to the enforcement and operation of the laws which govern our people; and its members, more often than those engaged in other occupations, are called to a participation in making these laws. Besides, they are constantly brought to the study of the fundamental law of the land, and a familiarity with its history. Such study and familiarity should be sufficient of themselves to increase a man's love of country; and they certainly cannot fail to arouse his veneration for the men who laid the foundations of our nation sure and steadfast in a written constitution, which has been declared, by the greatest living English statesman, to be "the most wonderful work ever struck off at a given time by the brain and purpose of man."

Washington had more to do with the formation of the constitution than our enthusiasm for other phases of the great work he did for his country usually makes prominent. He fought the battles which cleared the way for it. He best knew the need of consolidating under one government the colonies he had made free, and he best knew that without this consolidation, a wasting war, the long and severe privations and sufferings his countrymen had undergone and his own devoted labor in the cause of freedom, were practically in vain. The beginning of anything like a public sentiment looking to the formation of our nation is traceable to his efforts. The circular letter he sent to the governors of the States, as early as the close of the War of the Revolution, contained the germ of the constitution; and all this was recognized by his unanimous choice to preside over the convention that framed it. His spirit was in and through it all.

But whatever may be said of the argument presented in support of the propriety of giving the law classes the management of this celebration, it is entirely clear that the University herself furnishes to all her students a most useful lesson when, by decreeing the observance of this day, she recognizes the fact that the knowledge of books she imparts is not a complete fulfillment of her duty, and concedes that the education with which she so well equips her graduates for individual success in life and for business and professional usefulness, may profitably be supplemented by the stimulation of their patriotism, and by the direction of their thoughts to subjects relating to their country's welfare. I do not know how generally such an observance of Washington's birthday, as has been here established, prevails in our other universities and colleges; but I am convinced that any institution of learning in our land which neglects to provide for the instructive and improving observance of this day within its walls, falls short of its attainable measure of usefulness and omits a just and valuable contribution to the general good. There is great need of educated men in our public life, but it is the need of educated men with patriotism. The college graduate may be, and frequently is, more unpatriotic and less useful in public affairs than the man who, with limited education, has spent the years when opinions are formed in improving contact with the world instead of being within college walls and confined to the study of books. If it be true, as is often claimed, that the scholar in politics is generally a failure, it may well be due to the fact that, during his formative period when lasting impressions are easily received, his intellect alone has been cultivated at the expense of wholesome and well-regulated sentiment.

I speak to-day in advocacy of this sentiment. If it is not found in extreme and exclusive mental culture, neither is it found in the busy marts of trade, nor in the confusion of bargaining, nor in the mad rush after wealth. Its home is in the soul and memory of man. It has to do with the moral sense. It reverences traditions, it loves ideas, it cherishes the names and the deeds of heroes, and it worships at the shrine of patriotism. I plead for it because there is a sentiment, which in some features is distinctively American, that we should never allow to languish.

When we are told that we are a practical and common sense people, we are apt to receive the statement with approval and applause. We are proud of its truth and naturally proud because its truth is attributable to the hard work we have had to do ever since our birth as a nation, and because of the stern labor we still see in our way before we reach our determined destiny. There is cause to suspect, however, that another and less creditable reason for our gratification arises from a feeling that there is something heroically American in treating with indifference or derision all those things which, in our view, do not directly and palpably pertain to what we call, with much satisfaction, practical affairs, but which, if we were entirely frank, we should confess might be called money-getting and the betterment of individual condition. Growing out of this feeling, an increasing disposition is discernible among our people, which begrudges to sentiment any time or attention that might be given to business and which is apt to crowd out of mind any thought not directly related to selfish plans and purposes.

A little reflection ought to convince us that this may be carried much too far. It is a mistake to regard sentiment as merely something which, if indulged, has a tendency to tempt to idle and useless contemplation or retrospection, thus weakening in a people the sturdiness of necessary endeavor and diluting the capacity for national achievement.

The elements which make up the sentiment of a people should not be counted as amiable weaknesses because they are not at all times noisy and turbulent. The gentleness and loveliness of woman do not cause us to forget that she can inspire man to deeds of greatness and heroism; that as wife she often makes man's career noble and grand, and that as mother she builds and fashions in her son the strong pillars of a State. So the sentiment of a people which, in peace and contentment, decks with flowers the temple of their rule, may, in rage and fury, thunder at its foundations. Sentiment is the cement which keeps in place the granite blocks of governmental power, or the destructive agency whose explosion heaps in ruins their scattered fragments. The monarch who cares only for his sovereignty and safety, leads his subjects to forgetfulness of oppression by a pretense of love for their traditions; and the ruler who plans encroachments upon the liberties of his people, shrewdly proceeds under the apparent sanction of their sentiment. Appeals to sentiment have led nations to bloody wars which have destroyed dynasties and changed the lines of imperial territory. Such an appeal summoned our fathers to the battlefields where American independence was won, and such an appeal has scattered soldiers' graves all over our land, which mutely give evidence of the power of our government and the perpetuity of our free institutions.

I have thus far spoken of a people's sentiment as something which may exist and be effective under any form of government, and in any national condition. But the thought naturally follows, that, if this sentiment may be so potent in countries ruled by a power originating outside of popular will, how vital must its existence and regulation be among our countrymen, who rule themselves and make and administer their own laws. In lands less free than ours, the control of the governed may be more easily maintained if those who are set over them see fit to make concession to their sentiment; yet, with or without such concession, the strong hand of force may still support the power to govern. But sentiment is the very life blood of our nation. Our government was conceived amid the thunders that echoed "All men are created equal," and it was brought forth while free men shouted "We, the people of the United States." The sentiment of our fathers, made up of their patriotic intentions, their sincere beliefs, their homely impulses and their noble aspirations, entered into the government they established; and, unless it is constantly supported and guarded by a sentiment as pure as theirs, our scheme of popular rule will fail. Another and a different plan may take its place; but this which we hold in sacred trust, as it originated in patriotism, is only fitted for patriotic and honest uses and purposes, and can only be administered in its integrity and intended beneficence, by honest and patriotic men. It can no more be saved nor faithfully conducted by a selfish, dishonest, and corrupt people, than a stream can rise above its source or be better and purer than its fountain head.

None of us can be ignorant of the ideas which constitute the sentiment underlying our national structure. We know they are a reverent belief in God, a sincere recognition of the value and power of moral principle and those qualities of heart which make a noble manhood, devotion to unreserved patriotism, love for man's equality, unquestioning trust in popular rule, the exaction of civic virtue and honesty, faith in the saving quality of universal education, protection of a free and unperverted expression of the popular will, and an insistence upon a strict accountability of public officers as servants of the people.

These are the elements of American sentiment; and all these should be found deeply imbedded in the minds and hearts of our countrymen. When anyone of them is displaced, the time has come when a danger signal should be raised. Their lack among the people of other nations—however great and powerful they may be—can afford us no comfort nor reassurance. We must work out our destiny unaided and alone in full view of the truth that nowhere, so directly and surely as here, does the destruction or degeneracy of the people's sentiment undermine the foundations of governmental rule.

Let us not for a moment suppose that we can outgrow our dependence upon this sentiment, nor that in any stage of national advance and development it will be less important. As the love of family and kindred remains to bless and strengthen a man in all the vicissitudes of his mature and busy life, so must our American sentiment remain with us as a people—a sure hope and reliance in every phase of our country's growth. Nor will it suffice that the factors which compose this sentiment have a sluggish existence in our minds, as articles of an idle faith which we are willing perfunctorily to profess. They must be cultivated as motive principles, stimulating us to effort in the cause of good government, and constantly warning us against the danger and dishonor of faithlessness to the sacred cause we have in charge and heedlessness of the blessings vouchsafed to us and future generations, under our free institutions.

These considerations emphasize the value which should be placed upon every opportunity afforded us for the contemplation of the pure lives and patriotic services of those who have been connected with the controlling incidents of our country's history. Such contemplation cannot fail to re-enforce and revive the sentiment absolutely essential to useful American citizenship, nor fail to arouse within us a determination that during our stewardship no harm shall come to the political gifts we hold in trust from the fathers of the Republic.

It is because George Washington completely represented all the elements of American sentiment that every incident of his life, from his childhood to his death, is worth recalling—whether it impresses the young with the beauty and value of moral traits, or whether it exhibits to the wisest and oldest an example of sublime accomplishment and the highest possible public service. Even the anecdotes told of his boyhood have their value. I have no sympathy with those who, in these latter days, attempt to shake our faith in the authenticity of these stories, because they are not satisfied with the evidence in their support, or because they do not seem to accord with the conduct of boys in this generation. It may well be, that the stories should stand and the boys of the present day be pitied.

At any rate, these anecdotes have answered an important purpose; and in the present state of the proofs, they should, in my opinion, be believed. The cherry tree and hatchet incident and its companion declaration that the Father of his Country never told a lie, have indelibly fixed upon the mind of many a boy the importance of truthfulness. Of all the legends containing words of advice and encouragement which hung upon the walls of the little district schoolhouse where a large share of my education was gained, I remember but one, which was in these words: "George Washington had only a common school education."

I will not plead guilty to the charge of dwelling upon the little features of a great subject. I hope the day will never come when American boys cannot know of some trait or some condition in which they may feel that they ought to be or are like Washington. I am not afraid to assert that a multitude of men can be found in every part of our land, respected for their probity and worth, and most useful to the country and to their fellow-men, who will confess their indebtedness to the story of Washington and his hatchet; and many a man has won his way to honor and fame, notwithstanding limited school advantages, because he found hope and incentive in the high mission Washington accomplished with only a common school education. These are not little and trivial things. They guide and influence the forces which make the character and sentiment of a great people.

I should be ashamed of my country, if, in further speaking of what

Washington has done for the sentiment of his countrymen, it was necessary to make any excuse for a reference to his constant love and fond reverence, as boy and man, for his mother. This filial love is an attribute of American manhood, a badge which invites our trust and confidence, and an indispensable element of American greatness. A man may compass important enterprises, he may become famous, he may win the applause of his fellows, he may even do public service and deserve a measure of popular approval, but he is not right at heart, and can never be truly great, if he forgets his mother.

In the latest biography of Washington we find the following statement concerning his mother: "That she was affectionate and loving cannot be doubted, for she retained to the last a profound hold upon the reverential devotion of her son; and yet as he rose steadily to the pinnacle of human greatness, she could only say that 'George had been a good boy, and she was sure he would do his duty.' "

I cannot believe that the American people will consider themselves called upon to share the deprecatory feeling of the biographer, when he writes that the mother of Washington could only say of her son that she believed he would be faithful to the highest earthly trusts, because he had been good; nor that they will regard her words merely as an amiably tolerated expression of a fond mother. If they are true to American sentiment, they will recognize in this language the announcement of the important truth that, under our institutions and scheme of government, goodness, such as Washington's, is the best guarantee for the faithful discharge of public duty. They will certainly do well for the country and for themselves, if they adopt the standard the intuition of this noble woman suggests, as the measure of their trust and confidence. It means the exaction of moral principle and personal honor and honesty and goodness as indispensable credentials to political preferment.

I have referred only incidentally to the immense influence and service of Washington in forming our Constitution. I shall not dwell upon his lofty patriotism, his skill and fortitude as the military commander who gained our independence, his inspired wisdom, patriotism, and statesmanship as first President of the republic, his constant love for his countrymen, and his solicitude for their welfare at all times. The story has been often told, and is familiar to all. If I should repeat it, I should only seek to present further and probably unnecessary proof of the fact that Washington embodied in his character, and exemplified in his career, that American sentiment in which our government had its origin, and which I believe to be a condition necessary to our healthful national life.

I have not assumed to instruct you. I have merely yielded to the influence of the occasion; and attempted to impress upon you the importance of cultivating and maintaining true American sentiment, suggesting that, as it has been planted and rooted in the moral faculties of our countrymen, it can only flourish in their love of truth and honesty and virtue and goodness. I believe that God has so ordained it for the people he has selected for his special favor; and I know that the decrees of God are never obsolete.

I beg you, therefore, to take with you, when you go forth to assume the obligations of American citizenship, as one of the best gifts of your Alma Mater, a strong and abiding faith in the value and potency of a good conscience and a pure heart. Never yield one iota to those who teach that these are weak and childish things, not needed in the struggle of manhood with the stern realities of life. Interest yourselves in public affairs as a duty of citizenship; but do not surrender your faith to those who discredit and debase politics by scoffing at sentiment and principle, and whose political activity consists in attempts to gain popular support by cunning devices and shrewd manipulation. You will find plenty of these who will smile at your profession of faith, and tell you that truth and virtue and honesty and goodness were well enough in the old days when Washington lived, but are not suited to the present size and development of our country and the progress we have made in the art of political management. Be steadfast. The strong and sturdy oak still needs the support of its native earth, and, as it grows in size and spreading branches, its roots must strike deeper in the soil which warmed and fed its first tender sprout. You will be told that the people have no longer any desire for the things you profess. Be not deceived. The people are not dead but sleeping. They will awaken in good time, and scourge the moneychangers from their sacred temple.

You may be chosen to public office. Do not shrink from it, for holding office is also a duty of citizenship. But do not leave your faith behind you. Every public office, small or great, is held in trust for your fellow-citizens. They differ in importance, in responsibility, and in the labor they impose; but the duties of none of them can be well performed if the mentorship of a good conscience and pure heart be discarded. Of course, other equipment is necessary, but without this mentorship all else is insufficient. In times of gravest responsibility it will solve your difficulties; in the most trying hour it will lead you out of perplexities, and it will, at all times, deliver you from temptation.

In conclusion, let me remind you that we may all properly learn the lesson appropriate to Washington's birthday, if we will; and that we shall fortify ourselves against the danger of falling short in the discharge of any duty pertaining to citizenship, if, being thoroughly imbued with true American sentiment and the moral ideas which support it, we are honestly true to ourselves.

To thine own self be true,
And it must follow as the night the day:
Thou can'st not then be false to any man.

Throughout the entire address, which was delivered in a little less than forty minutes, the ex-President was given the strictest attention, and frequently was interrupted by sustained applause and resounding cheers. When Mr. Cleveland, in ringing tones, adjured his hearers not to surrender their faith to "those who discredit and debase politics by scoffing at sentiment and principle, and whose political activity consists in attempts to gain popular support by cunning devices and shrewd manipulation," the house literally rose at the speaker, while cries of "Hill, Hill!" went up in every direction. Again, when the ex-President asserted in trumpet voice that "the people are not dead but sleeping," a salvo of terrific applause greeted his utterance. Mr. Cleveland is an exceptionally easy speaker, makes very few gestures, but has the faculty, as happy as it is rare, of investing all that he says with the earnestness that dominates his every act. . . .

President Angell presented to the audience the five governors and former governors in attendance—Winans, Campbell of Ohio, Felch, Begole, and Jerome. Next he introduced Don M. Dickinson as a graduate of the Law Department and a distinguished member of Mr. Cleveland's cabinet. Mr. Dickinson was cheered to the echo as he rose to respond and was applauded most enthusiastically as he said:

I have always been proud of my state and her crowning glory, the University of Michigan. I am especially proud of her today, and I congratulate her law school especially for this very successful celebration on Washington's birthday.

President Angell then presented Chief Justice Morse, Judge Cooley, and the members of the law faculty, Professors Knowlton, Thompson, Griffin, and Abbott, and Justice Champlin. While the band played the audience dispersed, and members of the faculty and their ladies ascended the platform and were presented to Mr. Cleveland.

Beginning at seven o'clock, at a public reception in the courthouse, Mr. Cleveland and his party received for two hours an unending stream of people. The party then returned by the special train to Detroit and to the home of Mr. Dickinson.

In the same issue with its account of Cleveland's Ann Arbor visit, the *Detroit Free Press* commented editorially in part as follows:

> The address which ex-President Cleveland delivered at Ann Arbor yesterday, before the University of Michigan, is given to the readers of the FREE PRESS in its entirety. Any attempt at a mere synopsis would detract from its force, impair its beauty and mar that symmetry so characteristic of Mr. Cleveland's efforts from the rostrum. "Sentiment in Our National Life" was his happily chosen subject, for the suggestions of the day and the presence in which he talked were an inspiration to his theme. Among those who laid broad and deep the foundations of the republic, Gen. Washington was pre-eminent. The hope of its perpetuity and growth along the lines of approved development, rests in those about to enter upon the stage of public action.
>
> To meet the highest and noblest suggestions of these truths Mr. Cleveland is admirably equipped. His public career exemplifies the sincerity of his utterances and shows that he holds the integrity of his opinions, as bearing upon the nation's welfare, in higher esteem than the advancement of personal interests. His address carries the weight of sincerity. It contains the sentiments of a man who has sought to shape his life under their guidance. Few men of the age have been such exemplars of what constitutes the best citizenship, and none can better impress upon the youth of the day the sure course to the patriotic service of their country.

As an interpretation of the spirit of the Cleveland Era and as the background for these sketches, we have the words of Mr. Cleveland himself, spoken on a great occasion, before an audience which included many University of Michigan staff members and alumni who were in public service during one or both of the two Cleveland administrations.

E. D. B.
L. G. V.

Henry Carter Adams

1851	*Born in Davenport, Iowa*
1874	*Graduated from Iowa College (now Grinnell College)*
1875–76	*Attended Andover Theological Seminary*
1878	*Received the Ph.D. degree from Johns Hopkins University*
1878–79	*Studied in England, France, and Germany*
1879	*Lectured at Johns Hopkins University*
1880–83	*Lectured at Cornell University*
1880–87	*Lectured at the University of Michigan*
1886	*Dismissed from the faculty of Cornell University*
1887	*Appointed professor of political economy at the University of Michigan*
1888	*Appointed chief statistician of the Interstate Commerce Commission*
1890	*Married Bertha H. Wright*
1913	*Selected by the Chinese government as adviser on railroad accounting*
1921	*Died in Ann Arbor, Michigan*

HENRY C. ADAMS

Henry Carter Adams

By Marvin B. Rosenberry

HENRY CARTER ADAMS, economist and statistician, was born in Davenport, Iowa, on December 31, 1851, and died at his home in Ann Arbor, Michigan, on August 11, 1921. His contributions to economic thought had already given him prominence in professional circles when his appointment as statistician to the Interstate Commerce Commission in Cleveland's first administration brought him nation-wide notice. While still in his thirties, Henry Carter Adams had come to be looked upon as one of the nation's greatest economists in both the philosophical and the practical sense.

Adams' outstanding individualism, which was one of the most important factors in his rapid rise to prominence, was no doubt in large part attributable to his family background. Ephraim Adams, the father of Henry, was descended in the eighth generation from William Adams, who came from Shropshire, England, in 1628. The family moved ultimately to New Ipswich, New Hampshire, and it was from that home that Ephraim Adams went to Phillips Academy, Andover, Massachusetts. He was one of a group of fifty who left the Academy when they were forbidden to form an antislavery society. He graduated from Dartmouth College in 1839 and in 1843 from Andover Theological Seminary. With a group of fellow students from Andover, Ephraim left Albany, New York, on October 4, 1843, to enter upon missionary work in what is now the state of Iowa. The labels on the books and other belongings of the young men, "Burlington, Io., via New Orleans," gave an indication of the difficulties of transportation from the Atlantic seaboard to points west of the Mississippi in 1843. The journey from Albany to Chicago required two weeks. Another week was consumed in the journey from Chicago to Denmark, Iowa.

The exact date upon which the group arrived in Denmark does not appear, but the members of the band who reached Iowa, among whom was Ephraim Adams, were ordained at a Congregational church service at Denmark on November 5, 1843. Shortly thereafter, each departed for the settlement which he had chosen as his field. Ephraim went first to Mount Pleasant, then in 1844 to Davenport, Iowa, where he ministered to the Congregational church from 1844 to 1855. On September 16, 1845, he married Elizabeth Douglas of Hanover, New Hampshire, who was to share with him during the next sixty years the joys and sorrows of the life of a pioneer clergyman.

While serving with the Congregational parish at Davenport, Ephraim associated with other Congregational clergymen in the organization of Iowa College, which opened at Davenport in 1848. Upon its organization, Ephraim was elected a trustee and continued to serve as such to the time of his death. His son, Henry Carter Adams, was given his middle name because a contributor named Carter gave a large sum to the struggling college. Iowa College was moved from Davenport to Grinnell, Iowa, in 1859, and in 1909 its name was changed to Grinnell College.

After two years spent in raising funds for Iowa College, Ephraim in 1857 began a ministry at Decorah, Iowa, which extended over a period of fifteen years. After the close of his ministry at Decorah in 1872, he served ten years as superintendent of home missions. He then spent another year in the service of Iowa College, which was followed by ministries of six years at Eldora and fourteen years at Waterloo, Iowa. He died in 1907 at the age of eighty-nine, just two years after the death of his wife.

We have very little information, practically none, in regard to Henry Carter Adams' mother. During the first eighteen years of his life, the boy was in very frail health—so frail, indeed, that in his infancy physicians advised his parents that Henry would in all probability not live to the age of fourteen.

From this we may infer his mother gave days and nights to the care of her son, with a full measure of devotion.

As soon as Henry was able to manage them he was given a saddle pony and a gun. Thus equipped he roamed the prairies of Iowa as the family moved from one missionary home to another. This out-of-door life endowed him with a love of nature; at the same time he acquired an intimate knowledge of the way other people lived. He never lost either his love of nature or his respect for and understanding of the average man.

Henry received no formal instruction until his nineteenth year, but meanwhile his father taught him Greek, Latin, and Hebrew, and no doubt instructed him in mathematics, literature, and other branches of learning. The impressionable years of his childhood and youth were spent in a home in which the tenets of Puritanism were taught and practiced. The responsibility of the individual, the absolute distinction between right and wrong, with all the resultant duties and prohibitions, set the standards of his mature as well as his early life.

It was assumed by his parents and by Henry himself that he was to become a clergyman and follow in the footsteps of his father. Very early in his scholastic training, however, doubts arose in his mind as to the propriety of this course. To use his own words he was "plagued by doctrines" from the time he went to the Academy. Assailed by skepticism, he underwent a terrible heart-searching, which can be understood only by those who have experienced it. While all his early training and his deep affection for his family drew him one way, mental integrity drove him another. During his first years at Iowa College his interest was not enlisted in the subjects he studied, but, in his junior and senior years, when he came to history, philosophy, and social problems, Henry was aware of a new and lively enthusiasm for his college work.

After his graduation from Iowa College in 1874 with a Bachelor of Arts degree, he taught for a year at Nashua, Iowa. Then, in accordance with his parents' wishes, he entered Andover Theological Seminary. Here, to use his own language, he was "to try himself out"—to discover whether preaching was a possible career for him. By the spring of 1876, he had decided irrevocably that he could not with a clear conscience follow his father's profession. While he could not comply with his parents' wishes, his decision did not mean that he repudiated their ideals. As was said of him after his death:

> . . . although he abandoned certain theological formulas, the footfall of spiritual things ever echoed through his character. The union of winsome gentleness with stern devotion to humanitarian ideals, so distinctive of Professor Adams, rooted in the persistent influence of the New England conscience.

The missionary spirit of the father was not lost in the son, but was turned into different channels.

When Adams felt obliged to give up the ministry as a vocation, he determined to study economics, not so much for itself as because it constituted an avenue through which he hoped to reach his goal of ethical reform. Johns Hopkins University had opened its doors to students on October 3, 1876. Adams heard of the new institution at Baltimore and determined to enter it. In competition with more than three hundred applicants, he wrote an article for one of the new fellowships and was fortunate in being one of ten to receive an appointment. Life at the university opened up for him new opportunities. He had always been fond of good music, and here for the first time he heard the classics in music. He played in the church; he sang in the choral union while a young professor. He served as an assistant in Johns Hopkins Library not for the salary, which was meager, but for the opportunity to have access to books. He said, "I am reading myself full." To fit himself physically for the strenuous university year, he spent several summers in his native state working in the fields.

In 1878 Adams received the degree of Doctor of Philosophy, the first conferred by Johns Hopkins University. While studying for his doctorate, Adams had attracted the attention of President Daniel Coit Gilman, who after his graduation told him: "You must go to Europe." The reply was: "I can't. I haven't a cent," to which Gilman replied: "I shall see what can be done." The result was that a benefactor, Mr. Francis

White of Baltimore, found the requisite funds. Adams was at Oxford and Paris; longer at Berlin and Heidelberg; in all he was abroad for fourteen months.

In the summer of 1878, President Andrew D. White * of Cornell, who at the time was traveling in Germany, summoned Adams to discuss a vacancy at Cornell. As the interview progressed, Adams discovered, much to his disappointment, that White had mistaken H. C. Adams, the budding economist, for H. B. Adams, the budding historian. President White, however, proved to be also interested in economic questions. Adams said to him that he thought he had a message to give and could say something of value to the boys at Ithaca. White asked him to draw up a syllabus. Adams worked all night and handed White a syllabus in the morning, with the result that when Adams returned to this country he was invited to deliver lectures not only at Cornell but also at Johns Hopkins and at Michigan. So meager were the facilities then offered in the general field of the social sciences that Adams in 1879–80 gave one semester of work each at Cornell and Johns Hopkins. The same arrangement was continued with Michigan substituted for Johns Hopkins. Adams delivered his first lectures at Michigan in the fall of 1880. Thus began his outstanding career as a teacher. He himself said that he "gave up three careers, preaching, journalism, and reform," to devote himself to teaching, where he believed his mission lay.

In 1886, Adams was expelled from Cornell University for reasons that today seem totally insufficient. During that year what was known as the Gould railroad strike occurred. This strike was to form the subject of a discussion at Cornell University, and an engineer who had been invited to speak could not be present. At a moment's notice Adams was asked to step into the breach and to address the students, with the understanding that other members of the faculty were to speak also.

* Andrew Dickson White, LL.D. 1867, professor of history and English literature, 1857–63; professor of history, 1863–67; resigned from the University of Michigan to accept the presidency of Cornell University.

Adams described the occasion:

> The room was crowded for, besides the engineering society, my own students, getting word of it, came over to the Physical Laboratory room where the addresses of the Society were given. A more inspiring audience no man could have, and I spoke with ease, with pleasure and, from the way my words were received, with effect. The New York papers reported what I said and, three days after, Mr. Henry Sage, than whom I know no more honest hypocrite or un-Christian a Christian, came into the President's office, and, taking the clipping from the *New York Times* out of his pocket, said, "This man must go, he is sapping the foundations of our society." It was not until then that I thought of putting what I said into print, but then I did it, following as nearly as possible what I said and the way I said it.

The address was published in the August 21, 1886, *Scientific American Supplement* (No. 555, p. 8861). As published, it is so closely knit and the arguments so dependent on what precedes and follows that it is difficult to make a fair quotation from it. The whole address might well have served as a polemic in support of the right of labor to have the benefits which were ultimately conferred upon it by the Wagner Act. The outstanding fact is that Adams was fifty years ahead of his time. He attacked the very citadel of capital with arguments that today seem unanswerable. As an example, he said:

> While industries were numerous and small, while workmen were themselves owners of the places in which they worked, of the tools with which they worked, and of the materials upon which they worked, and at the same time had access to a comparatively steady market for the sale of product, the ordinary rights of personal freedom were ample to secure to men the enjoyment of the fruits of their labor. But now, under the regime of great industries, when the laborer is proprietor of nothing but himself, and is dependent upon the owner of machines, of material, and of place for the opportunity to work, and where the market, though broadened and extended, presents an unsteadiness that the old society never knew, it is folly to say that the same law of liberty will produce parallel results. The truth is that the theory of liberty upon which the French revolution was fought to a successful issue, which placed the personal right to acquire property

on the same footing as the right to security of life, is no longer applicable to modern society. It does not fit into the regime of great industries. Men knew the evils of concentrated irresponsible political power, but of the pernicious results of the concentration of power that comes with the accumulation of capital they were wholly ignorant. And this is the reason why it was reserved for the present generation, impelled by the same hope of personal freedom and by the same appreciation of social fairness and social equality that inspired the leaders of the English and the French revolution, to impose such conditions upon the exercise of industrial power that the material progress of our century may become the source of highest blessings to all . . .

We need not follow at greater length the specific claims of the laborers as displayed in this controversy, for enough has been said to show that the question of wages was subordinated to the question of internal organization. In this fact, which so surprised the public, lies the significance of the latest phase of the labor controversy. What the workmen demand is such an organization of the industries to which they give their time that certain rights shall be granted to them, even though they are not proprietors, in the ordinary acceptance of that word. In some instances, such rights have been secured.

Referring to agreement that an employee should not be discharged without cause and in another instance that wages should fluctuate with profits, Adams continued:

This necessarily means a permanent board of arbitration within the concern, before which the books of the company may be scrutinized. Such decisions as these are in perfect harmony with the views expressed in the first part of my address. They admit the claim that capital can no longer be regarded as bearing purely a private character, and that proprietorship in productive agencies can be admitted only on condition of strict responsibility. Such decisions as these may be regarded as prophecies of a new industrial organization.

The doctrine expressed in this address no doubt aroused the ire and the active opposition of many capitalists besides Mr. Sage. To one argument—"Did not the rise of free labor, consequent upon the fall of feudalism and the guilds, secure for men, as members of industrial society, all rights and all freedom now enjoyed by them as members of political society?"—Adams presented the following reply:

That the right of personal freedom was necessary as preparing the way for the social movements of the last three centuries, none will care to deny; but that the liberties of men should be judged by the wording of the law, rather than by the actual condition in which men find themselves for maintaining their independence, is open to reasonable doubt. This question, if intended as a criticism upon my statement of the labor problem, indicates a failure to appreciate the fundamental idea upon which Anglo-Saxon institutions rest. The purpose of both English and American law is to attach a duty to every right. It recognizes no liberty except as held to strict account. Nothing, indeed, can be so foreign to the spirit of our institutions as the granting of any privilege, whether political or proprietary, freed from the restraints of responsibility.

The address as a whole shows a deep insight on the part of Adams into the problems of labor and capital as they have developed over the years. As labor relations have since developed, the address seems a prophecy which in the present time is substantially fulfilled. It has taken fifty years for the country as a whole to catch up with Adams and come to a realization of the fact "that the liberties of men should not be judged by the wording of the law but rather by the actual condition in which men find themselves."

It was with real reluctance that President White, recognizing Cornell's debt to Sage, complied with his demand and dismissed Adams. The alumni of Cornell wished to make a test case of the episode, but this Adams would not permit. He quietly left Cornell.

President James B. Angell, LL.D. 1912, himself an economist of note and an administrator who quickly recognized outstanding ability when it came within the range of his vision, saw in Adams' dismissal from Cornell an opportunity for Michigan. Almost immediately he extended to Adams an invitation to associate himself permanently with the University of Michigan. It was, however, characteristic of President Angell that he should first have satisfied himself as to the precise limits of Adams' liberalism before extending him a permanent appointment. Several long letters from Adams in the Angell papers give clear evidence that President Angell had propounded some rather searching questions for Adams to answer. The replies must have been satisfactory; in June of 1887 the Regents of the University voted Adams a full professorship in political economy, to become effective October 1 of that year.

From that time on, Ann Arbor was Adams' spiritual home as well as his domicile. In this connection, however, it should be noted that in 1890, while Mr. Henry Sage was still a member of the board of trustees, the board voted unanimously to invite Adams to return to Cornell. In the meantime, he had become so attached to Michigan and the opportunities given him were so attractive that he declined this very flattering invitation. The family home in Ann Arbor, established upon his marriage in 1890 to Bertha H. Wright, A.B. 1888, of Port Huron, Michigan, became a center of gracious and generous hospitality. Three sons carry on the Adams tradition of public service: Henry Carter Adams II, A.B. 1913, M.S. 1915, who is now associate professor of naval architecture and marine engineering at the University of Michigan; Theodore W. Adams, B.S. 1918, M.D. 1920, specialist in gynecology and obstetrics, residing in Portland, Oregon; and Thomas Hammond Adams, A.B. 1922, lawyer, who is a partner in the firm of Hill, Hamblen, Essery and Lewis, of Detroit, and lives in Birmingham, Michigan.

In January, 1887, the American Economic Association published an essay by Adams entitled "The Relation of the State to Industrial Action." Previously, Adams had been invited to address the Constitution Club and the Institute of Social Sciences, both of New York City. The essay was a revision and extension of these addresses. It was a gem, and its influence in the field of economics was as great as that of Frederick J. Turner's *The Significance of the Frontier in American History,* in the field of American history. Its publication was said by Richard T. Ely to have had a profound influence not only upon economic thought but also upon economic legislation.

In the main the essay is a refutation of the doctrine of laissez-faire, which had been strongly supported by John

Stuart Mill and upheld by the so-called Manchester School. Adams attacked the two basic assumptions of laissez-faire philosophy: first, that the interests of human beings are fundamentally the same, and second, that individuals know their interests in the sense in which they are coincident with the interests of others and that in the absence of coercion they will, in this sense, follow them. He was so convincing that it is difficult for any unprejudiced person to reject his conclusions. He summarized his views as follows:

> Society is the organic entity about which all our reasoning should center. Both state action and the industrial activity of individuals are functions of the complete social organism. The state is not made out of the chips and blocks left over after framing industrial society, nor does industrial society serve its full purpose in furnishing a means of existence for the poor unfortunates who are thrust out of the civil or the military service. Society, as a living and growing organism, is the ultimate thing disclosed by an analysis of human relations; and because this is true it is not right to speak of a presumption in favor of individual initiative or of state control, as though these stood like contestants opposed to each other. It is not proper to consider individual activity as supplementary to state powers, or to look upon the functions of the state as supplementary to personal activity. It is futile to expect sound principles for the guidance of intricate legislation so long as we over-estimate either public or private duties; the true principle must recognize society as a unity, subject only to the laws of its own development.

Adams then stated the fundamental principle which he thought should govern the relation of the state to industrial action:

> This presentation of the problem suggests a general principle according to which the relation of governmental agency to industrial affairs should be adjusted. It should be the purpose of all laws, touching matters of business, to maintain the beneficent results of competitive action while guarding society from the evil consequences of unrestrained competition. This may seem a truism, but its statement is necessary as the starting point for constructive study . . . There is no presumption for or against either the one or the other in itself considered, for both are essential to the development of a highly organ-

ized society, and the purpose of constructive thought should be to maintain them in harmonious relations.

He next considered the beneficial workings of competition, naming the important evils of unrestrained competition and indicating the function of the state in the regulation of industry. In that connection he argued that the state may determine the plane of competitive action and may realize for society the benefits of monopoly, things which cannot be done without state interference. He then divided industries into three classes and stated the limitations which should obtain in state regulation as applied to each of these classes. Adams concluded his analysis with the following statement of his position:

> For myself, professing to be neither a fatalist optimist nor a fatalist pessimist, but professing rather to recognize the social destiny of man to lie largely in his own control, this mingling of races and of diverse ideas serves only to impress strongly upon my mind that the present is a critical epoch in the history of the American people . . .
>
> The opinions expressed in this essay are motivated by the theory of individualism, and not by the theory of socialism . . . It is true that the theory of governmental action, for which this essay contends, would press the principle of personal responsibility farther than it has yet been applied; but it is nevertheless conservative, for its aim is to bring industrial society into harmony with the fundamental thought of our political constitution. There is no other escape from socialism.

It is interesting to note that in concluding his analysis of the relation of the state to industrial action Adams made the following observation:

> It follows then that the labor question is not, and from its nature can never become, a political question, and they deceive themselves who suppose a well-crystallized political party may be erected upon the interest which it represents. And it should be noticed that the rules of interference of government with industrial action, which have been stated above, do not contemplate the solution of the labor problem. Indirectly, it is true, the state may lend its influence in such a solution by enacting laws for raising the plane of competitive action. Possibly, also, boards of legal arbitration may be established with some degree

of success for some particular industries; but such measures do not touch the vital point of the labor controversy.

A study of the essay irresistibly leads the reader to speculate upon what Adams would have thought of the development in labor relations in this country and in England over the last decade. In connection with the rise of the Labor Party to power in England he would undoubtedly point out that although the party is primarily representative of the interests of labor, it deals with the general problems of government in its internal and external relations in much the same way that the Liberal Party dealt with them. In spite of the victory of the Labor Party, it remains to be seen whether "a well-crystallized political party may be erected upon the interest which it represents."

As regards labor relations in this country Adams would undoubtedly point out that much of the criticism now leveled at labor policies would have been avoided and a better result reached if his suggestions had been followed. That his address on "The Labor Problem" and his essay on "The Relation of State to Industrial Action" powerfully influenced economic thought in this country during the nineties will be admitted by every well-informed person.

In the matter of human relations Adams had a sixth sense which enabled him to lay bare the crux of any problem dealing with this fundamental subject. He showed clearly the error in the German system, which exalted the state at the expense of the individual, and at the same time he pointed out the defects in the English theory, which tended to restrict state action to the exercise of police power, thus leaving the individual to work out his own salvation in a world dominated by the machine.

In 1887, Adams published his first book, dedicating it to his benefactor, Mr. Francis White. It bore the title, *Public Debts:—An Essay in the Science of Finance.* In the preface he explained:

It is the purpose of this treatise upon Public Debts to portray the principles which underlie the use of public credit. The essay is neither statistical nor historical, although it relies upon statistics and makes frequent appeals to history. In one respect it differs from works upon the same subject by German or French writers, for it recognizes a distinction between National Deficit Financiering and Local Deficit Financiering, and lays down rules for the latter not in complete harmony with rules applicable to the former. This peculiarity in structure was imposed upon the essay by the fact that, being addressed to Americans, it was obliged to conform to the characteristic features of American public law.

In 1898, he published a second work entitled *The Science of Finance*, which was designed as a textbook upon the subject for the use of colleges and universities:

> . . . to contribute something to the development of a financial system that shall satisfy the peculiar requirements of Federal and Local government in the United States . . . In all important cases it applies the administrative test to theoretical conclusions, and insists that every constructive proposal should be judged by its adaptation to existing conditions. It seems proper to make mention of this fact because those suggestions which give character to the programme of financial reform here submitted cannot be appreciated except the reader recognize the emphasis placed upon administrative considerations.

Speaking of these treatises, Professor E. R. A. Seligman commented:

> So far as the content of the work (*The Science of Finance*) is concerned, however, it was a remarkable performance and like its predecessor on Public Debts shot through with the American spirit. Adams here again very clearly shows that he was above all a thinker. This was so widely recognized that his colleagues elected him, after John Bates Clark, to the presidency of the American Economic Association, thus confirming the general verdict that he was after Clark the ablest thinker of the time in this country . . . He never lost interest in the problems of public finance. He felt convinced that they were the most important problems that confronted us.

In 1887 Congress had passed an act to regulate commerce and had authorized the organization of the Interstate Commerce Commission. The enactment of this law marked the beginning of the decline of individualism in industry and transportation. During the next third of a century, Adams was to witness the application of the principles set forth in his essay, "The Relation of the State to Industrial Action," by the enactment of regulatory laws both by Congress and by many of the state legislatures. Before Adams died in 1921, the Interstate Commerce Act (1887) and the Sherman Antitrust Act (1890), had been in substance re-enacted in many of the states. Workmen's compensation acts had been enacted in many states in an effort to equalize the losses necessarily incident to the operation of manufacturing plants and various other establishments.

These were followed by the Norris-LaGuardia Anti-Injunction Act (1932) and the National Labor Relations Act (1935). While it cannot be said that the later acts were prompted by the work of Adams, they were in conformity with the principles laid down by him in his essay "The Relation of the State to Industrial Action."

In 1887 President Cleveland appointed Thomas M. Cooley, LL.D. 1873, former chief justice of the Supreme Court of the state of Michigan, to be a member of the newly created Interstate Commerce Commission, and the commission immediately elected him its chairman. It soon became evident that the services of a specialist were needed to supervise the statistical work of the new agency. Cooley had known Henry Carter Adams intimately ever since Adams' first association with the University of Michigan faculty. It was, accordingly, not surprising that before the close of the commission's first year Adams had become chief statistician.

Accepting the appointment as statistician to the Interstate Commerce Commission, Adams began a long career of activity in public affairs. When he assumed his position, he was the department's only statistician; at the close of his tenure, in 1911, the statistical section employed 250 persons. His twenty-four years as head of the department witnessed many significant contributions to the regulatory process.

Adams' thorough study and serious consideration of the problems accompanying the organization of the statistical department is clearly indicated in his first annual report, on railway statistics in the United States for the year ended June 30, 1888, to the members of the commission. A major part of the report presents the results of the first attempt at compiling uniform railway statistics for the entire country. Less than six months had elapsed since the work of compilation had begun. Adams believed that "the framers of the 'Act to regulate commerce' intended to provide for comprehensive and authoritative railway statistics." To achieve this purpose he outlined a plan of procedure which would realize uniformity in railway statistics.

The railroads had resisted previous attempts to unify their reports, and the courts had ruled that there was no power granted to the commission to compel unification. As statistician for the commission, Adams immediately discovered that each company was making reports on its own basis—a practice which made almost impossible a satisfactory comparison and analysis of the reports.

Adams' proposed solution of the problem was tactfully presented to the railway officials in a paper on "Uniform Railway Statistics" written for a General Conference of Railway Commissioners held at Washington, D. C., March 5–7, 1889. In the years immediately following, many state legislatures were presented with bills looking toward the adoption of uniform statistical methods. Presumably, many of the state railway commissioners had carried home from the 1889 conference the lesson Adams had tried to teach. Further support from the railways themselves came when Adams encouraged them to present their individual suggestions as to the form of the blanks which should be employed by the commission in collecting the necessary data.

Final victory for the plan was realized in 1906, when Adams secured the adoption by Congress of an amendment to the "act to regulate commerce" which required railway companies to make uniform reports in accordance with regulations set by the commission; heavy penalties were imposed for failure to comply with the requirements. The amendment authorized the statistical department to make as complete as possible its file of railway statistics. For administrator Adams this posed a new problem. He found it difficult to discover well-equipped men to carry out his plans for conducting the work. In a letter of May 31, 1910, to United States Senator Francis W. Newlands, Adams wrote:

> I had assumed that all that was necessary was to provide the machinery and that a sufficient number of skilled men could be obtained for the government service to make that machinery effective. I had also assumed that the officials of the railways would readily appreciate the social and political meaning of supervised accounts. Neither of these assumptions seems to have been well-founded and I have been forced to the conclusion that a considerable body of young men must be educated to understand, not only the technical rules and scientific principles which underlie a system of accounts, but also the analysis of the political conditions and industrial relations to which those accounts address themselves, before we can hope to realize fully the possibilities which lie in the Twentieth Section of the Act.

With the hope that he could effect at least a partial remedy of the situation, Adams inaugurated a course in railway administration at the University of Michigan in 1910. Though the course was an "experimentation," Adams had great faith in its usefulness toward accomplishing his purpose. Fearing, however, that the Regents might not be favorably inclined to support such "experimentation," he attempted to interest prominent people throughout the country in giving the plan financial support for five years. He was confident that he could prove the value of the course within that period.

Financial assistance came from Joseph Boyer of Detroit, president of the Burroughs Adding Machine Company, and from other interested individuals. Letters to Adams—among them two from Senator Newlands and Elmer E. Brown,* of the United States Bureau of Education—furnish evidence of the enthusiastic approval accorded Adams' plan for educating

* Elmer Ellsworth Brown, A.B. 1889, acting assistant professor of the science and the art of teaching, University of Michigan, 1891–92; commissioner of education of the United States, 1906–11; chancellor of New York University, 1911–33.

young men to take over the supervision of transportation accounts. His efforts in this field mark one of his most effective contributions to the public service.

Adams' work as a statistician had received wide publicity and had come to the notice of the Chinese government, which retained Adams as its adviser in working out a system of accounting adapted to the Chinese system of railroads. He went to China on this mission in 1913 and remained there for four years. In recognition of his valuable services, the Chinese government caused a marble monument to be placed on his grave on February 22, 1922, with appropriate ceremonies. Doctor Chang, who delivered the address, translated the Chinese inscription as follows:

> In the memory of Professor Henry Carter Adams, this monument is erected by his colleagues of the Ministry of Communications, Republic of China, this tenth month of the tenth year of the Republic, where, as adviser, his wisdom and kindly temperament, his knowledge of economics and railway statesmanship were effective in unifying the accounting system of the Chinese Government Railways. We, strangers in the land, come in mourning to his grave. Our tears pay tribute to his honest and able help in our time of need. We commend his example to future generations.

Professor Frank H. Dixon,* for many years closely associated with Adams, had this to say of his contributions in the field of accounting:

> The accounting system has since been extended to other utilities, and into other jurisdictions, but the regulations have all been based upon this pioneer work. The accounting system for public utilities is the work of Mr. Adams and the service that this system now performs for the nation is a monument to his labors. Mr. Adams had the misfortune that his work was never fully appreciated by the commission during his years of service. But he never faltered in his purpose or in his conviction as to the significance of his work. It was his belief, amply

* Frank Haigh Dixon, Ph.B. 1892, Ph.D. 1895, assistant in political economy, 1892–95, instructor in history, 1896–97, assistant professor of political economy, 1897–98, University of Michigan; assistant professor of economics, 1898–1903, professor of economics, 1903–19, Dartmouth; professor of economics, 1919–44, Princeton University.

justified since, that the success of administrative regulation rested upon sound, intelligible, uniform standardized accounts. The Commission realizes this now and calls constantly upon its Bureau of Statistics and Accounts to aid in the solution of its problems of regulation.

It would be well within the truth to say that after 1887, Adams spent his entire life in serving the public. As a teacher, as a lecturer, and as a writer he dealt with matters related intimately to the public welfare. In addition to the publications already referred to, he contributed many other articles dealing with industry, corporate abuses, taxation, regulation of railway rates, principles of public accounting, and problems of budgetary reform and was among the first to call attention to intangible value in public utility valuation. Nor was his work confined to discussion. He was an active and effective participant in putting into practice many of the principles which he had developed in the course of his lectures and writing. He was also instrumental in the work of the tax commission of Michigan, a part of which related to the valuation for tax purposes of Michigan railroads.

Professor Seligman, a contemporary, in a memorial address thus appraised his work:

> When the history of economics comes to be written, I think it may be said without peradventure of doubt that Adams will occupy a place in the forefront ranks of American economists. In public finance, in railroad transportation, in industrial regulation, he made notable and permanent contributions to economic sciences.

So diverse were his activities and so extensive was the influence he exerted through teaching, lecturing, and writing, and through participating actively in public affairs, that it is very difficult to appraise the services of Henry Carter Adams to the public. All of his contemporaries awarded him first rank as an economist, statistician, and teacher.

A former student * discloses the key to Adams' outstanding success as a teacher in the following tribute:

* Ira A. Campbell, B.L. 1900, LL.B. 1902, lawyer, New York City, author of the chapter on "Alumni in Congress" in this volume.

His forte as a teacher lay not only in the soundness of his thinking and the foresightedness of his views, but in the personality which won the admiration and regard of his students. His fine appearance, handsome and always well groomed, the buoyancy of spirit with which he addressed his classes, and the modulated voice in which he spoke, not only held the attention and gained the confidence of his students, but developed a personal liking that amounted to affection. Possessing with this the ability and ease of clear statement of the subject matter he was discussing—taking it apart and putting it together again to test its truthfulness—made attendance at his lectures a pleasure rather than an activity to be endured for the profit to be gained. The result was an acquisition of knowledge that made study under his direction a delight and aroused in his students an eagerness for learning. To those who had the privilege of studying with Professor Adams, it was the fine personality of the man, even more than the principles he taught, that lived on and constituted his greatest influence on their after years.

One of the leaders * of the succeeding generation of economists said of Adams:

It is gratifying to the admirers of Henry Carter Adams that the tributes paid him when he died a quarter-century ago are as fresh and true today as when they were first delivered. The passing of the years has not dimmed either the lustre of his achievements or the influence of his rare personality on the lives he touched.

We hail him today as a pioneer in the field of public finance. We recognize him as a pathfinder in the effective regulation of the railways through the uniform accounting systems he helped to make mandatory, and the statistical controls he established. But most of all, we still honor him as a great public servant of the highest ideals, seeking always to instill them in the governments he served and the devoted students he trained.

If the careers of the many students who were profoundly influenced by his teaching and writings could be followed, one would beyond doubt find that the contributions of Henry Carter Adams to the polity of the state and the nation have been incalculable.

* Professor William H. Kiekhofer, University of Wisconsin.

James Burrill Angell

1829	*Born in Scituate, Rhode Island*
1849	*Graduated from Brown University*
1850	*Traveled in the South*
1851–53	*Traveled in Europe*
1853	*Appointed professor of modern languages at Brown University*
1855	*Married Sarah Caswell*
1860	*Became editor of the* Providence Journal
1866	*Appointed president of the University of Vermont*
1871	*Appointed president of the University of Michigan*
1880	*Appointed minister plenipotentiary and envoy extraordinary to China and chairman of the Treaty Commission*
1887	*Selected as a member of the Canadian Fisheries Commission*
1896	*Appointed chairman of the Deep Waterways Commission*
1897	*Appointed minister to Turkey*
1909	*Retired from the presidency of the University of Michigan*
1916	*Died in Ann Arbor, Michigan*

James B. Angell

James Burrill Angell

By Wilfred B. Shaw
With suggestions from James R. Angell

WHEN the President of the University of Michigan, James Burrill Angell, became minister plenipotentiary and envoy extraordinary to China in 1880, following the similar designation the year before of President Andrew Dickson White, LL.D. 1867, of Cornell University, as minister to Germany, a breath of air stirred through the musty corridors of Washington's State Department. A new element in American public service was rising, a leaven destined to become increasingly important with the succeeding years. The peculiar fitness of university administrators and scholars for diplomatic service was becoming definitely recognized, and these appointments became the first of many similar calls upon university leaders, tributes to maturing American scholarship.

This migration of scholars from the academic world into diplomacy not only foreshadowed a broader view of our relations abroad, based on experience in foreign ways and thought, but it also recognized the desirability of a certain proficiency in history, politics, and languages on the part of our diplomats. Moreover, it served to improve the standards of our foreign service at a time when too many of our representatives abroad were selected solely upon the basis of political expediency and a private income.

Actually, the entrance of university executives and teachers into this new field could not have come much before the appointments of White and Angell. American colleges had provided little in the way of preparation for diplomatic service; and it was not until a new approach to the study of contemporary history was recognized and political science became an accepted element in the college curriculum that Washington finally turned toward qualified members of college faculties.

The University of Michigan, the liberal educational policies of which had always been recognized, played an important role in the lives of both White and Angell. In his earlier and formative years Andrew D. White had been influenced by the progressive spirit of the young institution in the West, where in 1857 he became one of the first college teachers in America to occupy a chair devoted solely to the teaching and study of history. Likewise, James Burrill Angell, in 1872, had been one of the first to offer courses on international law and political science and later became the outstanding representative of the University in the eyes of the nation.

While Angell is to be regarded, like Eliot of Harvard and White of Cornell, as one of the great university leaders of his period, his diplomatic career as minister to China and, later, to Turkey and as a member of the Canadian Fisheries and Deep Waterways Commissions was distinguished. If he had not given himself wholeheartedly to university administration and had turned definitely to diplomacy, which might have been possible "if ministers could have counted on a permanent tenure," history might well regard him as one of America's foremost exponents of forthright, honest, and, at the same time, realistic policies in international relations. As it was, his pre-eminence as an educator gave him special prestige, particularly in China, where an immemorial regard for the scholar made his appointment peculiarly acceptable. As a diplomat his actions and policies were tempered and governed by his scholarly outlook; as a college president he was always the diplomat, as many of his colleagues, sometimes ruefully, were wont to testify. Throughout his career, moreover, the homely contacts of his early life, his travels, his experiences as a newspaper editor, and his firsthand studies of European politics proved invaluable.

There was still another quality in the man which colored and strengthened his services as a diplomat—his essentially American personality, with a native shrewdness and philosophy reminiscent of Benjamin Franklin. The resemblance might easily be overemphasized, but a similar New England background projected a broad and keenly observant appreciation of world problems, giving the personal relations and negotiations of both a simple directness and candor, tempered always by a keen and tolerant, often humorous, appreciation of human foibles.

James Burrill Angell was born in Scituate, Rhode Island, January 7, 1829. The place and the time are both significant. The austerities of a New England background in his case were tempered by the more liberal outlook of his Rhode Island forebears, early protestants against Puritan intolerance, and his formative years marked a period when the country as a whole was fast becoming aware of the vast areas beyond the Alleghenies.

The farm on which he was born was originally settled by the grandson of the first of the American family, who had come from England in 1631. The farmhouse, built in 1810, stood on a turnpike leading into Providence, and his father accordingly had combined farming with innkeeping. Of this element in his early development Angell later remarked, "I have always felt that the knowledge of men I gained by the observations and experiences of my boyhood in the country tavern has been of the greatest assistance." Here was human nature in every guise, and the boy acquired early an ability to adapt himself to all kinds of men.

When about eight years old, young Angell began his formal schooling in a series of local academies, which, despite many defects, rendered, in his mature estimation, a "valuable service" and resulted in what was deemed an adequate preparation for college. But he was only fourteen, and it was decided that vigorous outdoor life would be better for the somewhat delicate boy. For two years he was put to work on his father's farm, an experience that enabled him "to see how the world looks from the point of view of the laboring man."

Young Angell's interest in practical political and constitutional questions was also stimulated by the problems involved in the Dorr Rebellion of 1842 in Rhode Island, still governed under a colonial charter which restricted the suffrage to qualified landowners. With the growth of manufacturing following the War of 1812, the propertyless mill operators and mechanics demanded the vote, and a new constitution was promulgated by the people. Under its extralegal provisions Thomas W. Dorr, "a most worthy and capable man," was elected governor, but when an attempt was made to take possession of the state administration forcibly, Dorr was charged with treason.

Feeling ran high throughout this struggle. Angell's father, a member of the legislature, was a supporter of the old regime, although most of his neighbors in the adjacent factory village were Dorrites. Thus, his son's introduction to fundamental political problems took an immediate and practical form. Eventually, a more liberal constitution gave the vote to all citizens of American birth.

When he had reached the ripe age of sixteen in 1845, Angell was finally permitted to enter Brown University. There he found a faculty of seven under one of the great college presidents of his era, Dr. Francis Wayland, who "deserved to be ranked with the strongest men our country has produced." It is perhaps significant that one of Wayland's courses was political economy, which then comprised much of what is now included in political science.

The first few postcollege years, including an eight-month horseback trip through the South with his lifelong friend, Rowland Hazard, added new facets to Angell's widening experience. Starting down the Shenandoah Valley, the travelers progressed through the seaboard states to Florida, thence to New Orleans and up the Mississippi to Tennessee and Kentucky—an illuminating experience for two thoughtful young men.

Upon his return Angell planned to study for the ministry, but found that his delicate throat would always make much public speaking inadvisable. He fell back upon his mathematics and entered the office of Boston's city engineer, where his familiarity with the calculus gave him an immediate advantage over his associates with their rule-of-thumb practice. This work, an interesting and valuable experience, was brought to an end after a few months by another period of travel, a "grand tour" of France, Italy, Austria, and Germany, again in company with Hazard.

While in Vienna Angell received an offer of a professorship, in either civil engineering or modern languages, at Brown; he accepted the second. Returning to Paris in June, 1852, he began an intensive study of French, followed by a similar German program in Brunswick and Munich. The following summer he returned to become at twenty-four the youngest member of the Brown faculty.

President Wayland had advanced ideas, and the new professor was encouraged to develop in his classes original methods, which were greatly appreciated by his students, among whom were two future secretaries of state, Richard Olney and John Hay. Angell also began to capitalize upon his firsthand acquaintance with contemporary European politics in a series of leading articles in the *Providence Journal*, one of the outstanding newspapers of the period. This work led to his acceptance of the editorship, a position he held throughout the Civil War, important years for the still youthful editor, for his competence in national and international problems brought him into close and fruitful contact with many important leaders in public life.

The strain of newspaper life began to affect his health, however, and an offer of the presidency of the University of Vermont made possible a return to the more normal tempo of academic life. In August, 1866, he entered upon his lifework of forty-three years as a university administrator.

The task before the incoming president was to harmonize the traditions of a small conservative institution with the new and very practical dispensation in agricultural training provided by the Morrill Act. Within a few years the effects of his efforts became widely recognized. Younger men were brought into the faculty, and the president himself added to his already heavy program courses in rhetoric, history, German, and international law.

In the midst of this encouraging progress an offer to Angell of the presidency of the University of Michigan fell like a bombshell and precipitated a crisis for Vermont. He gave the subject careful study as his published correspondence reveals; but in the end declined the offer in October, 1869. Two years later, however, the offer was renewed, and this time he accepted.

When he entered upon his new duties at Ann Arbor in September, 1871, he found a situation very different from that in Vermont. The University of Michigan, new and progressive, was already one of the largest in the country. It had just received assurance of support from the state legislature; an integration with the secondary educational system of the state had been effected; and after some years of agitation, the revolutionary step of admitting women as students had been approved.

Michigan's new and progressive ideals in education had been ably set forth by the University's first president, Henry P. Tappan, who had envisioned with uncanny foresight the educational possibilities of the state university, but two decades passed before it fell to President Angell to give them practical form and to make Michigan a real university.

In the words of his son, President James R. Angell, A.B. 1890, A.M. 1891, LL.D. 1931, of Yale University:

> He saw at once that his commanding duty, as well as his dramatic opportunity, was not to be found solely in the wise and effective administration of the University, which he conscientiously sought and achieved, but quite as much in the development within the commonwealth of Michigan, and through her in the entire Mississippi Valley and the West beyond, of an ineradicable resolution to foster and protect the invaluable blessings of sound education, and especially in the creation among the people of an imperative demand for universities of the highest quality.

The early years at Michigan were by no means entirely free of problems and difficulties. Despite the legislative support, through a tax upon assessed land values, financial problems continued acute; a proposed homeopathic medical school was bitterly opposed; the constitutional powers of the Regents were not yet firmly established; and a series of minor discrepancies in the chemical laboratory accounts became a state-wide *cause célèbre.* Yet, throughout everything, the University grew and flourished and became the great exemplar of the state university idea; its president without question counted among the great educators of the post-Civil War era.

Accordingly, Angell's appointment to an important diplomatic service was approved throughout the nation. The call was apparently a total surprise. It came on February 20, 1880, in the form of a letter from Senator H. P. Baldwin, of Michigan, informing him that Secretary of State William M. Evarts desired to see him on a matter of public interest, but only during the course of his first interview with Evarts was Angell enlightened as to the task for which he was being considered.

Chinese immigration was creating many acute problems which, it was feared, might soon threaten the American political and economic system. Violent opposition in California led to "disgraceful legislation against the Chinese" and "to still more disgraceful treatment of them by the roughs and hoodlums of San Francisco." These difficulties made it sufficiently evident that some measure of control over Chinese immigration must be exercised if the status of the American workingman on the coast was to be maintained. There might be some immediate benefits for employers, but this influx of cheap laborers threatened the American standard of living for the average citizen.

The difficulty lay in the treaty negotiated for the Chinese by Anson Burlingame in 1868, which provided for free immigration of Chinese. To exclude them summarily would be a breach of good faith and would expose this country to the charge of deliberately breaking a treaty. The situation manifestly called for delicate and understanding negotiation. Senator George F. Edmunds, an old friend of Vermont days, suggested President Angell for the task. Mr. Evarts later told him that he had been chosen, in part at least, because he represented education, which the Chinese so highly honor.

It was first suggested he serve as one of two commissioners, but Angell was doubtful of the effectiveness of such a commission and cited Rome's consular difficulties. Accordingly, a commission of three members was finally authorized; one member to come from California, one from the Eastern seaboard, with Angell, as minister plenipotentiary and envoy extraordinary, to be the commission's head.

Angell did not accept the appointment immediately. In his reply on March 11, he wrote that if "direct and formal prohibition of Chinese immigration" was desired, someone else should undertake the work, but that if this correction "should work as a restraint on immigration," he was willing to undertake the task. He also desired it to be widely understood that he was undertaking the mission only as a special exigency.

Nothing in Angell's letter was incompatible with the President's purposes, and his nomination was confirmed on April 9, 1880. The other two commissioners were John F. Swift, of California, and William H. Trescot, of South Carolina. Swift, who "had no diplomatic experience or reading and no diplomatic instinct," definitely represented the point of view of California and was an advocate of exclusion; Trescot took Angell's views of the main question and of modes of procedure.

Subsequent interviews with Secretary Evarts, in which Trescot participated, served to define further the scope of the mission. The principal problems considered were diplomatic and commercial relations; the difference between European and Asiatic immigration; the commercial questions involved in the *likin* tax, which hampered the export of American goods; the importance of an American policy not tied to England; the expediency of dispersing Chinese in this country; and, above all, the importance of impressing the Chinese government with our desire to be fair and even generous. It was concluded informally that if the Chinese were unwilling to negotiate on these fair terms, the American government would be free to take legislative measures.

In commenting on these interviews Angell observed in his diary that "Mr. E's ideas [are] not yet brought out to sharp points." It was this very lack of "sharp points" that was responsible for some of the differences among the American commissioners and that helped to make Angell's task difficult.

Before sailing from San Francisco on June 19, Angell had informed himself as fully as possible on the whole problem of Chinese-American relations. He read diplomatic correspondence and books on China assiduously and interviewed, among others, Dr. Peter Parker, a former medical missionary at Canton, and the veteran George Bancroft, who "sympathized with the Pacific coast view." He consulted returned missionaries, as well as Frederick Ferdinand Low, governor of California from 1863 to 1874 and, later, a consular officer in China, who had doubts as to the mission. He found however "less difference of opinion among sensible men than . . . expected." On shipboard Angell's unaffected interest in everyone about him and his insatiable appetite for information led him to cultivate all those who could conceivably contribute information on China.

Hardly had their vessel cast anchor in Japan before a question of the status of Swift and Trescot arose. The American admiral in Yokohama gave the official salute to Angell alone and then rather pointedly called upon him, neglecting the other two commissioners, who were, naturally, offended. Angell unofficially informed the admiral of his mistake, and the trouble finally was settled amicably. It was explained that Navy protocol had ranked commissioners only as chargés, but Angell pointed out that commissioners with full powers to negotiate a treaty were of a higher grade. Had they been made envoys or ministers extraordinary, a usual designation, the question would not have arisen.

The naval officers on the three American vessels, the "Richmond," "Ashuelot," and "Monocacy," obviously were not enthusiastic over taking the party to the Chinese coast, but Angell again diplomatically pointed out to the admiral that it was important that the commissioners be carried to their destination by United States naval vessels. As a result the party was properly convoyed.

The party landed in Chefoo on August 1. Angell left immediately to arrange for the negotiations. On the way the new minister was cordially received in Tientsin by the great Chinese viceroy, Li Hung Chang, who expressed warm friendship for the United States and quickly returned Angell's call, bringing to the "Ashuelot" a large retinue, including General Charles ("Chinese") Gordon, later killed at Khartoum, who had come to China to persuade the government to avoid a threatened war with Russia over a troublesome boundary dispute.

In Peking the new minister was introduced at the Tsung Li Yamen, the Chinese foreign office, by his predecessor as minister, George F. Seward. Angell very quickly became aware of hidden opposition on Seward's part and of his attempts to undermine the new commission. Seward was not popular with the Chinese, however, and it was, in part, their opposition to him which had been responsible for his recall by Washington.

The political situation in China in 1880 was far from favorable for negotiations. Signs of the breakup of the old regime were already evident. The emperor was only a boy, and control rested in the ultraconservative hands of the empress, who was surrounded by politicians and bureaucrats, most of them venal and constitutionally opposed to Western ideas. The outlying provinces were controlled by local officials, who co-operated with the central government only when it suited their pleasure. Communications were slow. There were no railroads, although one small line was under construction. A telegraph line from Shanghai to Tientsin was opened in 1881.

Even the decrees of the Imperial Government, particularly those favorable to foreigners, were often ignored until their effectiveness was nullified, while a continual series of "incidents" made all too plain the Chinese feeling toward the "Western barbarians." Chinese evasiveness and lack of logical thought processes according to our standards made a further difficulty in negotiations. In Angell's words, "These keen reasoners were almost absolutely devoid of mathematical or scientific education. I sometimes doubted whether in reaching their conclusions they were aware as we are of taking certain logical steps."

Nevertheless, Angell came to have a high regard for some of the Chinese officials and found that he was able to deal with them on a man-to-man basis; this was particularly true of Li Hung Chang, who had evidently formed a high opinion of Angell also and had talked with him very freely.

Angell was received with great courtesy by Prince Kung, head of the Chinese Foreign Office, and by members of the Yamen, and his official call was quickly returned. The Chinese officials "seemed to present a combination of childlike simplicity and ignorance with the statesmanship of their sort." It was this quality of the Chinese, combined with cross currents of political intrigue, which made the mission difficult and led some members of the diplomatic corps to predict its eventual failure, possibly in some cases a wish-fathered thought.

Angell quickly became acquainted with members of the other legations in Peking, among whom he rated the German minister, von Brandt, as one of the ablest, but Germany's policy, with that of Russia, was aggressive and even warlike, in contrast to the attitude of the Americans and English. Sir Thomas Wade, the British minister, and Thomas Hart, head of the Chinese customs (who later became Sir Thomas Hart), with both of whom Angell became intimately acquainted, emphasized British peaceful policy against the saber rattling of Germany and Russia.

The Americans were apprised in a communication from Prince Kung of the appointment of two Chinese commissioners who were of high rank and members of the privy council. Pao Chun, a Manchu distantly related to the royal family and president of the Imperial College of Literature, was understood to be "conciliatory and progressive in his policy," but Li Hung Tsao, a Chinese tutor of the late emperor and a profound scholar, was "credited with being anti-foreign or reactionary in his views."

Before actual discussion was inaugurated on October 1, the

American commissioners agreed on a memorandum, prepared largely by Trescot, setting forth the American position, together with a draft of possible treaty articles to be presented if the Chinese asked for it. Some disagreement arose over this treaty draft, which originally proposed a mutual exclusion of laborers. Angell objected to this provision on principle, and his view, that it should be conceded only if demanded by the Chinese and if the power of the United States to regulate immigration were finally approved, was accordingly made implicit in the American proposal. Swift, however, demanded an article "stopping immigration unless Congress should by act open it." Angell and Trescot opposed this proposal, and Swift perforce yielded, "but not without some feeling."

It was Swift's position that the "commission was sent to stop immigration by treaty and not to leave Congress to fight on," but his associates, more familiar with Washington's view through their interviews with Evarts, maintained that the matter must rest with Congress, and since at that time the United States did not have the right to pass such legislation, it was the task of the commission to ask for such a right. Swift wished his statement pressed and that further instructions be requested from Washington, but the other two maintained the commission already had sufficient discretion. Mr. Swift once more "had much feeling."

On meeting the Chinese, only the memorandum was presented; it was deemed wiser to postpone submission of the treaty draft. The Chinese, upon reading the American statement, remarked upon its "cordiality" and stated that while there were difficulties, in the words of Pao, there were "none which were not capable of adjustment." "He was very jolly and cordial," but Li had "a less promising aspect." The beginning thus seemed favorable, but when the Chinese reply came a week later, it proved "inconsequential in reasoning . . . although . . . capable of an interpretation not discouraging."

At the next meeting, October 15, the Americans pointed out that they were present by order of the government and not, as the Chinese note implied, as a result of Irish discontent in

California. The Americans took sharp exception to the Chinese suggestion "that the government of the United States [was] merely speaking the language of 'violent men'" and stated in pointed language that the United States could not "allow the representatives of China to go behind . . . a commission upon a subject of grave interest in respectful and friendly language . . . and either criticize [the government's] motives or deny the good faith of its representatives."

The Chinese promptly disclaimed any intention of being offensive; their only desire was "to discuss and settle these questions upon the basis of mutual amity." Apparently, they had been somewhat misinformed upon American policy by Seward, who had suggested without proper authorization that steps be taken to prevent the immigration of four classes of Chinese citizens—coolie laborers, criminals, prostitutes, and diseased persons. The American commissioners, however, made it plain that Seward's "propositions in no way furnished the basis of any negotiation which they were willing to undertake." They maintained that "the Government of the United States thought it ought to have the right to decide to what extent and under what circumstances immigration is wholesome, and to stop it when it became injurious." The Chinese, asked whether "they could in no case consider the modification of the Burlingame treaty," replied that they were anxious to do nothing in direct opposition, but were willing in effect to consider modifications.

The American commission then submitted its modification of the existing treaty. The first of the three articles guaranteed mutual rights and privileges of residence to nationalists of each country who came "for the purpose of trade, travel, or temporary residence for the purpose of teaching, study, or curiosity." The second and most important article provided that the United States might "regulate, limit, suspend, or prohibit" the residence of Chinese laborers whenever the interests of the United States were affected; the third merely guaranteed the rights of Chinese subjects already in the United States.

It was recognized in advance by the American commissioners

that the use of the word "prohibit" in this second article would probably be unacceptable to the Chinese, but, following a cardinal rule of diplomacy, they were "prepared at the proper time to withdraw this extreme claim in concession to a final advance on the part of the Chinese commissioners to such a degree of discretionary power on the part of the United States as we deemed practically sufficient to secure the control of Chinese immigration."

The Chinese, as expected, at once questioned the use of the word, maintaining that "regulate" would suffice. They also suggested that they would "like to hear" what the American idea as to limitation might be. The Americans then stated their view that such limitation should be in the discretion of the United States government, and that the desired modification of the Burlingame Treaty would enable it, without raising unpleasant questions of treaty construction, to exercise that discretion.

While the American commissioners were encouraged by a general agreement upon which further negotiations could be based, it is obvious that great differences existed, not only in language, but in fundamental points of view. These differences, as well as the sharp disagreement among the American representatives, made Angell's task none too easy.

When the Chinese presented their treaty project on October 31, several features proved entirely unacceptable. It was specified that the limitation of Chinese immigration be confined to the state of California alone, that artisans, as distinguished from laborers, were not to be excluded, that there be no punishment of those who entered the United States in contravention of the treaty, and that only Americans be prohibited from importing and employing Chinese labor.

The American counterproposal was presented to the Chinese on November 2. The two plans had proved so divergent that the American commissioners had been forced to return to their original draft, omitting the word "prohibit" and retaining certain unimportant provisions suggested by the Chinese. But they were finally successful in maintaining that the proposed laws should be operative throughout the United States, and that the regulations should be applied there, rather than resting with the authorities in China, who had no jurisdiction over emigration from Hong Kong and Singapore.

The Chinese had already agreed that artisans should not be excluded from the treaty when it was made plain that actually it was skilled labor which caused the special embarrassment the United States was seeking to avoid. Also, to permit French, German, English, and Chinese residents, but not Americans, to import labor, would merely prohibit cheap labor to American citizens. That proposal, therefore, was also dropped.

When the commissions met on November 5 for a most anxious, and, as it proved, decisive session, both the Chinese and the American proposals were presented. The Americans made it plain they could not consent to any settlement which did not recognize the entire discretion of the United States in immigration policy. At first there appeared to be no common meeting ground in the limitation of immigration, which in the Chinese view should be temporary, with the "number allowed by the regulations not excessively small, nor the term of years excessively long." Angell, in his diary, reported that the other commissioners thought they had reached the end. But "I saw the Chinese were discussing among themselves, and asked for patience. We might as well spend an hour here now. Never will our time be more valuable. Let us leave this article and go to the last. Let the fish chew the bait awhile."

Accordingly, other sections were then discussed; a Chinese provision that no laws should be passed by the United States which would be operative until approved by the Chinese was recognized as unreasonable and was soon waived by the Chinese commissioners; likewise, an article in which the Chinese seemed to ask that students and merchants be allowed to take with them not only body servants but employees was settled satisfactorily when it was made plain that only household servants were meant.

Upon returning to the first article, the Americans were able to show that a limitation of the powers of the American government as to numbers or length of stay was not appropriate to a treaty and would only cause discussion, and accordingly that demand was also dropped. As to penalties, the Chinese wished only to guard against personal abuse and maltreatment, to which, of course, the Americans agreed. This meeting of minds finally paved the way for dovetailing the first articles of both drafts, and the work was done.

Subsequently, the Chinese officials, in submitting the treaty to Prince Kung, omitted a definition in Article 1 of the word "laborer." This greatly annoyed the American commissioners, but the Chinese maintained the word was virtually defined in the second article, and that it was "disagreeable to them to state the thing so sharply." The Americans finally yielded; the Chinese had, in fact, made many concessions.

The question of a second treaty to deal with commercial relations was then discussed. The Chinese felt that the existing treaties were one-sided; they wished equal commercial privileges abroad, with rates of tonnage and import duties fixed on the same scale for both nations. Since America had always been their friend they preferred to take this matter up with the United States first. The American commissioners responded cordially, feeling that we could lose nothing; it made the Imperial Government directly responsible in cases of customs maladministration, for which there was at the time no practical redress, and the implied reduction of the powers of provincial officers was a distinct gain.

When finally signed, this second treaty not only included a provision for the "future extension of commercial relations," but it also provided for the trial of a person in the court of his own nationality, including "what had never yet been granted . . . the right of the plaintiff's counsel to present, examine, and cross-examine witnesses." A regularization of the formalities of communication between the officials of the two governments was also suggested, but the Chinese were unwilling to include such a stipulation without general negotiations with all the treaty powers.

Then the Chinese raised the question of the prohibition of

trade in opium, a request made, it was generally understood, at the suggestion of Li Hung Chang. While there was some question among the commissioners as to their authority, they finally decided to include such an article, believing that it would meet with general American approval, although Angell had some doubt as to the British reaction.

The two treaties were finally signed on November 17 and sent to Washington for formal ratification. The forty-eight days of negotiation represented an unheard-of speed in dealings with the Chinese Foreign Office. The diplomatic skill of President Angell, not only in his relations with the Chinese but also in overcoming differences among the American commissioners, made the final outcome a distinct personal triumph. The Senate duly approved the treaty, the ratifications were exchanged in Peking on July 19, and it was proclaimed on October 5, 1881. Within eight months Congress passed the Chinese Exclusion Act of May 6, 1882, suspending Chinese immigration for ten years.

The net result, superficially at least, was a great gain for the United States, with few corresponding benefits for China. Nevertheless, the Chinese continued to enjoy larger privileges in this country than Americans had in China, even though in some cases the situation was reversed. Other factors undoubtedly influenced the Chinese. They wished, above all, friendly relations with the other great power across the Pacific and were willing to make concessions over a few thousand coolies in view of future American friendship. Moreover, their friendly spirit led to the ready American acceptance of the limitation of the opium traffic, greatly desired by the Chinese. In this matter there was no question of a *quid pro quo*, since the immigration question had been settled before the question of the opium traffic was raised. The Chinese, in Angell's words, might have said, "We will make you some concession provided you will help us in our attempt to prevent the importation of opium." But no such bargain was even suggested.

With the settlement of the two treaties Trescot and Swift returned to America, while Angell, as minister, remained in

China. Though the tasks he performed during his year of service were less important than the negotiation of the treaties, he was zealous in promoting friendly relations with the Chinese Foreign Office, and he participated actively in the conferences of the foreign diplomatic corps, which was discussing certain matters involving all the nations represented at Peking, particularly those questions affecting foreign trade with China.

Among these was the dredging of the Woosung Bar across the mouth of the Shanghai River, which the Chinese felt was "a heaven-sent barrier" against war vessels of heavy draught. Another question, debated throughout Angell's whole period in China, involved the tribute, or "squeeze," upon imports over and above the regularly imposed duties at the port of entry. Minor taxes, or *likin*, were demanded at each stage of transport into the interior, with the result that, not far inland, prices became prohibitive. The central government was unable, or unwilling, to deal with the local officials, whereas consular offices were overwhelmed with complaints and demands for redress. The diplomatic body, therefore, suggested a set tax to replace the exactions of the local officials.

Angell also protested vigorously against the granting of an exclusive license to a Danish company to construct a telegraph line from Shanghai to Tientsin and Peking. This monopoly apparently had been secretly supported by Li Hung Chang, and Angell received nothing but evasive answers from the Chinese officials.

A diplomatic incident with repercussions sixty years later concerned Japanese negotiations over the Loo Choo (now Ryukyu) Islands. The Japanese minister, Shishido, had negotiated a treaty providing that part of the islands should be held by Japan and part by China, but the Chinese failed to sign the treaty. The Japanese minister, therefore, felt that he had no recourse but to return to Japan. Upon being privately asked his opinion by Shishido, Angell said that if the Chinese had refused to sign the American treaty, he should have certainly felt bound to leave. Apropos of this conversation, James G. Blaine, Secretary Evarts' successor, wrote Angell that while no "censure . . . is intended," such a withdrawal, if necessary, would have been a subject for decision by the State Department, and that "scrupulous impartiality" was necessary in our relations with both China and Japan.

Throughout his stay in China, Angell made an especial study of American missions, and his diary is filled with references to them. He was active in adjusting their not infrequent difficulties, particularly depredations against them in outlying localities, and in securing property rights for the missions where Chinese opposition existed. He also secured a remission of the taxes upon the Protestant church bodies for support of Chinese religious ceremonials, already granted to Catholic churches but apparently by inadvertence omitted in the case of Protestant churches.

President Angell took every opportunity to familiarize himself with Chinese life. He read widely and took occasion to discuss with many authorities Chinese social, religious, and political questions. He even undertook a study of the Chinese language under the tutelage of his friend Sir Thomas Wade.

This interest and sympathy were greatly appreciated by the Chinese. At the close of the World Exposition in New Orleans in 1885, the Chinese government presented the whole of its elaborate exhibit to President Angell, a gift significantly made to him personally, although it is now a part of the anthropological collections in the University of Michigan. Today the University has one of the largest, if not the largest, enrollment of students from China. Many of these students come as a direct result of Angell's interest in China, and they continue to further the mutual understanding he inaugurated so long ago.

Angell's year of service in China came to an end on October 4, 1881, when he began the first stage of his long trip home by way of Europe. He arrived in Ann Arbor on February 24, 1882.

Following his return President Angell devoted himself for six years to his tasks as university president, but in 1887 he was again called into public service by President Cleveland to serve as a member of a joint British-American commission to settle, if possible, the long-standing dispute between the United

States and Canada over the North Atlantic fisheries. His acceptance of the appointment came in part as a result of the urgent request of E. J. Phelps, United States minister to Great Britain, through whose hands the correspondence of our government with the British had passed.

Fishing was one of the most important industries of the New Englanders. During colonial days they had enjoyed fishing rights over the whole North Atlantic coast, and they stoutly maintained, although with doubtful legality, that these were "natural rights." After the Revolutionary War, they continued to fish in what became Canadian waters. The Canadians, particularly in Nova Scotia and Newfoundland, many of them émigré loyalists, looked with disfavor on the American fishermen and were responsible for various oppressive measures which sought to prevent the Americans from buying supplies or using Canadian coastal areas for drying and curing their fish.

In a treaty signed in 1818 these questions had been settled to the satisfaction of both parties. The Americans renounced "forever any liberty heretofore enjoyed or claimed" as to fishing within three miles of Canadian coasts, bays, creeks, or harbors, although they were permitted to enter the bays and harbors for four purposes—shelter, wood, water, and repairs. This settled the dispute for a time, but within twenty years the British were insisting that the treaty excluded the Americans from larger bodies of water such as the Bay of Fundy, as well as from navigating the Strait of Canso. The British sought to control the waters of a bay as measured from "headland to headland," and the Americans insisted on following the three-mile limit, maintaining that the term "bay," in general, implied only an indentation of such size and shape that to enter it a vessel must approach within three miles of land.

What the Americans sought was the privilege of "inshore" fishing, that is, within the three-mile territorial limit; what the Canadians desired was free access to the markets of the United States. Both these aims were finally satisfied in 1854 by a treaty in which American fishermen again gained the liberty to fish in Canadian bays, harbors, and creeks, which they had had in the final settlement after the Revolution. The Canadians gained access to American markets, through the admission duty-free of a long list of commodities, including fish and fisheries products.

Relations improved immediately, and trade increased by leaps and bounds, but, unfortunately, this harmony was short-lived. Sympathy with the South during the Civil War, shown in some Canadian localities, was resented in the United States, and complaints of the unfairness of the reciprocity treaty grew with the growth of high-tariff policies. In consequent, the treaty was abrogated in 1866, and the old troubles once more arose. The situation grew so acute that in the Treaty of Washington signed in 1871, provision was made for a cash payment by the United States for inshore fishing privileges in Canadian waters, in addition to the admission of fish and fish oil duty-free to the United States. As a result the United States paid $5,500,000 to Great Britain, the sum finally fixed by an international commission, which met in Halifax in 1877 and which was, in American opinion, unduly sympathetic to the British point of view. Nevertheless, the dispute was again settled.

In 1885 the rising tide of protectionism in both countries led once more to the abrogation of the fishery articles in the treaty of 1871. Canadian authorities again began merciless seizures of American fishing craft, and, as a result, the American Congress passed a retaliatory law, although no action was ever taken under its authority.

Meanwhile, President Cleveland and Secretary of State Thomas F. Bayard, LL.D. 1891, in corresponding with the British, became convinced that an international commission might reach a peaceful and satisfactory settlement. Cleveland, therefore, despite strong opposition from a Republican Congress, in the fall of 1887 appointed Bayard, President Angell, and William L. Putnam, a lawyer from Portland, Oregon, who had served as a government counsel in fishery cases, as American members of such a commission, with Bayard as chairman.

The British appointed Joseph Chamberlain, Sir Charles Tupper, premier of Canada, and Lord Sackville-West, the British minister at Washington. Angell's appointment led his son Alexis, A.B. 1878, LL.B. 1880, LL.D. 1915, to observe that he was "glad the entry of fish and of Chinese is to be regulated by the same mind."

In contrast to his experience in China, Angell found the American commissioners in agreement upon practically all the questions involved. Thomas M. Cooley, LL.D. 1873, then in Washington as the first chairman of the Interstate Commerce Commission, wrote in his diary (October 8, 1887) that Angell considered Bayard "a man of fine feelings, who . . . desires that all our dealings with other nations should be considered in a spirit of fairness and amity. The Fisheries difficulty the Secretary expects to succeed in arranging with little trouble . . . President Angell is not so confident."

The British point of view differed radically from that of the Americans, as can be seen from Lord Salisbury's letter of October 24, 1887, to the British plenipotentiaries:

> . . . it is not the wish of her Majesty's Government that the discussions . . . should necessarily be confined to that point [the fisheries] alone, but full liberty is given to . . . [consider] . . . any questions which may bear upon the issues involved . . . which the United States' Plenipotentiaries may be authorized to consider as a means of settlement.

With this directive in mind, the British proved reluctant to confine the discussion to the fisheries question. The Americans, however, insisted on limitation of the negotiations, well aware of Republican opposition in Congress to the discussion of even the main question, to say nothing of tariff modification. The difficulties were pointed out by Judge Cooley in a letter (September 24) to James Bryce, LL.D. 1887, in which he said that he had talked over with Angell the whole matter of the appointment, and it developed that "probably no treaty can be agreed upon that the country as a whole will accept . . . and the Senate has put itself upon record against an attempt by the Commission to make one. But my opinion is he ought to accept, and I think that is his own inclination."

Judge Cooley's diary gives interesting sidelights on the progress of the negotiations. On October 30 he reports that "Mr. Angell is studying up the Fisheries question in its history. He is just now reading John Quincy Adams on Jonathan Russell, which he finds very spicy reading."

As early as November 10, Angell informed Cooley that the American commissioners "were united and would be firm," and that "the British party must come to their terms." Two weeks later Cooley reported that Angell and Putnam had a confidential talk with Chamberlain, "who now for the first time gets an insight into the American position."

Phelps wrote to Angell from England on October 29, warning him of the probable British tactics. He feared that Mr. Bayard would "begin with concessions which though right should be held to obtain other concessions from them. England will promptly accept everything that magnanimity will give her, but will never give a hair's breadth in return unless compelled."

The meetings began auspiciously on November 21 and were held two or three times a week at the State Department. On November 26 Angell suggested that "within a week it might be definitely reported whether the negotiation was to be a success or a failure." At that time Chamberlain was "inclined to think the Americans are in the right; and as they have taken their stand . . . it now becomes a question merely whether Sir Charles Tupper will come to their terms. The Canadians have come here expecting to sell a privilege . . . merely to dicker about a price; the [Americans] refuse altogether to talk about a purchase."

Chamberlain and Tupper were the important members of the English commission. In Cooley's estimate, "Sir Lionel West is an insignificant man in appearance and is generally regarded as insignificant in fact." In his *Reminiscences* Angell remarked that during the three months' discussion West never contributed anything "except a move to adjourn." It will be remembered that he was recalled the following year at the instance of President Cleveland because of a letter to a fictitious Charles F. Murchison, recommending that he vote the Democratic ticket.

On December 1 Angell reported to Cooley that all was "in the clouds yet"; he believed "the best settlement would be on the basis of free fishing and free fish, and that this would be assented to by the British commissioners but not sanctioned by the Senate." Two days later, however, the "negotiations were not looking well." The English had expected a treaty of reciprocity and were "disappointed and grieved to find our commissioners would not even consider the subject." Mr. Chamberlain had "counted confidently upon it, so much so that he seems to feel hurt and wronged." The American commissioners did not, per se, object to such a treaty, but they felt sure "it would not at this time be ratified by the Senate."

By January 10, 1888, the negotiations were apparently at a standstill. The British charged Bayard with giving them to understand he would accept certain terms they had "prepared the Canadians to receive, [and] he now refuses to abide by." But Bayard denied any such offer. Angell noted that the British commissioners throughout "assumed from time to time that the Americans had said something, or taken some position they never thought of taking or saying."

The British kept insisting the joint commission was "to consider the fisheries only as a part of our commercial relations, including, in fact, the tariff." Although Bayard was able to refute this assumption by submitting his correspondence with Salisbury and by showing that Congress alone could change the tariff, more than once they returned to this point of view with much apparent feeling.

On January 20 the negotiations "took a queer turn." The British presented an ultimatum, which, Cooley says, was "rejected finally and unhesitatingly." It was assumed this was the end, but the British came forward with "propositions that conceded nearly everything the Americans had asked for." Cooley observes, "Why the change no one can tell, but agreement now seems almost certain." Negotiations still dragged on for another three weeks, but on February 10 the treaty was agreed upon.

At the last minute there was a hitch when Sir Charles Tupper made certain inconsequential objections in the matter of phraseology, but the American commissioners would not "budge a hair," and Angell thought "Chamberlain will compel Sir Charles to concur." Putnam felt Sir Charles was "captious and troublesome from the start; oftentimes unfair." Nevertheless, everything was finally ironed out, and the treaty was duly signed on February 15. The following day President and Mrs. Angell started for home.

Cooley reported that Putnam had "brought a paper he had been preparing and which was to be submitted to the President with the Treaty and explanatory of it. It is a strong paper, but Mr. Angell would have put it in better shape and presented the salient points more clearly."

The treaty, "essentially a compromise, as indeed all such treaties must be" (Bourinot), provided for a commission to designate the Canadian areas in which American fishermen were to have full rights to fish and envisaged a more liberal view of the term "bay." Free navigation of the Strait of Canso was also assured. But fishing grounds within three miles of the coast were to be exclusively Canadian. The treaty also made a more satisfactory provision in Canadian ports for American vessels in distress, but the purchase of bait, fishing tackle, and the shipping of cargoes on land and the shipping of crews would be allowed only if, and when, American duties on fish were removed.

Since the treaty was signed just before the fishing season opened, a *modus vivendi* to cover the following two years was agreed upon at the suggestion of the British commissioners. This gave permission to American fishing vessels to enter Canadian bays and harbors and, upon payment of a license fee of $1.50 a ton, the right to purchase bait and other supplies. In his subsequent lectures to his students upon the History of Treaties, Angell was accustomed to praise this "liberal step" on the part of Canada.

This favorable outcome of the negotiations was not greeted with any enthusiasm by Congress. It became at once a matter of party politics in a presidential election year. The Republicans maintained, largely for party consumption, that the treaty contemplated the surrender of bay fishing, which would increase rather than diminish disputes with Canada. The legality of the American commission was also questioned, and Secretary Bayard, however patriotic and praiseworthy his motives, in their estimation had been "bamboozled by his diplomatic opponents" on every point. But Cleveland, in submitting the treaty to the Senate, observed that it "supplied a satisfactory practical and final adjustment upon a basis favorable and just to both parties." Democratic support was only halfhearted, however, and when a final vote was taken the treaty was lost by a vote of twenty-seven to thirty; the British and Canadian governments both ratified it, although there was some criticism in the Canadian Parliament.

Thus, while the work of the American commissioners might appear to have been in vain, as a matter of fact it marked a definite step forward. The *modus vivendi* was renewed for many years following the treaty, so that, as Angell observed in 1912, "in a sense we have been living under the treaty." Public opinion, so far as it took cognizance of the treaty, was, in general, favorable, although some criticism of its alleged surrender of American rights arose.

Angell's former colleague on the Chinese commission, Trescot, wrote a critical review in the *New York Herald*, and the qualifications of the American members of the commission were bitterly criticized by Senator Hoar of Massachusetts. He said that he respected President Angell highly, but that he was not aware that Angell "ever saw mackerel until it came from the gridiron." He knew President Angell to be pre-eminent in science, but he had never heard that any of the American commissioners "had had occasion to inform himself thoroughly in regard to the practical rights and interests of the vocation of the American fisherman."

Bayard commented on Hoar's attack in a letter to Angell: "You see by the Senate debate—and notably Mr. Hoar's invective—how little the merits of the proposition are weighed, and how the heats of party warp the judgments of men." Putnam, in letters from Portland, maintained that fishermen in great measure favored the treaty: "I live right here in the midst of the fishing interests, and am satisfied that I have never done anything in the course of my life which so commends me to the better part of the public of both parties, as my part in negotiating this treaty."

A further favorable comment came from George B. Davis, later judge advocate general and a delegate to two European peace conferences in 1906 and 1907, at the time serving as assistant professor of law at West Point:

> The treaty has greater value, from the point of view of the instructor in international law, than any instrument of the kind of which I have any knowledge. It illustrates the theory of territorial sovereignty, the doctrine of the three mile limit, the treatment of questions as to headlands and the bodies of water included within them. Indeed, there is hardly a point that can arise as to the marginal sea, or anything connected with it, which cannot be authoritatively illustrated from the text of the treaty.

Angell's services on the fisheries commission were evidently appreciated by President Cleveland. When, during the latter's second term, on the initiative of William F. Vilas of Wisconsin, Congress authorized a study of the question of a deep waterway from the Great Lakes to the sea, President Cleveland appointed Angell chairman of the commission thus created, with John E. Russell, of Massachusetts, a former member of Congress, and Lyman E. Cooley, Eng.D. 1915, of Chicago, a well-known member of the engineering profession, as the other members. The corresponding members of the Canadian commission were Oliver A. Howland, M.P.P., of Toronto, Thomas C. Keefer, C.E., of Ottawa, and Thomas Monro, C.E., of

Coteau Landing, the last two being engineers long in the service of the Dominion government.

The question of the feasibility of a seaway from Chicago and Duluth through a series of canals had been under discussion for some time, but this was the first official consideration given the problem. The appropriation was a small one amounting to only $10,000, which provided no compensation for the commissioners and permitted only a formulation of the initial engineering problems and possibilities and the collation of such information as was already available in the two countries.

Cleveland made Angell's appointment known on November 4, 1895, and on the following January 15 the American commissioners held their first meeting in Detroit during the annual meeting of the Lake Carriers' Association. Here the commissioners met with shipowners, masters, and merchants, who furnished the commission with much valuable information. Three days later the Americans met with the Canadians and planned as far as possible the scope of the survey. Throughout the investigation there was close agreement between both commissions; the Canadians co-operated in every way, furnishing valuable information from government files, and even making certain special surveys.

The industrial, economic, and political issues involved were not, however, considered as within the commission's province; the actual problem was considered to rest largely in the field of engineering, with a great part of the real work falling to Cooley of the American group. He was authorized to secure competent assistants, to set up an office in Chicago, where he could gather as much information as it was possible to secure from all available sources, and to prepare maps and plans. The valuable and significant information he acquired proved of great importance and convinced the commission at least of the practicability of deep-water communication between the Great Lakes and the Atlantic.

A second meeting of the whole commission was held at Niagara Falls in July, 1896, although by that time the major part of the task had been completed. An extensive report, largely the work of Cooley, was approved by the American commissioners at a final meeting held in Detroit December 18 to 22, 1896.

In submitting this report to Congress President Cleveland expressed his opinion that it demonstrated the feasibility of "direct and unbroken water transportation" from the western states and territories to seaboard ports. The "increase of national prosperity which must follow . . . will not long escape American enterprise." The President also suggested further provision for the work of the commission, but Congress took no action, and this first consideration of what has come to be known as the St. Lawrence Waterway was carried no further, although Congress made public the report of the commission. The subjects examined in the volume included surveys of various possible routes, water levels of the Great Lakes for a period of twenty-five years, and such pertinent information as the effect of gales on Lake Erie and the ice season in the basin of the Great Lakes. Had the time been ripe and congressional interest more active the study of the whole problem might well have been pushed forward to a higher level.

While this study inaugurated a series of investigations continuing for over half a century, one aspect of the developing opposition is suggested in the concluding, and perhaps ironical, words of an editorial on the work of the commission in the *Railroad Gazette* for February 5, 1897: "It is possible that the economy of such a project can be demonstrated, and at any rate the study of it, like the study of astronomy, will stimulate the imagination and enlarge the intellectual field of those who undertake it."

President Angell's final venture in diplomacy was as minister to Turkey during the years 1897 and 1898. His appointment came shortly after President McKinley had succeeded Cleveland as the nation's chief executive and was the result of Angell's well-known interest in foreign missions. Protestant mission groups were definitely behind his selection; he was even approached by two of their representatives, who asked whether he would accept the position of minister to Japan or

Turkey. Discontent and criticism on the part of church bodies had, in fact, been accumulating, because the State Department and its representatives had been extremely lethargic in making any aggressive effort to rectify damage caused to mission school and college properties by Turkish citizens.

When the offer came in April, Angell accepted after some correspondence, and the appointment was promptly confirmed by the Senate. The Regents of the University gave him a leave of absence for a year, and the legislature of Michigan passed a vote of thanks to the President for the appointment.

Before Angell left for Constantinople, however, two dispatches almost resulted in his withdrawal. The first dispatch reported that in a speech in New Orleans he had charged Russia with fomenting disturbances in Turkey, and, therefore, his relations with the Russian ambassador would be strained; the second stated that the sultan objected because Angell was a Congregationalist. Secretary of State Sherman telegraphed at once a denial of the truth of the first dispatch, and it transpired that the sultan had confused the American Congregationalists with the congregation of the Jesuits, with which order the sultan had had controversies. The sultan accordingly withdrew his objections, and no one proved more cordial to Angell, on his arrival, than Mr. Nelidoff, the Russian ambassador. Moreover, Angell observed in his *Reminiscences* that the sultan was always most affable, even when a question involving missions was under discussion.

President Angell, accompanied by Mrs. Angell, reached Constantinople on August 18 and was greeted at the wharf by the American staff and a representative of the grand vizier. He found in Constantinople a very interesting and able body of diplomats with whom he formed some valuable connections. It may well be that through his relations with other foreign representatives Angell performed his most valuable service during his year in Turkey when the United States was at war with Spain, since the official questions he discussed with the Turkish government were for the most part of a minor character as revealed both in his reports to the State Department and in his *Reminiscences.*

At the time of his arrival the ambassadors of the six great powers were seeking to adjust the relations of Turkey with the Balkan states, and one of the first of Angell's dispatches reported the negotiation of a satisfactory treaty, although in his view the results were not very important and only served to show "*l'impuissance des Grandes Puissances.*" Perhaps his most serious problem concerned an American gunboat, the "Bancroft," which was fired on in the port of Smyrna, but after some diplomatic exchanges the Turkish government apologized and dismissed the officers responsible.

American war vessels had been ordered to the Turkish coast at Angell's special request to help in the enforcement of certain claims arising from the destruction of the property of American missions by Turkish soldiers, but with the declaration of war with Spain the vessels in Turkish waters had been ordered home, and the matter of the claims dragged on some years after Angell's time. The settlement was finally made by adding to the contract price of a Turkish warship built in Philadelphia the sum due, the builders remitting the excess to the mission board whose property had been destroyed. The building of this warship for Turkey was, in fact, one of the subjects Angell discussed with the sultan, who expressed a hope that some ships like ours could be constructed without the intervention of middlemen.

Diplomatic representations to the Sublime Porte were matters of exasperating delays before any action developed, although Angell's long experience with Oriental procedures and ways of thinking was of some service to him in his dealings with the Turks. After a transaction had dragged along for weeks, the only reply Tewfik Pasha, the Turkish foreign minister, could make to Angell's somewhat impatient representation was, "I can only say that is our way"—and that was the sole explanation.

Nevertheless, it may be said that, in general, Angell had

little trouble in his official contacts, even with the sultan, with whom he had no difficulty in securing an audience whenever necessary. It is possible his knowledge of French was in part responsible, since the sultan once observed that he was the only French-speaking American minister ever assigned to his court. Upon learning that Angell proposed to visit Jerusalem and Damascus, the sultan sent orders to all officials in the Holy Land to aid him in every way, which they did to an extent "sometimes almost embarrassing."

This friendliness indicated that in some measure at least he had made progress in the accomplishment of his chief task, better treatment for American missions and schools. The favorable settlements which were made later originated obviously from the pressures he first brought to bear. Among other matters Angell reported to the State Department were an apparent discrimination against American travelers in the interior of Turkey, Turkish opposition to the acquisition of property in Jerusalem by an American-Jewish citizen, and the special rights in the Turkish courts of a dragoman of an American consular agency.

President Angell had only accepted his appointment for one year, and, accordingly, on August 5, 1898, he was received in a farewell audience with the sultan; the talk ran mainly on our war with Spain and, again, the construction of a warship for Turkey. Some forty or fifty friends—missionaries, teachers, and diplomats—gathered at the ship on August 13 to say farewell when he and Mrs. Angell embarked for America.

This was President Angell's last venture in the field of diplomacy. Once more he took up his duties at the University of Michigan, which he carried on until his retirement in 1909, after thirty-seven years of service. Throughout this period he continued to give his well-known lectures on the History of Treaties and on International Law, courses which were taken by literally thousands of students. He died on April 1, 1916, in the house on the campus to which he had come forty-five years before.

President Angell's accomplishments in diplomacy from the

present-day background of world-shaking events may seem relatively unimportant. But that is only a matter of perspective. At least two of his excursions into foreign affairs—his negotiation of the treaties with China and the tentative settlement of the fisheries dispute—were at the time of paramount importance to the United States. His work on the problem of deep waterways foreshadowed a continued agitation of increasing importance from his day to the present. His ministry to Turkey led to reforms in the treatment of American missions and unquestionably made many friends for America as well at a time when the preponderant sentiment in Europe was hostile to this country.

Thus, it may be said that Angell's four diplomatic appointments form an important and honorable record in the history of this country's foreign relations. Moreover, his accomplishments in this field are particularly significant and noteworthy since they were only interludes in his long and better-known career as one of the great educators of his time.

Thomas McIntyre Cooley

1824	*Born in Attica, New York*
1843	*Moved to Adrian, Michigan*
1846	*Admitted to the bar of Michigan*
	Married Mary Elizabeth Horton
1848	*Became one of the leaders in organizing the Lenawee County unit of the Free Soil Party*
1854	*Returned to the practice of law in Adrian after a brief business career in Toledo, Ohio*
1857	*Appointed compiler of the statutes of Michigan*
1858	*Chosen reporter of the State Supreme Court*
1859	*Became a member of the faculty of the new Law Department of the University of Michigan*
1864	*Elected a member of the State Supreme Court; resigned as reporter*
1868	*Published his* Constitutional Limitations
1882	*Appointed member of the Trunk Line Rate Commission*
1885	*Defeated for re-election as a justice of the State Supreme Court; resigned from the Court*
	Became professor of history and dean of the School of Political Science
1886	*Appointed receiver of the Wabash Railroad property east of the Mississippi*
1887	*Became first chairman of the Interstate Commerce Commission*
1890	*Mrs. Cooley died*
1891	*Resigned from the Interstate Commerce Commission*
1893	*Elected president of the American Bar Association*
1898	*Died in Ann Arbor, Michigan*

Thomas M. Cooley

Thomas McIntyre Cooley

By Lewis G. Vander Velde

THOMAS McINTYRE COOLEY, LL.D. 1873, was already a well-known public figure at the time of his appointment, in 1887, to membership in the newly created Interstate Commerce Commission. Indeed, the appointment marked the climax of a long and distinguished public career. In view of his qualifications for governmental service, the wonder is not that he received a federal appointment, but rather that his talents had been so long overlooked. For twenty years he had enjoyed a nation-wide reputation as a distinguished jurist and as writer of authoritative works on the law, yet no president before Cleveland had seen fit to make his outstanding capabilities available to the Federal government.

Oddly enough, the work to which he was called was in a field—railroad administration—which he had first entered only five years before, and with an agency which was novel in Federal government history; flattering as the appointment was, it was scarcely a recognition of his well-known abilities as judge and writer. It is significant that in the hundreds of newspaper reports of President Cleveland's selections for the new commission, Cooley was invariably referred to as "Judge Cooley" and described as a "distinguished Michigan jurist."

Cooley was sixty-three years old at the time of this appointment. He brought to his new position a wealth of experience and accomplishment, but relatively little formal training. He was born on a farm near Attica, in western New York, eighth of the thirteen children of Thomas Cooley and his second wife, Rachel Hubbard Cooley. Both parents came from families that had long resided in Granville, Massachusetts. Like his three brothers, who were also farmers in the Attica neighborhood,

Thomas Cooley was a respected citizen; his means, however, did not permit advanced education for his children. Thomas McIntyre Cooley's formal education was limited to graduation from the "academy" in the near-by town of Attica. After a brief experience as a teacher in a country school, he studied law for a few months in an office in the neighboring town of Palmyra.

In the autumn of 1843, at the age of nineteen, he wended his way westward. Legend has it that Chicago was his objective, but that depletion of his funds cut his journey short when he had reached southeastern Michigan. If the story is true, fate was at least kind when she determined that Adrian, Michigan, should be the end of his journey, for the town was full of people who hailed from his home vicinity—New Yorkers for the most part just one generation removed from New England. Almost immediately after his arrival Cooley entered the office of one of the leading law firms and in 1846 was admitted to the bar. In the same year he married Mary Elizabeth Horton, daughter of a family which in 1837 had moved to Michigan from a New York farm not many miles from his former home.

Cooley's early years as a practicing lawyer gave little indication of his future eminence in the profession. His career in Adrian was interrupted from time to time by periods in law offices in Tecumseh and Coldwater, and in the real estate business in Toledo. For several of these years he shared with his father-in-law the responsibilities of operating a farm. In 1852–53 he edited Adrian's Democratic newspaper, the *Watchtower*. Throughout this period he found time to contribute essays and poetry to current periodicals and to give lectures before local literary societies. He was active as a member of a fire company, as an official of the county horticultural society, and as a director of the county fair. Politics also claimed his attention. In 1848 he was one of the two chief organizers of the Free Soil party in his county.

When free-soilism suffered a setback in the early 1850's, Cooley returned to his former party allegiance. In 1854, when most of his former antislavery associates in Michigan were busy in the organization of the Republican party, Cooley, a Toledo resident at the time, was a Democratic candidate for county judge in Ohio. Almost immediately after his defeat in the fall election, however, he moved back to Michigan, and before long he was counted an enthusiastic Republican.

It was not until his return to Michigan in 1854 that Cooley was able to make a real success of his law practice. A new partnership—with Charles M. Croswell, who had been secretary of the famous "Under the Oaks" convention in Jackson where the Republican party was born and who was later to become governor of the state—proved to be a fortunate one, and probably also helped to identify Cooley as a young Republican who could serve the party well. In 1857 he was chosen by the state legislature to compile the statutes of the state—a task to which his orderly mind was particularly well adapted, and which he performed to the great satisfaction of all who had occasion to use the published work. A year later, in January, 1858, the newly organized State Supreme Court chose him as its reporter. In 1859, thanks largely to the influence of an old-time friend and neighbor, Benjamin F. Baxter, of Tecumseh, then a Regent of the University of Michigan, Cooley was appointed a member of a faculty of three in the newly created Law Department of the University, being the only resident member.

The appointment was truly epochal in Cooley's life, for it marked his first association with an institution of higher learning. Despite his limited formal training, he soon distinguished himself as a University teacher of first rank. The records of the Board of Regents furnish impressive evidence that almost immediately he came to be counted upon as one of the strongest members of a strong faculty. Within a half-dozen years, the Law Department of the University of Michigan had become the largest law school in the land. By the time he was forty, Thomas M. Cooley had come to be recognized as a strategic figure in American legal education.

Meanwhile, he continued his duties as reporter of the Supreme Court—duties which took him to winter and summer terms in Lansing and spring and fall terms in Detroit. Detroit

—thirty-eight miles away—was readily reached by way of the Michigan Central Railroad and in the role of Michigan's metropolis was possessed of some attractiveness to a small town resident, but the court terms in Lansing Cooley found particularly burdensome. Just beginning its second decade of existence, Lansing was still a dreary village, not sufficiently important to have won adequate transportation facilities. The most direct routes to the capital from Ann Arbor required at least forty miles of stagecoach travel; the only all-railroad route meant two changes of trains, was more than twice as long, and over the last section of the route offered but one train a day each way.

In 1864 Cooley was elected to membership in the Court he had for six years served as reporter. There is no doubt that during the twenty years he served as a Justice of the Supreme Court, he was associated with a body which had no peer in the land. The personnel of the Court changed somewhat during these two decades, but invariably at least two of Cooley's three associates were, like him, jurists of the first rank. Indeed, those years when the Court consisted of Campbell,* Christiancy, Cooley, and Graves are still often referred to as the period of the "Big Four." For twenty years Cooley and Campbell were double colleagues—on the faculty of the Law Department of the University and on the State Supreme Court.

It was in the fourth year of his justiceship that Cooley brought out the volume which practically overnight gave him a national reputation and which soon made his name one of the most-quoted in court opinions. So great was the influence of this work, which appeared under the ponderous title, *A Treatise on the Constitutional Limitations Which Rest Upon the Legislatures of the Several States*, that its appearance in 1868 is sometimes rated as of equal significance with another outstanding event of the same year—the adoption of the Fourteenth Amendment. The coincidence of these two events, it is claimed, makes the year 1868 a great turning point in American constitutional history.

* James Valentine Campbell, LL.D. 1866.

The appearance of the *Constitutional Limitations* raised Cooley from local to national stature. Almost immediately began that long series of citations from Cooley with which the United States Court reports for the last three-quarters of a century have been so liberally sprinkled. Before long, lawyers had not merely one but several authoritative works by Cooley to use as references. In 1878 appeared *A Treatise on the Law of Taxation;* also a volume which developed the following year into *A Treatise on the Law of Torts.* In 1880, Cooley brought out *The General Principles of Constitutional Law in the United States of America. Cooley on Taxation, Cooley on Torts,* and *The Principles of Constitutional Law* all became standard textbooks in the various law schools of the country; none went through fewer than four editions. Nevertheless, the *Constitutional Limitations,* the first of the treatises, remained the most popular; 1878, the year of the appearance of *Taxation,* saw the fourth edition of the *Constitutional Limitations;* in all, there have been eight editions.

Cooley's treatises on the law immediately stimulated a demand for his services as lecturer and as essay writer. From the 1870's on, not a year—indeed, scarcely a quarter-year—passed without Cooley's name appearing on the title page of one or another of America's leading periodicals. The Cooley name carried weight. Daniel Coit Gilman was proud to obtain him as one of a group of distinguished scholars who were each to give a series of twenty lectures in 1876 at the newly established Johns Hopkins University; indeed, after the first series, Gilman did his best to make Cooley a permanent member of the Johns Hopkins faculty, urging him to undertake the organization of a department of jurisprudence which should embrace history, political economy, and law, with full authority to select his own associates. Similar offers came from other universities. He was an invited guest at Harvard's two hundred and fiftieth anniversary in 1886 and was honored by an LL.D. degree from the venerable institution. It was a proud moment in the life of this self-made Westerner who had never seen the inside of college walls as a student.

The clarity with which Cooley wrote and the ease with which he could discuss technical subjects in nontechnical terms led to countless invitations to address audiences and readers on nonlegal subjects. Most frequently such invitations came from the field of history, in which his most noteworthy achievement was his *Michigan—A History of Governments*, in the "American Commonwealth" series. Dozens of articles on history and government were written for publications ranging from almanacs and encyclopedias to the *North American Review* and the *Atlantic Monthly*. When James Bryce, LL.D. 1887, consulted Andrew Dickson White, LL.D. 1867—a colleague of Cooley's earlier days at the University—relative to obtaining American scholars to read critically the manuscript of his study *The American Commonwealth*, White suggested Cooley; in listing in the Preface to his completed work acknowledgments of assistance, Bryce placed Cooley's name first; in the body of the text he found occasion to quote Cooley some twenty times.

There is not the slightest question that from the appearance of his *Constitutional Limitations* in 1868 until his death three decades later Cooley was America's leading authority on constitutional law and that he was one of America's greatest judges. Urging him to accept the invitation to lecture at Johns Hopkins in 1876, Cooley's former colleague, Judge Isaac P. Christiancy, who had become Senator Christiancy, wrote, "I know that among Senators here (all of whom know you by your work on *Constitutional Limitations*), your authority is placed higher than that of any man on the Bench of the Supreme Court. . . ."

Why, then, one asks, was he not appointed to membership in that great tribunal? Cooley's contemporaries asked this question, too, over and over again. From the time of the death of Chief Justice Chase in 1873 until Cooley's final illness came upon him in the early 1890's, practically every vacancy in the Court was the occasion for bar associations, alumni groups, interested individuals, to request (often to demand) that Cooley be appointed to the Court. Among the relatively few copies of self-drafted letters which Cooley retained was one expressing gratitude to Edwin Willits, A.B. 1855, who, as a member of Congress, was urging Cooley's appointment to the Court in 1881:

Ann Arbor, Jan. 29, 1881

Hon. E. Willits
My Dear Sir:

I desire to express to you & to all the members of the Michigan delegation in Congress my grateful sense of the interest they have taken in the proposed nomination of myself to a seat on the bench of the Federal Supreme Court. I appreciate their efforts quite as sensibly as I should have done had they succeeded, know that their failure to succeed was due to no want of zeal on their part.

I cannot say that I expected the appointment at any time, & have felt sure for a considerable time that I should not receive it. It early became evident that Mr. Hayes intended to nominate the man he has. I am not therefore in any degree disappointed; & I hope Mr. Matthews may prove to be the proper man for the place.

Very truly yours,
T. M. Cooley

It is an amazing fact—and one which does not redound to the credit of the presidents from Grant to Harrison—that the requests for Cooley's appointment remained unfruitful. Certainly, not one of the twelve men elevated to the Court during the period from 1868 to 1893 could match Cooley in combined attainments as judge, producer of authoritative works on law, and experienced teacher of the law. The historian soon learns not to expect too much of most of the six men who occupied the presidency during this period; nevertheless, the overlooking of Cooley is so conspicuous as to require an attempt at explanation.

One factor is emphasis on geographical distribution. At a time when Supreme Court judges were still doing circuit duty, it was deemed imperative that each appointment be allocated to the section comprising the particular circuit to be served. This, in effect, reduced the opportunities for a potential appointee to one-ninth of the vacancies occurring. Specifically, between 1868 and 1893, only two of the twelve vacancies occurring were in the circuit to which Michigan belonged.

Political considerations also played an important part. Cooley had been a Republican from the early days of the party; three times he was elected to the State Supreme Court as a Republican. But he was suspected of voting for Cleveland in 1884, and he was openly critical of the high tariff policy of the party. To Republican presidents he was hardly a "sound" man. As far as Cleveland was concerned, no vacancy occurred in the Court prior to his appointment of Cooley as a member of the Interstate Commerce Commission; after this event Cooley himself expressed the conviction that Cleveland would not consider transferring him to the Court because the Interstate Commerce Commission position was so much more difficult to fill.

With his strong New England reserve Cooley refrained, in both his diary and his letters, from any direct expression of disappointment, but his frequent references to the concern of others in the matter lead one to suspect that he shared his friends' eagerness for this particular form of recognition of his talents as an interpreter of the law. Speculation as to how Supreme Court history during the last third of the nineteenth century might have been affected by Cooley's membership leads one inevitably to the conclusion that the failure of his friends' efforts to have Cooley elevated to the great tribunal was a catastrophe. With Cooley as a member, the Court personnel would have been impressively strengthened; with the benefit of his incisive mind it would have found much easier the solution of the baffling constitutional problems of the post-Reconstruction period.

Meanwhile, Cooley's rise in the professional world had been paralleled by his advancement as a man of affairs. Throughout his service on the faculty of the University of Michigan he had, in contrast to most of his colleagues, other sources of income. From 1859 to 1864 he received the profits from the volumes he brought out as Supreme Court reporter; from 1864 to 1885, salary as a Justice of the State Supreme Court; from 1868 on, a steadily mounting income from his writings and his lectures.

In 1853 when, at the age of twenty-nine, he temporarily left the profession of law to enter the real estate business in Toledo, his skill in business astonished his friends, who thought of him as primarily a literary man. His return to Adrian in 1854 marked his complete reconversion to the law. When, however, his various professional activities began, in the 1860's, to bring a considerable return, his interest in business was kindled anew. An immediate incentive toward investment was the embarkation of his son Eugene, A.B. 1870, upon a business career following graduation from the University. This incentive was doubled a few years later when a second Cooley son, Edgar, A.B. 1872, began the practice of law in Bay City. Partly to assist his young sons, partly for investment purposes, Cooley (with his neighbor, James Clements) contributed heavily to the financing of a manufacturing establishment in Bay City, and gas works and wagon works in Lansing. Both sons prospered; so, too, did most of Cooley's business ventures, with further substantial increment to his income.

The income was needed for the sort of life Cooley wanted to live. He had a large family to support, and among his numerous relatives were several who, from time to time, turned to him for financial assistance. Despite a natural shyness he loved companionship and was tremendously interested in people. Accordingly, the Cooley family progressed from residence in one of the four "Professors' houses" on the campus (Eugene Cooley, eighty years later recalled that as a nine-year-old, his happiness in this house had been marred when his rabbits were killed by President Tappan's dog, next door), to a somewhat larger house on Maynard Street, thence to a commodious stone house which the Judge in the 1860's built on State Street at the foot of South University Avenue. This home, enlarged in 1883, was, until the death of Mrs. Cooley in 1890, one of the chief social centers in Ann Arbor; as the residence of one of the University's greatest men it was a landmark to thousands of students until in 1916 it was torn down to make way for the building of the Michigan Union.

Among the homes of faculty families, the Cooley house was, next to the President's residence and the octagonal house of Alexander Winchell on North University Avenue, probably the best known to University students. Because of the distinction of its owner, of the closeness of the Cooleys to the Angells, and of the fact that for twenty-five years the six Cooley children were growing up there * (Eugene had graduated from the University before Thomas Benton and Mary were born), the Cooley home was a spot of peculiar interest to the campus.

Except for Thomas W. Palmer, A.B. 1876 (*nunc pro tunc* 1849), and J. Sterling Morton, A.B. 1858 (*nunc pro tunc* 1854), the subjects of the sketches in this volume belong to the Cooley period of the University. For those who were law students this meant classroom relationship with Cooley throughout the two-year course, with usually six courses under his direction, since the shortage of faculty members required an alternation of courses every two years. Even those students who were not in the Law Department had much opportunity to profit from his instruction. For several years Cooley gave courses in constitutional law and constitutional history in the Department of Literature, Science, and the Arts. Perennially, he accepted invitations to address the Students' Christian Association, to give moral discourses, to speak on public occasions. Thus, Lawrence Maxwell, B.S. 1874, A.M. (*hon.*) 1893, LL.D. 1904, Alfred Noble, C.E. 1870, LL.D. 1895, William E. Quinby, A.B. 1858, A.M. 1861, LL.D. 1896, Henry T. Thurber, A.B. 1874, Edwin F. Uhl, A.B. 1862, A.M. 1865, and Edwin Willits, A.B. 1855, A.M. 1858, who were not enrolled in the Law Department, nevertheless probably sat frequently at the feet of Judge Cooley.

Unless one has read Cooley's writings, the high praise which Cooley's auditors invariably paid to his effectiveness as a teacher is hard to reconcile with the facts of his physique and

* Eugene F. (1849–1938), A.B. 1870; Edgar A. (1852–1914), A.B. 1872, law 1872–73; Fanny C., later Mrs. Alexis C. Angell (1857–1932), Literary Department, 1873–74, 1875–76; Charles H. (1864–1929), A.B. 1887, Ph.D. 1894; Thomas B. (1871–1945), A.B. 1891, M.D. 1895; Mary B., later Mrs. G. W. King (1873–1944), Ph.B. 1900.

appearance. Cooley had a high—almost falsetto—voice, was awkward in bearing, slight of build, almost shy in manner; certainly he possessed little of the glamour which in his day was regarded as a prime requisite for a public speaker. But in composition and exposition he was a master. Clarity, the quality which above all others inspires confidence in a listener, was the most distinctive attribute of his style. Cooley's expression was not unembellished, however. Although his style was not flowery, he chose words for their sound as well as for their sense. "President Gilman persists in expressing admiration of the *English* of my lectures, as he did last year," he wrote his wife at the time of his second series of lectures at Johns Hopkins, "He told me last night he thought it superior to Professor Child's." President Gilman was a man of action and may have overrated directness of style; nevertheless, to be adjudged by one of America's leading university presidents as superior in written expression to Francis J. Child was no mean compliment—especially to a man so largely self-taught as was Cooley.

Another quality which made Cooley impressive to his auditors was character. A transplanted Yankee Puritan, he revealed to a marked extent the beneficent effects which transplantation often brings. The better elements of Yankee Puritanism were accentuated in him; to a striking degree, its more conspicuous faults were attenuated. Kindness, consideration of others, a high sense of duty, deep sincerity, intense devotion to work, thrift, complete honesty, generosity, and interest in religion were among the traits which most conspicuously marked him. Overseriousness and impatience were apparently his most outstanding faults; together with his exaggerated zeal for work, these must sometimes have tried the tempers of other members of his family, yet his obvious devotion and self-sacrifice were effective counteracting agents. Cooley was always doing things for someone else; giving or lending money to relatives, friends, students; remonstrating with his son for not appreciating the housekeeping burdens of his daughter-in-law; encouraging his young neighbor, Irving K. Pond, C.E. 1879—who, much to his father's disgust, had ambitions to be an artist

—by presenting him with his first book on art and by commissioning him to draw a set of cartoons of the Cooley family (the set, alas, has been lost!); devoting hours of time to counseling young men with respect to the law.

In view of Cooley's natural reserve and the fact that he was obviously busy, the freedom with which people came to him for advice and assistance is astonishing. He was repeatedly being importuned for legal advice, for his judgment on matters of business, for criticism of the literary efforts of others, for financial help, even for counsel in matters of love! Except when they exceeded the bounds of propriety, his generosity in meeting these demands was never failing.

Those who came to Cooley for counsel in their love affairs were perhaps prompted to do so by the obvious success of his own marriage. Mary Horton Cooley was a remarkably fine woman. Intelligent, sensible, self-sacrificing, with broad sympathies and a high degree of tolerance, she proved an excellent helpmate. The hundreds of letters which passed between her and her husband during his many absences from home reveal character and ideals of the highest order. At the time of her death in 1890, President Angell, in expressing his own and Mrs. Angell's sorrow, wrote, "I think that we never formed a stronger attachment to any person. She seemed to me one of the rarest and sweetest characters I ever knew."

At the time of this statement, the Angells had known the Cooleys for nearly twenty years. Almost from the moment of the Angells' arrival in Ann Arbor in 1871, the two families had been very close. It was most natural that the newly arrived president should have rejoiced that the deanship of the Law Department was in the hands of a man who had an established reputation as a scholar, teacher, administrator, and, in addition, years of experience in state government. Here was a man who, five years older than the new president, could be relied upon for sound and selfless advice. It soon became apparent that Mrs. Cooley was wholly trustworthy as a conveyor of information; over and over Mrs. Cooley's letters to her husband reveal this confidence. "Mrs. Angell tells me" she wrote, for example, in 1882, "that the Dr. finds the finances of the University in a fearful condition—worse than they have ever been since he has had anything to do with them. But very likely he wrote you something of it. He is greatly worried and nearly sick Mrs. A. says. She said she would not mention it to any one else, but she knew he would consult you about it, as soon as he saw you at least." Cooley, on his part, was deeply attracted to Angell, who had the urbanity and sophistication that Cooley himself lacked.

The two families became especially intimate after the marriage in 1880 of Fanny Cooley to Alexis C. Angell, A.B. 1878, LL.B. 1880, LL.D. 1915. Young Angell began the practice of law in Detroit; before long Cooley came to employ him in the editing and revising of his works. This assistance became all the more necessary because of the multiplication in the early 1880's of Cooley's professional tasks. During the years from 1880 to 1885, Cooley, besides preparing several scores of opinions for the Michigan Supreme Court reports, and bringing out the third edition of his *Blackstone's Commentaries* and the fifth edition of his *Constitutional Limitations*, published his *General Principles of Constitutional Law in the United States*, his *Michigan, a History of Governments*, and a dozen or more articles for law reviews and encyclopedias. Meanwhile he was giving frequent addresses, and carrying on his heavy duties as professor (and dean until 1883) in the Law Department and as judge of the State Supreme Court.

Among the tasks Cooley performed during this period, however, peculiar significance, in the light of his subsequent career, attaches to those in a field which first engaged his interest in 1882—the field of railroad regulation. In January of this year he accepted an invitation extended by the Trunk Line Executive Committee, representing five eastern railways, to serve, with Judge Allen G. Thurman, of Ohio, and the Honorable Elihu B. Washburne, of Illinois, as member of a commission to hear arguments by various trade bodies regarding differences in railway rates to and from the various terminal Atlantic ports, to process the information collected, and to report the conclusions to the railway companies. The reason for this invitation was mounting discontent over differentials in rates from Chicago and other western points to New York, as compared with those to Philadelphia and to Baltimore.

Some seven weeks of Cooley's time from February to July of 1882 were taken up by the work of the commission, which held hearings in New York, Philadelphia, Baltimore, St. Louis, Louisville, and Toledo, and sessions for consultation and deliberation in Toledo and New York. Observers quickly noted that Cooley outdistanced his colleagues in energetic and intelligent attack upon the problems before them. In April he was invited to accept membership, at a salary of $7,500, in the permanent Board of Arbitration of the Trunk Line Commission. Because of his obligations to his judgeship, Cooley declined the offer. After the final meeting of the Rate Commission in July, he again devoted himself to the law, and particularly to his writing in this field. In November, 1882, he began his teaching in the newly founded School of Political Science in the University, finding increasing pleasure in this particular work as the course developed.

Cooley had a deep interest in politics. Though he was a Republican, the fact that he came from that wing of the party which had a Democratic background made ticket-splitting much easier for him than for those Republicans whose background was Whig. At any rate, in the fall of 1882, Cooley reported in his diary that except for the nominees for governor and lieutenant governor, he had not the slightest interest in the Republican ticket, except in the defeat of the Republican candidate for senator. A few days after the Democratic victories, he remarked casually, "It seems probable now that the Democrats will elect the next President," adding, however, "It is very doubtful if as a party they can be induced to take ground in favor of a radical revision of the present iniquitous tariff."

To his diary Cooley confided his intense interest in the 1884 presidential campaign. Inevitably, he was attracted to Cleveland, who, with his honesty, courage, directness, and common sense, came closer to Cooley's simple democratic ideals than had any other presidential candidate since Lincoln. It was more than a coincidence that a statement which Cooley wrote in 1877, "a public office is a public trust," should, when used by Cleveland in his campaign, have been attributed to Cleveland's authorship. Cleveland may have independently invented the expression, for the principle enunciated is as typical of one of these men as it is of the other.

Nevertheless, despite his personal support of the Cleveland candidacy, Cooley was discreet in publishing his views. In September, Don M. Dickinson, LL.B. 1867, sent him a copy of a letter received from Senator A. P. Gorman, asking whether it was true that Cooley, notwithstanding his election to the bench by Republican votes, was "in reality a believer in the Jeffersonian theory of government." Pointing out that as a faculty member of a law department "where a large portion of the young lawyers of the Northwestern states were educated" and as the author of the *Constitutional Limitations* his political views had great weight, Gorman asked Dickinson to let him know where the judge stood in the current campaign. Dickinson's accompanying letter showed him obviously anxious for Cooley's views, but Cooley in a confidential reply expressed unwillingness to say anything for publication at the time. He admitted feeling very strongly "upon some questions, in respect to the candidacy of a particular person" but added, "while I remain on the bench I esteem it my first duty to preserve so far as I may possess it, the confidence of the public in my entire freedom from party or other bias in respect to all questions which may possibly come before me judicially."

To his diary, however, Cooley was frank with respect to his voting:

Tuesday, Nov. 4. A wet day. I spent it in judicial work. Of course, I voted in the morning, depositing a ballot for Cleveland & for Begole [for Governor]. I voted for Cleveland as a protest against public dishonesty & for Begole as a rebuke to Alger for outrageous expenditures of money in the caucus.

In a confidential letter of congratulation to Vice-President-elect Thomas A. Hendricks, he stated somewhat more fundamental reasons for his rejoicing over the Democratic victory:

> I was never reconciled to the manner in which a President was made in '76, & I have been long tired of the assumptions of those politicians who have held the views of power until they have come to look upon the government as an appurtenance to a political party, & any attempt at a change of rulers as a sort of treason. Moreover I have never unlearned my early lesson in Constitutional law, & still believe the States have rights which even at Washington are entitled to respect.

In his immediate relationship to politics Cooley was destined shortly to have an unpleasant experience. His term for Justice of the Supreme Court was to expire at the end of 1885. Despite considerable thought of not running for re-election, he finally consented to be a candidate in the spring election. He was badly defeated at the polls. There is some evidence that endorsement by the Prohibition Party, opposition by the Knights of Labor, and dissatisfaction with Cooley's railroad connections played important roles in the defeat. Nevertheless, President Angell was probably not far wrong when he attributed Cooley's defeat to the current "Democratic Deluge, sure to submerge even the mountain tops."

Cooley assured Angell that he was not deeply concerned; it is impressive, however, that in his diary, which received his full confidence, his defeat at the polls is scarcely mentioned. Coming after three successive elections to membership in the Court, and more than twenty years of service in that body, it could scarcely have been less than a shock to him. His term was not to end until January 1, but he chose to resign at the end of the summer. Reflecting on the previous year's developments in his political career, Cooley can hardly have escaped the conclusion that voluntary resignation from the Court in 1884 and public support of Cleveland would have served him better. He could thus, at least, have spared himself the humiliation of having lost the election. Whatever sentiments of this sort he may have had were no doubt aggravated by some of the thoughts expressed in a "private and confidential" letter from his friend

Don M. Dickinson reporting an interview with the President and Secretary of the Interior L. Q. C. Lamar, shortly after the inauguration in March:

> Michigan was somewhat discussed owing to the nature of my own business with the President and Secretary. The President himself first mentioned your name and in such high terms of praise as would have gratified your most sincere admirers. . . .
>
> Owing to the future outlook, and the needs of this administration, I cannot help regretting with more and more conviction, that we could not have had you with us publicly, and that your relations with the Opposition have been renewed. I know that this regret is deepened by my own sincere admiration for you, and my earnest pride in you as a Michigan man. Michigan needs you more in those places which are seeking, and will seek strong men under this administration, than you will need any place which you might personally desire. I am ambitious for the State, and it is a real bitterness to me that what would seem to be a series of accidents, should even retard the advancement of yourself—an advancement of which my party could be proud, and an advancement which the opposition has for years—and shamefully—neglected.

Having resigned his professorship in the Law Department the previous year, Cooley was now, for the first time in nearly thirty years, without a salaried position. Nevertheless, he at first resisted President Angell's persistent invitation that he return to teaching. In August, however, he accepted a new position as professor of history and dean of the School of Political Science at a salary of $2,200; a part of his duty was to give a course of lectures on constitutional law for the law students as well as for the students of the School of Political Science.

Cooley must have felt, in the fall of 1885, that a new era was beginning for him. For more than a quarter of a century, ever since he had become reporter of the Court in 1858, he had been required to spend a considerable amount of time, every three months, away from home. Now the tedious journeys to Lansing (since 1879, all of the quarterly sessions of the Court had been held there) were over; except for his teaching duties, his time was henceforth to be his own. To be sure, he would miss the $4,000 annual salary, but he could count on an increasing income from his writings and from services in railway matters; he might even undertake a career as a practicing lawyer. In fact, in 1884 he had seriously considered opening a law office in Chicago with his son-in-law.

Having returned to teaching, however, Cooley characteristically devoted himself wholeheartedly to the work—particularly to his course on constitutional history, a new one to him. At the end of the semester, he listed in his diary the topics of the twenty-nine lectures delivered and noted with satisfaction that "quite a number of the intelligent ladies of the city attended regularly, Mrs. Angell among them." (Cooley—perhaps because he was married to one of them—had a very high respect for the opinions of intelligent women.) The meetings of his historical seminary course he found increasingly interesting: "I dreaded them at first, but think I shall like them after a little, and make them interesting to myself as well as to the students."

In the spring of 1886, he served as arbitrator for the Association of the Railroads of Kentucky, Tennessee, and Arkansas; also as the arbitrator in a lumber controversy. In 1884, he had heard and determined certain controversies pending between railroads running east from Chicago. It was apparent that more and more he was coming to be regarded as an authority on railroad administration, on the practical as well as on the theoretical side. In September, 1886, Professor E. R. A. Seligman of Columbia College wrote him requesting copies of Cooley's articles on railroads for use in his classes.

In December, 1886, Judge W. G. Gresham of the Seventh United States Judicial Circuit, appointed Cooley receiver of the Wabash Railroad property east of the Mississippi in his circuit, with full authority to select his own subordinates. The appointment was widely acclaimed, and Cooley entered upon his new duties with enthusiasm. The work required his presence in the Wabash offices in Chicago, or at other important points of the system, from Monday to Friday. Saturdays and Sundays he spent in Ann Arbor.

Cooley welcomed the opportunity to be at home for the week end not only to see his family, to which he was deeply devoted, but also because it permitted him to attend his home church, for despite the fact that he never formally "joined church," he was a most faithful church attendant. His attendance was always meticulously recorded in his diary, with the subjects of both morning and evening sermons noted and usually a comment on the quality of the discourse. In Ann Arbor, the Cooleys worshiped with the Congregationalists; but absence from Ann Arbor—and Cooley's absences were many—was never used as an excuse for staying away from church. Indeed, to read Cooley's diary is to learn the names of the outstanding preachers of the various cities he visited. It is obvious that he went to church not only to satisfy his religious instincts, but to enjoy the sermons. At Harvard's two hundred and fiftieth anniversary, the Cooleys were the special guests of Dean and Mrs. C. C. Langdell. There was only one sour note in Cooley's account of the generous hospitality accorded them: "The Langdells are stiff Episcopalians, and as they were going to their own church in the morning, we went with them. We thus lost Dr. Peabody's address—had instead the reading of a pastoral letter from the Bishop." Sparse fare, indeed, for a staunch nonconformist!

Sunday for the Cooleys was a day apart; not severely puritanical, but a day for church and Sunday school, for reading, walks, and quiet calls. Cooley frequently expressed his annoyance when Sunday callers introduced such subjects as law or business. Thus, it is noteworthy that he entered no such expression in recording a particular call on Sunday, February 13, 1887:

> In the afternoon Don M. Dickinson called, having come out from Detroit that he might learn whether I would decline a commissionship if it was offered to me. We had considerable conversation on the subject, & it ended in my saying I was not a candidate, but the public

interests involved were so great that if the President thought my appointment desirable I should not feel at liberty to decline.

Cooley was not surprised at the character of Dickinson's errand. Two days before, he had written his wife:

I really begin to think I am in danger of being named on the Railroad Commission. The president I am told is talking about it, & though there is nothing conclusive in that, it indicates a danger. I don't think there is anything in it for one to feel elated over.

On March 11 came the formal invitation, in the form of a four-page letter written in President Cleveland's own hand on "Executive Mansion" stationery:

Hon. Thomas M. Cooley

My Dear Sir: Ever since the duty of appointing commissioners under the law to regulate Inter State Commerce has devolved upon me, & the subject has challenged the attention of the public, your name more than any other has been in mind & has been the oftenest mentioned in connection with such a place.

I have had an idea that you could be induced upon considering the public usefulness which would be accomplished by you as a member of the board, to consent to your selection as one of these commissioners.

It is almost necessary to a successful administration of this law that the confidence of the people in the men to whom it is entrusted should be gained at the outset. This will be secured very largely by your appointment, & I earnestly ask you to consent to serve us all in the capacity mentioned.

If this involves a sacrifice I beg you to make it for the public good. I will give you if you consent a long or short term as you desire, & will do my very best to appoint with you able & patriotic men.

I should be glad to be informed of your decision as early as practicable; & in view of the desirability of completing the organization of the commission speedily, should be glad to receive your answer by telegraph.

Yours sincerely,
Grover Cleveland

Under the terms of the Interstate Commerce Act, the five commissioners were to select their own chairman. It is clear from Cleveland's letter that the President expected Cooley to be chosen—as he was—to this post; this is also evident in the fact that he asked Cooley to name the date of the first meeting of the commission. Cooley chose March 31.

It was accordingly necessary for Cooley to close up speedily his work as receiver. He had enjoyed the receivership, and apparently his associates had enjoyed having him with them, for he wrote his wife, "I think I can safely say everybody from the Judge [Gresham] to the colored messenger boy was sorry to see me go." The judge-professor had made good in an important business position. Benefits had been mutual: the railroad had experienced a thorough reorganization, and Cooley had gained a firsthand knowledge of the intricacies of a large railway system.

Cooley had been deeply interested in the railroad problem ever since his arrival in Michigan in 1843. Adrian, his first Michigan home, was then already something of a railroad center—marking the intersection of the Erie and Kalamazoo Railroad (the first railroad west of the Alleghenies) and the Michigan Southern, which was being rapidly extended westward from Monroe to Chicago. During his newspaper editing days, in 1852–53, he had championed the adoption of a "general railroad law" which would provide for the general chartering of railroads, replacing the requirement of a special charter for each new road. From 1858, as his various state positions necessitated frequent and extensive travel, he had abundant occasion to appreciate the importance of railroad service. As far as the more recent years were concerned, so lively minded a man as Cooley could not have escaped concern over the railroads, for the matter of their regulation—what form it should take, how far it should go, and by whom it should be exercised—constituted one of the country's greatest problems.

From the 1870's, the people had been continuously hearing about the evils and the dangers of pools, passes, rebates, underbilling, discrimination in rates, not to mention the frequent charges of corruption, "undue influence," and intimidation. The first attempts at government regulation of the railroads had generally taken the form of state action, with the individual state legislatures setting up railroad commissions. Important as the commissions were, they fell short of effective cure of the chief railroad evils, and by the middle of the 1880's, there was widespread demand for a federal regulatory commission. Accordingly, the first Congress of the Cleveland administration in its second session passed the famous Interstate Commerce Act of 1887.

The Interstate Commerce Act was important not merely as an effort to provide a solution for an immediate problem, but chiefly because of the character of the solution proposed. Throughout nearly a century of existence, the Federal government, except for the early experiment with the establishment of the Bank of the United States and a persistent employment of protective tariffs, had pursued a laissez-faire policy toward business and industry; whatever action had been taken had been with the intent to be helpful, not regulatory. Now, in 1887, Congress set up a permanent regulatory commission of potentially great power.

There were many critics of this step. The Constitution empowers the Congress "to regulate Commerce . . . among the several States . . ." In the Interstate Commerce Act, Congress chose to delegate some of this power to an agency of its own creation—an agency whose personnel was to be appointed by the President and the Senate, and whose power, though nominally administrative, was likely to become at least quasi-judicial. Accordingly, critics were prompt not only to question the extent of delegation of power, but also to charge that into a government which the framers of the Constitution had intended to consist of three separate and balanced departments, Congress was now thrusting a fourth.

Whatever may be said of the merits of the arguments of the critics, the twentieth-century historian sees clearly that the adoption of the Interstate Commerce Act did indeed constitute a turning point in American history. Congress had learned how to give a double use to its powers; how to exercise them for regulation as well as for stimulation. It had discovered how to achieve a Jeffersonian end by a Hamiltonian means. At least,

Congress thought it had made this discovery; whether or not it had proved overoptimistic depended largely on the manner in which the first commission performed the functions entrusted to it. If the commission proved weak, the old policy of laissez-faire could go on untrammeled; if, on the contrary, the agency proved virile and effective, the precedent for federal regulation would have been established, with the inevitable ultimate consequence of vastly increased federal power.

Which of these roles was to be chosen by the commission depended, of course, largely upon the character of its original membership. Cooley's fellow commissioners were, like him, lawyers. The act provided that not more than three might be selected from a single political party. Cleveland named three Democrats: William R. Morrison of Illinois, Augustus Schoonmaker of New York, and Walter L. Bragg, of Alabama. Cooley was counted a Republican; the other Republican was Aldace F. Walker, of Vermont. Bragg had been president of his state's railway commission; Walker had been active in the promotion of state legislation with respect to the railroad problem.

Upon assembling in Washington, the commissioners promptly as a group paid their respects to the Chief Executive. Cooley reported to his wife with some satisfaction that the President was very cordial. "I have reason to think he is much pleased with the reception which has been accorded to his appointment of Commissioners," he remarked, adding, "I expect to like them all. They are evidently all men of ability."

Nowhere has the task faced by the new commission been more clearly defined than in the opening pages of its first annual report, drafted by Cooley. In the unimpassioned, direct, objective style so typical of him, he described how in the course of railway development in the United States the public had become alienated; he then explained how the act purposed to remedy the situation.

As was to be expected of one of his experience and interests, he began his report with a historical statement, pointing out how vastly commerce had changed in character since the framers enumerated as one of the powers delegated to Congress, the regulation of commerce among the several states. He explained why the power had been little used at first; how the invention of the steamboat had impelled steps in the regulation of maritime interstate commerce; and how the essentially intrastate character of the early railroads (and canals, as well) had left them apparently outside the realm of the interstate power of Congress. In these earlier years, when the power of the Federal government had been exercised at all, it had been by way of negation, rather than affirmation—that is to say, by the federal courts' restraint of excessive state power when it appeared. The effect of all this was, he explained, "to leave the corporations, into whose hands the internal commerce of the country had principally fallen, to make the law for themselves in many important particulars—the State power being inadequate to complete regulation, and the national power not being put forth for the purpose." As for regulation under the common law, Cooley went on to say, adequate remedy was not possible, chiefly, perhaps, because railroad transportation was wholly unknown to the common law.

In their double role of governing their own corporate affairs and at the same time of very largely determining at pleasure what should be the terms of their contract relations with others, those who controlled the railroads, Cooley explained, were able to determine in great measure what rules should govern the transportation of persons and property. This "indirect and abnormal law-making" was "exceedingly unequal and oftentimes oppressive," leading to overinvestment in railroad schemes, ruinous competition, instability, and gross inequities in rates ("the memorandum-book carried in the pocket of the general freight agent often contained the only record of the rates made to the different patrons of the road, and it was in his power to place a man or a community under an immense obligation by conceding a special rate on one day, and to nullify the effect of it on the next day by doing even better by a competitor"). Other evils resulting from this "abnormal law-making" were unjustified influence in the making and breaking of "trade centers," and enormous abuse of the practice of giving "passes," particularly to public officials ("for if any return was to be made or was expected of public officers, it was of something which was not theirs to give, but which belonged to the public or to constituents").

It was characteristic of Cooley, however, that he should have declared that even greater and more pernicious than these evils themselves were their indirect consequences, "for they tended to fix in the public mind a belief that injustice and inequality in the employment of public agencies were not condemned by the law, and that success in business was to be sought for in favoritism rather than in legitimate competition and enterprise." Thus, they built up a class feeling and embittered the relations between those who for every reason of interest ought to be in harmony.

Accordingly, adequate power should be put forth to bring these great evils to an end:

> Railroads are a public agency. The authority to construct them with extraordinary privileges in management and operation is an expression of sovereign power, only given from a consideration of great public benefits which might be expected to result therefrom. From every grant of such a privilege resulted a duty of protection and regulation, that the grant might not be abused and the public defrauded of the anticipated benefits.

The state legislatures, however, had proved inadequate to establish satisfactory regulation; the Federal government had to do with the commerce which these artificial entities of state creation might be concerned in; Congress, then, in the 1887 Act to Regulate Commerce had laid down certain rules to be observed by the carriers to which its provisions applied. These rules were emphatically rules of equity and equality "which if properly observed, ought to, and in time no doubt will, restore the management of the transportation business of the country to public confidence." Equity, equality, public confidence—here were ideals toward which Cooley, with his long judicial training, his puritan conscience, and his Jeffersonian faith, could give implicit devotion.

It was most impressive that in embarking upon this first adventure in regulation by commission, the object of regulation should be so vast an industry. Railroad mileage in 1887 was almost 140,000; the number of corporations represented was more than fourteen hundred; total cost of construction and equipment had been more than seven billion dollars, and the funded debt of the companies was nearly four billion. "The regulation of no other business," declared Cooley, "would concern so many or such diversified interests or would affect in so many ways the results of enterprise, the prosperity of commercial and manufacturing ventures, the intellectual and social intercourse of the people, or the general comfort and convenience of the citizen in his every-day life."

While the commissioners were all able men, there is overwhelming evidence that Cooley dominated the body. Certainly, he did far more than his share of the work. "Morrison told Mr. Angell yesterday," he reported in his diary, "that I liked to do the work and the others liked to let me do it; which is very near the fact." Besides bearing the chief burden of the work, he had difficult responsibilities with respect to personnel matters: one of the commissioners had inordinate political ambitions, another was objectionable to some of his colleagues because of what Cooley sarcastically referred to as his "plantation manners," and a third was difficult because of excessively sensitive feelings.

These difficulties were the more serious because of the heavy work load of the commission, a load made much heavier by the necessity of conducting long hearings in various parts of the country. During the year 1887, hearings in points ranging from Atlanta to St. Paul, and from New Orleans to Rutland, Vermont, occupied more than one-eighth of the time. In 1889, hearings were held from coast to coast, taking, in all, more than two months of the year. Not all of the commissioners found it convenient to attend all of the hearings; Cooley, however, was invariably there.

Moreover, returning to Washington from these strenuous trips afforded no rest. The daily routine there was taxing, and, as time went on, became more and more burdensome. More than one hundred cases came before the commission during each of the years of Cooley's membership. A calendar of the points decided during the first four years occupies eighty pages of the Fourth Annual Report and is forcefully impressive evidence not only of the amount of work accomplished, but also of the orderliness of the accomplishment.

By 1890, the clerical staff of the commission had increased to more than one hundred. This was in part attributable to the statistical work assumed under the able direction of Henry Carter Adams, whose appointment as statistician Cooley had obtained in 1888. In general, however, the increase in staff was indicative of an increase in Cooley's responsibilities rather than of a sharing of his work. In the fall of 1887, when he had been chairman for half a year, there appeared in his diary the first of a series of complaints that he was feeling the strain of overwork. Only a brief while before he had boasted of his great capacity for work; now he recorded, "I am *tired, tired, tired.*"

With his presence now required in Washington so much of the time, it might have been expected that Cooley would move his family there, as did some of the other commissioners. Cooley did not; Ann Arbor and his multiple family ties in Michigan meant too much to him. Invariably, as a vacation approached, the entry in his diary outlining the things he expected to do before departure would end with the words, "and then *home!*"

Despite his heavy duties, however, his time in Washington was not devoid of social life. The various members of the Supreme Court, several of the cabinet officers—including, of course, Dickinson—and other notables entertained him. When Mrs. Cooley visited him, the social engagements multiplied and included tea at the White House. During the weeks when President Angell was in Washington in connection with the Fisheries Commission, the two friends saw each other frequently and were entertained together. It was at this time that Cooley recorded in his diary, no doubt chuckling as he did so:

The *Free Press* of today contains a clipping from the New York *Sun* descriptive of Prest. Angell & myself, who are said to be great friends but wholly different in characteristics. The President is fond of society, for which I care nothing; he is plump, while I am thin & spare; he is particular about his dress, while I wear a shocking hat & a threadbare coat & so on. It is amusing, & has just enough *vraisemblance* to give point to what is said.

One wonders whether association with Supreme Court justices may not have given Cooley nostalgia for the far quieter judicial life he knew so well. Despite the heaviness of his work, however, he derived a great deal of satisfaction from his position. It was pleasant to have the commission receive general commendation from the press and particular congratulations from experts in the field, such as Professor Arthur T. Hadley of Yale. It was more than pleasant to have President Cleveland remark: "You fellows are the only men I ever appointed to office who never give me any trouble." Cooley must have been well aware that all thoughtful observers attributed the success of the commission to him. And what Republican—for Cooley was still at least nominally of that designation—would not have been flattered to be specially summoned by President Cleveland, as was Cooley, to discuss Don M. Dickinson, just prior to his appointment as Postmaster General?

In some respects the commission work was not greatly different from work on the bench. Cases were heard, arguments presented, decisions reached, opinions written. Indeed, Cooley's judicial experience and the lawyer membership of the commission made it inevitable that its proceedings should take on much of a courtroom character. There was, however, one extremely important difference. While the commission had duties of a quasi-judicial character impressed upon it, involving the investigation of important and intricate questions, it had not been given the power of enforcing its orders by its own powers. This was later to prove an increasingly serious handicap, for the federal courts in many instances failed to be the bulwark of defense which the commission needed. The lack of finality in the commission's power must have been trying to the judge who headed the body.

Cooley certainly found the timidity of some of his fellow commissioners annoying. To his diary he complained that his fellow members were content to have the body confine itself simply to hearings; he felt that its function was to develop a policy and program of regulation. He was particularly irritated when he could not obtain support for his plan to intervene in the great Burlington strike of 1889. Yet when, in a moment of discouragement over the commission's future, he discussed with Commissioner Morrison his thought of resigning, the latter reminded him that from the outset, despite any differences in view among the members, Cooley had been allowed to shape the action and policy of the commission. The statement was so true that Cooley could have no answer. Certainly, with students of the history of the Interstate Commerce Commission, the opinion is universal that the great power and usefulness which has been attained by the agency is largely attributable to the wisdom, foresight, and administrative skill of its first chairman.

To Cooley's devotion of time and energy to the commission must be attributed in large measure the physical breakdown which necessitated his resignation in 1891. The first serious break came in 1889 and forced his retirement to Ann Arbor for some time. The death of Mrs. Cooley in 1890 retarded his recovery. Though he lived on until 1898, giving occasional lectures and holding the presidency of the American Bar Association in 1893–1894, he was never again sufficiently well to do sustained work—a fate which to a man of his temperament was a particularly heavy tragedy.

One wonders whether the tragedy might have been avoided had the position he filled so ably been one less demanding of energy and physical strength—for example, the judgeship which he so abundantly merited. In such a position, however, his fame could hardly have been so great. Cooley would have been a distinguished member of the United States Supreme

Court, but as one of nine in a judicial body he could scarcely have had so challenging an opportunity to participate in the building of the governmental structure as was afforded him by the chairmanship of the Interstate Commerce Commission.

In fact, Cooley's achievements as a builder extended far beyond the commission itself, for the many federal administrative agencies which were set up in succeeding decades all reflect the influence of the Interstate Commerce Commission. President Cleveland had asked Cooley to accept an appointment on the new commission because he believed this would ensure it a successful start. History has proved this confidence was more than justified. Not only did the commission under Cooley's leadership have a successful start; but to the impetus he gave it is in large measure to be attributed the growth in effectiveness which the agency has experienced. This effectiveness, in turn, has proved an important factor, during the twentieth century, in the rapid extension of federal regulatory agencies.

Opportunity to exercise such influence in government comes to few men; Cooley had the requisite qualities of ability and character to meet effectively the challenge offered. It has been of profound significance to our country, not only during the Cleveland Era, but in the years which have followed, as well, that for his first Interstate Commerce Commission appointment President Cleveland chose a man who believed so implicitly, and who in the employment of his great talent for administration observed so faithfully, the principle that "a public office is a public trust."

Don M. Dickinson

1846	*Born in Port Ontario, Oswego County, New York*
1848	*Moved to the island in the St. Clair River, now known as Dickinson Island*
1852	*Moved to Detroit*
	Prepared for college under a tutor
1867	*Graduated from the Law Department of the University of Michigan*
	Admitted to the bar of Michigan
1869	*Married Frances L. Platt*
1872	*Selected member of the State Central Committee of the Democratic Party*
1876	*Elected chairman of the State Central Committee and delegate to the Democratic National Convention*
1880	*Chosen delegate to the Democratic National Convention*
1884	*Became member of the National Committee of the Democratic Party*
1887–89	*Served as Postmaster General of the United States*
1891	*Dickinson County was organized in the Upper Peninsula*
1892	*Chosen chairman of the Democratic National Campaign Committee*
1895	*Elected first president University of Michigan Club of Detroit, founded on October 21, 1895*
1896	*Appointed to represent the United States as senior counsel in the Bering Sea arbitration*
	Opposed Bryan's candidacy for the presidency
1902	*Served as member of the Court of Arbitration to adjust claims in the controversy between the United States and San Salvador*
1912	*Supported Theodore Roosevelt for the presidency*
	Retired from practice
1917	*Died in Trenton, Michigan*

DON M. DICKINSON

Don M. Dickinson

By Arthur Pound

NEW YORK STATE from the close of the American Revolution down to the Civil War was stopover land for countless migrating families of New England origin that eventually took root in Michigan and gave that young commonwealth a lead in law, politics, and customs. It is a commonplace for genealogists to find one generation shifting from New England to eastern New York, the next moving on to central and western New York, and the next settling in Michigan. This phase of the westward folk movement generated such political vigor that no less than twelve Michigan governors were born in New York, besides numerous other leaders of public life.

Among these none rises more commandingly from his time and place or shines with purer luster in the annals of the University of Michigan than does Donald McDonald Dickinson, LL.B. 1867. The practical idealist in politics always deserves the serious attention of thoughtful men, for in America his is pre-eminently the type which makes history. Colonel Asa C. Dickinson, his father, more idealistic and adventurous than practical, was one of many worthies on the New York frontier who, incident to the Mackenzie rebellion of 1837 and the following tumults, tried to unite the present province of Ontario with the United States. Although the movement was quite outside the law, not a few worthy characters joined in that dubious enterprise, which in the fullness of time no doubt will be rated merely premature rather than unwise. Among such parties to border strife were a number of New York militia officers. Discouraged and discredited by their failure, more than one New Yorker colonel packed his effects rather hurriedly and went west to Ohio or Michigan. About 1820, as a young voyageur, Dickinson *père* had traveled the Great Lakes by canoe, so when he left his New York home for the West in 1848, he made for the lovely seclusion of the St. Clair where that noble strait debouches into the lake of that name. The small island of which he took possession, lying northwest of the larger Harsen's Island, has since been known as Dickinson Island.

In this move the most precious baggage was the two-year old son, Donald, who had been born to Minerva (Holmes) and Asa C. Dickinson on January 17, 1846, at the old home in Port Ontario, Oswego County, New York. His mother was a daughter of the Reverend Jesseniah Holmes of Pomfret, Connecticut. Port Ontario, a more important place then than now, lies in the estuary of the west-flowing Salmon River, which enters Lake Ontario on its eastern shore. The site is of historic interest as an old trading beach for whites and Indians in colonial days, a stopping point for French expeditions on their way to attack Iroquois settlements in New York. The region was of such bad repute that it was for a time called "Hungry Bay" or "La Famine," owing to the misfortunes which overtook De la Barre's expedition thereabouts in 1684. Don M. Dickinson is properly listed in Spencer's *Roster of Native Sons (and Daughters) of New York* as a son of Port Ontario, with four other famous natives of Pulaski Township, but one wonders if he would have been heard of again if he had remained in that beautiful backwater.

As it was, Don Dickinson was carried on to busier waterways on the inland seas; but to the end of his days he resided within eyeshot of a river or lake. After four years on the somewhat inaccessible Dickinson Island, the family moved to Detroit, where their six-year-old son could have proper schooling. Public schools had been established in Detroit in 1842, and by 1863 high-school facilities flourished in the old Capitol Union. Nevertheless, many families did not trust this new institution to prepare their sons for college, and young Dickinson was prepared for the University of Michigan by private tutors. He matriculated in the Law Department at the age of nineteen. Little is now recoverable of his college days beyond the fact that his fraternity was Chi Psi, and the grace note that he wrote a poem in the Wordsworthian manner entitled "The Hills of Washtenaw," a subject favored by students in rhetoric. In March, 1867, he graduated as Bachelor of Laws. The law course then covered two winter terms of about six months each, which may account for the error, common to many Dickinson biographical sketches, that he graduated in 1866. He was admitted to practice on May 2, 1867, at the age of twenty-one.

A precocious youth, handsome and eloquent, Don made an early start in law and its sister profession, politics. He caught on almost at once with the excellent firm of Moore and Griffin, later Moore, Griffin, and Dickinson; then Griffin and Dickinson; then Dickinson, Thurber, and Hosmer; and, during the senior partner's more illustrious days, Dickinson, Thurber, and Stevenson. The private and corporate business of this firm has been well covered by Fred G. Dewey, A.B. 1902, in his sketch of Henry T. Thurber, A.B. 1874, which is included in this volume.

The young attorney, hungry for the briefs which win renown, does what he is told and is judiciously receptive toward the opinions of his seniors. When Dickinson became associated with the old firm, its senior partner was William A. Moore,* a Democratic stalwart who had been state chairman of the Democratic party in Michigan during the Civil War. In that

* All the partners were graduates of the University of Michigan: Moore, A.B. 1850, A.M. 1854; and Griffin, A.B. 1850, A.M. 1860. Later, after Dickinson became the senior member of the firm, the tradition was continued for a time when he took Henry T. Thurber, A.B. 1874, and George S. Hosmer, A.B. 1875, LL.D. 1910, into the firm. Hosmer left to become a circuit judge in 1887, and Thurber withdrew in 1897. There were numerous changes in the personnel of the firm which for a time was Dickinson, Warren, and Warren. One of the members was Charles Beecher Warren, Ph.B. 1891, A.M. (*hon.*) 1916, who was ambassador to Japan from 1921 to 1923 and to Mexico in 1924. As long as Dickinson remained senior partner of the firm, he always had at least one other Michigan man as an associate.

Of the present law firm, which is a lineal descendent of the Dickinson partnership, the senior members are Leo M. Butzel A.B. 1894, LL.B. 1896, Thomas G. Long, LL.B. 1901, Frank D. Eaman, A.B. 1900, LL.B. 1902, Rockwell T. Gust, LL.B. 1914, Charles A. Wagner, LL.B. 1913, and Fred J. Kennedy, LL.B. 1915. All are graduates of the University of Michigan. Eleven of the junior members also are alumni.

unhappy period, to be a Democrat in Michigan demanded stubborn independence. From 1868 Moore was national committeeman until 1876; his young partner succeeded to this post after an interval of eight years. In a state so solidly Republican that only four Democratic congressmen had been elected since 1856, young Democrats of talent were a bit scarce. Fortune rode gaily with the Republicans in Michigan, where the bloody shirt covered a good deal more than a battle-scarred back; it also covered frequent and sizeable raids on a public domain amply endowed with forest and subsoil resources which only recently had been mapped in detail.

Enlistment with the Democrats might, therefore, have been considered a little unworldly, especially since the young man had taken to himself a wife. She was Frances, daughter of Dr. Alonzo Platt, of Grand Rapids. After reading the Dickinson correspondence, one thinks of her as a well-beloved helpmate, comrade, and sustaining force through all the turmoil of her husband's lively public career. Fortunately, the young couple could not know what heavy sorrows were to come to them. In a single dreadful year their five children, the eldest less than ten years of age, died from spinal meningitis contracted during a summer vacation in Canada. Two other children, both of whom survived, were born respectively seven and twelve years after that tragic summer.

At the time when Dickinson threw in his lot with the Democrats, he was about the age at which a present-day lawyer graduates from law school. There is this merit in joining a minority party in a state in which it has no prospects: competition is scarce and one climbs fast. When Horace Greeley ran against President Grant for the presidency in 1872, Dickinson became a member of the State Central Committee of a party which had already felt his electric touch as National Committeeman Moore's "bright young man." Granted that Dickinson was precocious, something must be said for the opportunity which a gracious older time offered to talent by letting it loose for world conquest while still young.

Quite noticeably, although less so in rock-ribbed Republican

Michigan than elsewhere, the political tide had turned. In New York, Democratic Governors Seymour and Tilden had been elected, and these examples were not lost on Michigan. Democratic Senator Allen G. Thurman of Ohio, the "Old Roman," was giving his party strong leadership in Congress and in the Middle West. Political generations are only ten years in duration—from the eleven-year old who scarcely knows his President's name, to the twenty-one-year old who is expected to vote intelligently for town constables and presidential electors. Scandal after scandal during Grant's administration had confirmed the forebodings of the most doleful of Democratic Cassandras. Our young champion of the underdog took fire at Greeley's luminous campaign speeches, and when Michigan shook out its customary 55,000 majority for Grant's re-election, Dickinson was so chagrined by what he considered the defection of old-line Democrats from the "Liberal" Greeley that he vowed to desert the party. Dickinson always took party affairs with grim seriousness. Calmed by Chairman Moore, Dickinson was soon back in harness and virtually ran the 1874 campaign, in which Michigan Democrats elected three congressmen and the Republican candidate for governor squeezed through with a majority of only 2,000. The Republican majority in the legislature was torn with dissension: Senator "Zach" Chandler, Republican boss and United States senator since 1857, was defeated for re-election—omen of harsher retribution to come.

In the twenty years from 1856 to 1876, the Republican party had come far from Ripon and the Jackson Oaks. Victorious in Michigan in its first dash toward the presidency with Fremont, the new party had stoutly held the state ever since, while shifting from radical reform to ultraconservatism. Early deprived of Lincoln's idealistic leadership, it forthwith became the champion of rising industrial capitalism. This position had been sharply outlined in its platform of 1860; and, indeed, possessed merits of practicality and purposeful dynamics. Unity once assured by victory over secession, the nation was ripe for economic expansion commensurate with its immense natural resources. But, like the Crusaders of old, the Republicans soon took to looting. Rapacity coursed almost without restraint through railroad and corporate manipulations. When the G.O.P., which aged very rapidly indeed, showed no intention of restraining individual initiative, it left the door ajar for a new Democratic appeal to the masses in behalf of the general welfare.

By 1876, when Dickinson became state chairman, the Democrats were ready to elect a President—and did. By contesting elections in four states and rigging an electoral commission, the Republicans in Congress were able to count Samuel J. Tilden out and Rutherford B. Hayes into the presidency by one electoral vote, after shouldering the Democratic states of South Carolina and Louisiana to the Republican candidate. The swindle was so gross that many eloquent young men profusely vowed to right that sovereign wrong. Among them was Don M. Dickinson. What the nation thought of the 1876 affair is revealed by the solid way it plumped for a Democratic Congress in 1878.

Six years more would pass, however, before conversion could be accomplished on a national scale. Meantime, Dickinson developed as a public speaker and party organizer. His themes were the burning issues of the day—tariff reform, civil service reform, banking and railroad control. Spoilsmen were his enemies, spoilsmen in both public and private life, and in both parties. There were old-line, unregenerate Democrats to rout before one could come to grips with the enemy in full strength. Some of the unregenerate had the temerity to vote against Dickinson in the state convention of 1880, when he sought to be named delegate-at-large to the national convention. He beat them down with the resounding majority of 550 to 31, which fairly measures his ascendency. Thereupon, at the age of thirty-four, he became the unquestioned leader of a major party in a fighting state. In the convention he supported Justice Stephen J. Field against Tilden for the presidential nomination. The prize went to a dark horse, General Hancock, who lost to Garfield by fewer than ten thousand popular votes, whereas either Tilden or Field probably would have won.

For the 1884 campaign Dickinson moved up to the post of Democratic national committeeman for Michigan. By this time personally acquainted with the national leaders of his party, he took his stand with the progressive and reforming element ably led by Governor Grover Cleveland in New York, Senator Allen G. Thurman in Ohio, and Senator William F. Vilas in Wisconsin. As a result of steady organizing, Dickinson expected to break through at last in Michigan and can be pardoned for telling the national convention that his state could be counted for Cleveland and Hendricks.

To bring stubborn Michigan into line, Dickinson "made a treaty," as he phrased it, with the Butler Greenbackers, a treaty of which he was somewhat ashamed because he spoke of it as "a bitter thing for us." In manipulating the affairs of a minority party, he often had occasion to treat with lesser minority groups—Prohibitionists, Populists, Grangers, and what not. Sometimes these temporary alliances helped, sometimes they did not. In this instance, after promising to deliver the state on the prospect of the Greenback deal on electors, he was unhorsed by the Prohibitionists, who, still strong after a twenty-year trial of state prohibition which ended in 1876, held the balance of power between the two major parties. The Blaine and Logan electors won Michigan by a shady thirty-three hundred plurality over the Cleveland and Hendricks electors, and the Prohibitionist electors polled eighteen thousand votes. If the national election had gone against Cleveland, Dickinson's prestige would have suffered greatly, but a distant complex of involved partisanship gave Cleveland the victory. In his own state of New York, Cleveland won because about two thousand Conkling Republicans in Oneida County switched their votes in order to avenge former Senator Roscoe Conkling, against his archenemy, candidate James G. Blaine, because the Reverend Samuel D. Burchard alienated many Catholics from the Republicans by his "rum, romanism, and rebellion" speech, and because some Republicans voted for the Prohibition Party candidate, John P. St. John. Michigan's loss was overlooked in the hullabaloo of victory and in the tension following so narrow a squeak.

Dickinson hurried to national headquarters in New York City where, through several hectic days, it was feared that so slim a margin might be counted out. Arriving with a $50,000 "war chest," to which he had contributed $5,000 himself, the Detroit lawyer became by common consent spokesman for his party in that crisis. He informed the *Herald* that he suspected manipulation, had communicated with the district attorney, and would demand the arrest of certain poll officials. There was talk that he had engaged former Senator Conkling as counsel. These reports were sufficient to cool the clamor of the opposition. Conkling of the acid tongue and bitter soul knew too much; it seemed better to drop the whole thing. Dickinson sped back to Detroit for a monster celebration on November 9, by which time Cleveland's election was conceded.

No doubt Dickinson's fighting prowess at New York and his deft handling of the press endeared him to Cleveland and had no little to do with his later elevation to the post of national chairman. Four years later, when Senator Conkling died after exposure in the great blizzard of March, 1888, Dickinson announced that he would attend the Conkling funeral, and he suggested that Cleveland and Vilas go along—an indication that he thought they owed something to Blaine's chief foe.

No sooner was the Democratic victory of 1884 acknowledged than Dickinson had to stand on his rights as patronage dispenser. Although the party had declared in favor of civil service and against making spoils of public office, that noble sentiment did not slake the thirst of Democrats long separated from political fleshpots and juleps or the pride of those aspiring to award the plums. In the absence of United States senators of the party in power, state leaders customarily step into control of federal patronage, but the Democratic congressmen from Michigan resented Dickinson's recommendations. Meeting this congressional rivalry in Washington, Dickinson wrote a letter to Cleveland from the Hotel Arlington, evidently at the President's request, in which he firmly stated his position. His state committee, he declared, "had no slates":

> Both Mr. Eddy (state chairman) and myself prefer that any and all precedents resting on machine methods may be disregarded; and we are agreed that the competition for place should be open to all, and that, the question of fitness once settled, care should be taken to recommend those whose appointment would give the greatest satisfaction to the greatest number in the locality to be affected.

No better or more elevated statement of correct leadership with respect to patronage could have been written at that time.

This aloof and idealistic attitude often had to be tempered in the heat of conflict. Somewhat later in 1885, he wrote: "Please remember that from a Republican State, Michigan is being made Democratic, and that in their desperation to hold the state the other side are using all means, methods and men, which may be at hand" (including, he thought, Republican undercover backing of conservative, undeserving Democrats unpopular in their home towns). To check their stratagems local representatives of the administration known as "referees" were set up to advise on appointments.

Among Michigan Democrats, Dickinson distributed many major offices during Cleveland's first administration. Despite the fact that the University was barely a generation old, it was represented by several of its alumni: George V. N. Lothrop, of Detroit, minister to Russia; A. P. Swineford, of Marquette, territorial governor of Alaska; Martin V. Montgomery, of Lansing, United States commissioner of patents and later a justice in the District of Columbia; John C. Shields, LL.B. 1872, of Howell, judge of United States Court in Arizona Territory; Orlando W. Powers, LL.B. 1871, of Kalamazoo, United States judge in Utah Territory; Henry F. Severens, LL.D. 1897, of Kalamazoo, judge of United States District Court at Grand Rapids; Daniel J. Campau, of Detroit, collector of customs at Detroit; John B. Moloney, collector of internal revenue; Robert McKinstry, pension agent, Detroit District; Galusha Pennell, A.B. 1868 (in Law School 1868–1869) United States marshal; Cyrenus P. Black, district attorney for the Eastern District of Michigan; David R. Waters, marshal, and G. Chase Goodwin, district attorney for the Western District.

When President Cleveland realized Dickinson's abilities and deep personal loyalty, he sought to reward him. All that Dickinson would accept was an honorary and unsalaried appointment to the Board of Visitors at the United States Naval Academy at Annapolis. This post satisfied Dickinson's desire for social prestige and his lifelong joy in an occasional junket. Higher recognition came when Postmaster General Vilas resigned to become Secretary of the Interior. For the postmaster generalship, the Detroit lawyer was admirably fitted. Traditionally, it is the post of chief patronage dispenser, and in that role Dickinson's convictions paralleled those of his beloved "Great Chief." In a cabinet already overloaded with Easterners, the new appointee had to be a Westerner, and preferably from the Great Lakes area, since the Far West as yet had hardly grown up to full Cabinet stature.

That Dickinson did not seek Cabinet appointment is clear from his correspondence with Cleveland and with General John G. Parkhurst, of Coldwater. The latter, who ardently desired office himself and was finally rewarded with the post of minister to Belgium, observed that Dickinson received $8,000 a year as postmaster general and spent $30,000. Always lavish as regards living, clothes, and entertainment, Dickinson needed ample returns from his busy law practice, and it was clear that he literally could not afford public office. In addition, experience with patronage had made him a cynic on the whole subject; he had learned the hard truth that, with each appointment, he made, *à la Richelieu,* one ingrate and ninety-nine enemies. Writing to Colonel Daniel S. Lamont years later of I. M. Weston's desire for a Central American post, Dickinson recommended him as a man of ability and huge fortune, adding, "Why such a man wants public office is beyond my comprehension, but such men do and Weston does."

When nominated for the postmaster generalship, Dickinson was only forty-one years old; he was confirmed in office by the Senate on January 18, 1888, the day following the forty-second anniversary of his birth. He then became the youngest member of an able cabinet which contained such notables as Thomas F. Bayard, LL.D. 1891, of Delaware (State), James H. Manning, of New York (Treasury), and William C. Whitney of New York (Navy).

Dickinson's two years as postmaster general proved to be exciting and constructive. Amazed by the conservatism of the Post Office Department, which had changed little since Benjamin Franklin's days, the newcomer instituted wholesale reforms. He shook the railroads out of their complacent and legalistically permissive attitude toward the mails, made them acknowledge the Federal government as master, and enlarged service to foreign lands. His genius for organization brought forth a more economical administration along territorial lines, which greatly improved domestic deliveries. When Congress hesitated, Dickinson cited to them Supreme Court opinions to support his broad view of congressional powers and responsibilities. Charles B. Norton in *The President and His Cabinet* roundly declared that "the Post Office Department has accomplished more work at less cost and to the better satisfaction of the entire nation than has ever been done before." In general, Congress backed Dickinson, but not in his recommendation that the Post Office Department be given charge of the telegraph lines.

In two sledge hammer conflicts Dickinson emerged victorious. The first of these was against a ship subsidy measure under congressional consideration. He declared that the proposed bill would put the government at the mercy of shipowners and yet be of only temporary benefit to them. What shipping needed was more ocean freight, and the way to get that was to lower tariffs in order to cultivate closer commercial relations on a sound basis. If there must be a subsidy for American ships let the shipowner receive a rebate of half of the customs duties on the goods his vessels should bring to port.

For the time ship subsidy foundered on the rock of his logic.

A sharper conflict arose over the status of the mails during the railroad strike of 1888. Recognizing Chicago as the center of the disturbance, Postmaster General Dickinson had been forehanded in moving the headquarters of the railway mail service to that city and in sending one of his most energetic assistants there to marshal trainmen for mail movement. The railroad position was that hauling the mails, though under contract, was merely a part of their whole activity, for which the roads wanted government protection in its entirety. Dickinson's logical mind cut through this sophistry. To him a contract was a contract; the railroads had a contract to move the mails, and the mails must be moved. The Brotherhood of Locomotive Engineers would move the mails, but not passengers or freight. Men were available, and if the railroads did not move the mails, the government intended to do so with railroad employees and railroad equipment. Before the general strike was called, the Atchison, Topeka, and Santa Fe men already had gone out, and that railroad had flatly declared itself unwilling to move mail trains unless those trains also carried freight and passengers.

How the crisis was resolved is well related in Peter White's biographical sketch of his friend Dickinson; White indicated that he was told the story by the postmaster general, who said he was called to the White House at 11 P.M. to find the President besieged there by the railway committee. Wrote Mr. White:

> The railway committee labored to change the view of the Postmaster General, who simply said: "The mails must be moved." Just about midnight Nash (in charge at Chicago) telegraphed, "The Santa Fe gives up."
>
> Dickinson asked permission to open the envelope, read it and passed it on to the President. The President read it and said, "Anything further, gentlemen?"
>
> "No, sir, we have had our say."
>
> "I think we will leave it there then," said the President. "Have you men enough, Dickinson?"

"I think so, sir."

"Well," said he (Cleveland), turning to his desk, "Let me know your needs." . . . The meeting broke up at half-past twelve.

Dickinson was still at the wire at 3 o'clock (A.M.), when he heard from Scott (of the Pennsylvania Railroad and chief railroad negotiator): "The railroad companies will move the mails tomorrow and regularly thereafter." He took it to the White House and found the President still at his desk.

The President said, "I congratulate you and think we had both better go to bed . . ."

Thus, without espousing the cause of either the striking railroad employees or the operating corporations, Dickinson kept the mails moving and upheld the principle that the public welfare should be the first concern of a democratic government.

The Dickinson–Cleveland correspondence is full of allusions to the close association which existed between the two families and indicates that the Dickinsons fully enjoyed the gay social seasons of the capital. The friendship with the Clevelands endured far beyond the turn of the century; to the year of Cleveland's death the Dickinsons sent him birthday gifts and many were the epistolary exchanges on blessed events, millinery, dresses, and parties between the two families.

If the Republicans lost by a blunder in 1884, the Democrats were victims of misfortune in 1888. Had they been able to present a ticket with a well-known Hoosier like Hendricks in second place to counterbalance the Republican ticket with the less popular General Benjamin Harrison in first place, they might have carried Indiana, but Hendricks' death precluded that possibility. Instead, they gave the vice-presidential nomination to the "Old Roman" of Ohio, Allen G. Thurman, on the mistaken supposition that this switch would carry Ohio. The pestiferous Prohibitionists were again compromising a clear verdict, and there appeared out of nowhere a Union Labor party, never seen before or since, which cut into Cleveland's vote in vital industrial centers. As a result, although Cleveland received 110,000 more popular votes than Harrison, the Hoosier had 233 electoral votes to Cleveland's 168. Never has the clumsiness of the electoral college device been more completely exposed.

With the rest of the administration Dickinson retired from public life to reflect upon the American habit of voting against the "ins," and to recoup by professional exertion the financial ravages of official entertaining. Out of federal office, Dickinson applied his political genius to his home state with striking results. The year 1890 saw one of those off-year tidal waves in which a disillusioned electorate swamps an unpopular administration. In Michigan a startling phenomenon appeared—the entire Democratic state ticket was elected, and Michigan chose Democrats for eight of her eleven seats in the House of Representatives. The Democrats had a majority of the state representatives, and were able to control the Senate also by the vote of the lieutenant governor. This legislature put through the Australian ballot, gerrymandered congressional seats, and installed a system of choosing presidential electors by congressional districts instead of on a state-wide basis. There were precedents for this method, but it was adopted then and there as a fighting measure by a party sure of carrying Detroit and some other urban centers and determined to benefit thereby in the next election.

In the 1892 campaign, which had thus been realistically prepared for, it was the Republicans who made the blunders, the Democrats who benefited by a favorite slogan of that era—"put the rascals out." Cleveland, made of the granite that wears well, was by all odds the logical choice, having twice outrun the Republican candidate. Nevertheless, there were powerful Democratic leaders who opposed naming him, chiefly because he frowned on their machines, stratagems, and obscure aims. Chiefs of this coalition were the wily Arthur Pue Gorman, of Maryland, and "Clawhammer" David B. Hill, of New York. How they were outwitted by the secret conference of Clevelanders at William C. Whitney's residence in New York City is well told by Earl D. Babst in his account of Edwin F. Uhl, A.B. 1862, A.M. 1865. Dickinson, long suspicious of Gorman's intentions, became a natural leader in the Cleveland preconvention campaign and also on the floor of the convention.

To the leaders in that campaign it was clear that victory depended on the Lake States of the Middle West. Normally, all were Republican. Since 1860 only Indiana had gone Democratic, first for Tilden in 1876, then for Cleveland in 1884. As for Michigan, that state vied with Vermont and Maine for first place in percentage of the electorate that voted Republican—a rivalry which it consistently maintained in every presidential election up to 1936. Cleveland picked Don M. Dickinson for national chairman, and the latter concentrated money and attention where it was effective. Cleveland, with Adlai E. Stevenson as his running mate, carried this time, not only Indiana, but Illinois and Wisconsin as well, and picked up five of Michigan's fourteen electoral votes on the congressional district basis. This bloc provided the margin for a sweeping victory. Cleveland received 375,000 more votes than did Harrison, in spite of the heavy drag of the Populist candidate, who was given more than a million votes. Not since Grant's last campaign had a plurality of that size in the popular vote been scored by either major party in a presidential election. Dickinson's fellow townsmen accorded him a grand reception at the Hotel Cadillac, and congratulations poured in from press and public. Their tenor was felicitously phrased in an editorial in the St. Louis *Republic* by C. H. Jones, who sent it on to Dickinson with a letter saying, "You have done gloriously." But the hero, as he later wrote to Cleveland (March 31, 1896), said that he came out of the 1892 campaign "gray and bald and old."

Dickinson's return to power over patronage enabled him to place another group of Michigan men in official positions. Accounts of some of these, as alumni of the University, are given in this volume; among the others were Allen B. Morse, of Coldwater, defeated Democratic nominee for governor in 1892, to be consul at Glasgow, and Charles S. Hazeltine, *med.* 1865–66, of Grand Rapids, to be consul at Milan.

General Parkhurst, already mentioned in connection with Dickinson's attitude toward appointments, corresponded extensively with Dickinson; his letters, now in the Michigan Historical Collections of the University, are of interest. Both Parkhurst and Dickinson had been approached in connection with the vice-presidential nomination in 1888. Dickinson had been, as usual, nonreceptive, giving the suggestion no shadow of encouragement. Parkhurst was definitely receptive and permitted himself to hope, but accepted disappointment in good spirit and a little later was rewarded with a pleasant berth as minister at Brussels.

Again, Dickinson became a cyclone center for patronage seekers. This time he contended not merely against the hungry wolves of Michigan, but against ravening packs of claimants from all parts of the Union. Some aid came from Secretary of War Daniel S. Lamont, whose former place as personal secretary to President Cleveland had been filled at Dickinson's suggestion by the latter's law partner, Henry T. Thurber. Lamont was politically minded, and to him Dickinson willingly passed on the burden of choice whenever possible, but that did not save the Detroiter from being harassed by office seekers.

Occasionally, he had to put on pressure to get the man desired. Filling the office of secretary of state proved to be a difficulty. Rumor had it that Dickinson himself was a candidate; he deprecated the rumor, and there is no good reason for thinking that Cleveland ever seriously considered his national chairman for that place. Dickinson wanted the banner Cabinet position to go to the Middle West as a reward for hard-won success in that area and recognition of that triumph in high Democratic councils. Ordinarily the office of secretary of state went to the Atlantic seaboard; to fill it with a Westerner would mark a new era in sectional politics. The man selected was a Republican supporter of Cleveland, the gifted and already well-known Judge Walter Q. Gresham of Indiana, postmaster general and secretary of the treasury in President Arthur's administration. To Dickinson was assigned the duty of tapping Gresham and bringing him into line, against the wishes of Mrs. Gresham, who objected that her husband's health would not stand the strain of office. Dickinson persisted and succeeded, but Mrs. Gresham was right, for her huband died in office in 1895.

Cleveland offered Dickinson the honorary post of government director on the board of the Union Pacific Railroad, which he declined with thanks at great length in a letter that left no doubt of his yearning to avoid public office and of his wish to concentrate on his law practice. Prominent Democratic lawyers in Michigan endorsed a proposal to have Dickinson appointed to the United States Supreme Court in 1893. Dickinson wrote Thurber that he would have none of it and that he had checked the suggestion on a previous occasion. There were two vacancies on the Court in 1893; apparently, he was considered for each of them and also for the position of attorney general. Peter White, A.M. (*hon.*) 1900, of Marquette, no mean witness, said definitely in his sketch of Dickinson published on July 15, 1903, that he was offered the attorney generalship and also a place on a commission against the opium traffic—both promptly declined. But, informally and unofficially, Dickinson was "keeper and guardian of the President," as a New York correspondent described his activities at the inauguration of March, 1893. What the President thought of this shepherding is revealed in his letter of the following October: "I wish there were about twenty Dickinsons in the country." *

By 1893 the bloom was off the electoral peach and bitter grew its flesh. Misery stalked the land as overexpansion of credit took its usual toll in hard times—"boom and bust," the characteristic American cycle. The Democrats, less to blame than their adversaries, went into office just in time to catch the blow. The most optimistic of national chairmen could hardly hope to carry the midadministration election of 1894, which developed into a smashing pro-Republican overturn in Congress. Thereafter, Dickinson gave up hope of a Democratic victory in 1896 and strove chiefly to keep the party from what he termed the "free silver heresy." As the heresy gained steam-

* Cleveland to Dickinson, October 9, 1893, in Allan Nevins' *Letters of Grover Cleveland,* Houghton, Mifflin Company, Boston, (1933) p. 337.

roller headway, he grew concerned with holding his place as head of the Michigan delegation to the national convention. Enthralled by Bryan's oratory, the party swallowed with utmost enthusiasm the sixteen to one potion which turned Dickinson's stomach.

There were three ways of meeting this crisis. One could stick to the party, bolt to the Gold Democrats, or go over to the enemy. The first was submission, the second was evasion, the third was open resistance. Dickinson resisted, took the stump against Bryan, and helped to organize "sound money clubs" throughout the state. A host of Michigan Democrats followed him, enough to give Michigan back its old-time overwhelming Republican majority of the days of Grant. For the next sixteen years the cause of the Democratic party in Michigan was lost.

Old Dickinsonians who clung to the party in spite of free silver never forgave him for deserting to the enemy. Factionally, he had earlier quarreled and made peace with Daniel J. Campau, who, when Dickinson could no longer command a substantial following, became his successor as national committeeman from Michigan. Campau was a rich and consistently regular politician, now chiefly remembered for a bland cocktail which he invented and which is still served at the Detroit Club.

Don M. Dickinson's constructive political career came to an end with the 1896 campaigns. Although only fifty years old, he had been in politics for thirty years, climbing the ladder from local to national leadership. He had found his state overwhelmingly and traditionally Republican and had transformed it into a battleground where a few thousand votes tipped the balance and where victory hinged on details of organization or negotiation. Succeeding where others had failed, he moved to high office, but risked his national leadership to fight spoilsmen in Detroit regardless of party.

In 1893, when his prestige in the nation stood at its peak, Dickinson leaped to the support of Republican Mayor Hazen S. Pingree in his fight against the streetcar interests, declaring that Republican leaders were backing the Democratic nominee, William G. Thompson. This instance of nonpartisanship in local affairs is the more noteworthy because it was Pingree who in 1889 had broken the long series of Democratic victories in Detroit engineered by Dickinson in his effort to overturn Republicanism in the state.

An earlier instance of his stark political probity still lives in the annals of Detroit, which long ago began to dispense with partisanship in local affairs. Appearing before a canvassing board he insisted that its members correct a clerical error of record in order not to thwart the will of the voters. As a result the Democrats lost two aldermen, and the Republicans gained two. But, usually, Dickinson's well-led cohorts carried the city of Detroit. It is said that resistance to his iron rule throughout the state drove many Democrats into the free-silver camp, which was as much the refuge of the aggrieved and affronted as it was of the opinionated. Yet this adroit and vigorous political manager became an early champion of primary elections, which the Democratic party platform accepted in 1904.

Professional recognition at the hands of the government came to Dickinson when he was appointed senior counsel in the famous fur seal arbitration. He prepared his case so thoroughly and argued so effectively before the International High Commission on Bering Sea claims that the commission scaled the claims against the United States down from $150,000,000 to $264,000. One of his proudest achievements was his part in this prolonged litigation, and when his brilliant mind began to wander, toward the end of his days, he talked overmuch of that cold sea separating Alaska and Siberia. Indeed, the first sign of breakdown came in a Detroit court in 1911, when, in the midst of discussion of goods in storage, he drifted back to the Bering Sea arguments of fifteen years before. Reluctantly, the court had to admonish the great man that this was a simple case to replevin merchandise, not an international proceeding.

In a lesser litigation, arising over the protection of American property rights in San Salvador, Dickinson served in 1902 as American member of a court of arbitration and wrote its decision, highly esteemed for both style and substance, which upheld the contentions of the United States. That result was somewhat clouded by the fact that the award, as far as can be learned, was never paid. Salvador would not guarantee, with a part of her customs, the bonds she offered in satisfaction of the award, and the interested American banks refused to accept the settlement otherwise.

Charles W. Casgrain, a retired Detroit lawyer, once gave the writer this description of Dickinson in the fullness of his professional career:

> Like all leaders of the Detroit bar in this period, Dickinson dressed the part fully and punctiliously. He customarily wore a silk tile or, as we call it, a "plug hat," a frock or cutaway coat, striped trousers, patent leather shoes, and a heavy watch chain against a comfortably filled but not unduly obtrusive waistcoat. This garb was the uniform of leaders of the bar as well as of many prosperous business men, auctioneers, patent medicine vendors and theatrical stars. Don M. had short arms, fine nervous hands, and a quick step; he walked with something of a swagger which made him seem larger than he was. In height he was average, five feet seven or eight, but appeared larger, especially when in action. It was a memorable sight to behold Don M. Dickinson enter a courtroom, swing down the aisle with the air of owning the place, dramatically remove his gloves, hang up his plug hat, step to the counsel table and bow to the court.

In action Dickinson was a passionate advocate, one whose oratory usually brought beads of sweat to his forehead and conviction to those who heard him. Though his whiskers were luxuriant burnsides of the full Dundreary type, he exercised commendable restraint and tugged at these adornments only under stress, and not ever and anon, after the manner of his similarly decorated contemporaries. It was his habit to stride up and down in front of the jury box. To stress a point he took all possible liberties with court etiquette, occasionally entering the jury box itself. In almost any case, large or small, he roared so much that he would wear his voice to the breaking point. He tried his cases with all powers extended, and this accounts to a large extent for his many courtroom successes and the accompanying popular acclaim, for it was a day when legal spectacles were rated high drama by the public.

Part of Dickinson's success was certainly due to his thoroughness in preparing cases. Judge George S. Hosmer, A.B. 1875, LL.D. 1910, used to relate in delightful detail how Dickinson sailed into the office of his law firm at 4 A.M., silk tile and all, ready for work. Returning to Detroit late at night Hosmer, then a junior in the firm, went to sleep on a couch in the office, only to be awakened when the senior partner came in and turned on the light. With an important case to try that day, Dickinson had been unable to sleep because of some legal quandary, and had come to spend a few more hours of preparation before court convened. Insomnia became a curse with advancing years and contributed to his apparent breakdown in 1911 and virtual withdrawal from practice in 1912.

This prodigious care in the preparation of cases was once duly acknowledged in the United States Supreme Court. Presenting his side of the famous telephone case, which finally settled the validity of the Bell patents, Dickinson produced so many witnesses that the jurists were impressed. His prize discovery was one Drawbaugh who, it was alleged, had preceded Bell in voice transmission over wire but not, as the majority of the court held, to the Patent Office. In a bench of seven judges, three, including the chief justice, were so impressed by Dickinson's case and presentation, that they filed a dissent against the majority verdict concurred in by the four who held for Bell. The chief justice remarked on the flood of Drawbaugh witnesses; yet when the case went against him, Dickinson asked for a retrial on the ground that he now had discovered additional witnesses. The court, however, concluded that it had heard enough and must get on to other business. Many years later, as "a quiet gentlewoman of the old school sitting in a rocking chair in the library of their home" in Trenton, Mrs. Dickinson recalled to a reporter how her husband had shut himself up in a hotel room in New York City for a week to master certain details of this intricate case.

In the years of his strength Dickinson practiced widely in

New York as well as before the Supreme Court in Washington. How this came about is related by Mr. Casgrain. Newcomers in old firms usually were given the commercial or collection accounts. When Dickinson joined them, Moore and Griffin had as clients the leading Jefferson Avenue wholesalers, mostly Jewish. As a young man he helped them collect accounts from upstate retailers; then, gaining their confidence, he represented these substantial merchants in negotiations with Eastern jobbers, manufacturers, and bankers. Eventually, his New York clients kept him much of the time in the metropolis, where the firm was known as Dickinson and Griffin, not Griffin and Dickinson, as in Detroit. In the course of these transactions Dickinson became acquainted with the famous Field family and other Eastern notables in the profession. For instance, young Robert Lansing, son-in-law of John W. Foster and later secretary of state under President Wilson, is said to have been impressed early in his career by Dickinson's powers as an advocate. He came to Detroit and warmly urged Dickinson to accept President Cleveland's tender of the position of chief counsel for the United States in the Bering Sea fur seal dispute. In his letter of June 27, 1896, Cleveland wrote that "a young man by the name of Lansing who is quite familiar with the details will assist." Lansing zealously acted as Dickinson's junior in that protracted case, which capped the career of one distinguished lawyer and started the other toward eminence.

Dickinson's untrammeled fluency of expression was aptly characterized by a brother attorney, Otto Kirchner, A.M. (*hon.*) 1894, LL.D. 1919, who called Dickinson a "walking hyperbole." This inspired characterization was voiced in the trial of a suit against parties who had purchased property across from the Dickinson residence at Fort and Fourth streets with the intention of erecting a factory or warehouse there. Dickinson filed suit on the ground that this would constitute a "nuisance," and hired for his attorney John Atkinson, LL.B. 1862, like himself a luminary of a bar shining with stars. In Detroit legal annals the courtroom duels between Dickinson and Atkinson were famous in a day when such bouts were well attended and long remembered. Usually, if one can believe reminiscent hearsay, Dickinson, the impassioned advocate, won against the precise but frigid Atkinson. When Dickinson had to hire a lawyer, however, it was to his steadfast adversary that he went for help. If Atkinson in defense of Dickinson had any demurrer to enter against his client's being designated as a "walking hyperbole," it has been lost in oblivion, but the phrase lived on as description somewhat valid because of Dickinson's soaring vocabulary and his superb confidence that he was ever and unequivocally right.

Dickinson often interrupted his lucrative practice to take up cases without fees. For years he wrestled with certain railroads of the Upper Peninsula and with the Department of the Interior as attorney for groups of poor settlers who had been attracted there by corporate agents and whose land titles under the Homestead Act were in jeopardy. The sacrifice of time and money he made in this protective action led the beneficiaries to have spacious Dickinson County organized and named in his honor in 1891. There was, no doubt, a political advantage to this particular out-of-pocket case. In the Upper Peninsula, then a frontier region, the lumberjacks and miners were voted Republican by their strong-arm bosses, who as yet were undeterred by the Australian secret ballot. It is related that the first practical political use of the long distance telephone in Michigan was on an election day when the downstate G.O.P., having ascertained how many votes they were short at the closing of the polls, telephoned their needs to the Upper Peninsula, where polls were conveniently kept open to a late hour for just such a contingency. But apart from politics Dickinson took many cases for poor folk in Tennessee and elsewhere from whom neither revenues nor votes could be expected. These cases usually involved public education and other social causes in which he was interested.

Dickinson continued his correspondence with national leaders, but after 1900 his letters to Cleveland are tinged with reminiscent melancholy. The good old times were gone forever for the team of Cleveland and Dickinson. The latter supported

Woodrow Wilson in the 1912 primaries, but he had known Theodore Roosevelt for twenty years, liked both his personality and program for social justice, and in the three-way campaign of that strange year supported the Bull Moose candidate, who carried Michigan. Psychologically, Dickinson was more akin to the forthright Teddy than to the austere Princeton professor in politics.

Grover Cleveland, however, was for Don Dickinson ever the Great Chief. On March 23, 1895, in a reminiscent letter to Cleveland, Dickinson summed up the difficulties which beset his chief during his second administration. Those trials in office included a profound business depression, which well earned the homely phrase of "hard times," a bitter coal strike, the march of Coxey's Army of the unemployed upon Washington, and disturbing fiscal complications for the government. Of Cleveland's heroic part therein, Dickinson not unjustly, but with characteristic hyperbole, wrote:

> History will set down your four years as the most difficult years—war not excepted—in the life of this government . . . and history will surely set down against this epoch, that the chief, standing alone, was great in his place, equal to every occasion, a patriot always, and in and of himself the bulwark that turned back the flood of destruction.

In that same letter he quotes a verse from Smollett which brightly reflects his own feeling for Cleveland:

> Thy spirit, Independence, let me share,
> Lord of the lion-heart and eagle-eye,
> Thy steps I follow, with my bosom bare,
> Nor heed the storm that howls along the sky.

Great souls have a way of bringing others up to their standards. Here were two men of lofty motives who had need of one another, and who clove together for nearly thirty years through success and failure, without either ever finding anything to criticize in the other. Such robust, enduring, and faithful comradeship, rare in American politics, shows forth in the unpublished letters of both men, always constant to high political morality and to each other.

Nearly all of Dickinson's political letters to Cleveland, Lamont, and others are handwritten in a round, open, vigorous hand easy to read. Not so Cleveland's replies. His handwriting is almost as difficult to read as a foreign script. Like an adagio dancer, it hovers and twitches inordinately in one spot, then leaps in almost a straight line across the page to another twitching point. It is difficult to reconcile this chirography with Cleveland's steady, hew-to-the-line character. But Dickinson's script is one with his character and message as outgiver of affection, loyalty, courage, and hope.

Don M. Dickinson was a friendly, clubby person, a man's man, and elderly acquaintances in their off-hour gatherings still talk of his vibrant power and personality; most of all, probably, in the Detroit Club, of which he was first president and a founder. It is recalled there that his usual drink was claret, a mild vintage ever soothing to the questing legal mind. His other Detroit clubs were the Boat Club, the Country Club, the University Club, and the Bankers. He was a member of the Huron Mountain Club, to which retreat he went for quiet, and whither he tried to lure President Cleveland on several occasions. Elsewhere, he was a member of the Pilgrims in London and of the following New York clubs—the Manhattan, the National Democratic, and the Pilgrims of the United States. He belonged to a host of societies, legal, financial, and historical, in many of which he served as trustee or president, or both. He was a trustee of the Detroit University School, a director of the First National Bank, and a president of the Detroit Bar Association.

His home and family life was warmly gracious beyond the average. He enjoyed a glowing and enduring marriage, the fond love of children, and, as he aged in grace and wisdom, the goodly company of great books. If other poems followed his college verses on the beauties of Washtenaw's glades and groves, such effusions were suppressed by a young lawyer who had his way to make in the world and who knew that poets are suspect among the solid men of law and trade. In his homes on Fort

Street, at 666 Jefferson Avenue, and in Trenton, the library was his place of refuge and delight, and in communion with the great he gained right to the oft-bestowed title of "the scholar in politics."

In the last year of Dickinson's life, John Fitzgibbon of the *Detroit News* visited him in the spacious "Yellow House" at Trenton on the river below Detroit, where the Dickinsons resided after his retirement from active practice. The interviewer found Dickinson feeding his Wyandotte chickens in Horatian calm but ready to indulge in reminiscences in the rotund periods of an earlier day. The luxuriant burnsides had vanished, revealing at long last a "strongly limned, smooth shaven face," parchment white but animated by "snapping brown eyes." Dickinson related to Fitzgibbon a number of stories of encounters in courtrooms, convention halls, and hotel lobbies, where fisticuffs sometimes had the last word. When, after the Salvadoran award, a *señor* from the region came toward him with a revolver, our lawyer "swung from the floor" and laid his attacker low. He told his visitor that he admired Cleveland and Roosevelt because they were fighters and that he disliked Wilson's lack of firmness in Mexico. One is reminded of Browning's line, "I was ever a fighter and so one fight more, the last and the best."

Death came to Don M. Dickinson on October 15, 1917. His estate as probated was small; apparently his widow had been deeded all major assets during his semi-invalid but comfortable retirement. Other survivors were his daughter Frances (Mrs. George Barbour) and Don M. Dickinson, Jr., both of Detroit. The former leader had been in a backwater for more than five years and out of national politics for more than twenty years. In the meantime Detroit had grown from a colorful little city of 200,000 to a crashing industrial giant of a million. But the story of his life was then well reviewed, and Detroit felt again the impact of a personality who, entering early the soiled palace of politics, never stooped to meanness there.

Flags stood at half-staff in all post-office buildings in the

United States during his funeral. Services were conducted by the Reverend John Wellington Hoag of the Woodward Avenue Baptist Church, Detroit, at the Elmwood Chapel. Participating in the service were his Episcopalian minister, Dr. W. H. Thomas, and the Reverend John Richard Command. Burial was in the family plot in Elmwood Cemetery. Thirty-five of the leading citizens of Detroit were honorary pallbearers. The Detroit bench and bar appointed thirty members to serve as a guard of honor. A telegram of sympathy was received from Secretary of State Robert Lansing appropriately honoring his former colleague in important cases.

The *Detroit Free Press* said, editorially:

> . . . so long as scholarship in public place, gameness in contest, kindness to the vanquished political foe and fine old-fashioned camaraderie shall be appreciated in Michigan at their par value, there will be someone left to voice an appreciation of the warm-hearted son of Michigan who has gone to his long rest.

Thirty years after his death, Don M. Dickinson's place in the life of his times can be assessed with some definiteness. He was a reformer without cant, one who became opulent through driving effort, but kept free from arrogance. He was a cleanser and purifier, an honest, able man with a gift for political negotiation and management who took politics seriously as an agency for good. Party was to him important, but not all-important; on a point of principle he could tramp a lonely road. There were enough men of that kind then alive to rouse the nation from complacent materialism, and through twelve years of crisis and narrow margins, this way or that, they held the fort of conscience and compelled their G.O.P. adversaries to mend their ways. It is a battle which must be fought over and over in a democracy where rampant change crushes everything except political forms and usages, where graft eternally battles virtue, and where the impatient machine age is forced to putter along with an arthritic electoral college.

To the public arena Don M. Dickinson took the sane and

lofty ideals taught in his University, used them for the purging of evil, and thus wrought a career which both directly and indirectly stimulated both the University and its alumni to serve the nation with zeal like his own.

Lawrence Maxwell

1853	*Born near Glasgow, Scotland*
	Brought to Cincinnati, Ohio
1873	*Participated in the invitation to Theodore Thomas and his orchestra to inaugurate the Musical Festival Association in Cincinnati*
1874	*Graduated from the University of Michigan*
	Entered the Cincinnati Law School
1875	*Graduated from the Cincinnati Law School*
	Admitted to the bar of Ohio
1876	*Married Mrs. Clara (Barry) Darrow*
1884	*Argued his first case in the United States Supreme Court*
	Became a partner in the firm of Ramsey, Maxwell and Matthews
1893	*Appointed solicitor general of the United States*
1895	*Argued the case of the* United States *v.* E. C. Knight Company
	Resigned as Solicitor General of the United States
	Became a nonresident lecturer in the University of Michigan Law Department
1896	*Became a member of the Cincinnati Law School faculty*
1905	*Appointed chairman of the American Bar Association's Section on Legal Education*
	Chosen president of the Cincinnati Music Festival
1927	*Died in Cincinnati, Ohio*

LAWRENCE MAXWELL

Lawrence Maxwell

By Henry M. Bates

THE heritage of Scottish ancestry and the environment and opportunity of America combined to give to the University of Michigan a loyal and a helpful alumnus, and to his home city of Cincinnati, to his state of Ohio, and to the United States a very able, vigorous, and patriotic citizen, the Honorable Lawrence Maxwell, B.S. 1874, A.M. (*hon.*) 1893, LL.D. 1904.

Lawrence Maxwell was born near Glasgow, Scotland. He was the son of Lawrence and Alison (Crawford) Maxwell, who were natives of Scotland, but who came to this country soon after their marriage. The senior Maxwells immediately entered vigorously and cordially into the life of their adopted country. Lawrence Maxwell, Sr., engaged in the wholesale plumbers' supply business in Cincinnati and soon became a partner in the firm of Maxwell and Gibson. He volunteered to serve in the Union Army in the Civil War, but was rejected because of a bad heart. He did, however, help to repel the so-called Morgan Raiders during that war.

Not long before the birth of Lawrence, Jr., his mother journeyed to Scotland in a sailing vessel, which encountered very severe storms during the seven weeks on the water. Mrs. Maxwell wanted to be with her mother at the time of the birth and perhaps had some desire that the child be born in Scotland. Lawrence was born on May 4, 1853, and after a few months his mother returned with him to Cincinnati. As Mr. and Mrs. Maxwell had become naturalized before his birth, young Lawrence was an American citizen despite the fact that he was born abroad; subsequently, however, he had difficulty in obtaining a passport to European countries for the reason that the records of the naturalization of his parents had been destroyed in the Cincinnati courthouse fire in 1884. After some delay it was proved that Maxwell, Sr., had voted at several elections and that his name appeared in the records of the board of election commissioners as a citizen and voter.

At an appropriate age, young Lawrence Maxwell entered the public schools of Cincinnati and graduated from the Woodward High School of that city. In the fall of 1871 he entered the University of Michigan, from which he graduated in 1874 with the degree of Bachelor of Science. He had early acquired an ambition to become a lawyer, and during his college course at Ann Arbor, in addition to his regular work, he spent some time in studying law and in attending classes in that subject at the University. This enabled him, after his return to Cincinnati, to enter the Law School of that city with advanced standing. He received its law degree in 1875. Some months after this graduation he was admitted to the Ohio bar and became a member of the firm of King, Thompson, and Maxwell. In 1884 he became a partner in the well-known firm of Ramsey, Maxwell, and Matthews, subsequently reorganized under the name of Maxwell and Ramsey, and remained a member of that firm until his death.

During the period of his law study and apprenticeship in Cincinnati, in order to relieve his father of some of the expense of his education, he resumed what he had begun during his high-school days, regular employment during vacation times as an accountant for the Singer Sewing Machine Company. In that capacity he examined and passed on the complicated accounts of the Singer Company, covering its business throughout the world. He wrote a brief, published by the company and distributed to its agents throughout the United States, in which the rights of vendors under conditional sales contracts were clearly and accurately stated, with citations of the controlling decisions in every state. This experience was to prove invaluable to him later in the practice of law, for it gave to his vigorous and eager mind an acquaintance with business organization and finance which was highly useful to him in much of his important trial work. Few, if any, of the lawyers he met were able to match his quick and thorough understanding of the intricate problems of modern business and corporate life.

In December, 1876, Maxwell married, at Ann Arbor, Michigan, Mrs. Clara (Barry) Darrow, the daughter of Robert J. Barry, of Ann Arbor. Mr. and Mrs. Maxwell had two children, one of whom is now the wife of Joseph S. Graydon, who from the time he was admitted to the bar was associated in the practice of law with Maxwell and who is now a member of the firm of Graydon, Head, and Ritchey, successors to the firm of Maxwell and Ramsey. The other daughter is Mrs. William J. (Jean) Sturgis. By her first husband, Mrs. Maxwell had a son, Eleazar Darrow, A.B. 1892, now of Cincinnati. The Maxwell family residence for many years has been on Edgecliff Road, Walnut Hills, on the picturesque Cincinnati bluffs overlooking the Ohio River and the Kentucky hills.

From his earliest years in practice, Maxwell was a conscientious citizen, taking intelligent interest in the affairs of local and state government and in the election of competent and honest men to office, but his energy and ability as a lawyer soon brought to him so great a volume of important and exacting law practice that he had no time to devote to candidature for public office. He was persuaded, however, to accept appointment as solicitor general of the United States, and his nomination by President Cleveland was confirmed on April 6, 1893.* He retired from the office, by wholly voluntary resignation, on January 30, 1895. The reasons for this will appear later in this sketch.

Maxwell's extraordinary mental vigor, his habit of close analysis and thorough preparation, as well as his aggressive conduct of legal business and his tenacity of purpose, highly qualified him for success at the bar, and almost from the beginning of his practice his services were sought in litigation and other legal work of great importance.

The first case to bring widespread recognition of the unusual

* Charles H. Aldrich, A.B. 1875, A.M. (*hon.*) 1893, one of the most brilliant lawyers in Chicago in his time, was Maxwell's immediate predecessor as Solicitor General. The two men were very close friends and student associates in college as members of the Michigan chapter of Psi Upsilon.

abilities of Maxwell was *McArthur* v. *Scott* (113 U.S. 340), which involved the validity and construction of the will of General Duncan McArthur and was of enormous complexity, as to both the law and the facts. The will was probated in 1839, and clashing interests of beneficiaries, as well as of trustees, under the will, soon led to litigation in the lower courts. This continued for many years and, in addition to the legal problems indicated above, involved almost every possible aspect of the common law and of Ohio statutory rules against perpetuities. In 1884 the case had reached the Supreme Court of the United States and was to have been argued by William M. Ramsey, a senior member of Maxwell's firm. Ramsey, however, was taken ill suddenly, and the entire burden of the argument for the appellants was thrown upon Maxwell, who was then only thirty-one years of age and had never before argued a case in the Supreme Court. Maxwell, who had made an exhaustive study of the case, without hesitation stood in the breach and made the argument. Owing to the complexity of the case, the rule limiting the time for arguments was suspended, and Maxwell spoke for more than two hours in an argument whose excellence and profound scholarship is still remembered by older practitioners.

Justice Stanley Matthews had been associated with the firm of Ramsey, Maxwell, and Matthews and therefore did not participate in the hearing of the case but, as he afterwards wrote, he stepped behind the screen placed back of the justices in the old courtroom, intending to listen for a few minutes; Maxwell's argument proved so profound and powerful that, without realizing it, the justice stood for more than an hour and a half and heard substantially the entire argument. Later, he wrote to Rufus King, who earlier had been associated with the firm, that the evening after the argument he had attended a dinner with his colleagues of the Supreme Court, and, in the inevitable discussion of the case, they all agreed that Maxwell's presentation was one of the finest efforts to which they had ever listened.

Justice Matthews also wrote to Mrs. Maxwell about the argument, and a facsimile copy of that letter, which has been made available through the kindness of Mr. Graydon, reads in part as follows:

[The case was opened by] Mr. Maxwell in a speech of two hours and fifty minutes, the time having been extended. I heard it in part from behind a screen and the judges, whom I met that night at a dinner party, were unanimous and enthusiastic in their praises of it, the Chief Justice speaking of it as equal to any he had ever heard in the Court.

The case became recognized as a leading one in all of its main features. It has been cited hundreds of times in other cases that subsequently reached the United States Supreme Court and probably thousands of times in state courts from coast to coast. It was a decisive factor in the career of Maxwell, for it revealed him as thoroughly grounded in his profession, keenly analytical and penetrating, and possessed of exceptional intellectual capacity. Moreover, it demonstrated that he had the invaluable quality in a good lawyer of always being ready and prepared in the firm's cases, and, furthermore, that he had well-founded confidence in his own ability to meet situations as they arose. He was now firmly established as one of the foremost lawyers in the entire Middle West.

As solicitor general, Maxwell was associated with the case of *United States* v. *E. C. Knight Company* (156 U.S., 1, decided January 21, 1895), which is of great historical interest and which remained for many years the controlling authority upon one aspect of the scope of the Sherman Antitrust Act passed by Congress in 1890. The case had already been tried in the United States District Court, which had held that there had been no violation by the American Sugar Refining Company, of which the Knight Company and others were subsidiaries. The case was appealed to the United States Circuit Court of Appeals, which affirmed the opinion of the lower court. Appeal was taken from this decision to the United States Supreme Court. This case was the first one of importance brought by the government charging violation of the Sherman Antitrust Act, which reached the Supreme Court. There had been several cases in the lower courts. The government charged that the sugar companies had violated the provisions of the act, which made unlawful "every contract, combination, in the form of a trust or otherwise, or conspiracy in restraint of trade or commerce among the several states."

The defendants pleaded that they had formed no such contract, combination, or trust in restraint of trade. It was found by all three courts that the American Sugar Refining Company had achieved control of the business of refining sugar, but they held that the business was not "commerce" but "manufacture" and hence that the Sherman Act, which forbade only restraints on commerce, had not been violated. In other words, the Court treated the business of refining as a distinct act in itself and no part of commerce. There was a strong dissenting opinion by Justice Harlan, who maintained that the refining of sugar and its marketing and shipping in interstate commerce constituted integral and inseparable processes. Some of the sugar shipped by the company out of the state of Pennsylvania had apparently been refined with reference to pre-existing contracts of sale.

The holding of the Supreme Court, that the refining or manufacture and the marketing of such sugar were wholly separate functions, prevailed for many years, but for fifteen years or more the Court has nibbled away at this doctrine until little, if anything, remains of it. In fact, the Supreme Court has once or twice referred to the Knight case as in effect an overruled decision. The consequence of these later holdings is that an enormous amount of business, theretofore held to be local and within the state, is now drawn within the scope of the Antitrust Act. The records reveal no connection of Maxwell with this case in the two lower courts, but in the Supreme Court the government's case was briefed by "Lawrence Maxwell, Jr., Solicitor General, and Richard Olney, Attorney General, with whom was associated Samuel F. Phillips."

Perhaps the case of greatest national importance in which Maxwell was a participant was *Pollock* v. *Farmers Loan and Trust Company,* which was finally decided by the Supreme

Court of the United States, as reported in 158 U.S. 601, in 1895. This was the famous case involving the federal income tax provision in the Wilson Tariff Act, which was enacted by Congress during the second Cleveland administration.

The validity of the income tax provision was contested by the Trust Company on the ground, among others, that the tax was a direct tax upon property and was not apportioned among the states according to population, as direct taxes are required to be by Article 1, section 9, paragraph 4 of the Constitution. Attorney General Richard Olney believed that the tax was constitutional, claiming it was not a direct tax, but Solicitor General Maxwell believed the tax invalid and made most careful preparation to argue the case before the Supreme Court. The custom had been, and this was the general understanding of lawyers practicing before the Supreme Court, for the attorney general, who was a member of the President's Cabinet, to act as adviser to the President and to Congress, and in general to decide the over-all policy of the government in regard to legal matters. It was generally accepted that the solicitor general should argue the important cases before the Supreme Court. Olney, however, decided, especially in view of Maxwell's belief that the statute was unconstitutional, that he, Olney, would argue the case for the government. There was a very vigorous argument between the two men, but Olney insisted upon presenting the case, and on January 30, 1895, Maxwell resigned as solicitor general. Both men were able and conscientious and, equally, both were aggressive and dominant personalities. Maxwell, however, felt that he could no longer work with Olney on questions such as those involved in this case. By his resignation, the government lost a very able lawyer, strong in counsel, in organizing government litigation, and in argument in the Court.

The Pollock case was argued by Olney; the Court held that the income tax was a direct tax and hence that it violated the constitutional requirement of apportionment, thus agreeing with the views held by Maxwell. Subsequently, as thousands of us can testify with some degree of anguish, upon the adoption of the Sixteenth Amendment, Congress lost its constitutional inhibitions with respect to levying an income tax.

In 1887 an ambitious financier, known as "Young Napoleon" Ives, endeavored to throw the Cincinnati, Hamilton and Dayton Railroad Company into the hands of a receiver. As counsel for the railroad, Maxwell defeated this attempt by securing a decision of the Circuit Court of Hamilton County, reported as *Duckworth* v. *Cincinnati, Hamilton and Dayton Railroad Company* (2 Ohio cc 518). The decision was affirmed by the Supreme Court of Ohio and is still the leading authority in that state on the jurisdiction of courts in equity in the appointment of receivers.

In 1903 a contest between James R. Keene and the E. H. Harriman interests for the control of the Southern Pacific Railroad properties reached the United States District Court for the Western District of Kentucky (122 Fed. 147) and was finally determined in the Circuit Court of Appeals for the Sixth Circuit (129 Fed. 1007). Many eminent lawyers appeared in this case; among them, besides Lawrence Maxwell, were Senator Joseph B. Foraker, former Governor A. E. Willson, of Kentucky, Maxwell Evarts, and Eugene Treadwell, of the firm of Hoadley, Lauterbach and Johnson. Maxwell wrote briefs for his client, E. H. Harriman, and opened his argument at nine o'clock, continuing until half-past twelve. When the judges had left the courtroom, one of Maxwell's associates noticed that his left hand was badly swollen. When Maxwell was asked about the swelling, he said, "I think I broke my arm this morning." He had, in fact, slipped on the tile floor in his bathroom, inflicting a severe break at the elbow. The incident is illustrative of Maxwell's courage and persistent performance of his duty.

In 1914, after the Department of Justice had spent several years of exhaustive preparation of the case against the firm, John H. Patterson and other officers of the National Cash Register Company of Dayton, Ohio, were indicted for violation of the Sherman Antitrust Act. Maxwell, with John A. McMahon and John F. Wilson, of Columbus, represented the defendants in a prolonged trial before the United States District Court, with Judge Howard C. Hollister and a jury, the tribunal. The jury brought in a verdict of guilty, and Patterson and several other defendants were sentenced to imprisonment. The case was appealed to the United States Circuit Court of Appeals for the Sixth District, with Justice William R. Day, B.S. 1870, LL.D. 1898, associate justice of the Supreme Court and circuit justice for this district, and Judges A. M. G. Cochran and Edward T. Sanford, sitting. The case was elaborately argued on both sides, and on March 13, 1915, the verdict and sentence were reversed and the case remanded for a new trial. The Circuit Court of Appeals made a most meticulous study of the proof offered by the government of monopoly and conspiracy to monopolize and was unanimous in holding that the government had not made out a case. The opinion of this court was so decisive that the government suspended the prosecution, and no further attempt to prosecute was made. The case is reported in 222 Federal Reporter 599.

In the year 1900, Maxwell was employed as special counsel for the Commonwealth of Kentucky in the litigation growing out of the violent contest and disputed election returns for the offices of governor and lieutenant governor. In the election of November, 1899, William Goebel and J. C. W. Beckham were the Democratic candidates for these offices, and W. S. Taylor and John Marshall, the Republican. The State Board of Election Commissioners on the face of the returns certified the election of Taylor and Marshall by approximately 2,400 votes. Goebel and Beckham thereupon instituted contest proceedings in the state legislature, and a joint committee of four from the Senate and seven from the House was set up. All of the members except three were Democrats.

Charges of all kinds of fraud were made and considered. The committee reported that fraud had been proved and that Goebel and Beckham had been duly elected, and the legislature approved their report. Goebel took the oath of office on February 3, 1900, but died a few hours later from gunshot wounds inflicted on January 30. Beckham, who had already taken the oath required for lieutenant governor, immediately after Goebel's death took the oath as governor. A large number of men were indicted for the crime of killing Goebel, among them a former officeholder, Caleb Powers, who was charged with being an "accessory before the fact." Two of the numerous defendants were acquitted. The others were found guilty and were sentenced to death in some cases, and for various terms of imprisonment in others. Powers was sentenced to life imprisonment.

In the meantime, Taylor, having claimed election and having taken the oath of office as governor, immediately pardoned Powers and some others. The pardon was treated as of no effect. On the strength of it, however, the defendant secured two new trials at successive periods, but at each of them he was again found guilty. In the meantime, several of the defendants, including Powers, had begun to serve their sentences of imprisonment. Powers petitioned for a writ of habeas corpus and also for removal of his case to the Federal Court. The District Federal Court ordered the state authorities to release Powers. They refused to do so, and successive appeals were taken to the circuit court and to the United States Supreme Court. The latter court, in an opinion by Justice Harlan which was concurred in by the entire court, declared that no cause of federal action was involved and remanded the case to the state court for further proceedings.

As stated above, Maxwell was employed as special counsel for the Commonwealth of Kentucky, in both the removal case and the case of *Beckham* v. *Taylor*. In the latter case (178 U. S. 540) Beckham, who had assumed the governorship on the death of Goebel, sued Taylor and Marshall for usurpation of office. A majority of the court, in an opinion written by Chief Justice Fuller, confirmed the judgment of ouster against Taylor and Marshall rendered by the Kentucky Court of Appeals. Dissenting opinions were written by Justices Brewer and Harlan. Justice Brown concurred with Justice Brewer.

Maxwell argued each of the cases orally and filed briefs which apparently greatly influenced the dissenting justices, as shown by their opinions. There was not much that was novel or unusual in the law problems involved in this extraordinary series of events, but the controversy was the most dramatic and exciting political feud ever waged in this country, and the entire state was aroused to a pitch of excitement incredible to us of this day. Hundreds of armed men roamed the streets of Frankfort; threats were hurled by each side against the other, and Frankfort was on the verge of something like civil war. The fever gradually abated, however, and the prison terms were begun by those who had been sentenced. Powers served eight years and three months of his term and then, with others, was pardoned by Governor Willson in 1909. After his pardon, he returned to his home in the Kentucky mountains, where he was repeatedly honored by the voters of his congressional district, who elected him to four terms in the lower house of Congress.

The cases referred to above are perhaps the best known and among the most important in a long list of important cases in which Maxwell participated, usually as leading counsel. Other cases which deserve mention are: *Terre Haute and Indiana Railroad Company* v. *Indiana* (194 U. S. 579), in which were considered certain state laws impairing the obligation of contracts in railroad companies' charters; *Adams Express Company* v. *Iowa* (196 U. S. 147), *American Express Company* v. *Iowa* (196 U. S. 133), *American Express Company* v. *Kentucky* (206 U. S. 139), *Adams Express Company* v. *Kentucky* (214 U. S. 218), and several other cases involving the transportation and delivery of intoxicating liquors in interstate commerce; *Cincinnati Packet Company* v. *Bay* (200 U. S. 179), considering contracts in restraint of trade affecting steamer traffic; *Ballman* v. *Fagin* (200 U. S. 186), involving constitutional rights against self-incrimination; *Adams Express Company* v. *Kroninger* (226 U. S. 491), dealing with the validity of limitation of value clauses under the act to regulate commerce; *United States* v. *Adams Express Company* (229 U. S. 381), a prosecution under the Interstate Commerce Act; *Hamilton Brown Shoe Company* v. *Wolff Brothers* (231 U. S. 756), dealing with trade-marks and unfair competition; *Toledo*

Newspaper Company v. *United States* (247 U. S. 492), a contempt case against the publisher of a newspaper; *Hawke* v. *Smith* (253 U. S. 221), which dealt with the submission of the Eighteenth Amendment to the referendum in Ohio.

Maxwell was recognized during most of the period of his practice as one of the really great lawyers of the country. He achieved this reputation because he never failed to make a most painstaking investigation, both as to facts and law, of all matters confided to his care. His was a powerful mind, and he possessed the genius for analytical study. The law, its practice and its development, was the dominating interest of his life, but he was not merely a great trial lawyer. He was perhaps even more outstanding as an adviser, and no man could have achieved what he did who was not possessed of a lively and yet realistic imagination. His eminence in the profession and his understanding of its problems were recognized by his appointment in 1911 as chairman of the Committee of the Bar of the Supreme Court of the United States on the Revision of the Rules in Equity, and it may be said that in large part the present simplified rules in equity practice are to be credited to Maxwell's labor in that field.

Maxwell early recognized the importance of developing and extending throughout the country a sound program of legal education, to follow the example set by a few of the better law schools. It was natural that he should take an active interest in the work of the University of Cincinnati Law School, of which he was a graduate. That school had had a long history, and, judged by the quality of its faculty and alumni, an honorable one. It was founded as the Cincinnati Law School in 1833 by Edward King (the son of Rufus King, United States senator from New York), Timothy Walker, and John C. Wright, who had been a judge of the Supreme Court of Ohio. Timothy Walker became the dean and the most active professor in the law school. His deanship began in 1844. Walker was the author of what is commonly known as Walker's *American Law*, which came to be recognized in legal circles everywhere, and was undoubtedly one of the most useful and comprehensive books on American law ever published.

In 1896, after the school had gone through a period of vicissitudes involving its association at times with the College of Cincinnati, a number of prominent Cincinnati lawyers undertook a complete reorganization. William Howard Taft became dean and taught constitutional law. Judson Harmon, formerly attorney general of the United States, was active in both its administration and its courses of instruction. Gustavus Wald, author of Wald's *Pollock on Contracts,* and Rufus B. Smith, judge of the Superior Court of Cincinnati, took the courses in contracts and quasi contracts; and Harlan Cleveland, the United States district attorney, taught criminal law. Maxwell took pleading and jurisprudence for his subjects. It was characteristic of him that, although he appreciated the value of Langdell's *Case Book on Equity Pleading,* he decided not to use it in his course, but prepared a list of his own cases, which emphasized the practical side of equity rather than its historical and philosophical background.

Maxwell taught civil procedure, common law, procedure in equity, and jurisprudence, until 1907. During the next ten years he did not teach regularly, but the annual catalogues announced: "The Honorable Lawrence Maxwell will give a course of lectures during the year, subject and hours to be announced later." He did lecture frequently in the school during that decade, but gave no regular courses. In 1918, a majority of the shares of stock in the old law school having been transferred to the University of Cincinnati, the school became a permanent part of the University.

Maxwell was also active as an adviser to the Law Department of his alma mater, the University of Michigan. In 1895, he accepted appointment as a nonresident lecturer on legal ethics in the University of Michigan Law Department and held that appointment until 1912, often coming to Ann Arbor at great inconvenience to himself, year after year, to lecture to the senior class. It need scarcely be said that with his wealth of experience, his sound judgment, and the high standards of professional practice which he always insisted upon, his lectures were of great interest and importance to his hearers and to the Law Department.

For many years Maxwell had been active in the American Bar Association, frequently speaking in the important discussions of its problems. In 1905 he was appointed chairman of the association's section on legal education, and his committee made an important report which is published in the proceedings of the association.

Another indication of Maxwell's breadth of view and his desire to aid in worth-while activities was his thoughtful and very helpful aid given the University of Michigan from time to time. As a student at the University he took a keen interest in all wholesome student activities. He was a member of the Psi Upsilon fraternity, and the records of the local chapter show that he held practically all of the offices of this chapter. At the public literary exercises of the 1896 national convention of Psi Upsilon, held in University Hall, he delivered an address on the "Relation of the University to the Teaching of Law." He showed that the United States was in advance of England and contended that even more attention should be given to our law schools. That he had become recognized as one of our most helpful graduates is shown by the fact that he was selected to deliver the commemorative address at the brilliant celebration in 1912 of what was then considered the seventy-fifth anniversary of the founding of the University. He made his address a historical treatment of the founding, growth, and development of the University. The address, it is believed, is the most understanding and effective summary treatment of the life of the University which has been made at any time. It is far more than a mere recital of dates and facts; it indicates deep understanding of the function of education in a democracy and sympathetic observation of its achievements.

Another instance of Maxwell's helpful consideration of important activities of the University was the part he played in the long struggle, beginning locally in 1903 to 1904, to establish the Michigan Union and to obtain for it the means to build a home which would be adequate and helpful to the University. After the organization and incorporation of the Union under the laws of the state, Maxwell was soon appealed to for advice. He responded immediately and during the years that followed made several trips to Ann Arbor for conferences here; he gave the use of his name and a substantial money contribution, as well as his own personal assistance in raising money in Cincinnati and elsewhere.

There were a few alumni, called in in this way, who felt that the committee in charge was proposing to raise a larger amount of money than would be needed. Their criticism made a rather tense situation, but Maxwell spoke vigorously in several conferences in favor of the large sum which the Union committee had in mind. The committee's estimated need and half a million dollars more were ultimately raised and expended, and no one having the slightest acquaintance with the present situation doubts that all the money was needed and well spent. It is hard to conceive of the University operating at the present time without the aid which the Union gives in housing visiting alumni and guests and in affording a place for all kinds of University affairs and for numerous gatherings of the faculty and students for purposes definitely related to the primary work of education. All of this Maxwell foresaw and vigorously stated at a time when such aid was critically needed.

In 1911 the well-remembered National Dinner was held in New York. This project was conceived by another generous and helpful alumnus and friend of the University, Earl D. Babst of the Literary Class of 1893 and the Law Class of 1894. This was probably the most effective and brilliant event of the kind ever successfully projected by the alumni of any university. It was distinctly the product of Babst's loyalty to his alma mater and his organizing ability; but Maxwell was characteristically active in arousing interest on a national scale.

One of the indirect results of the National Dinner was the great benefaction of William W. Cook, A.B. 1880, LL.B. 1882, of New York. A direct result was the recognition by the alumni,

President Hutchins, Ph.B. 1871, LL.D. 1921, and others of the University, that appeals to the alumni for financial aid should be under the official control of the University. Again, Babst supplied the spark which led, with the approval of President Hutchins, to the adoption of this pioneer plan designed to prevent conflicts between different groups.

It was the era of the Alumni Advisory Council, and Maxwell, James R. Angell, A.B. 1890, A.M. 1891, LL.D. 1931, and Babst were serving as its executive committee. Maxwell, deeply interested, guided the framing of the resolutions outlining the plan and secured their adoption at the annual meeting of the Alumni Association at the time of the 1911 Commencement.

The main feature of the plan was the requirement that proposals for soliciting funds for any purpose from the alumni should first be submitted to the President of the University and be approved by the Board of Regents. The solicitation of funds for the various needs of the University became increasingly important in succeeding years. Treatment of the matter took present form at the meeting of the Board of Regents in December, 1926, as follows:

> The President reported certain recommendations, regarding procedure in the solicitation of funds from alumni and other private individuals for the benefit of the University, made by a group of members of the Faculties and others consulted by him. The Board adopted these recommendations, approved the appointment of a committee to advise with the President on matters of this nature, and adopted the following addition to the By-Laws (page 107):
>
>> Chapter V, Sec. 17 *a* (*a*) All solicitations for the benefit of the University by members of its staff, shall be with the consent of the President, who may appoint an advisory committee to consider and report to the Regents through him such measures germane to the subject as they may deem desirable (cf. By-Laws, Chapt. VI, Sec. 9, for regulations concerning solicitation by student organizations).
>>
>> (*b*) Gifts to the University shall at stated times, to be designated by the President, be reported to him by the proper authorities.

The plan, as finally worked out, provides for intelligent, harmonious co-operation of the President of the University and other officials with the parties interested in soliciting funds for any University purpose. It has resulted in the elimination of some projects not deemed expedient or practicable and especially in concentrating all the strength of the University back of those projects officially approved. The result cannot fail to be of continuing benefit.

The story of this important development is well summarized by Babst in an address delivered at a memorial meeting in honor of the late President Hutchins, held by the University on November 28, 1930, in Ann Arbor. Excerpts from the address, bearing on this matter, follow:

> The difficulties arising from the lack of harmony in alumni effort prepared the way for a unified policy. It had long been the practice of alumni wishing to promote some particular objective to form a committee and to launch their effort on their own initiative, soliciting the alumni far and near. Often the alumni were confronted with appeals from a number of such committees. Women campaigned among their own numbers and sometimes approached the men to cover the difference between expectation and reality. Religious organizations had their own campaign lists. Student organizations sallied gayly forth. There were appeals for subscriptions to University periodicals, for portraits, for exploration, for excavation, for the purchase of manuscripts and collections, for the establishment of research, and for scholarship funds. And to these were added the appeals of the general alumni association and of the local alumni associations. It is not difficult to understand the confusion of effort which resulted. The belabored alumni were almost forced at times to hide their identity.
>
> Judge Claudius B. Grant (A.B. 1859, A.M. 1862, *law* 1865–66, LL.D. 1891, Regent 1872–80) and his associates in carrying through the project of Alumni Memorial Hall were the innocent victims of this antiquated system. Infinite labor and undeserved disappointment were behind the first sentence in Judge Grant's presentation address of May 10, 1910: "We celebrate tonight the consummation of a work of seven years." The building was not paid for when he spoke those words. A group of younger alumni already had formed another committee to launch a campaign for the Michigan Union and were clamoring for

alumni support. The 1910 annual meeting of the Association had certain tense moments. It led, however, to a happy and far-reaching solution the following year through the efforts of the Alumni Advisory Council under the guidance of Lawrence Maxwell, '74, (*hon.*) '93, (*hon.*) '04, in co-operation with President Hutchins. The Alumni Association took then the high ground which it continues to hold. It can best be stated in the simple preamble of its official resolution:

"The General Alumni Association desires to serve the University and so meet those needs regarded by the Regents and the Senate as most urgent."

This resolution is the source of our strength for united and harmonious action; it has become not only a policy but a tradition. . . .

Under this policy the Michigan Union and the Michigan League building projects have been carried to successful conclusion. The alumni have been freed from continuous solicitation and their generosity has been cheerfully marshaled for the larger needs of the University as they have been officially declared from time to time to be most urgent.

It may be added that the Union movement was inaugurated by a small group of students and faculty members in 1903 and that the Union was incorporated in 1904. This group carried on for several years until it had raised a fund to defray the correctly anticipated heavy expenses of the campaign, and then a general campaign for the building fund was instituted among all of our alumni.

One who knew Maxwell only as the scholarly, aggressive, and successful lawyer knew him only in part. There was another side to his nature than that called into play by his law practice, a side which gives a fair conception of the breadth of his character and interests and one which undoubtedly added greatly to his enjoyment of life and to the constructive and imaginative manner in which he approached the problems of his profession. That was his great lifetime avocation, the study, practice, and love of music.

Maxwell was one of the founders and, until his death, one of the dominant, creative, and leading members of the Cincinnati May Festival Association. He was made president of the Association in 1905 and held that office until his death. In 1873, the year of the first festival, he was one of a committee of seventy citizens who invited Theodore Thomas to bring his Chicago orchestra to Cincinnati for the purpose of carrying out a plan for permanent festivals, a plan which had already been conceived by a committee, of which George Ward Nichols was president, John Shillito, treasurer, and Bellamy Storer, secretary.

During the life of Theodore Thomas, and afterward, when the festivals were held under the direction of Van der Stucken, Elgar, Ysaye, and other directors, Maxwell co-operated in making the programs, and he gave his personal attention to the selection of soloists and the arrangement of contracts with them. For many years he made special trips to Europe and to important musical centers in this country for the purpose of judging the ability of various soloists. J. H. Thuman, secretary of the Festival Association, wrote of him at the end of his career:

> The death of Lawrence Maxwell removes from the life of Cincinnati one of her most noted and unselfish idealists. His accomplishments in the field of Law were but one phase of his notable career that made him nationally famous. But the side which placed him in his most engaging mood was his sincere and earnest devotion to music. He brought to the appreciation and understanding of this art those same remarkable powers of discernment and intelligent analysis which must have marked his devotion to legal problems. Only the finest and the best appealed to him and only the greatest masterpieces in music met with his sympathetic approbation. His ideals in the cause of music were of the highest.
>
> In his early years Theodore Thomas had been his mentor and his friend, and the ideals of that great pioneer in the cause of good music in America became his ideals and were preserved throughout his life. They found their most practical expression in his devotion to the May Festivals, with which he was so intimately identified for more than 50 years. When Theodore Thomas died in 1905 there were those who thought that the festivals would die with their founder, but Lawrence Maxwell undertook to carry on, to uphold and develop those same

ideals. His courage, his foresight and his intimate knowledge of music were unselfishly devoted to the cause. For more than twenty years he carried on where Thomas had left off; never for one moment was there any deviation from the straight and narrow path. The May Festivals meant as much to him as his legal profession. Music was his all-absorbing hobby and it was this fact, this devotion to the cause, which sustained the festivals on their high plane and advanced them as the appreciation of the public grew.

On one occasion in a group of men, including Maxwell and Theodore Thomas, there was conversation about the rumor that the President had offered, or was about to offer, a place on the Supreme Court to Maxwell. The latter made no comment about it whatever, and one of the lawyers remarked that he thought it would be the ambition of any lawyer to sit on that court, to which Theodore Thomas replied that he believed Maxwell's greatest ambition was to have two or three hundred school children carrying, between their homes and schools, the Bach "Passion" music, in preparation for a Cincinnati Music Festival. Not many years had passed before that was actually brought about. Maxwell was greatly interested in having young children acquire a knowledge and appreciation of good music, and he contributed effectively to that end.

About a year before his death, ill health compelled Maxwell to discontinue the active practice of law. During that period he was practically confined to his home and unable to pursue his lifelong habit of intense industry. Shortly before his death, he seemed comfortable so that there was no great apprehension of a fatal termination; but suddenly he suffered a cerebral hemorrhage and died on February 17, 1927.

The Commercial Club of Cincinnati said, in a memorial resolution:

Lawrence Maxwell, leader of the bar, giant of intellect, patron of music, outstanding citizen and social leader [is dead]. His course through life was that of a strong man of high character and in a field of endeavor that went far beyond his individual concerns.

His lofty attainments in the profession, in which he rendered services of the highest order to his government and to his private clients as well, are attributable to a greatness of mind, such as is vouchsafed to few individuals, fully balanced by an equal breadth and integrity of character.

The Cincinnati *Enquirer* remarked editorially:

Death last night ended the brilliant career of Lawrence Maxwell; . . . a man of high attainments embodying all the romance and culture that are associated with the profession of the law. He was one of the foremost attorneys in the country, and became so prominently associated with cases involving Federal constitutional and legal questions that interest in his appearance often overshadowed the issues at bar.

Indeed, it must appear from this brief sketch of Maxwell's life, that not only was he one of the country's greatest lawyers in his generation, but also, and even more important, he was a great human being, conscientiously and effectively serving his many interests in life. His genuine love of music, already referred to, reveals him as valuing highly the finer things of life. An incident of his law practice is illustrative of his human sympathy and his desire to help less fortunate fellow beings. Although he was legal counsel for several railways, he once brought suit, without compensation, against a railway company, for a penniless small boy who had been injured in a railway accident.

Lawrence Maxwell was a man who asked no favors, no guaranties of security, no rights or privileges at the expense of others or of the community, a man of high standards for the activities that count most in a good life. His achievements made him a towering figure. To have acquired such wide and recognized standing as a lawyer was enough in itself to bring great distinction. But he was far more than a gifted and successful lawyer. Undoubtedly, he would have strengthened and adorned the Supreme Court of the United States.

The late Howard C. Hollister, judge of the Federal District Court in the Southern Ohio District, told some friends that he had sat next to Justice Holmes at a men's dinner in Washington and had asked the justice who, in his opinion, was the ablest advocate that had appeared before the court in his time. Holmes answered that he would mention two names without preference. The men thus mentioned were the outstandingly able John G. Johnson of Philadelphia and Lawrence Maxwell of Cincinnati. No man could wish for higher commendation.

J. Sterling Morton

1832	*Born in Adams, Jefferson County, New York*
1834	*Moved to Monroe, Michigan*
1846	*Attended Wesleyan Seminary, Albion, Michigan*
1850	*Entered the University of Michigan*
1853	*Published* The Peninsular Quarterly and University Magazine, *first University of Michigan student publication*
1854	*Expelled from the University*
	Became a reporter for the Detroit Free Press
	Married Caroline Joy French
	Moved to Nebraska Territory
1855	*Elected to first territorial legislature*
	Became editor of the Nebraska City News
1858	*Received A.B. degree (class of 1854),* nunc pro tunc *from the University of Michigan*
1858–61	*Served as secretary of the Nebraska Territory*
1872	*Established Arbor Day*
1873	*Elected president of the Nebraska State Board of Agriculture*
1893	*Appointed Secretary of Agriculture by Cleveland*
1902	*Died in Lake Forest, Illinois.*

J. Sterling Morton

J. Sterling Morton

By William D. McKenzie and Paul A. Leidy

IN THE FALL of 1850, a freshman arrived in Ann Arbor, who, forty-three years later, would become Grover Cleveland's secretary of agriculture: the earliest University of Michigan student to be honored by appointment to a presidential cabinet.

Had the young man been required to fill out the registration record card familiar to modern University of Michigan students, it would have disclosed these facts: name, Julius Sterling Morton (as time went by he would discard the full first name and use the initial only); born, April 22, 1832, in the village of Adams, in Jefferson County, New York; father, a merchant in Monroe, Michigan. The new student justified his admission to the University by showing the satisfactory completion of the course of study at Wesleyan Seminary at Albion, Michigan.

The campus to which young Morton had come was situated at the edge of the little town of Ann Arbor. It is described, in an article by Charles M. Perry, Ph.D. 1911, "Dr. Tappan comes to Michigan," * in this fashion: "The campus itself looked like a large farm meadow, and was indeed mowed regularly for the crop of hay it yielded." Moreover, when the young freshman went "down to Ann Arbor," the atmosphere he found must have contrasted sharply with that of his home town. The University, which had just become a university in fact through the establishment of a Medical Department, in addition to the Literary Department opened nine years before, dominated the village. Monroe, as the eastern terminus of the Michigan Southern Railroad, had not given up hope of attain-

* *Mich. Hist. Mag.,* vol. 10, pp. 194-211.

ing the importance which had been commonly expected for her. When the elder Mortons moved west from Adams, New York, Monroe was a thriving community, as populous and as important, commercially, as Chicago, Illinois, and her citizens confidently expected her to maintain a position of leadership as a Great Lakes port and a railroad terminus. Ann Arbor, on the other hand, was essentially a rural community; its prospects for growth depended largely on the future of the University.

J. Sterling Morton was assigned a room on the fourth floor of "the dormitory," which occupied all floors but the first of the building known as North College. He and his new roommate could have walked around the campus, visiting all of the University buildings, in but a few minutes. In addition to North College, there were only "South," four houses occupied by members of the faculty, and a part of a building designed for the Medical Department. The library and the museum were on the first floor of "North."

In the excellent biography of J. Sterling Morton by James C. Olson, an entire chapter is devoted to Morton's college career. In a brief consideration of its high lights it may be hoped, however, that a hasty glance will make possible an appreciation of some of the characteristics of this student who was to be a central figure in a campus *cause célèbre* late in his senior year, the founder of Arbor Day in the early seventies, the stormy petrel of Cleveland's second-administration cabinet, and, for fifty years, a powerful figure in Nebraska and the Middle West.

J. Sterling Morton was probably not an excellent student. His diary and correspondence suggest that he might not have deserved to be called a conscientious student; he promised himself, from time to time, to "turn over a new leaf," and alter his attitude toward classroom assignments. He was, however, a lively member of the literary society to which he belonged, and he seems to have been active, strangely enough, in at least two fraternities, though evidence indicates that his membership in, and loyalty to, Chi Psi fraternity was the more enduring. In fine, his interests appear to have been concentrated in the field of extracurricular activities. He was the founder, editor, and probably the chief contributor of the first student publication to appear on the campus of the University of Michigan—*Peninsular Quarterly and University Magazine.* His interest in journalism was a most natural one. His grandfather, Abner Morton, had owned and edited a newspaper in Adams, New York, and shortly after the arrival of the Morton family in Monroe, Abner and a son, Edward, had started a newspaper there. What developed into a lifelong interest in journalism, on the part of Edward's nephew, was undoubtedly due, in large part, to the influence of this uncle. It may be noted, in passing, that a similar devotion to the Democratic party may be traced to the same source. J. Sterling Morton was to be known as a man of strong convictions, but he would be the first to admit the effect of early environment. "Uncle Edward" was always one of his idols; while Sterling and his father disagreed, sometimes rather violently, over the years, there is no tangible evidence of a failure to see "eye to eye" with the father's brother.

The *Peninsular Quarterly* was not Morton's first venture into the field of student journalism. At Wesleyan Seminary, as president of "The Clever Fellows," a literary society, he had led that little group into the publication of a magazine. Its first issue appears to have been its last, but its sudden demise did not deter its founder and editor from attempting a similar effort at the University. *Peninsular Quarterly and University Magazine* was also short-lived, but available copies of two issues demonstrate the young editor's literary interests. They also confirm the estimate of Professor Whedon, Morton's "landlord" during his second year on the campus. In a letter written to the lad's father, Whedon described Morton's literary ambition as "intense," and said of the young man himself that he was "more a universal reader than a laborious student." Buried not too deeply in later paragraphs of this same letter are references to certain traits of the son which may give explanation to the most colorful event of his college career—his expulsion. "He seemed to be one of that class of students," Professor Whedon wrote, "who derive more benefit from the libraries and literary associations than from the laboratory or the classroom. He shone better in debate than in recitation."

Young Morton would not have denied the implications of Professor Whedon's analysis. Apparently, the neighbors back in Monroe regarded him as somewhat of a "spoiled child," one who "wouldn't mind his parents." In later years he himself recalled his early interest in chicken fighting and the cultivation of intimate friendships in a stratum of Monroe society which was distinctly "not aristocratic"; in fact he described himself as a "general vagabond." Since he was describing himself as he had been when only twelve years old, one may discount this not too pleasant picture; he was prone to extreme statement, and he had a good sense of humor. There is ample evidence, however, of his love of argument and of his flair for the dramatic in speech and writing. After all, this would not be surprising in a lad admitting hero worship for an uncle who himself had been characterized as "sharp, incisive, and keenly alive to the weak points of the enemy." Both the uncle and the nephew were to find many "enemies" to attack as time went on. And both of them seem to have taken up the search relatively early in life.

As was to be true of nearly every controversy in which Sterling Morton was involved—and there were many—reports differ, and reporters are in direct conflict as to the merits of his position, the extent of his dereliction, and the propriety of the disciplinary action taken with respect to him by the University administration. With even a most charitable attitude, however, one is driven to the conclusion that it was Morton's love of argument, and his penchant for taking strong positions on controversial matters, which summarily ended his career as a Michigan student just a few weeks before graduation.

The specific event which brought about this drastic action may have been merely the ultimate in a series of clashes with the faculty; in letters to his family and friends he rather boasted of numerous pranks; and University records, though scant, suggest numerous absences from class and other failures to perform seriously the academic tasks assigned to him. In any event, the proverbial last straw was typical: Morton was asked to leave the University because of the part he took in an obviously lost cause in which one of his *fratres in facultate* played the major role. On May 4, 1854, the Board of Regents dismissed one of the members of the Medical Department faculty, Dr. J. Adams Allen. That evening, at a citizens' meeting called to protest Dr. Allen's dismissal, Morton took the platform on behalf of his friend and fellow Chi Psi. Though friends described his remarks as unexpectedly temperate, the young man was advised, the next day, by the secretary of the faculty, that he had been "removed from the privileges of the University." This summary action by the University officials, following so closely the dismissal of a prominent faculty member, precipitated letters to the editor and editorial attacks in various Michigan newspapers, a hasty reconsideration on the part of President Henry P. Tappan and the faculty, and reinstatement. Two weeks later, however, young Morton was re-expelled; this time the action was final, and the young man left the campus and returned to his home in Detroit. The elder Mortons had moved there, from Monroe, some months earlier.

Apparently, Morton never quite forgave the University for his failure to receive his degree with his class. Although he did accept the bachelor's degree in 1858, he declined the offer of an honorary degree in the nineties. His letter of declination must have been typically Mortonesque, for President Cleveland, to whom he submitted it, though appreciative of its stinging humor, significantly suggested that it was "just too bad that you cannot send it." Further evidence of Morton's attitude is found in his letters to his father, who had been keenly disappointed over his son's failure to graduate from the University. In later years the son seemed to take special delight in granting favors to not-too-successful Michigan graduates, and then reminding his father of the relative failure of these possessors of "Dr. Tappan's diplomas!"

His career as a university student at an end, Morton secured a position as a reporter for the *Detroit Free Press*, then edited by Wilbur F. Storey. Storey, an extremist like Edward Morton and J. Sterling Morton, was the type of editor who admittedly delighted in "printing the news and raising hell." It was, no doubt, an appealing situation for the youngster who had himself so recently been engaging in a little of the latter activity. He stayed with the *Free Press* but a few short months, though his friendship with Storey was to be lifelong, and he was to make numerous contributions to the columns of Storey's *Chicago Times* in later years.

While a student at the seminary in Albion, Morton had fallen in love "at first glimpse" with a fellow student, Caroline Joy French, of Detroit. When he was fifteen, and she but fourteen, the young couple had become engaged. Upon completion of her studies at Wesleyan Seminary, Caroline enrolled in the Misses Kelley's School at Utica, New York. She returned to Detroit upon graduation from this leading girl's school just as young Morton was beginning his brief reportorial assignment with the *Free Press.*

Of more than casual interest to many residents of Michigan in 1854 was the settlement of two new territories, made possible by the passage of the Kansas-Nebraska Bill. Among those to whom such territorial pastures seemed greener than those nearer home was J. Sterling Morton. Encouraged by Lewis Cass, then senator from Michigan, and by his employer, Storey, he decided to try his fortune in Nebraska. The elder Morton had become a prominent figure in the commercial life of Detroit; he was president of one of the banks and general agent of the New York Central Railroad. The future in Detroit could not have looked entirely black for the son of a successful business man. However, the father, who had himself left a future almost certain to be prosperous in New York, to risk failure in Michigan in 1834, could not object seriously to a similar venture on the part of his son twenty years later. On October 30, 1854, J. Sterling Morton and Caroline Joy French were married; on that same day they started on a most unusual honeymoon—a tedious, tortuous trip from Detroit to St. Louis, and from there to Bellevue, Nebraska.

The young couple was destined to enjoy a happy and successful life together in Nebraska. They raised a splendid family, four stalwart sons, one of whom became Secretary of the Navy in Theodore Roosevelt's cabinet, and two of whom founded and carried on the Morton Salt Company. They enjoyed the honors which accrued to Morton's prominence in political life and the comforts which are afforded to persons of affluence. Above all, they reaped that rich harvest of satisfaction which comes only to those who have "grown up with" a community and who have been wise enough to appreciate and to assume the responsibilities of the more fortunate in such surroundings. One may hazard the guess, however, that in their early Nebraska days there were periods of doubt, and many nostalgic heartaches, especially in those first few months at the edge of civilization. Morton himself gave some clue as to just what the young couple faced when, in an address given nearly forty years later, he said: "It was my fortune to look out from my log cabin on the bank of the Missouri River upon the prairies of Nebraska, as a settler there in 1854, when, beyond that domicile there was not a single permanent habitation of civilized men until you reached the valleys and mountains of Utah."

There were, though, some ties to Michigan, even to the University of Michigan! The wife of Fenner Ferguson, the first chief justice of the Territory, was an Albion girl, and she and her jurist husband lived on a claim adjoining that taken up by Sterling and Caroline Morton. At that time the secretary of the territory was Thomas B. Cuming, a member of the first class to graduate from the University of Michigan (1845). And there was Andrew J. Poppleton, A.M. (*hon.*) 1895, another ardent young Democrat from Detroit; it was "Pop" who had agreed to go to Nebraska and report back to Morton; his favorable report finally prompted his young friend to take the venturesome step. Moreover, the Mortons were young, ambitious, and devoted to each other. Even frontier life was not without its compensations to such a couple.

To an observer of present-day politics, conversant with the

normally slow climb up the ladder of political preferment, the careers of men like J. Sterling Morton are almost unbelievable. He had left Detroit on October 30, 1854; yet, on January 3, 1855, he was one of three delegates representing the town of Bellevue at a convention called to select an acceptable candidate to succeed the unpopular acting governor—Thomas Cuming! Two weeks later Morton, not yet twenty-three years old, was the almost unanimous choice of the voters of Bellevue as one of their three representatives in the first territorial legislature! True, success was to be remarkably evanescent: Cuming refused to recognize the three Bellevue representatives, and the citizens of Bellevue failed in their efforts to have their town selected as the territorial capital. Yet as far as vote-getting was concerned, Morton had demonstrated his ability in his first political venture. He soon had an opportunity to try his hand in the field of journalism, his other major interest.

Selection of Omaha as the territorial capital had an immediate reaction in Bellevue; the local newspaper, the Bellevue *Palladium*, closed its plant. It was apparent to young Morton that his future lay elsewhere. His father urged him to return to Michigan and suggested that he study law or go into business. "Shun the papers, and politics, as you would the 'Devil and Dr. Tappan.' " the elder Morton advised. But Sterling was not persuaded. Instead, he accepted an offer from the promoters of the town of Nebraska City, purchased some of the equipment of the defunct *Palladium*, became the first editor of the Nebraska City *News*, and in April of 1855 moved his bride of six months to the little village which was to be home to them throughout the rest of their lives.

Politics, journalism, farming, and, above all, his family were the absorbing interests of the man who was to play a dominant part in the development not only of Nebraska City but also of the territory and state of Nebraska from 1855 until his death in 1902. Because of the nature of the volume of which this sketch is a part, it must be left to others—to his capable biographer, Dr. James C. Olson, for example—to make detailed examination of these various interests. A proper appreciation of his contribution, insofar as it had sectional and national significance, requires special emphasis on his political career; the other interests are touched, in the main, only when they impinge upon this.

Politics to Morton meant partisan politics; specifically, he was a member of the Democratic party. Only once did he definitely bolt the party, and, for one of his strong convictions, the experience must have been a most trying one. It is in the field of partisan politics, and particularly during the Civil War period, that one finds apparent evidence of the tremendous influence exerted on the younger Morton by his Uncle Edward. His father, Julius D. Morton, could apparently take his politics or leave it. Not so Uncle Edward, nor Uncle Edward's nephew. One hesitates even to intimate that it was party first, and then country, but correspondence between the father and son during the early sixties shows no such hesitation on the part of the troubled parent. "You are like Ephraim of old, joined to your Idol, and that Idol is party which overrides all love of country and gives the party the whole party and nothing but the party," he wrote, in apparent exasperation, in August of 1863. Meantime, during that period, Edward Morton, back in Michigan, was blaming the war on "greed of office" on the part of Northern abolitionists, and was vehemently asserting that the Republican party in Michigan was as much "in rebellion" as the state of South Carolina.

Perhaps one does the younger Morton an injustice in emphasizing the possible influence of his rather belligerent uncle. It is not impossible that the uncle and nephew reached their similar conclusions, and displayed their similar attitudes, entirely as a matter of coincidence. After all, the father, too, appears to have been a person of strong convictions; in any event his letters to his son Sterling were at times most unrestrained. But the father had always been in business, where a certain measure of "give and take" was required to win and hold the good will of customers and suppliers. The uncle, like the grandfather, had preferred the editor's chair, and the editors of that early period were not disinclined to take extreme positions and to defend them vigorously, especially in matters touching partisan politics. Stinging sarcasm, and the not too sparing use of epithets—these, rather than calm, cool, calculating analysis, were the tools of the journalist of the fifties and sixties. And J. Sterling Morton, like Abner Morton and Edward Morton, was ever the journalist. Certainly, in part, young Morton's tendency to take a controversial position may be attributed to the influence of the journalistic Mortons of the preceding generations.

Reference has been made to the prominence Morton was to attain in the political life of the territory and state of Nebraska. Prominence in his case, however, rarely meant what is popularly regarded as success. He was destined to be of the opposition throughout the greater part of his political life; continually an "out," an "anti," "against." True, Buchanan was President from 1857 until 1861, and, as early as 1858, young Morton had become a sufficient factor in territorial politics to warrant attention from far-off Washington. In the main, however, his was the minority party; in the territory and in the state after admission, he would be fighting losing battles and championing lost causes. Most of his life was to be spent in political situations not unlike the Dr. Allen incident of campus days. He was to be a leader, always, but to him the political wars were to afford only an occasional foray into the political promised land.

In 1855, at the age of twenty-three, Morton was elected to the second territorial legislature. Once seated, he was made chairman of the committee on public grounds and buildings, a post he had sought in order to continue his fight against his now sworn enemy, Thomas Cuming, the Michigan graduate who had refused him a seat in the first legislature. The history of that session, described at length by Morton's understanding biographer, furnishes ample evidence of the fighting qualities of the Morton of twenty-three. He had been elected by the Nebraska City voters to undo the work of the previous session insofar as it related to the selection of a territorial capital. As

Cuming had been the power behind the rejection of Nebraska City and the selection of Omaha, Morton introduced resolution after resolution to embarrass and harass Cuming. He even suggested secession and introduced a memorial to Congress which, if approved, would have annexed the South Platte section to Kansas. His every effort failed, and Cuming and the Omaha group continued in power. At this same session Morton offended his credit-hungry constituents by voting against several banking bills which gave tremendous inflationary powers to inexperienced financial groups. Ever an exponent of sound money, support of which was to result in his bolting the party forty years later when William Jennings Bryan and the Populists were advocating cheap money, he could not vote for wildcat banks and their attendant evils. He was defeated for reelection and did not sit in the third territorial legislature.

In 1857, however, after the prompt failures of the banks organized under the banking bills denounced by him had brought on a panic, Morton regained his popularity, and his seat in the legislature, and from then until the inauguration of Abraham Lincoln, he took his proper place in Nebraska politics. He was one of the two leading candidates for speaker of the territorial house in 1857, at the age of twenty-five. Though unsuccessful, he attracted the attention of powerful Democratic politicians, and in 1858 he was appointed secretary of the territory, a position he held until replaced in 1861 by a Lincoln appointee.

The positions Morton assumed during the days of those early territorial legislatures serve to illustrate the nature of the man. They help to confirm his biographer's statement that, while a man of strong convictions, he often "backed into" those convictions. He loved a good fight; he never avoided an argument; he seemed to thrive, physically and mentally, on controversy. And he was willing to change his mind. Consistency, at least the constant maintenance of a position once assumed, was to him no virtue. For example, in 1856 he had been elected by constituents who were definitely of the opinion that Omaha was not the place for the territorial capital. In 1858, when they returned him to the legislature, they were still of that opinion. Nor had there been indication, during the campaign, of a change of attitude on Morton's part. Yet, with full recognition of the unpopularity of his new position, Morton worked against the South Platte group, and with the Omaha group, because, as he explained afterward, it was a losing battle at best (this alone would hardly have deterred a Morton!) and there were "more important matters," more "useful and important legislation," which required attention. When a majority of the legislature withdrew and organized a rump legislature in another city, Morton stayed in Omaha with the minority (Cuming's crowd!), and he even wrote the committee report which took to task the majority group, including his fellow townsmen, for "seceding."

It was shortly after this legislative session that Morton received from President Buchanan appointment as secretary of the territory. His long fight with Cuming, his fellow student at the University of Michigan, was at an end. One may suspect that the victory was just a little hollow because Cuming had died before his ultimate defeat. From the date of his confirmation by the United States Senate in 1858 until May, 1861, he was secretary, and, for a brief period, acting governor of the territory, and a powerful factor in territorial affairs. The young man who had left the campus of the University but four years before was, at the age of twenty-six, in a position to remind his father, not too apologetically one suspects, that he had "appointed—a graduate of the University of Michigan" (this part underlined!)—"a notary public." "Things change," he continued, "when men are thrown out into the world to scramble for themselves, and he whom Doct. Tappan & other learned snobs diplomaed & titled asks & gets place & emoluments from one whom that same Dutch Dr. Tappan & other learned snobs considered unworthy of their benign patronage & fit only to be crushed out of decent society as soon as possible." Though claiming that he "cherished no vengeance except to help those who hated and abused me then but whom I have so far distanced that I can afford to be generous now," it seems clear that dismissal from the University still rankled. As forty years had gone by at the time he sarcastically declined an honorary degree in the nineties, we make no mistake in assuming that expulsion from the University left a deep and abiding scar.

From 1861 until 1885 there were to be no Democratic presidents; and Nebraska was to remain Republican. A Democrat, even the most influential, was to find the situation exceedingly difficult. This was especially true of the war years.

In August, 1860, J. Sterling Morton conducted a successful campaign for nomination as delegate to Congress from Nebraska Territory. The elder Morton expressed deep regret upon learning of his son's candidacy. "It being a presidential election, Buchanan the most unpopular of all the Presidents, & you his appointment—it is a hard road to travel," he wrote in October of that year. It was. There was the customary series of debates, and that part of the campaign must have been a joy to the lad who, on the campus, "shone in debate rather than recitation." There were letters to the editor to define the issues and the candidates' positions; this, too, could not have been displeasing to one with the journalistic flair and training possessed by Morton. But, though the local count showed his election, Morton lost in the ensuing contest; the Republican Congress recognized Morton's opponent and denied Morton's request for certification, on May 7, 1862.

On May 8, 1862, the now famous "Democratic Address" was issued. Though regrettable, it is not surprising that young Morton played some part in the preparation of that address. It had been the author of the address, the notorious Vallandigham, who had urged Morton to move back east, to Ohio, so that he could assist with greater effect in the opposition to the Republican conduct of the war. It had been Vallandigham and others of his group who had fought the losing battle for Morton in Congress. Morton was ever loyal to those who supported him. He was, withal, a sincere believer in the two-party system, in war as well as in peace. Fusion, even during a Civil War, was unthinkable. He would remain anti-Lincoln, antiwar, anti-abolition, and above all, anti-Republican throughout the war years.

He hired a substitute to enlist in the Union Army in his place, and he himself was a captain in the Nebraska City Cavalry Company, formed in anticipation of possible Indian raids during the absence of the "regulars." But his support of Vallandigham, and his partial advocacy of Vallandigham's proposed "Northwest Secession" quite naturally made him suspect; like other Northern Democrats who remained definitely partisan, he was referred to as a "Copperhead," "disloyal," and a "traitor." His own father, as early as April of 1861, expressed a hint of doubt as to Sterling's loyalty: "I hope," he wrote "you will be a loyal citizen." Since he was not the type of man to be definitely disloyal, one may assume his loyalty; there is certainly no evidence to the contrary. There is plenty of evidence, however, that he continued to be extreme of statement, ever reminding his readers of the past and present errors of the Republicans. He kept the opposition party alive in his area and assisted in doing so on a national scale. He was continually looking for issues around which dissidents could rally. He ridiculed Lincoln and the Emancipation Proclamation in a particularly bitter contribution to his friend Storey's Chicago *Times*. In that article, with a customary tendency not to overlook any error on the part of the opposition, however remote, he sarcastically castigated George Washington, referring to him as a "poor old fogy" and "an ass." Washington's handling of the Whisky Insurrection during the last decade of the preceding century was, it seems, the vicious precedent for Lincoln's current error! Edward Morton must have enjoyed that particular blast from the pen of the nephew.

The great public issues of the quarter of a century following the Civil War naturally commanded much of Morton's attention—particularly the railroad problem and the economic and scientific needs of the great farm areas of the Middle West. Morton was throughout his life a firm believer in the railroads. An ardent member of a party which directed its appeal to "the common man," here was a leader in that party who could without any qualms of conscience be an agent (a lobbyist, his enemies said) for the never too popular railroads. His interest could be justified, it is true, on the ground that they were necessary to the development of Nebraska and that section of the country. In pointing with pride, in after years, to the enormous advance in land values in Nebraska, he could find the foundation for that advance largely in "the effort put forth by capital to build railroads which serve to relate those lands and the products thereon intimately and profitably with the great cities and populational centers of the East." But, over and above the local justification for the railroads themselves, he left no doubts as to his personal convictions on questions economic. Here was no Populist or hater of "Capital"; nor did he frown upon wealth or the accumulation thereof. He would have, he told his listeners during one address, "a copy of Adam Smith's *Wealth of Nations* in every farmhouse." (He would, as might be expected, also have "the daily newspaper from a great city at every farm fireside.") "It is the business of government," he argued, "to give each citizen an equal chance, within the limits of the public good, for life, liberty, the accumulation of property, and the pursuit of happiness."

While using his talents as a journalist and a public speaker, to "sell" the railroads to his fellow Nebraskans, he recognized, far earlier than many others, the need for the development of better crops, better grades of farm animals, and—probably above all—for trees. Therefore, there were many Morton addresses during this era, and many communications in newspapers throughout the Middle West, devoted to such mundane matters as the advisability of converting Iowa corn into pork, the introduction of a new variety of swine, and the necessity for the planting of trees. At the same time there were letters to the editors, such as one to his friend Storey for publication in the Chicago *Times*, anent the "element of damphoolism" strong enough to influence the passage of a statute giving the state legislature the power to set maximum freight and passenger rates.

There were, too, bitter attacks upon the National Grange; for Morton always deplored the "professional farmer," the demagogue who would "farm the farmer," as he quaintly phrased it. At the same time there was a strong devotion to the work of the Nebraska State Board of Agriculture, to which he gave of his time, effort, and money, and to the International Society of Arboriculture, of which he was the first president. There were "side trips" into the affairs of such national organizations and movements as the "Free Trade Convention," the "Sound Money League," and, at a still later period, the "Anti-Imperialist League." It will be his "Arbor Day" and his excellent work as secretary of agriculture, however, which will be remembered long after these other interests are forgotten.

It may not be surprising that the man who had called his Nebraska farm home "Arbor Lodge" should be the founder of "Arbor Day." The surprising feature, perhaps, was the speed with which the movement progressed, and its tenacity. Having "invented" Arbor Day in 1872 Morton may have been guilty of exaggeration when he claimed in 1874, "my invention now has become a public holiday"; by 1882, however, it had become a matter of annual observance in the schools of Cincinnati, Ohio, and by 1892 it had become a holiday in every state in the Union but one. Indeed, it has international significance. Nationally, it was the forerunner of many related conservation movements, and its success has given heart to many who have watched with dismay the waste of national resources.

The most surprising feature of his appointment to President Cleveland's Cabinet was the fact that it was made. Few presidents could have been so forgiving as even to consider it. J. Sterling Morton had been a bitter opponent of Cleveland at the Democratic Convention in 1884. In 1887 he took occasion to remind a friend of that opposition; he frankly gloried in it. "Every month," he wrote, "I grow prouder and prouder of my position regarding candidates—in 1884. —We were New Yorked to death. —The President has a big belly. His brains are not proportioned to it." Publicly, too, he advertised his extreme dislike of Grover Cleveland. "I see no reason to be discouraged," he told a New York reporter after Cleveland's defeat in the 1888 election, "We are fortunate in getting rid of Cleveland. —I regarded him as one of the most unfit men for President who ever occupied the position."

Yet this "unfit" President was big enough and his detractor prominent enough in the "Democracy of the West" to make possible Morton's elevation, in 1893, to the Cabinet. However difficult Morton may have found it to overlook personal considerations, Grover Cleveland did not let them enter into account. Here was a sound money Democrat, with a proper attitude toward that political football, the tariff problem, a proponent of economy in government, and a practical farmer. Why look farther? Having found the man, why deny him the appointment because he had worked, written, and spoken for the opposition? As far as Morton was concerned, for twenty-five years—ever since Nebraska had become a state—he had failed in every attempt to be elected to office. Now in what was to be the last decade of a long and active political life, he received an appointment which gave him national recognition, at the hands of one who, though a fellow Democrat, was nevertheless a political "enemy."

Morton administered the Department of Agriculture efficiently and economically. Useless positions were abolished, expenses cut, extravagant practices stopped, agricultural experiment stations, even some of those in Nebraska, were closed, and an attempt was made to discontinue the distribution of seeds at government expense. Unsuccessful in his attempt to stop the congressional appropriation, Secretary Morton essayed to do by indirection what he could not do directly—he refused to spend the moneys appropriated. Congressional wrath followed this inaction; one prominent statesman said: "The devil, to use a Western phrase, has owed the party a grudge, and has paid us in a Secretary of Agriculture." But Morton stood by his guns; he has the unique record of having returned to the Treasury nearly 20 per cent of the funds appropriated for his department during his four years as secretary of agriculture.

When his term had ended, the "stormy petrel" of Cleveland's second Cabinet could point to a most unusual record: a nearly 20 per cent saving in the cost of operating his department; a 10 per cent reduction in the department staff; the application of civil service to nearly every important position in the department, an accomplishment which caused Theodore Roosevelt to praise him for his "manful work for civil service reform"; an improved and expanded Weather Bureau; a new section of foreign markets; and the introduction of several lines of scientific investigation, including the study of soils and the improvement of roads.

Nearly every man in public life has his bitter enemies and his loyal friends. Readers of a later generation may be led to erroneous conclusions by the mere choice of sources. That the reader of this sketch may be in a position to make his own determination as to just what manner of man J. Sterling Morton was, statements from sources not unfamiliar with the man himself, his principles, and his prejudices, are offered:

> Morton believed in contention for contention's stormy sake. Peace was the only failure, war ever a success in Morton's eyes. . . . Bent for conflict, he must be the opposite of an environment. Being among free-soil folk, he had been for slavery; coming from a silver region—he was a fierce champion of gold; finding protectionists all about him, he was for free trade; hemmed in at home by a solid wall of Republicans, he was a Democrat. . . .

Thus wrote Alfred Henry Lewis in the *Saturday Evening Post* in 1903, less than a year after Morton's death.

In 1895, when many newspapers were outspoken in their advocacy of his nomination as the Democratic candidate for the presidency, an article in the *Atlantic Monthly* contained these significant observations:

> He has acquired the habit of mind of one always in the opposition, which for a man of courage readily takes the form of recklessness of speech. The astute politician who wishes to shape Mr. Morton to his own ends will encounter a difficulty in the honesty and the shrewdness of the man. Mr. Morton himself is not an astute politician and he

never will manage conventions or intrigue for power. Nevertheless, he has in him the sort of stuff out of which *better Presidents than presidential candidates are made.*

In 1902, at the time of his death, the *Chicago Tribune,* never a supporter of Morton and seldom a believer in the principles for which he stood, said:

He was a man of steadfast convictions, unswerving honesty, and undoubted ability. He has frequently been alluded to as the most prominent citizen of Nebraska, but his prominence extended all over the United States.

Perhaps the following words were designed to furnish Morton's own analysis of his character and creed. They were inscribed by him on the flyleaf of a copy of Robert W. Furnas' *Arbor Day,* by way of advice to the youthful owner:

Oaks thrive in the tempests that would rend them, and draw nutriment from the howling storms. Men of right fibre are like oaks, and develop best in antagonisms; and by constant attrition with adverse criticisms, and harsh opposition, establish, at last, good name and high character.

Alfred Noble

1844	*Born in Livonia, Wayne County, Michigan*
1862	*Enlisted in Company C, Twenty-fourth Michigan Infantry*
1870	*Graduated from the University of Michigan*
1871	*Married Georgia Speechly*
1873	*Appointed United States Assistant Engineer, Sault Ste Marie*
1894	*Opened an office as a consulting engineer in Chicago*
1895	*Member of the Nicaragua Canal Board*
1897	*Member of the United States Deep Waterways Commission*
1899–1903	*Member of the Isthmian Canal Commission*
1905	*Consulting engineer of the Panama Canal*
1910	*Awarded John Fritz Medal for notable achievement as a civil engineer*
1912	*Awarded Elliott Cresson Medal of the Franklin Institute*
1914	*Died in New York, New York*

Alfred Noble

Alfred Noble

By Henry E. Riggs

ALTHOUGH the Department of Engineering was not formally established by the Regents as an independent department until 1895, instruction in civil engineering was included in the scientific course of the Department of Literature, Science, and the Arts as early as 1852. From 1857 to 1872, Professor DeVolson Wood, M.S. 1859, taught the engineering subjects, for the greater part of the time alone or with only one assistant. The first degrees in civil engineering were conferred upon two members of the class of 1860.

During these early years the number of engineering degrees granted was small, ranging from one or two in the Civil War years to sixteen in 1871 and 1872; during the period of twelve years 105 engineering students graduated. A surprisingly large percentage of these men achieved national prominence. Fifteen of them received honorary degrees from universities for outstanding professional work; the records of eleven of them appear in *Who's Who in America.*

Among these outstanding leaders of the profession it seems proper to mention Stillman W. Robinson, C.E. 1863, Sc.D. 1896 (Ohio State), inventor, teacher, and dean of engineering at Ohio State University; George Y. Wisner, C.E. 1865, internationally known hydraulic engineer; George H. Banzenberg, C.E. 1867, Eng.D. 1912, Sc.D. 1911 (University of Wisconsin), designer and builder of many great waterworks plants; William B. Rising, M.E. 1867, Ph.D. 1871 (Heidelberg), for more than forty years professor at the University of California; Ebenezer S. Wheeler, C.E. 1867, M.S. (*hon.*) 1897, builder of the Soo Locks and chief engineer of the Nicaragua Canal; Joseph Baker Davis, C.E. 1868, A.M.

(*hon.*) 1912, greatly loved professor of engineering at Michigan; Albert A. Robinson, B.S. (C.E.) 1869, LL.D. 1900, builder of the Sante Fe Railroad system; Charles F. Brush, M.E. 1869, M.S. (*hon.*) 1899, Sc.D. (*hon.*) 1912, Ph.D. 1880 (Western Reserve), LL.D. 1900 (Western Reserve), LL.D. 1903 (Kenyon College), world-famous pioneer in electrical development; Benezette Williams, C.E. and M.E. 1869, M.Eng. (*hon.*) 1914, engineer of the Chicago Sanitary District; Henry C. Ripley, C.E. 1870, Eng.D. 1913, builder of the Galveston sea wall; Henry G. Prout, C.E. 1871 (*nunc pro tunc* 1879), LL.D. 1911, A.M. 1902 (Yale University), pioneer developer of railway signal and interlocking plants; Horace G. Burt, C.E. 1872 (*nunc pro tunc* 1900), builder of the Salt Lake cut-off, president, Union Pacific Railroad; Cornelius Donovan, C.E. 1872, Eng.D. 1912, whose entire professional life was devoted to the building of the jetties at the mouths of the Mississippi; Otto J. Klotz, C.E. 1872, Sc.D. (*hon.*) 1913, LL.D. 1904 (Toronto University), LL.D. 1916 (University of Pittsburgh), His Majesty's Royal Astronomer in Canada; Robert S. Woodward, C.E. 1872, Ph.D. (*hon.*) 1892, LL.D. 1912, LL.D. 1904 (University of Wisconsin), Sc.D. (*hon.*) 1905 (Columbia University), Sc.D. (*hon.*) 1905 (University of Pennsylvania), LL.D. 1915 (Johns Hopkins University), president of the Carnegie Institution; and Alfred Noble, C.E. 1870, LL.D. 1895, LL.D. 1904 (University of Wisconsin), who became one of the most outstanding and best loved men in the engineering profession in the English-speaking world.

The University can set no higher inspiration before its students than the life and work of Alfred Noble. No man in the engineering profession has ever left a finer record of patriotism, of high professional ideals, of incorruptible honesty, of outstanding achievement in widely different engineering fields, or of splendid service to the nation.

He was a man whom success could not spoil. Throughout his career, from student to world leader in his profession, he was a quiet, modest, and lovable gentleman as well as a hard-working, straight-thinking, square-dealing executive. The attempt is here made to tell the story of one of Michigan's greatest sons in such a way as to emphasize his fine personal traits and the wide range and great importance of his work.

Alfred Noble was born on August 7, 1844, at Livonia, Wayne County, Michigan. He was the son of Charles and Lovina Douw Noble; his ancestors saw military service in the American Revolution; his grandfather, Norton Noble, was a soldier in the War of 1812. Until he was eighteen his life was spent on his father's farm. He helped his father and brothers in the work of clearing, draining, and cultivating land in the newly developed Michigan country. When very young he began attending a near-by district school, and as soon as he was able to ride a horse he attended the Union School at Plymouth, where the remainder of his early education was obtained. A boyhood friend, neighbor, and schoolmate, Judge Edgar O. Durfee, wrote of him in 1914: "From his earliest school days he always excelled in all his studies. He was very studious, and as a boy was always truthful and always lived up not only to the letter but to the spirit of his promises."

On August 9, 1862, two days after his eighteenth birthday, he enlisted in Company C, 24th Michigan Volunteer Infantry, a regiment raised principally in Wayne County. The regiment was first in action in December at Fredericksburg, and from that time until February, 1865, Alfred Noble took part in all the principal engagements of the Army of the Potomac. At Gettysburg his brigade bore the brunt of the first day's fighting, and his regiment lost 80 per cent of its men. Noble went through the war without receiving a wound. He was very loath to speak of his war experiences. On one of the rare occasions when he was induced to talk of the subject, he described the qualities of a good soldier as "ability to withstand hunger, fatigue and hard marching, . . . but to be a good runner was often a useful attribute."

From July, 1865, to September, 1867, he was a clerk in the

adjutant general's office in the War Department in Washington. During this time he prepared for college, and in the fall of 1867 he entered the University of Michigan. He graduated with the class of 1870, although for several months he was absent from college, working as a recorder on the United States Lake Survey. The late Justice William R. Day, B.S. 1870, LL.D. 1898, of the United States Supreme Court, was a classmate and fraternity associate of Noble; both were members of Alpha Delta Phi. Under date of November 3, 1914, Justice Day wrote of him as follows:

> I well remember when Alfred Noble came to the University of Michigan, where he entered the sophomore class in the fall of 1867. He was somewhat older than the rest of us, and, in my opinion, far more able than any of us. He had had three years' experience in the army, and those who knew him there said that he had been a faithful and valiant soldier. I do not think that any of his classmates ever heard him speak of his army career. . . . I think his army experience had matured him at an earlier age than men usually reach a proper view of the responsibilities of life. . . . He was modest, kindly, industrious and capable as a boy and man. I need hardly say to you that he had particular aptitude for the science of engineering and unusual skill in the higher mathematics. While he was easily, in my opinion, the first man in our class, I do not think that any of his fellow students had the slightest feeling of envy or jealousy toward him. By common consent he was our intellectual leader.

The extent of Noble's modesty is illustrated by an incident related as occurring at the Michigan National Dinner of 1911, at which Justice Day was a guest of honor, Noble having rallied a reunion of their class of 1870. When Noble called on the next day to say good-by to his classmate, Justice Day remarked casually, "Alfred, I came through your Pennsylvania Railroad Tunnel yesterday." Noble merely nodded. Justice Day smilingly ventured again, "Alfred, you must have had some pretty difficult engineering problems in that tunnel." After a pause Noble's answer came slowly and quietly, "No, we went down on this side and came out beyond the hills on the other side." Naturally, the eyes of his classmate fairly danced. Doubtless, another story had been captured for the next conference with his associate justices at Washington.

Immediately upon graduation in June, 1870, Noble entered government service on harbor surveys on Lakes Huron and Michigan. In October he was transferred to Sault Ste Marie. His marriage to Georgia Speechly, of Ann Arbor, took place on May 30, 1871. A son born of this marriage, Frederick C. Noble, B.S. (C.E.) 1894, C.E. 1904, followed his father in attaining prominence in the engineering profession and now is a consulting engineer in New York City.

In 1873 Noble was appointed United States assistant engineer in charge of building a new lock and of straightening and dredging the channel of the St. Mary's River. This work was completed in 1882. A letter dated June 5, 1914, from the late Joseph Ripley, class of 1876, consulting engineer, New York State Canals, who served under Noble at the Soo, tells of his work there:

> While at the Soo Mr. Noble designed and built the Weitzel lock, St. Mary's Falls Canal. It was a bold undertaking, for in lift and size it was a wide departure from any existing locks. Previous lifts in locks had been limited to about 10 feet, the Soo lock provided for 20 feet at extreme lift. It was 515 feet long between hollow quoins, 80 ft. wide in the chamber narrowing to 60 feet at the gates and with a depth of 17 feet of water on the mitresills. The masonry was the finest of its kind ever built in this country. The filling and emptying culverts were located under the floor of the lock, the gate hangings and the hydraulic operating machinery were all new features.

With the completion of the work at the Soo, Noble resigned and accepted a position as resident engineer on the Shreveport, Louisiana, Red River bridge under L. F. G. Bouscaren. Ripley states that whereas Noble's salary as United States Assistant Engineer had been $3,000 a year, in his new position it was only $2,100 a year. After twelve years of work on harbor and lock surveys, design, and construction, having had responsible charge of work costing more than $3,000,000, and having obtained a fine foundation of experience in that branch of hydraulic engineering, he ventured into the radically different field of the construction of bridges.

During the ten-year period from August, 1882, to May, 1892, Noble served as resident engineer on construction of great bridges, thus acquiring expert knowledge in this field. In these years he had charge of the Red River bridge at Shreveport, Louisiana; the Snake River bridge at Ainsworth, Washington, under General Adna Anderson; the replacement of a timber bridge over Clarks Fork of the Columbia near Belknap, Montana; the foundations of a high trestle near Missoula, Montana, and the foundations of the bridge over St. Louis Bay, Duluth, Minnesota. From May, 1885, to October, 1886, much of his time was spent in shop inspection of ironwork for the St. Louis Bay drawspan, in supervising its erection, in inspecting bridge manufacture in the shops, and on temporary duty as acting principal assistant engineer of the Northern Pacific Railway.

In 1886–87, under the late William R. Hutton, Noble was resident engineer on the Washington Bridge over the Harlem River at 181st Street, New York City. From July, 1887, to October 1889, he was resident engineer of the Illinois Central Railroad bridge over the Ohio at Cairo, Illinois, serving under the late George S. Morison and Elmer L. Corthell. In November, 1889, under Morison, he became resident engineer of the railroad bridge over the Mississippi at Memphis, Tennessee. On its completion in May, 1892, he formed a partnership with Morison which lasted for two years. During this partnership he was assistant chief engineer of bridges over the Mississippi at Alton, Illinois, and over the Missouri at Bellefontaine and at Leavenworth. In April, 1894, the partnership was dissolved, and Noble opened an office as consulting engineer at Chicago.

With this background of twenty-four years of intimate experience in the construction field—experience bringing knowledge of all types of foundations and of the processes of manufacture of steel—Noble was undoubtedly far better qualified than most engineers for the solving of great problems of design and construction. During the first two years of his private practice he was connected with several projects, such as the regulating works of the Chicago main drainage channel, the power canal at the Soo, and bridges and building foundations in New York City.

In April, 1895, came the first of a series of important calls for service to the United States government. In that month he was appointed by President Cleveland a member of the Nicaragua Canal Board. An account of Noble's career which appeared in *Engineering News* (April 23, 1914) tells of the occasion for the appointment:

> In 1895, Congress was on the point of passing a bill providing for a government guarantee of the bonds of the Nicaragua Canal Co. . . . The assurances held out were that the entire cost of building a ship canal across Nicaragua connecting the two oceans would be only $65,000,000. . . . In its stead an act was passed creating the Nicaragua Canal Commission. . . . This commission with a very small appropriation and a very limited time in which to work, was required to report as to the feasibility of the Nicaragua canal enterprise. President Cleveland appointed as the members of that commission, Colonel William Ludlaw from the Army, Mordecai T. Endicott from the Navy, and Alfred Noble from civil life.
>
> The situation was one which demanded engineers of ability with sufficient independence to form their own opinions and not be swerved from a straight course by the strong influences brought to bear by the corporation whose plans were under investigation. The report made by this commission showed that the advantages of the Nicaragua canal route had been greatly over estimated and that the cost of building a canal there would be far greater than the estimates made by the canal company.
>
> . . . The sound advice of these engineers saved the nation from lending its credit to a private corporation which, if it had undertaken the Nicaragua work, would have inevitably met failure.

His second great opportunity to place his technical knowledge at the service of the Federal government came four years later, under President McKinley, when Congress created the Isthmian Canal Commission, which was to find the best possible route for a ship canal across the Central American isthmus.

Noble was appointed one of the members of this commission; his former partner, George S. Morison, was another of the members. These two men were immediately recognized as the leading engineers of the commission and no doubt played major roles in determining its conclusions. After two years of surveys and investigation the commission recommended that the United States should adopt the Panama route. This decision has been generally commended since, and its wisdom has been borne out by experience.

The distinguished services rendered by Noble as a member of the Nicaragua Canal Commission in 1895 and of the Isthmian Canal Commission from 1899 to 1903 paved the way for a still more important service during the administration of President Theodore Roosevelt. This service was effectively recounted in the 1914 article about Noble in *Engineering News:*

> It was seven years later when Mr. Noble had the opportunity to render what was, without doubt, the greatest public service of his life. The government had started construction work on the Panama route, and the question came up for a decision as to whether a sea level canal or a lock canal should be undertaken. To advise upon this momentous question, President Roosevelt created an International Commission of Engineers, made up of five eminent members of the engineering profession representing foreign countries and eight prominent American engineers.
>
> . . . all the foreign engineers and three of the American engineers united in a majority report advising the construction of a sea level canal. Five American engineers, with Mr. Noble at the head, stood out in favor of a lock canal. We say "Mr. Noble at the head" because from his strong experience with the lock at Sault Ste Marie, he was better able than any engineer upon the commission to speak authoritatively with respect to the construction and operation of great ship canal locks.
>
> To Alfred Noble's discerning wisdom and independent judgment and to his willingness to stand in a minority in defense of what he believed to be right, the country owes it today that it did not undertake what we now know to be the folly of a sea level canal in Panama.
>
> In the struggle which followed the submission of these two conflicting reports, Mr. Noble's ability and strong forceful personality had

much to do with the final decision by which those in authority rejected the majority report and adopted that of the minority.

In summarizing Noble's services to the Federal government, *Engineering News* declared:

We believe it is within bounds to say that there are few men to whom the people of the United States owe a greater debt of gratitude for important services rendered at a time of crisis than to Alfred Noble.

. . . [In particular] it will be universally agreed that his name deserves high prominence in connection with our greatest national engineering work, the Panama Canal. It detracts nothing from the honor due to those who have borne the burden and heat of the days and years during the long period of construction at Panama to give honor to the great engineer whose sound judgment and incorruptible integrity enabled the nation to steer a straight course in undertaking this hugest of engineering feats and avoid the disgrace attendant upon disastrous failure.

It is impossible in this article to do more than list a few of the other great projects which were handled by Alfred Noble during his years of consulting practice. In July, 1897, he was appointed by President McKinley a member of the United States Deep Waterways Commission which was to make surveys and estimates of cost for a ship canal from the Great Lakes to deep water in the Hudson River. In the spring of 1898 he was appointed by his former classmate, William R. Day, then assistant secretary of state, as arbitrator in a dispute between a citizen of this country and the government of San Domingo, an appointment which necessitated a visit to that country.

In the fall of 1900 he was made a member of an engineers' board to advise the state engineer of New York concerning the plans and estimates for a barge canal across that state. He was a member of the board of engineers that planned the Galveston sea wall and the raising of the city grade. With the late Ralph Modjeski he designed and built the massive bridge over the Mississippi at Thebes, Illinois. He passed upon vital problems of design and construction on the Panama Canal, such as the Gatun Dam and lock foundations. He spent months at Honolulu in a study and report on the Pearl Harbor dry dock. He reported to the Canadian government on the plans for the new Welland Canal and advised on the foundations for the new Quebec bridge after the fall of the old structure. He was consulting engineer for New York City on the many miles of tunnels for the Catskill aqueduct and on the deep tunnels under the boroughs of Manhattan and Brooklyn and under the East River, and also on the four subway tunnels under the East River. He made many extensive reports on power projects on Lake Superior, at Niagara, on the Susquehanna River, and in California.

Noble's most striking undertaking is the Pennsylvania Railroad terminal in New York City. In 1902 he was appointed a member of the board of engineers to direct the operations of the company in tunneling under the North and East rivers and under the borough of Manhattan and in establishing the great railway station. Noble, besides serving on the board, was chief engineer of the East River division.

The construction designed and built by Noble cost many hundreds of millions of dollars. All of it received close personal attention from him—a record of professional practice that has been rarely, if ever, equaled.

Many honors were conferred upon Alfred Noble, notably by his fellow engineers. His honorary degrees have already been listed. Most of his other honors came from the engineering profession. He served as president of the Western Society of Engineers in 1898, of the American Society of Civil Engineers in 1903, and of the American Institute of Consulting Engineers in 1913. He had served on the boards of these societies and of the American Society of Mechanical Engineers and was active in technical society committee work; he was author of eleven papers read before the American Society of Civil Engineers, and of a number of other published articles.

In 1910 Noble was awarded the John Fritz Medal for "notable achievements as a civil engineer." This medal is the outstanding engineering award, given annually by the national societies of civil, mechanical, electrical, and mining engineers. In 1912 he was awarded the Elliott Cresson Medal of the Franklin Institute for "distinguished achievements in the field of engineering." In 1911 he was elected an honorary member of the Institution of Civil Engineers of Great Britain, the oldest of all engineering societies, a distinction enjoyed by no other American engineer. He was a member of many technical and scientific societies and of several clubs in New York and Chicago.

Alfred Noble's death occurred on April 19, 1914, less than four months before the Panama Canal, in the construction of which he had played so significant a part, was opened to traffic. His life had been an eventful and influential one—particularly since the occasion, nineteen years before, when President Cleveland had first set him upon what proved to be a highly important career of public service.

Engineering News, the most prominent of professional journals of his time, closed its evaluation of his career with the following tribute (April 23, 1914):

> It can be said of Mr. Noble, without fear of contradiction, that he won his way to the foremost position which he occupied as the leading American civil engineer of his time by sheer force of ability. Mr. Noble was always a quiet and modest man, absorbed in his professional work. He never tried to advertise himself nor attempted to put his professional work in any way on a commercial basis. The great responsibilities which were laid upon him came to him because he was a man who inspired confidence both in his integrity and ability.

Thomas Witherell Palmer

1830 *Born in Detroit, Michigan*
1845 *Entered the University of Michigan*
1848 *Traveled in Spain and South America*
1850 *Moved to Appleton, Wisconsin*
1853 *Returned to Detroit*
1855 *Married Lizzie Pitts Merrill*
1876 *Received A.B. degree* (nunc pro tunc 1849) *from the University of Michigan*
1878 *Elected to the Michigan Senate*
Elected chairman of the legislative caucus which nominated Zachariah Chandler to the United States Senate
1883 *Chosen United States Senator from Michigan*
1889 *Appointed Minister to Spain*
1890 *Appointed Commissioner at Large and President of World's Columbian Commission at Chicago*
1893 *Presented Palmer Park to Detroit*
1899 *Elected president of University of Michigan Club of Detroit*
1913 *Died in Detroit, Michigan*

Thomas W. Palmer

Thomas Witherell Palmer

By Henry E. Bodman

THE CAREER of Thomas Witherell Palmer was marked principally by his service as United States senator, minister to Spain, and president of the World's Columbian Commission. In his private life and in his participation in the affairs of the city and state in which he lived, he was equally distinguished as a man of culture, of exceptional character, and of great philanthropic interest. His public services, reflecting credit upon his name and upon the University of Michigan, entitle him to be memorialized in this volume.

Senator Palmer came from pioneer stock. His father, Thomas Palmer, moving west in 1807 from Connecticut, settled temporarily at Malden (Amherstburg), Canada, near the mouth of the Detroit River. With the outbreak of the War of 1812, Palmer and the other American citizens resident in Malden were imprisoned. Some of these took the oath of allegiance to Britain and were released. Thomas Palmer and his brother refused to do this and were held in confinement. Later they were freed and went to Detroit. On Hull's surrender of Detroit, Palmer was returned to Malden on parole, but later took up residence at Detroit, engaging in business as a merchant. He also carried on extensive lumbering operations in Michigan, especially at what is now St. Clair (then called Palmer), Michigan.

In 1821, Thomas Palmer was married to Mary Witherell. She was born in 1795, in Fairhaven, Vermont, where her father, James Witherell, occupied successively the offices of circuit judge and member of the state legislature and of Congress. He had also served in the Continental Army throughout the Revolutionary War. In 1808 he was appointed by President

Thomas Jefferson to be judge of the Territorial Supreme Court (Michigan) and served as one of the "Board of Governors and Judges" until 1828, when he was appointed secretary of the territory. He was an able and distinguished citizen. As testimony of his service to the territory and to the city of Detroit, Witherell Street was named for him. The street so named was the most important thoroughfare of the city, being that part of the present Woodward Avenue extending north from Grand Circus Park, the hub of the city. Later, because confusion arose from the use of two names for the same street (Woodward Avenue from the Detroit River to Grand Circus Park and Witherell Street beyond the Park), the name Witherell was given to the street which now skirts Grand Circus Park on the east.

On their wedding trip, Thomas and Mary Witherell Palmer traveled in the East. On their return they took passage from Buffalo to Detroit on the first steamer ever to navigate the Great Lakes, a vessel familiar in the early prints of Detroit, the "Walk-in-the-Water." This vessel was regularly towed through the upper part of the Niagara River into Lake Erie by sixteen oxen pulling a 600-foot towline, the vessel having insufficient motive power to make headway against the current of the Niagara River.

The "Walk-in-the-Water" had completed her maiden voyage in 1818, less than ten years after Robert Fulton had first demonstrated the practicability of navigation by steam. The first voyages of the "Walk-in-the-Water" created tremendous excitement among the inhabitants of the frontier settlements on Lake Erie. Wherever the vessel landed, crowds of spectators were on hand, bands played, public ceremonies were arranged —all of which is easily understood when it is realized that for the first time these people were seeing a vessel propelled by its own power. They were not witnessing an experiment but the actual transporting of one hundred to two hundred passengers and tons of merchandise. The name of the vessel was supposedly derived from the expression of the Indians who, first seeing a steamboat plying the Hudson River, had described it as a boat or canoe that could walk in the water. The "Walk-in-the-Water" made regular trips between Buffalo and Detroit, and on one occasion carried passengers and freight as far as Mackinac Island and across Lake Michigan to Green Bay, Wisconsin. A voyage on the "Walk-in-the-Water" remained a real adventure for Detroiters, since the novelty of steam navigation did not wear off for several years following her initial voyage.

Thomas Palmer and his bride, however, on taking passage on this vessel, set forth on a particularly fateful trip. No sooner had the vessel entered Lake Erie than she encountered a November storm of great intensity. The vessel began to leak, and being insufficiently powered to make headway against the wind and seas, turned back, but, as it was night, was unable to enter the Niagara River. An attempt was made to anchor near the shore in the vicinity of Buffalo. To avoid foundering it finally became necessary, however, to cut the cables and allow the vessel to be driven ashore. The passengers were all taken off in a thrilling rescue; the vessel, however, was wrecked beyond repair, and, for the time being at least, the Great Lakes were again without a steamboat. Mr. and Mrs. Palmer hired a wagon and driver to convey them through Canada to Detroit. This trip was completed, after much hardship, in nine days.

On January 25, 1830, there was born to Thomas and Mary Witherell Palmer a son, Thomas Witherell Palmer. In view of his ancestry and environment, it is not surprising that from early youth Thomas Witherell Palmer took a vital interest in the life of the community. He was born in the very heart of the Detroit of 1830, in a brick house standing on the southeast corner of Griswold Street and Jefferson Avenue. In some of his later writings he gave a vivid description of the community in which he was born and reared. To those who are familiar with Detroit, it will seem almost incredible that the sprawling city of today with a population of nearly two million could have undergone such changes from the relatively short time since Senator Palmer's early boyhood—a period of about one hundred years. Senator Palmer related that in 1840 there were no stores on Woodward Avenue, north of Larned Street; that is, four blocks from the Detroit River. Jefferson Avenue, the principal east–west thoroughfare, ended in a rail fence at Russell Street, three-fourths of a mile from the center of town. Fort Street ended in a rail fence, separating the farms beyond, at Cass Avenue (within one block of the present post office), less than half a mile from the site of the present city hall. The Michigan Central station was situated where the city hall now stands. Many old French windmills lined the banks of the Detroit River from Amherstburg (near its mouth) to St. Clair, fifty miles north of Detroit. Senator Palmer mentioned a fishery on the bank of the river near the center of the present Detroit where he had seen five thousand whitefish and many sturgeon five to six feet in length taken from the river in a single day. Years later, the seriousness of the decline of the lake fisheries was accentuated in his mind by these recollections, and as a senator he worked hard for legislation to protect this important industry.

In the 1820s the first steam ferry was built at Detroit. On this ferry Palmer's father had taken passage on a weekly trip up the river, across Lake St. Clair, and then up the St. Clair River to Palmer (now St. Clair), where the elder Palmer operated a sawmill. This trip of fifty miles was made in sixteen hours.

Yet small as the settlements of the city and state were at that time, young Palmer entertained a strong faith in their future growth, and while neither he nor any other person could foresee the extent of that growth, with his father he staked his hopes on the outcome. Both were to reap large material rewards. As will be seen later, Senator Palmer was not content simply to reap profit from this growth, for he early felt the urge to lend a guiding hand in civic affairs.

Young Thomas W. Palmer was a healthy boy, fond of adventure and the out-of-door life. He was fortunate, moreover, in having a mother who knew the value of bodily vigor when directed and controlled by an educated mind, and largely under her tutelage he prepared for college. He became a member of the Class of 1849 at the University of Michigan, where he joined the Chi Psi fraternity and entered actively into college life. The University, which had held its first Commencement only a few months before his admission, had an enrollment of seventy-seven students. Only the Literary Department was in existence, and seven years were to elapse before the University obtained its first president. Nevertheless, the institution was a thriving one, and in later years Palmer's reminiscences of student days were a never-failing resource at alumni gatherings. He was always a loyal Michigan man, and in 1899 and 1900 served as the fourth president of the University of Michigan Club of Detroit.

In 1848, at the age of eighteen, Palmer was forced by failing eyesight to leave the University. In company with five other students, including his cousin, James B. Witherell, A.B. 1848, who was also a grandson of Judge James Witherell, he took passage on a sailing vessel to Spain and thence to South America. It was thought that a sea voyage would be beneficial to his health. It is a matter of fair speculation whether the idea of a sea trip to improve the eyesight of a boy of eighteen could have been suggested by the experience of the hero of *Two Years Before the Mast.* Dana's book was in wide circulation at the time Palmer set forth. Benjamin G. Stimson, a Detroit boy, whose name was afterwards given to Stimson Place, was a member of the crew of Dana's vessel. Thus, it is not unlikely that Palmer's trip was prompted by Dana's voyage.

A very brief diary kept by Palmer during his voyage is preserved in the Burton Historical Collection of the Detroit Public Library. It throws interesting light on the youth's journey. It records, for example, how on some of the thirty-four days of the voyage to Spain, Palmer's companions read aloud to him as he lay in his berth, and one notes with interest that the reading was from the classics. Evidently, notwithstanding considerable seasickness in the earlier part of his trip, Palmer's health improved.

Little could this boy have imagined on landing at Cadiz, Spain, that one day he would return to it as the accredited representative of his own country, that he would then find occasion to celebrate at Cadiz the forty-first anniversary of that landing, nor that he would be the president of a world exposition, participated in by nearly every civilized nation, to commemorate another voyager who had set forth from that port some three and one-half centuries earlier to discover the New World. From Spain the party progressed on its travels to South America. Little record of this part of the journey has been preserved, but one may assume that to youths who were sufficiently serious to spend their time on shipboard reading the classics, the experience must have been enlightening. Whether Palmer regarded this as sufficiently compensatory for his not graduating with his University class is also a matter of conjecture. At any rate, in 1876 the University conferred upon him the degree of Bachelor of Arts, as of the Class of 1849, and he thus became a full-fledged alumnus.

Returning from his voyage to Spain and South America, Palmer began earnestly to engage in business, part of the time in Detroit and part of the time in Wisconsin. In 1853 he settled permanently in Detroit. A few years later he became associated with Charles Merrill, a successful lumber operator, whose daughter he married on October 16, 1855. On the death of her father Mrs. Palmer inherited his interest in the business. Both Senator Palmer and his wife became rich; when Mrs. Palmer died in 1918, her estate, valued at $6,500,000, was said to have been the largest ever probated in Wayne County up to that time.

By the year 1873 Palmer had begun to take active part in civic affairs: he became a member of the first Board of Estimates of the city of Detroit. In 1878 he was elected to the State Senate of Michigan. During his incumbency he was instrumental in the passage of a bill creating the State Industrial School for Girls; he also sponsored a bill providing for the establishment of an elaborate boulevard system for Detroit and for the acquisition of Belle Isle, situated in the middle of the Detroit River, as a park for the city. He was chairman of a legislative caucus which in 1879 nominated Zachariah Chandler for the United States Senate, to complete the unexpired term of Isaac P. Christiancy, who had replaced Chandler four years before.

In 1883, Palmer himself was chosen United States senator from Michigan. This choice, ushering in his appearance upon the national stage, came at the end of some very spirited and protracted balloting by the members of the Senate and House of Representatives of the Michigan legislature in joint convention. The convention balloted for 122 candidates at one time or another, including such men as James B. Angell, LL.D. 1912, Thomas M. Cooley, LL.D. 1873, Don M. Dickinson, LL.B. 1867, Austin Blair, LL.D. 1890 (former governor of Michigan), Julius Caesar Burrows (afterward elected to the United States Senate), G. V. N. Lothrop (afterward minister to Russia), and others of almost equal prominence. Finally, after the eighty-first ballot, the president of the Senate, on March 1, 1883, announced that Thomas W. Palmer had received a majority of all votes cast and had been elected for a six-year term beginning March 4, 1883.

Palmer served only one term in the United States Senate, most of it during the first administration of President Cleveland. He was well liked and respected in the Senate and became a close friend of Benjamin Harrison, then senator from Indiana. In those instances in which he took a firm and influential stand, he evidenced sound and liberal views and broad vision. One of the causes close to his heart was woman suffrage. In December, 1883, he was appointed a member of a committee of the Senate to deal with that subject and subsequently reported favorably on a proposed joint resolution to amend the Constitution so as to provide for woman suffrage. Although the resolution was not adopted, Palmer battled uninterruptedly for this cause. His address in the Senate advocating a change in the Constitution to bring about this reform was forceful but unsuccessful.

Another subject to which Palmer addressed himself was immigration. He did not believe in unrestricted immigration and he opposed the contemporary practice of subjecting immigrants to examination only after their arrival in this country; he demanded that the examination should be made before the immigrant was permitted to begin his voyage. A bill introduced for this purpose did not pass, but Congress ultimately adopted Palmer's plan for such an examination under the supervision of our representatives in foreign countries, and much credit is due him for advocating and helping to bring about this practical and useful reform.

Palmer voted in favor of a bill to amend the act regulating Chinese immigration so as to exclude all Chinese laborers from entering the country. He advocated much closer scrutiny in the admission of immigrants, declaring that the contemporary policy of indiscriminate admission was making the United States the dumping ground for the "vicious and delinquent human product of other nations." In a speech in the Senate he maintained that we were admitting "social wolves, honoring no flag, revering nothing as sacred, denying and despising all laws and rights of persons and property." He argued that through unregulated immigration our country would experience not "the survival of the fittest" but "the degradation of the best." He could see "a growth of classes, un-American and hard of assimilation, which menace the public and threaten to overturn all established law and usages."

These words, uttered in 1887, were significant and prophetic. Although the measures he proposed to correct these abuses were not immediately adopted, Congress did, at a later date, enact statutes to correct the evils of which he complained.

Palmer had much to do with the creation of the Department of Agriculture. He introduced and advocated the passage of a bill for the creation of a bureau of animal industry and another aimed at the extirpation of contagious and other diseases among domestic animals. He was a pioneer in this field. When one considers what has since been done to preserve the public health and safety, his foresight and progressive ideas must be recognized.

Always interested in all measures for the improvement of navigation on the Great Lakes, Senator Palmer served at different times as president of the deep waterways conventions, including those held at Sault Ste Marie and at Detroit in the eighties and nineties.

On March 6, 1889, Palmer was appointed by newly inaugurated President Benjamin Harrison to be envoy extraordinary and minister plenipotentiary to Spain, in place of Perry Belmont, resigned. From the point of view of diplomatic relations the period was a very quiet one; no matters of great importance appear to have required his attention during his official residence in Spain. Perhaps he found diplomatic life of this sort uninteresting after his experiences in public life at home; at any rate, after thirteen months in Spain, he resigned his post and returned to America.

Senator Palmer had been at home but a short time when he was appointed by President Harrison as a commissioner-at-large to the World's Columbian Commission—to conduct the World's Columbian Exposition at Chicago in 1892, actually held in 1893. In addition to eight commissioners-at-large, two commissioners were appointed to represent each state and territory. Palmer was elected by these commissioners as president of the World's Columbian Commission. This Exposition of 1893 was planned and conducted on a grand scale. The site, in Jackson Park and the adjoining Midway, included nearly seven hundred acres, of which two hundred acres were covered by buildings. It was a remarkable enterprise and an artistic triumph. The attendance during the six-month period of the Exposition was about 21,500,000—a number equivalent to approximately one-third of the population of the United States at the time.

It was a distinguished gathering of national figures that participated in the dedicatory exercises of the World's Columbian Exposition. A naval parade of war vessels of various countries had taken place at New York and a dedicatory meeting was attended by the Vice-President of the United States, many cabinet members, senators, representatives, governors of states, and representatives of the Army and the Navy. Senator Palmer delivered an address formally presenting the magnificent buildings of the exposition. Chauncey M. Depew delivered the Columbian oration. Among other speakers were Henry Watterson and Cardinal Gibbons.

The exposition was formally opened by President Cleveland, who delivered an address before a tremendous throng. Among the millions who visited the exposition were many distinguished guests, foremost among them being the Duke of Veragua, a lineal descendant of Columbus, and his family. After visiting President and Mrs. Cleveland at the White House, they had been taken to Chicago where they were received by a special committee headed by Senator Palmer. Later, Senator Palmer tendered the ducal party a banquet at a hotel in Chicago.

The closing exercises of the exposition in the fall were in sharp contrast with those which opened it. An elaborate program had been prepared, but was all but abandoned due to the assassination of Carter H. Harrison, mayor of Chicago, who had taken a prominent part in the planning and construction of the exposition. Senator Palmer, as president of the commission, made appropriate reference to this tragic event and, after a prayer had been offered, declared the exposition at an end.

His cultural attainments, his business, governmental, and diplomatic experience, and especially his graceful and genial personality well qualified Senator Palmer for the position of president of the commission. He possessed a marked talent and facility for public speaking and was continually being called upon to preside at public meetings, particularly when distinguished visitors were being entertained in his home town.

Senator Palmer's services were not, however, confined to public office. He had a deep and constant interest in philanthropy and in the encouragement of the arts. He was one of the founders and the first president of the Detroit Museum of Art. The State Industrial School for Girls, at Adrian, Michigan, was established chiefly through his influence. He was the founder of the Society for the Prevention of Cruelty to Animals, in Detroit, and for a long time allotted a part of his own offices as the headquarters for that society. In 1893 he and his wife presented to the city of Detroit the large and beautiful

Palmer Park, which has been one of the chief recreational centers of the city.

Among the pamphlets and articles written by him, the following may be mentioned: "Detroit Sixty Years Ago: An Address Before the Unity Club" (1897); "Sketch of the Life and Times of James Witherell" (*Michigan Pioneer and Historical Collections*, Volume IV, 1906); "Detroit in Its Relation to the Northwest: Bicentenary of the Founding of the City of Detroit" (1902).

Senator Palmer at different times was president of the following business organizations: Preston National Bank, Michigan Mutual Life Insurance Company, Percheron Steam Navigation Company, American Horse Breeders Association, and the *Detroit Journal* Company. On the edge of Detroit, in what was afterward Palmer Park, he built the famous Log Cabin. Here he was the genial host to many friends and many important persons who came as visitors to Detroit. In 1904, in recognition of his many public services, Albion College conferred upon him the degree of Doctor of Laws.

Senator Palmer died on June 1, 1913, having attained the age of eighty-three; he left a widow and two adopted children, Harold Palmer (mentioned above) and Grace Palmer Rice. His widow survived until 1918. As a monument to her memory she heavily endowed the Merrill Palmer School for Home Making, in Detroit, so that, according to her will, girls and young women could be "trained for the functions of wifehood and motherhood."

Thomas Witherell Palmer by birth and ancestry, by his education and natural endowments, and by his broad sympathies and enthusiastic belief in the future of his city, state, and nation and in the soundness of the principles underlying the national structure was fully qualified to play his part in the public and private life of his time. It is fitting that his character and accomplishments should be recorded in this account of alumni of the University from which he derived an inspiration that directed and, perhaps, determined the entire course of his life.

William Emory Quinby

1835	*Born in Brewer, Maine*
1836	*Moved to Lisbon, Maine*
1850	*Moved to Detroit, Michigan*
1858	*Graduated from the University of Michigan*
1858–59	*Studied law with the firm of Charles I. Walker, E. C. Walker, and Alfred Russell in Detroit*
1859	*Admitted to the bar of Michigan; practiced law and served as court reporter for the* Detroit Free Press
1860	*Married Adeline Frazier*
1861	*Became acting city editor of the* Free Press
1862	*Became city editor of the* Free Press
1863	*Purchased interest in the* Free Press
1872	*Became the principal owner and editor-in-chief of the* Free Press
	Supported Greeley for President
1881	*Established the London edition of the* Free Press *(weekly)*
1893–97	*Served as Minister to the Netherlands, May 24, 1893, to July 31, 1897*
1898	*Elected president of the University of Michigan Club of Detroit*
1899	*Elected president of the University of Michigan Alumni Association*
1904	*Appointed member of the building committee, Alumni Memorial Hall*
1907	*Retired from the* Free Press
1908	*Died in Detroit, Michigan*

William E. Quinby

William E. Quinby

By Brewster P. Campbell and Edgar A. Guest, Jr.

WHEN, one day in 1863, William E. Quinby, A.B. 1858, A.M. 1861, LL.D. 1896, purchased a part interest in the *Detroit Free Press* no fanfare heralded the transaction. Quite possibly there was no call for demonstration, for the *Free Press,* in that early day, wielded no particular influence. Detroit, though a thriving town of some fifty thousand population, had not yet dreamed of putting the nation on wheels and of becoming the symbol of an industrial age which was to remake the world. William Emory Quinby, himself, then out of the University of Michigan only five years, had as yet given no evidence of the important role he was to play in both civic affairs and the field of journalism. Yet his purchase at the age of twenty-eight of a part interest in the *Free Press* was in fact no whit less important than it must have seemed to him. Quinby was not to be content to see his paper grow with Detroit. He intended to make it a vital and ever-increasing factor in the city's steady growth.

The city in which Quinby took up his editorship was not new to him. He was born December 14, 1835, in Brewer, Maine. His father, Daniel Franklin Quinby, within a year after William's birth, had moved his little family to Lisbon, Maine, where they stayed for fourteen years before venturing westward. William Quinby knew Detroit first, then, as a school child, attending Capitol High School and John M. Gregory's Preparatory School, an institution with an excellent reputation in its day.

The years 1854–58 that he spent at the University of Michigan were good years, which Quinby was to cherish throughout his life. He joined Alpha Delta Phi fraternity and made friendships and associations which were to be lifelong. The many attachments he formed at the University made him its unflagging champion throughout his career. His championship was to be evidenced in many ways, especially through the columns of his newspaper.

So strong were the ties he had made, so lasting the associations, that in 1898 he was elected president of the University of Michigan Club of Detroit, and a year later president of the general University of Michigan Alumni Association. The Detroit alumni group became the parent of the Alumni Association, which in turn served to bind together University of Michigan graduates not only all over the country, but all over the world. Quinby's enthusiasm for this organization was one of the vital factors in its early success.

With his course not yet set when he graduated from the University with a Bachelor of Arts degree, young Quinby immediately entered the law offices of Charles I. Walker, LL.D. 1874, Kent Professor of Law 1859–76, 1879–81, 1886–87, E. C. Walker, and Alfred Russell, of Detroit, intent upon studying law and gaining admission to the bar. So well did he apply himself that in 1859 he was able to begin practice as an attorney.

Already, however, there was evidence that printer's ink flowed in his veins. Whether his desire for a journalistic career was acquired from his father remains unknown, yet such might have been the case. Certainly, while in Detroit, the elder Quinby had joined forces with J. K. Wellman to publish *Wellman's Literary Miscellany.*

At any rate William Emory Quinby had scarcely been well launched as an attorney when he turned to the newspaper business. Within a year he became court reporter for the *Free Press.* In the following year he married Adeline Frazier. Only a year later, in 1861, he became acting city editor of the *Free Press* and at the same time received a Master of Arts degree from the University.

Apparently, by this time the die was cast. Quinby deserted the law as a profession and turned his talents and all his attention to newspaper work. In 1862 he became full, rather than acting, city editor of the *Free Press,* and in the following year he became part owner of the paper.

The streets which Quinby trod that year of 1863 must have been cobbled, if they were paved at all. The streetcar, horse-drawn, was a new thing in Detroit. Two four-storied buildings were the town's skyscrapers, and as yet Detroit boasted no organized police or fire department, though volunteer firemen were ready to man the city's three steam pumping engines. Fur trading still prospered in the city, but side by side with the old frontier occupations new activities were appearing. Already the area was becoming an important seed center, and the varnish industry, which was to flourish mightily at a later date, had been launched.

The city was the natural wholesale center of a considerable area, and hardware and drygoods firms prospered in supplying near-by merchants with their stocks. The drug and chemical business, for which Detroit later was to become famed, was making a modest beginning in 1863. In the same year the First National Bank of Detroit was established.

Two railroads, the Michigan Central and the Detroit and Milwaukee, served the city, which also had access to the Great Western Railroad, but this was a Canadian line and, unfortunately, had a different gauge track from the American lines. At this time it was still by way of the Detroit River and the Great Lakes that the bulk of Detroit shipping was carried.

Neither signs nor portents foretold the future greatness of the city in which Quinby had cast his lot, but he would seem to have had every right to take a certain satisfaction in his new acquisition. There is little in the printed record to indicate the problems in his new wartime venture. Quinby, who was to devote the greater share of the remainder of his life to the business of chronicling the events of his era, left surprisingly little information regarding the part he played in those events.

When Quinby became one-eighth owner of the *Free Press,* the paper had at least one correspondent, and possibly more, at Washington, the fountainhead of information, to gather news of the Civil War. Yet, in common with many other publishers, the owners of the *Free Press* were not satisfied with the news-gathering facilities available to them. In the East there was the Associated Press, the forerunner of the great news agency which still bears that name. Its activities did not extend to the "West." In an attempt to do something to improve the situation, a meeting was held in the *Free Press* office, and the problems of war coverage and the general gathering of news were discussed. It was here that the Western Associated Press, which later merged with the New York Associated Press, was formed.

Whatever the problems the owners of the paper encountered, Quinby seems to have been a major factor in surmounting them promptly—and his rise on the *Free Press* was rapid. Very shortly after becoming a part owner of the paper he became managing editor. With his new status, apparently, came even greater faith in the future of the publication and of the city which it served, for it is certain that Quinby continued to acquire additional *Free Press* stock over the years, with the result that by 1872 he was virtually a 50 per cent stockholder in the concern. In 1872 politics forced Quinby to make a definite decision as to his future with the *Free Press.*

At their national convention in 1872, held in Cincinnati, Ohio, the Democrats saw no possibility of nominating a member of their party who had even an outside chance of defeating President Ulysses S. Grant for a second term. Faced with what seemed to them certain defeat if they nominated one of their own men, the Democrats turned to a Republican who had opposed Grant's nomination in 1868 and who had been a bitter critic of the Grant administration in the ensuing years—Horace Greeley, New York newspaper publisher. The move was a strange one, for Greeley had fought everything the Democratic Party had espoused over the preceding twenty-five years. He was as implacable a foe of the Democrats as he was the bitter enemy of the Grant administration.

The *Detroit Free Press* was then a Democratic newspaper and like any other newspaper supporting the Democratic cause, faced a difficult problem. The Democratic Party itself was split asunder. A not inconsiderable minority of members of the party repudiated the candidate entirely. They wanted no traffic with a "renegade Republican" and preferred to go down to what they considered "honorable defeat" with a member of their own party rather than to take the chance of winning with a political foe.

Colonel Freeman Norvell, part owner of the *Free Press*, took this attitude. Quinby, on the other hand, felt that for a Democratic newspaper to refuse to support the Democratic nominee was unthinkable. He believed that desertion would lose the *Free Press* party good will and the confidence of all loyal Democrats.

Colonel Norvell was adamant in his stand, and Quinby heard rumors that if the *Free Press* opposed Greeley other Democrats would establish a rival paper in Detroit. He thought it wiser to support Greeley than to bring ruin to the newspaper.

Since these men could not reconcile their views, Norvell offered to buy Quinby's interest or to sell his own. There was no question in Quinby's mind as to what he wished to do. By this time he had come to consider the *Free Press* his lifework—the career to which he was determined to devote himself. Detroit was his home town, and he looked upon the *Free Press* as his newspaper. Yet there remained the very considerable question of money if it was actually to become his newspaper. He was faced with a major problem: to acquire the paper quickly if he did not wish to lose all connection with it.

It was, we know, a dejected Quinby who walked out of the *Free Press* office, once the meaning of the alternative which had been put to him was clear. As he walked northward on Griswold Street, toward Jefferson, he must have given much thought to the years of planning, the long hours of joyous labor, his dreams for the future. Were all these to be wiped out? True, there were other newspapers and other cities, but there was only one *Detroit Free Press*, just as, to him, there was only one Detroit.

Quinby recalled A. G. Boynton, a Detroiter, who, like himself, hailed originally from Maine, and who had expressed a desire to become a newspaper man. It might be possible to obtain from him the money he so sorely needed. Quinby would have preferred, possibly, to take an experienced newspaperman as a partner, but this time there was no opportunity to make a choice. Boynton, a member of the Detroit bar and a police court judge, had long wished to enter the newspaper business and fancied himself in the role of a writer of editorials. If he was to have an inexperienced man as a partner, Quinby felt that he could go to no finer person than A. G. Boynton.

The judge, for reasons best known to himself, perhaps because of the problem of raising the amount of money immediately, could not give Quinby an immediate answer. For several days Quinby must have suffered torments of uncertainty.

Boynton finally made whatever arrangements were needed, however, and became one-fourth owner of the *Free Press* by purchasing Norvell's stock. Quinby was now in undisputed control of the property. The association was a happy one. Boynton, realizing his great desire, served for years as chief editorial writer. This left Quinby in a position to raise the paper to new and greater heights, to place it, in fact, among the great papers of the time.

Not the least of Quinby's many and unquestioned attainments was his ability to surround himself with outstanding talent and to give that talent every opportunity to develop to its fullest. The names of those who won fame on the *Free Press* under Quinby may mean little today, for newspaper fame is fleeting, indeed, but at the time its roster of "stars" was certainly second to none in this country.

Strange as it may seem to modern newspaper readers, the *Free Press*, under Quinby's guidance, first acquired outstanding fame as a humorous journal. This can be attributed largely to this roster of "stars." Included among them was Robert Barr, who became widely known as a humorist under the name of Luke Sharp in his *Free Press* days. Later, Quinby was to send Barr to London to institute the *London Free Press*, the first newspaper published abroad by the publisher of an American daily. After serving as editor of this edition, Barr gained added fame as a novelist in Britain.

C. B. Lewis was another *Free Press* staff member to become noted for his humorous writings. Lewis had started in the newspaper business as a printer in Pontiac. He had a great desire to become a writer, however, and from time to time would set up humorous paragraphs of his own devising and see that they found their way into print. Quinby noticed some of these paragraphs and employed Lewis as a reporter. He soon managed to prove that he had no great ability or genius in this capacity, but he continued to try his hand at humor and eventually hit upon a sort of forerunner of today's gossip columns. His "Lime Kiln Club" featured stories of Negroes who carried on discussions of politics and other matters of current importance. Though not written in true Negro dialect, the "Lime Kiln Club" stories had a distinctive flavor which won them immediate attention and a regular following. Lewis' nom de plume, "M. Quad," a printing term, became one of the best-known names in the journalistic world of the time.

A third *Free Press* "great" of the time was George P. Goodale, A.M. (*hon.*) 1915, whose theatrical criticisms made history, and whose knowledge of the stage and the people of the stage remains a legend.

These are but a few of the many important figures in the newspaper world who worked for Quinby during the years of his editorship. They will serve to indicate the quality and capabilities of the men Quinby gathered about him. More and more, as time went on, the paper began to veer from what may have been an overemphasis on humor to a solid basis of reporting the news and of commenting on questions of politics.

Still staunchly Democratic, Quinby took the stand that neither he nor any *Free Press* employee would go into politics or accept political appointment. He wished to keep himself and his newspaper free to criticize and to praise political moves and political personages.

This rule of aloofness from political office remained unbroken until Grover Cleveland appointed Quinby minister to the Netherlands in 1893. Even then the publisher hesitated to lay aside his journalistic duties and accept the presidential appointment.

The hesitation may have been due to an embarrassment natural in a man of Quinby's punctilious regard for the ethics of journalism. The *Free Press*, for about six weeks prior to his appointment, had been waging a front-page campaign for recognition of Michigan Democrats in the distribution of patronage. On April 16, 1893, the headline, "What Will Michigan Get?" was followed by the comment that thus far there had been only five appointments from Michigan requiring senatorial approval and that only one of the five was for an office outside the state.

On April 19 after the line "Good Places to Give Out," came a plaintive "Michigan Men Are Waiting for Them." Articles assessing the prospects for Michigan men appeared regularly every few days: on May 4, "Michigan Men Likely to Be Remembered Soon"; on May 11, "Detroiters Want Office"; on May 18, "Their Turn is Coming; Michigan Men May Get Good Places"; on the twentieth came a list of Michigan men at the capital, with the statement that there was "no effort to disguise the fact" that they were there "to see what will be done about Michigan appointments."

After these headlines the sudden and surprising news of his appointment to The Hague must have been almost as embarrassing to Quinby as it was gratifying. The *Free Press* of May 26, under a Washington dateline of May 25, announced: "To The Hague; A Citizen of Detroit is highly honored; William E. Quinby selected for Minister to the Netherlands." It is doubtful whether in all the land there was any more surprised person than Quinby when the news appeared in his own paper. He could hardly believe it, for he had not sought political favor nor had he been informed that it was about to be thrust upon him.

It was not, in fact, until he received congratulations from Don M. Dickinson, LL.B. 1867, a fellow alumnus of the University of Michigan and an outstanding power in Michigan Democratic politics, that he fully realized that this honor had been accorded him. It was Dickinson who, without telling the publisher of his intentions, had urged the appointment of Quinby.

Any misgivings Quinby may have had, however, with respect to the propriety of his accepting the appointment must have been allayed by the enthusiasm with which it was greeted. Once the news of the appointment was made public, congratulations began to pour in upon both President Cleveland and Quinby. The recognition was amply deserved, in the public mind, not only by reason of the ardent support which he had accorded the Democratic Party throughout the years, but also because of his high qualifications for a diplomatic post.

Even such an honor as this could not, despite the generous popular approval it had met, overcome Quinby's scruples against mixing journalism and politics. When he decided to accept the post abroad, he immediately severed his connection with the *Free Press*, leaving it under the direction of two of his sons, Theodore E. and H. W. Quinby.

The relations of the United States with the Netherlands during the years when Quinby served as envoy were, as usual, placid, and there is little in the record to indicate what his activities were while abroad. The meager details available record on July 20, 1893, "Mr. Quinby is in Washington. He has received his final instructions and will sail for The Hague on Saturday, July 22." On August 10, 1893, The Hague *Dagblad* records a "socio-official function was held in connection with the arrival at The Hague of Minister Quinby and the departure of his predecessor." The "function," it appears, was a dinner given by Quinby as a farewell party for the Honorable Samuel R. Thayer. The event was held at the Hotel Den Ouden Doelen in a dining room decorated with American flags. Following the dinner Quinby accompanied Thayer to the railroad station, where the latter entrained on the first part of his journey home.

Quinby returned to Detroit for a time in the spring of 1896. He felt that he was needed to take care of certain business matters in connection with the *Free Press*, and the trip gave him the opportunity of going to Ann Arbor to attend the exercises marking Dr. Angell's twenty-fifth year as President of the University of Michigan. Mr. Quinby's interest in the University had never flagged; his paper had been its staunch champion throughout the years. It gave the publisher-envoy real pleasure to be able to time his visit home so that he could be present at the ceremonies honoring Dr. Angell.

In company with more than 150 other Detroit alumni of the University, Quinby made a special train trip to Ann Arbor on June 24, 1896. Alumni President Don M. Dickinson and Secretary Earl D. Babst had done their work well. The attendance for the occasion certainly attained the very peak of anyone's expectations.

Among the honored guests seated on the platform in University Hall were Quinby, Dickinson, Levi L. Barbour, A.B. 1863, LL.B. 1865, A.M. 1876, and the presidents of numerous universities. At the alumni dinner that night, Quinby was seated at the speaker's table, and the following day he received a Doctor of Laws degree from the University.

Only a little more than a year later, Quinby was again back in Detroit, this time to remain, his duties in The Hague having been completed. The publisher plunged at once into the work which he loved best and which was to occupy him from that time virtually until his death in 1908.

Throughout the years William Emory Quinby had done much for the newspaper business and for the city in which he resided. He is generally credited with having brought the web printing press and typesetting machinery to Michigan. The Michigan Bell Telephone Company credits Quinby with having helped to introduce the telephone to Detroit in 1877, just one year after its invention by Alexander Graham Bell. Quinby, the company points out, installed one of the first two experimental telephone lines in Michigan. It was set up between the *Free Press* office and the American District Telegraph office.

The years had seen the *Free Press* grow in influence as it had grown in circulation to become a tremendously powerful force for good in the community. Its support of a project was of invaluable aid, and Quinby, realizing fully the responsibility that goes with such power, did not lend the paper's support lightly. Many of the civic improvements of the day stemmed from suggestions made by Quinby through the pages of his publication, and the success of many other worthy projects could be traced directly to his editorial endorsement of those movements. As a result Quinby became a figure of great power in Detroit, yet he remained the same unassuming person he had always been.

Perhaps one of the finest tributes Quinby, or any other publisher, ever received was that accorded the owner of the *Free Press* on his seventieth birthday, December 14, 1905. The tribute, presented by George P. Goodale at a surprise party, included autographed photographs of his friends who were present, and the following sentiments:

> The neighbors and friends whose names accompany this expression of admiration and friendship offer their dearest felicitations for your having so happily arrived at seventy years.
>
> To have come through the storm and stress of an active public life with so much of youth preserved, so much of energy remaining and with so high and so many honors as those that are linked with your name, is to have compassed much of the truest and best happiness that man may hope to enjoy . . .
>
> The half-century mark of your career as a representative American journalist is visible over the near horizon. That career has been characterized by tenacious adherence to principle, sometimes at the cost of great personal sacrifice; by enduring regard for the best interests of your people and country; by the authoritative word, timely spoken, in behalf of exalted ideals and in opposition to encroachments by selfish greed; by intrepid service for the decent and clean in human intercourse; and by personal conduct that has engraved the image of manly nobility in the hearts of your friends . . .

Only shortly before this event Mrs. Quinby had died—a heavy loss. To the sentiments expressed in the testimonial tendered him on this seventieth birthday, Quinby feelingly replied:

"Someone has said, 'Life has only three things—anticipation for youth, memory for old age, friends for both.' " The roster of Quinby's friends present on this occasion reads like a "Who's Who of Detroit." Among them were such men as R. H. Fyfe, Levi L. Barbour, Don M. Dickinson, Senator Thomas W. Palmer, A.B. 1849 (*nunc pro tunc* 1876), John R. Russel, A.B. 1879, M.D. 1882, Colonel Frank Hecker, W. C. McMillan, and the Reverend Dr. A. H. Barr.

Within two years, because of failing health, Mr. Quinby retired from the *Free Press*. The following year, on June 7, 1908, he died at Grace Hospital in Detroit.

The publisher's life had been a long and useful one. Though little is recorded of his personal career, it is known that he reared his family of three sons and three daughters in one of the city's most gracious and pleasant homes.

Quinby was described as "a journalist of the old school," "a scholarly, dignified and high-toned gentleman," "always approachable, a most courteous and affable gentleman, possessing qualities which greatly endear him to his friends and associates," "modest as he is energetic; suave, patient, methodical; a warm friend and an agreeable companion."

Quinby had a deep sense of the obligation of a newspaper editor to his community. In a paper entitled "Reminiscences of Michigan Journalism," written from the vantage ground of nearly a half-century's experience as an editor and read before the Michigan Press Association in 1903,* he declared:

> The noblest profession on earth is that of the Editor. Affording the opportunity for noble deeds, for beneficence, for aiding all good works, it carries with it also great responsibility. No man should have or does have, a greater sense of this responsibility, than does the conscientious editor. So believing I take to myself also that which I say to you, as St. Paul said to Timothy, "Oh, Timothy, keep that which is committed to thy trust." It is indeed, my friends of the press, a good heritage that we have, a sacred trust.

* Published in the *Michigan Pioneer and Historical Society Collections*, XXX, pp. 507-17.

Examining the history of the *Free Press* during the period of his control of the paper, one finds, indeed, ample proof that Quinby regarded his editorship as "a sacred trust."

The task of painting a word picture of Quinby is no simple one. There are few men in Detroit today who knew him at all well, and Quinby's reticence about himself was so great that the written record concerning him is exceedingly meager. Would that he had but heeded the moral of a story he himself related! This story with which he opened his "Reminiscences" address is, incidentally, of interest not only for its own sake but also as evidence of Quinby's sense of humor:

> Saith Rip Van Winkle, "how soon we are forgot." I remember an illustration of this. One of those exaggerations characterizing American humor and yet carrying its moral. At one of the famed Gridiron Club dinners years ago, witty Dick Merrick, the noted Washington counsellor, was talking with Senator Sherman. He said: "We fade away like a tale that is told, so soon, alas. The other day," said he, "ex-President Hayes came to Washington to attend a chicken convention and he walked the entire length of Pennsylvania [Avenue] with his linen duster in one hand and his luncheon wrapped up in a newspaper in the other and not one man saluted him. Finally he entered the grounds of the White House and there but one man spoke to him. He was a policeman and he said 'please keep off the grass.'"

One who does recall Quinby is James S. Holden, a distinguished business and civic leader who was an intimate friend of Quinby and who served as executor of his estate until a few years ago. It is by drawing upon Holden's memory that we are able to give a picture of the kind of man Quinby was, as he guided the *Detroit Free Press* during those turbulent days.

Quinby was not a large man, although photographs of his head and shoulders might lead one to believe he was a giant. Personal neatness amounted almost to a fetish with him. He was always groomed to perfection, and he particularly favored a frock coat as the proper and dignified mode of dress. He had a full white mustache, and there are those who feel that in his jovial moments he somewhat resembled the humorist Mark Twain. According to Holden, Quinby neither smoked nor gambled. He did not play cards; he drank with extreme moderation. On state occasions he permitted himself a glass of wine. He was a member of the Detroit Club, going to the club merely for social relaxation. It is fairly certain that he engaged in no sports, not even golf, which was the popular sport of his contemporaries.

Quinby owned a summer home at Port Austin, Michigan, about 125 miles due north of Detroit, which in those days was almost an all-day ride on the Pere Marquette Railroad, and when he felt he could spare the time away from his desk he relaxed there. But no record indicates that he had any hobby to occupy his mind other than his work and his deep interest in the affairs of the University.

The sideboard of his home, at 777 East Jefferson Avenue, was decorated with an elaborate and rather expensive set of Dutch ware of the delft variety, which he had purchased, or which had perhaps been presented to him, during his years at The Hague. But by no stretch of the imagination could china collecting be rated as a hobby. He collected nothing, with the possible exception of books. He was an avid reader, and his knowledge of current affairs, both foreign and domestic, was comprehensive. Even while he was occupied with the duties of his office at The Hague, Quinby kept himself thoroughly informed of the march of events at home, especially in Detroit.

Mr. Holden declares that Quinby was both a social and a sociable man, Detroit's quasi-official host during his days on the *Free Press*. Whenever the city paid homage to a celebrity, Quinby could usually be counted on to voice the tribute in his quiet, dignified, gentlemanly manner. He had a leading part in many of these functions, often to the discomfort of Mrs. Quinby, who had little liking for the social life at which her husband was adept. He punctiliously observed the social graces and earned a reputation as a delightful raconteur, but his favorite stories have not come down to us.

That he possessed a great store of personal courage is unquestioned. He was a man who fought for what he believed to be right, regardless of the odds and of the possible consequences. His devotion to his ideals is no better demonstrated than by the decision he made in the spring of 1896 that ended the *Free Press* support of the Democratic Party.

The *Free Press*, under Quinby, had always been staunchly and unswervingly Democratic. It battled with all its strength not only for the tenets of that party but against all opposition to the party. But Quinby could not accept the nomination of William Jennings Bryan and the 16 to 1 silver policy. He did not make the decision hurriedly, but when he made it, he made it for good. The *Free Press*, in July, 1896, announced publicly that it could no longer support the Democratic Party and that henceforth it would consider itself "independent." A month later the paper carried a story to the effect that it had been expelled by the Democratic Press Association. Quinby commented editorially: "It comes a little late, this expulsion, inasmuch as the *Free Press* declared itself to be independent of any party affiliation more than a month ago." This statement took courage of the highest order, but Quinby was more than equal to it. With the same vigor and intelligence that characterized his earlier efforts in behalf of the party, he resisted all pressure to bring the *Free Press* back into the fold.

William Emory Quinby made a mark upon his generation in Detroit. Quietly and unostentatiously he did much for the University from which he graduated and which he never ceased to love. Even though his objections to mixing journalism and politics had led him in 1892 to decline a proferred appointment as regent of the University, he admitted that his interest in educational questions had strongly tempted him to accept. This interest may, however, have served the University equally well through the consistent support given by Quinby's paper in such matters as the mill tax and the constitutional control of the University by the Board of Regents. Certainly his services as minister to the Netherlands reflected honor upon the University with which he had been so closely identified as well as upon himself and upon President Cleveland who had appointed him.

John Mahelm Berry Sill

1831 *Born in Black Rock, New York*
1834 *Moved to Oberlin, Ohio*
1836 *Moved to Jonesville, Michigan*
1854 *Graduated from Michigan State Normal School*
Married Sally Beaumont
1859 *Appointed principal of Michigan State Normal School*
1863 *Elected superintendent of Detroit Public Schools*
1865 *Became proprietor and principal of the Detroit Female Seminary*
1867 *Appointed regent of the University of Michigan*
1875 *Re-elected superintendent of the Detroit Public Schools*
1886 *Re-appointed principal of the Michigan State Normal School*
1894 *Appointed minister to Korea*
1897 *Returned to the United States from Korea*
1899 *Became member of the Detroit Citizens Committee on Education*
1901 *Died in Detroit, Michigan*

John M. B. Sill

John M. B. Sill

By Shirley W. Smith

ON TUESDAY afternoon, February 27, 1894, in the Wagner palace car "Khedive," a man who had won distinction and honor in the educational field in Michigan was approaching the borders of the state that had been his home for more than forty years, outward bound for a country that was not merely foreign but "hermit." There he would represent the United States of America as its minister resident. He was entirely confident that honors as a diplomat waited to be added to those he had won as an educator.

He was John Mahelm Berry Sill, principal, for the eight years just preceding, of the Michigan State Normal School (now College) at Ypsilanti. This was a position of distinction, and Mr. Sill had honored it no less than it had honored him. With him on his long travels to Korea were Mrs. Sill, a cultivated, courageous, sweet-spirited victim of asthma and arthritis (they called it "rheumatism"), her sister, Mrs. Alice Graham, and the Sills' son Joseph, who was to return the following winter to graduate from the University of Michigan as Bachelor of Arts in 1897 and as Doctor of Medicine in 1899. The minister himself had received from the University an honorary Master of Arts degree in 1870. The Sills had left behind them in Michigan a daughter and her husband, a little granddaughter and grandson. They were a most devoted family. No one could read the letters that went from the travelers, en route or after arrival, to those at home without being charmed by the happiness they all found in one another.

Sill was in his sixty-third year, aging, doubtless, but not old, and looking forward with untroubled, vigorous complacency to being able to fill completely and perhaps to expand the position awaiting him. This writer believes his self-confidence was reasonably well justified, not only on the basis of past achievement but in the events as they were to unfold in the future. When he arrived at his new post, however, he was to be precipitated into a situation that neither he nor his sponsors nor President Cleveland, who had appointed him, could possibly have foreseen.

Instead of the peace and tranquillity suggested by Korea's characterizations as the "Hermit Kingdom" and the "Land of the Morning Calm," the new minister found himself in the midst of a full-dress rebellion, to be followed immediately by a war between China and Japan, with Korea as the scene of conflict—fought with a savage disregard of human life and suffering that we sometimes characterize as "Oriental." It was a war watched with close and suspicious attention by Russia, England, and other European powers as its shifting tides affected their interests in the Far East.

There were other difficulties. The missionaries, in spite of their ideals and their professions, were but human after all; they were bound to be a source of trouble now and then in a strange land where they had no legal standing—where, indeed, they were banned by royal decree, which, though not currently enforced, was nevertheless always "there." Their deep religious convictions and their sense of first loyalty to a divine higher power often brought them into collision with Korean laws. Naturally, too, they had their full supply of the sectarian prejudices of those days.

In Minister Sill's time the government was centered absolutely in one man, the king; in its ramifications it was hopelessly corrupt. The minister relates in one of his early letters how, when the king was to make a royal progress between palaces, his advisers found it desirable to clean up and renovate that part of the capital city of Seoul through which he was to pass, so that he might not learn the facts of life as it was lived in Korea. Naturally, it was worse in the provinces. which he never saw. An instance illustrating the difficulties in the way of social progress had occurred a few years before

Sill's arrival, when an effort to establish a missionary hospital at partial government support had encountered opposition on the ground that several hundred years earlier, when the dynasty was more vigorous, it had itself made provision for a hospital. This institution had had only a most shadowy existence and save for its payroll had ceased altogether to function for over a hundred years; the "staff" of the old "hospital" naturally did not want another that would threaten if not wholly destroy a source of income. The king was amiable, well-meaning, and "progressive," ignorant of what was going on about him, necessarily deferential to the vigorous Chinese resident, Yuan Shih Kai (later to be president of the Chinese Republic), in great fear of his aged father, the former regent, and in general inclined to show cowardice. The queen was much the abler person of the royal pair, a fact for which she paid with her life during Sill's residence.

A young naval officer, Lieutenant Lucius Allyn Bostwick of the U.S.S. "Palos," wrote some verses that amused Mrs. Sill so much that she copied them and sent them home to the family for entertainment and instruction. While the lines could not be called immortal, they are still lively. Three of the seven stanzas are as follows:

I

There's a singular country far over the seas:
To the world it is known as Korea.
Where there's nothing to charm one and nothing to please,
And of cleanliness not an idea.
Where lucid descriptions of persons and things
Quite baffle the cleverest pen,
And stir up strange qualms in the poet who sings
Of that far-away land of Chosen.

II

Where the houses they live in are mostly of dirt
With a tumble-down roof made of thatch;
Where soap is unknown, it is safe to assert,
And vermin in myriads hatch.

Where the streets are all reeking with odors more rife
Than the smells from a hyena's den.
One visit is surely enough for one life
To that far-away land of Chosen.

VI

Where the King, in a manner befitting a prince,
Is charmed with each innovation
And plays with post-offices, steamers, and things
At a grievous expense to the nation.
Where gullible strangers big contracts have made,
But they find, when they ask for their yen,
It's a very cold day when employees are paid
In that far-away land of Chosen.

But Minister Sill was to have another problem that he could hardly have foreseen. This problem was embodied in the secretary of the legation, Dr. Horace N. Allen. Dr. Allen, a graduate of Ohio Wesleyan University and of the Miami (Ohio) Medical College, was at the time of Sill's arrival only thirty-six years old and had already been in Korea ten years. He had been secretary of the legation under Sill's predecessor, Augustine Heard, for four of the ten years. He was the first missionary in Korea—to survive. He had come to Korea under the auspices of the Presbyterian Church. In view of the current active ban on missionaries as such, he "sneaked in by a ruse" (to use his own words) as a doctor. It was by no means the only ruse that was to contribute to the doctor's successes in Korea. But almost immediately—and not by any ruse—he had the good fortune and the skill to bring back to life and health a favorite official and relative of the king who had been left for dead or dying from many sword slashes received in one of the numerous revolutionary outbreaks. Promptly thereafter Allen was appointed royal physician—and was one of the few men ever admitted to the presence of the queen. He became physician to most or all of the legations. It was he who brought the new hospital into being, and he continued in active charge. Moreover, he soon became the trusted confidant of the king in matters far afield from medicine. Allen admitted freely and with utter truth that he was neither a personal pacifist nor a mediator; when the quarrels that had broken out among the missionary brothers and sisters even on the ship bringing Allen over to China en route to Korea were no longer to be endured, the king came to his rescue and sent him to the United States as official secretary of a Korean delegation whose principal objective was the negotiation of a loan.

The story of Allen's difficulties with his delegates, who had not the slightest knowledge of Western usages, such as smuggling, plumbing, soap, insecticides, or the social position of women, would have furnished George Ade situations with which he might well have outdone the success of his popular comic opera, *The Sultan of Sulu.* Allen did not succeed in getting the loan, but he did get back to Korea alive and in his right mind, and, of almost equal importance for his future, without loss of the king's favor. He came back as a Presbyterian representative once more, but soon resigned again to become a salaried official adviser to the king. He also continued in his medical and surgical activities, partly because his public, Oriental and Occidental, would not allow him to do otherwise and partly because his own brand of human nature never allowed him to let go of anything he had once had in his hands. He might ostensibly cease being a missionary or a royal counselor—actually he always continued to give matters his personal and detailed attention. He was courageous, ubiquitous, and indefatigable. In 1890 his talents were recognized by his appointment as official secretary of the American legation under Minister Heard, and he stayed on under Minister Sill. Until almost the last, Allen's relations with Sill were of the friendliest. It was as if the minister felt he could not live without him, even though sometimes he could hardly live with him.

The secretary was so tireless, so "resourceful," and so bold with the Korean government in behalf of the Korean groups or individuals, and in behalf of Americans desiring concessions of wide variety, that now and then he brought down the wrath of our thoroughly isolationist State Department. Unavoidably, the secretary's activities involved the responsible minister, who seems unprotestingly to have accepted blame when it came. Allen was naturally sensitive, quick-tempered, and quarrelsome, though with some justice it might be argued that he had troubles enough to warrant. He knew so much more about Korea than any other American in sight that it is no wonder Sill thought him a jewel whose imperfections might justifiably be ignored. Allen wrote later: "I did his work; he got the credit." It is clear that the doctor yearned for the credit he was not getting. Sill was to wake up later to the fact that he had an assistant more ambitious, more widely informed, with broader contacts, and far more aggressive, than himself; yet without invariably fixed high principles. Allen admitted that he not only had received cash "presents" from entrepreneurs whom he had aided, but that he had also at times suggested the desirability and propriety of such acknowledgment of his efforts. Allen was "loyal," but when the time came that it was a basic question of Sill or Allen, he was wholeheartedly and undividedly loyal to Allen. In 1897 he became his "Gold Democrat" chief's Republican successor, and he stayed on as minister until March, 1905, when, in a White House interview, he had disagreed bluntly and persistently with Theodore Roosevelt. Not even Allen's resourcefulness could undo that error.*

* Horace N. Allen's life has lately been presented in a volume of 355 pages by Professor Fred H. Harrington, now of the University of Wisconsin. The work bears the comprehensive and, as regards Allen's activities, significant title *God, Mammon, and the Japanese* (Madison: Univ. Wisconsin Press, 1944). It represents much careful research and is unusually well written, though some of its conclusions and characterizations do not seem to me to be justified. It is unfair to Mr. Sill, usually speaking of him patronizingly at the best; for example, Professor Harrington's early direct mention of Sill as "one of Cleveland's ministers," "the school superintendent from Michigan who succeeded Heard," with no reference anywhere in the book to the important post Sill had left to assume the duties of minister; his assertion that Sill's political friends had "wanted to give the old man a rest and an opportunity to study the flowers of Korea," and that "he echoed his subordinate." In "the final quarrel" attending the struggle for appointment versus reappointment, Allen is recorded by Harrington as referring to Sill as "a spoiled old man in his dotage." These are characterizations not in harmony with Sill's reputation as I personally remember it; no person of sense who knew Mr. Sill in his lifetime with whom I have been able to make contact regards them as even remotely applicable to him. (It is interesting to note that Secretary of State John Sherman, a citizen of Ohio, whence Allen also came, warmed himself to the Allen candidacy with the words, "I remember Allen; he has red hair.")

I have devoted all these lines to Dr. Allen not merely because he was an actor on the Korean scene, but because he was an inseparable component of Sill's period of office and was finally the determining factor in Sill's failure to be reappointed.

What manner of man was Cleveland's minister when the President sent him to Korea? John Mahelm Berry Sill was born at Black Rock (now a part of Buffalo), New York, November 23, 1831. His parents brought him to Oberlin, Ohio, in 1834, and to Jonesville, Michigan, two years later. His father and mother died on the same day, when he was only eleven. From thirteen, he depended on his own resources. He taught school in Hillsdale County, and later at Ypsilanti, where he matriculated in the State Normal at twenty-two. When he graduated in 1854 he became the institution's first male alumnus. He must have been a respected, mature student for he was promptly made professor of the English language and literature and continued as such till 1858. The following year he was principal. From 1865 to 1875 he was proprietor and principal of the Detroit Female Seminary, and in 1863–65 and 1875–86, superintendent of the Detroit school system, which, in fact, as the second to bear the title of superintendent, he organized. In 1867 he was appointed to the Board of Regents of the University by Governor H. H. Crapo, a Republican, to fill out the term of Henry C. Knight, deceased. This term lasted until December 31, 1870, when he retired following defeat at the polls by a Republican, a foretaste of what was to happen to him as minister after the election of President McKinley in 1896. As a regent of the University, he was active and useful, and was selected as one of the committee of three who made the trip through the East that resulted in the first offer of the presidency of the University of Michigan to James Burrill Angell. In 1886 he again became principal of the Normal School at Ypsilanti, then relatively a more outstanding post than it could be today with four state normal colleges. During all these years he was a "head-man" in the educational field of Michigan. He wrote two textbooks: *Synthesis of the English Sentence* (1856) and *Practical Lessons in*

English (1880). It was the first of these two books that President Cleveland recalled as having used when at the suggestion of Don M. Dickinson, LL.B. 1867, former postmaster general, and Edwin F. Uhl, A.B. 1862, A.M. 1865, assistant secretary of state, he took Sill out of the Greek-honoring city of Ypsilanti and made him minister to the anything but Grecian country of Korea.

A student at the Normal School during Sill's incumbency as president gave these recollections of his appearance and personality: "He was not above average height, perhaps a little below, but he had great breadth of shoulders and a torso to match." In one of his letters home from Japan en route to Korea, Sill said that the emperor of Japan to whom he was presented under pleasant circumstances, "is about my height, but in latitude I am his superior." Of Secretary Allen he wrote: "He is more than six feet tall, but crosswise I am taller than he is." Sill once mentioned that he weighed two hundred pounds. According to his former student:

> He was not fat, but very solid and substantial appearing. His head was rather leonine, but lighted by shrewd and kindly eyes. His bodily presence was impressive. The magazine *Time,* so given to picturesque adjectives, might have called him "bumbling," but that could not have implied that he did not know very definitely what he wished and how to obtain it. He could be very severe, but I am sure his severity was always softened by mercy. It was his voice above all, especially in platform speaking or reading, which set him apart from the ordinary. He read Scripture in chapel as one might read aloud a narrative from the morning paper—made the Bible characters real, every-day people.* There was no attempt to be dramatic; with the wonderful tonal qualities and modulations of his voice he simply interpreted what was there to interpret. After fifty-three years his reading of the Bible and of certain poems still seems to me thrilling, exciting, magnificent.

Minister Sill was very much more than a run-of-mine "school superintendent from Michigan" as Allen's biographer characterized him.

* Sill was ordained as an Episcopal clergyman in 1890 and occasionally preached in the English churches of Japan and Korea.

The minister's party, on the voyage from Japan, stopped at Fusan in southern Korea where, as Joseph Sill wrote to his sister: "The flag brought all the Americans in town—seven—to the ship." They arrived at Chemulpo, the port for Seoul about twenty-five miles distant, on April 25. Thence they proceeded by a very small river steamer to within three miles of Seoul. These last three miles were covered in the legation sedan chairs brought by Allen. The minister's family were all intrigued by their first chair ride, and Mrs. Sill's sister recorded: "John headed the procession, and the coolies did some audible groaning before they landed *him* at the Legation."

The house itself was in Korean style. Mrs. Sill was to write in the coming December that the cold was too much for "our large, airy residence and its seven coal stoves." The usual Korean heating was by flue under the floor, as in the little house Joseph Sill was to occupy while with the family. Joseph wrote that his house was "two kongs long," a kong being eight feet square.

Exchange of letters with those left behind was begun at once by this devoted family. Many of these letters are in the Michigan Historical Collections of the University. Mail left every two weeks, and few letters were dispatched that did not contain something optimistic, sometimes seemingly with little basis of fact, with respect to Mrs. Sill's health. She herself promised to write "until her wrists gave out." Ultimately, she wrote a few lines each day, making what she called a "journal letter" and mailing it weekly to one or the other of her children. Her letters of the later years form actually the bulk of the collection. They are very much easier reading than are those of her husband. The minister's own letters are in a perfect but tiny script unusual for a man of his bulk, robust strength, and energetic temperament. It is like engraving—on the head of a pin—and is literally more easily read with a reading glass than without.

Seoul was a city of about two hundred thousand. Dr. Allen had maintained the legation staff of servants, eighteen in all, including a major-domo who took full charge of everything, purchasing the food and supplying the personnel. Mrs. Sill and Mrs. Graham write very happily of this man, a Chinese. Probably never before and never afterward was their housekeeping easier. There were, in addition, a cook, an assistant cook, and a houseboy, all Chinese. The other fourteen servants were Koreans: two interpreters, four chair bearers, two gatekeepers, one groom (there was a pony or two), and five *kisus* or guards whose principal duty was to run ahead of a chair and shoo the people out of the way—sometimes with a vigor that would not have been appreciated in the Occident.

The last dispatch from Minister Heard to Secretary of State Gresham went out on May 16; the first by Minister Sill, on the following day. In this era of almost instant communication, it is a shock to come face to face with the pace of fifty years ago. Except in the case of the comparatively few cables, it took four to six weeks for Sill to communicate with his chief. The *Foreign Relations* volumes list the dates of a dispatch and of its receipt. It was the period of two exceedingly able Chinese statesmen, old Li Hung Chang, the great viceroy, and the younger Yuan Shih Kai, the powerful Chinese resident in Korea from 1885 till military developments forced him to leave hurriedly in 1894. Sill was to have two chiefs (not including the Republican under whom he served but briefly): Walter Q. Gresham, Cleveland's secretary of state until his death on May 28, 1895, and Richard Olney from June 10, 1895, to March 4, 1897. These two men had on their hands matters of far more importance than Korea—even when it became the scene of war between China and Japan; namely, the "Hawaiian Question" bequeathed by the Harrison administration (the record of this affair fills a *Foreign Relations* appendix of 1,400 closely printed pages), and, under Olney, the question of the Venezuelan boundary, wherein the United States antagonized Great Britain. The secretaries might perhaps be excused if at times they seemed merely annoyed by the intrusion of the little business of Korea and her neighbors.

Sill's dispatch of May 17 reported disorders in three southern provinces and fear of their spread, since the people, first stirred by an Oriental religious motive, had risen against the oppression of the government officials. At the king's request Sill had called the missionaries in from the interior. The minister felt that more frequent visits of American warships would have a salutary effect, and he had forwarded to Admiral Joseph S. Skerrett a request from the king for a warship to be sent now to Chemulpo. Sill was later to write on the basis of his experiences: "Admirals are a cocky lot."

After some initial discussion with the Korean officials about which palace gate the new minister should use, and his ultimatum that if the most exalted gate were not open when he got there he should turn around and go home, he had his first audience with the king on May 30. (It was the king who settled the gate question instantly on hearing of it.) The party included the minister, Secretary Allen, and Frank G. Carpenter, a well-known correspondent of that time, who described the occasion in several copyrighted columns cabled to American papers. The minister's audience naturally came first, then the secretary's, and then Carpenter's. The intrapalace distances were considerable, but ultimately the party arrived in the royal presence. On entering, the Korean escort of high nobles prostrated themselves, touching the floor with their foreheads. Sill wrote to his daughter of his own procedure: "On entering I made one of my most graceful bows." Then he advanced to within six feet of the king, where he stopped and made another bow "which was grace itself." From this point he delivered his speech prepared in the best palaver of diplomacy. Then he presented his letter of credence, which the king received in his own hand after waving away an official who offered to take it from the minister. Then followed a quarter of an hour of interpreted conversation based on His Majesty's flow of kindly questions:

> How was I? How was my health? How was my wife who, he had heard, was ill? How was Mr. Cleveland? Were all the people of the United States well? Of course I told him that every last one of my countrymen was in bully good health. How old was I? Did I like the climate? What did I think of Korea . . .

There was a withdrawal backward and then an audience with the crown prince. While Sill, with Occidental eyes, saw the humor in all this ceremony, he came genuinely to like and respect and sympathize with the king, who in turn liked and respected him and sought his counsel. In the letter in which he described the audience to his daughter, Sill further said he was sure there would be fighting, but that both the Chinese and the Japanese would take care not to injure Americans.

On the very next day the State Department dispatched to Sill the first of its "regrets," namely, that Secretary Allen had on April 6 asked the American Consul General at Shanghai to use his good offices to the end that a Korean political assassin be given up at the request of the Korean Government. Not infrequently the secretary of state, far from the scene of activity, was to repeat in effect: "You must not meddle."

Already the southern rebels had been wholly successful in their first encounter with government troops. For a century or two Korea had paid tribute to China and had acknowledged Chinese suzerainty. This arrangement was not much publicized, but apparently everybody knew it but the Japanese. Not unlikely, they knew it too, but their plans were better served by ignorance of it, and, therefore, they were ignorant. The Korean king now asked China to send troops to pacify the land, and after some hesitation Li Hung Chang sent first fifteen hundred and then seven hundred men to the southern provinces. This was unfortunate, inasmuch as before the troops could possibly render any aid the Korean forces themselves had defeated the rebels. Meanwhile, Japan, asserting that it was also her duty to keep the peace in her neighbor's territory, sent fifteen thousand first-class troops. These did not go into the disturbed south, but promptly occupied and fortified every strategic point from Chemulpo to Seoul, inclusive. Then the king asked the Chinese to withdraw, and China assented provided Japan also left. The affair promptly became a case of Oriental Alphonse and Gaston, and both the foreign armies stayed on with their helpless host. A fight became inevitable.

On June 22, Assistant Secretary Edwin F. Uhl, A.B. 1862,

A.M. 1865, cabled: "In view of the friendly interest of the United States in Korea and its people, you are, by direction of the President, instructed to use every possible effort for the preservation of peaceful conditions." Sill was later to be severely censured for overemphasis on the words "every possible effort," and for his assumption that what a government says today it will be willing to say tomorrow. By June 24 Sill began to "suspect Japan of ulterior motives." This was perhaps because Japan had asked the king point blank, though in the sweet language of diplomacy, whether his country was a Chinese vassal. To this the Koreans concocted a reply that gave them great Oriental satisfaction in that it was both perfectly truthful and wholly misleading. By the end of June, Sill had pried loose from Admiral Skerett a legation guard of 120 men, though Skerett sailed away again during the first week in July with most of his men. He did not notify Sill of his intention, which placed the latter "in a humiliating and most perilous position." Two warships reappeared at Chemulpo, however, by July 17.

Meanwhile, a Japanese officer and troops took offense at the near approach to one of their encampments by the British consul general, his wife, and two Englishmen while the four were on the highway; accordingly, they hustled, beat, and dragged the consul and forced his wife's chair into the roadside ditch. Demand for apology was met with a straight-faced denial of all the essentially offensive acts; the Englishmen were referred to by the Japanese general merely as "foreigners," and the capsheaf of insult was added by the statement that "the soldiers had not perceived any lady present." Tension was increasing.

On July 18, along with a report of this roadside fracas, Sill sent to Gresham a transcript of demands made upon Korea through the Japanese minister, Otori. These demands included:

Eleven to be discussed within three days and to be decided and put into operation within ten days.

Ten to be discussed and put into operation within six months.

Ten to be discussed and put into operation within two years.

Many of these in all three classes would, if met, necessitate basic changes in Korean policy, which were bound to be unwelcome, however much agreement there might be among Occidentals as to their basic desirability. Korea could scarcely consider them seriously and remain free from vassalage to Japan. Korea's situation could not be much ameliorated, either, by the foreword: "The urgent demand for putting these things into operation is made as advice by my Government, but your Government has a perfect right to take the advice or not." In place of the final two words Korea might as well have read "or else." Certainly no diplomat but a Japanese could have joined together the foreword and the demands.

In the midst of all these alarms sounding before he had been in Korea over sixty days, Sill's dispatches and his letters home show no lack of self-confidence and no doubt of his ability to deal with the situation capably and without emotion. For an "old man who had come to Korea to see the flowers," as Allen's biographer has designated him, he was doing remarkably well with all the nettles. About this time Secretary Gresham was sufficiently impressed with the importance of Korea and possible European reactions to write to Ambassador Bayard, LL.D. 1891, in London a long letter summarizing developments in "the feeble country whose helplessness engages our sympathy." But he strongly emphasized United States isolationism. To use a characteristically pat rural phrase, the secretary "felt deeply for the Koreans—but couldn't reach them."

Then at 4 A.M., July 23, 1894, Japanese troops broke into the palace and took full possession. A few soldiers were killed, both Korean guard and Japanese. Later in the day, on request of the king in his distress and with a Japanese pass, the diplomatic corps visited His Forlorn Majesty, whom Sill reported in this case as showing courage and self-possession. The city was in turmoil. The legation was filling up with refugees, and the guard it had had was gone. Two days later Sill had fifty marines from the "Baltimore."

The Japanese in their diplomatic intercourse blamed their

presence in Korea on the "equivocal attitude of China which prevented Korea from adopting needed reforms." There surely was nothing equivocal on the part of the Japanese in taking possession of the palace by force, whatever might be said of their comments on the event.

Two days later, on the twenty-fifth, there came another example of Japanese aggressiveness. China had leased a British ship, the "Kowshing," to carry troops to Korea, with provision in the lease that, should war be declared, the ship would at once return to a Chinese port, where the Chinese flag would replace the British. On July 25, sailing under the Union Jack with some fifteen hundred troops aboard, under a British captain and officer crew, and accompanied by a Chinese dispatch boat, the "Kowshing" was overhauled by four Japanese warships and commanded to follow into a Japanese port. The Chinese troops refused to permit the captain to obey this order, saying they would rather be drowned than captured. The Japanese took them at their word, and promptly torpedoed and sank the ship, British flag and all. The only surviving European was a German, Major von Hannekin, who after swimming several hours was picked up by a Korean junk.

Formal declaration of war by both countries followed within a week, and Japan placed her interests in China under United States protection; the Chinese placed their interests in Korea with the British. By August 16, Sill had notified Secretary Gresham that under Japanese pressure Korea had abrogated all previous agreements with China. Any savageness on the part of Japan was fully equaled by that of China. Charles Denby, American chargé in China, sent Gresham a Chinese government list of rewards, of varying values, offered for Japanese heads; the document reads like a game warden's list of bounties on a wide variety of noxious animals. On July 25, Korea, in writing, gave Japan a commission to expel all Chinese from the country.

From the point of view of contest it was not much of a war. The Japanese destroyed, one after another, Chinese armies and fleets; they captured stronghold after stronghold. China early began to try to secure peace. But since the Occidental powers would intervene only in mildest fashion, and since envoy after envoy from the Chinese was refused conference by Japan as not of sufficiently dignified status, these efforts were fruitless. From Pekin, Denby wrote to Gresham on November 4, "China will acknowledge independence of Korea and will pay indemnity." Her request "pathetically sets forth the sorrows of the Emperor and the Empress Dowager, and piteously invokes aid of foreign powers in this great crisis." Li Hung Chang was blamed and censured and to a certain degree degraded by deprivation of his principal imperial decorations, the Three-Eyed Peacock Feather and the Yellow Riding Jacket!

Japan meanwhile, according to Sill's dispatches, was showing great lack of wisdom in her Korean policy by so obviously coercing the king. Under pressure, a new set of reforms was almost daily recommended by the Korean Council for royal adoption. There were eighty of these in all from July 31 to August 28, and they ranged from the abolition of the pseudo-slavery of Korea and the management of the ginseng business, to the remarriage of widows and the length of sleeves. Sill significantly wrote that the promulgations by the King were "obeyed in Seoul." Outside Seoul there seemed to be no efficient government, and the authorities, so far as there were any, disregarded orders they believed forced from a helpless king. There was widespread mob rule, with all its horrors, Oriental style.

But in the midst of wars the Sills as a family pursued a peaceful line. They gave their first official dinner to the diplomatic corps on November 4. Mrs. Sill described pleasantly the table, the "sixty-five cream-colored roses," the place cards made by Mrs. Graham—and then her hand "gives out." They gave a Thanksgiving reception for "sixty foreigners" in Seoul, and in preparation for "an old fashioned Christmas" sent to China for a turkey. From Korean friends, Christmas brought to the minister "a pot of honey, one hundred eggs, six pheasants, walnuts, chestnuts, and a silver nail shield (for the finger)." To Mrs. Sill came fine cloth and mats from the queen, and from the Japanese legation, "most exquisitely made artificial flowers." On New Year's Day, "nearly eighty calls were received." Early in December, however, Joseph Sill had gone back to enter the University of Michigan, leaving a great void in the family circle. And there were other things to bring personal depression; in January Sill wrote to his daughter: "Again I have had to draw in advance for my salary in order to help out the Korean representatives in Washington"—surely a proof of friendship for the country to which he was accredited.

On January 7, 1895, the Japanese exacted from the king a new oath of office in fourteen sections—or perhaps "movements" is the word. One of the difficulties the Japanese had been having in their attempts to reform Korea rather significantly appeared in the section wherein the king swore that thereafter "Her Majesty the Queen, the royal secondary wife (concubine) and the royal relations shall not interfere" in political affairs. It would have been better for the queen and her clan, known as the Min family, had she lived up to this engagement of her royal spouse.

Finally, on May 10, 1895, a peace treaty ended the war. Li Hung Chang, himself, his Three-Eyed Peacock Feather and Yellow Riding Jacket restored, was received by the Japanese, though it was on this occasion that, upon his arrival in Japan, he was promptly shot in the face by a Japanese fanatic. He recovered, however, and negotiated the treaty, that is, he accepted the offered terms. Sill wrote his son the day the treaty was signed, "The tug is yet to come," in reference to the opposition on the part of Russia, France, and, perhaps also, England and Italy to Japan's having Port Arthur and the Manchurian peninsula.

The war was to have one more savage flare-up in Korea itself. The queen, implacably anti-Japanese and abler than her husband, continued to manipulate palace affairs, political and governmental. Meanwhile, Japan replaced as minister the comparatively gentle, if scheming, Count Inouye; his successor was Viscount Miura, who said of himself that he was "by profession a soldier with no experience in diplomacy," though he "had a diplomacy all his own which he proposed to try out in Korea." The sequel was the murder of the queen by some thirty Japanese in civilian dress who invaded the palace early in the morning of October 8, the day after Korea had dispatched a royal prince to thank Japan for liberating the country from China's yoke. Three of the queen's ladies met death with her. Her body was wrapped in cloth, soaked with kerosene, thrown outdoors, and burned.

Sill was on vacation in Japan, and Dr. Allen in response to the king's instant request hastened to the palace with the Russian resident. They found that the king's father, decrepit physically but not in mind, ambition, or ferocity, a long-time enemy of the queen and her family, was telling the king what to do and working hand in glove with the Japanese as they saw fit to use him. The queen's death was not "announced"—this for the double purpose of "degrading" her and her family (thus making all members ineligible to hold office) and of avoiding a three-year period of expensive mourning. The grounds for the "degradation" were that the queen had absented herself when the king needed her; that is, she was not dead but had fled away.

Sill hastened back and on October 26 cabled that Allen's conduct of affairs in the crisis had been "excellent." A few days later he cabled further that Count Inouye, who had been sent to replace the blunt Miura, would "restore" the king if the step were approved by the foreign powers and asked our State Department's permission to participate. Secretary Olney on November 11 cabled curtly: "Intervention in political concerns of Korea not among your functions and is forbidden." On November 20, there arrived another cable in the same tenor, followed by a long letter dated November 21 elaborating on this theme. On December 1, long before this letter was received, a loyalist uprising to free the king occurred in Seoul. The movement was abortive, though furthered in its initial steps by three revolver-armed missionaries inside the palace grounds, to which they had secured admission on legation cards furnished them by Allen.

To Sill and Allen sitting in the capital of the "forlorn little Kingdom" and moved by daily talks with the "forlorn little King," it was impossible that a fellow man, even at a distance of ten thousand miles, could be so bloodless and automatic as Olney. The legation was full of refugees who, if surrendered, would be first tortured and then killed by the bloody old man who, with the backing of Japan, had possession of the king. Sill wanted to know if he might send these unfortunates out on the "Yorktown." His cable was promptly answered by a dispatch from Olney packed with refusal and frigidity: "The Department sees with disfavor your disposition to forget . . ." On January 10, 1896, Olney cabled again: "Your course in continued intermeddling in Korean political affairs in violation of repeated instructions noted with astonishment and emphatic disapproval. Cable briefly any explanations you have to make. Also answer whether you intend to comply with instructions given."

The next day there was dispatched more of the same in letter form, with severe express disapproval of Sill for having communicated to the king in an interview his satisfaction that the royal decree degrading the queen had been revoked. In general almost the whole of Sill's course since the queen's murder, including the acts of Allen which Sill had manfully taken on his own shoulders, was condemned. Even the missionaries who had been consistently favored by the Department came in for a reprimand because of their very human reactions to the way their friends had been treated by the conquerors:

> You should on receipt of the present instructions, inform all Americans resident in Korea that they should strictly refrain from any expressions of opinion, or from giving advice concerning the internal management of the country, or from inter meddling in political questions. . . . They should strictly confine themselves to their missionary work, whether it be teaching in schools, preaching the gospel, or attending the sick, for which they went to the country. Use such other

arguments as you properly can to discourage and stop, if possible, the habit which has steadily increased since the arrival of American citizens in Korea, of irresponsible persons advising and attempting to control through irregular channels the Government of the country.

This was a considerable order. Imagine American citizens, ten thousand miles from final authority, on secretarial fiat, giving up their birthright by bottling up their sympathies! Olney must have known this himself as his petulance and his "if possible" indicate. Olney was correct, but Sill and Allen were human, and at times most of us prefer to be human, right or wrong.

But at last Sill had to believe that Olney meant it. There was no use arguing with a superior whose veins ran neutral icewater. Sill first cabled on January 13 and then wrote on January 20 his regrets for the past and his resolves for the future. A more imaginative man than Richard Olney might have read into Sill's letter of January 20, 1896, a still burning wonder that such things as Sill had seen could be regarded in Washington merely as within routine.

The remainder of Sill's term, to judge from available records, was less troubled. During part of the king's detention by the Japanese, his fear of poisoning was so great that wives of missionaries prepared his food for him. (Had Mr. Olney been informed, would he have regarded preparation of the "royal victuals" as involving the interior affairs of the government?) The measure that most stimulated the successful plot for the king's escape had to Occidental eyes its comic side. By Japanese-instigated royal decree the Korean "topknot" was outlawed. This monumental hair-do was the Korean badge of manhood; to give it up would be a national humiliation. Farmers refused to bring food to town for fear they would be seized and barbered, and there was a really serious uprising. If his majesty could only escape from Japanese hands there would be an end to such tyranny. Thus, very early in the morning of February 11, 1896, when a palace woman known to the guards passed out in her chair accompanied by a coolie and another woman on foot, none of the party was stopped. The "coolie" was in fact the king, and the "other woman" was the crown prince. Once outside they made all haste to the Russian legation, where they were given hospitality for a year. From there the king instantly revoked the "topknot" decree and numerous other decrees. Greatly encouraged, loyal Koreans developed mob man hunts, with unfortunate results for many collaborators with the Japanese, among them five cabinet ministers. The loyal minister of foreign affairs wrote Sill a note in which he observed, "very sorry that traitors were killed in accident without legal trial."

The present writer has omitted practically all references to the ubiquitous activities of Secretary Allen in behalf of the interests of Americans who were in Korea strictly as businessmen rather than as missionaries; or of several among the latter group who did not overlook what they regarded as their reasonable opportunities. Allen gave far more attention than Sill to the "development" of the country in trade, transportation, industry, and mining, obtaining, during Sill's time, American concessions for mines and a railroad. Sill signed the reports concerning these, and he may, though it seems unlikely, have known all about them. The coming of the Japanese, the Russians, and then the Japanese again, wrecked some of these enterprises as American ventures. A chief result for the two men of "Allen's work for Sill's credit" was that the business people on the ground, wanting "more of the same"—and even the king—were for Allen when the choice had to be made between him and Sill.

In spite of lifelong and sincere Democratic affiliations, Sill, like a good many others, had been thoroughly anti-Bryan. He wrote to his son in America that there was no need to justify the latter's vote for McKinley: "Had I been at home I should have voted as you did had I believed it necessary in order to defeat the wild schemes of the Chicago lunatics who paraded as Democrats." Mrs. Sill wrote in November, 1896, that they "had news of the election of McKinley, for which we feel thankful although it probably means that your Father will have his successor appointed. But in such a crisis as this has been, no true American could possibly let any selfish motive have any influence." For eight months more the family was not finally to know its diplomatic fate, and it was ten months before the complementary letters of recall and appointment arrived. Somewhat earlier Mrs. Sill had written, "Your Father is very happy here, and now that his debts are out of the way each year here means adding to his capital." The Sills were no longer young, he had no position or even a house of his own to which to return, the suspense itself was humiliating, and the anxiety they felt was pathetically natural. In April, 1897, when they were packing in preparation for what they regarded as the inevitable, Mrs. Sill wrote, "Every month we are actually here we are a few hundred dollars better off." If their son's college course could once be finished, "we will get along comfortably if all goes well." Happily, they did not know for how short a period they would have to "get along."

Meanwhile, Mrs. Sill recorded life in the legation with its problems of the household and of officialdom. There was more illness, more pain. The summer of 1897 was the "rainingest" rainy season they had ever had—nearly fifty inches in all, with "mould on everything." "The rain keeps the city cleaner but it is not favorable for rheumatism," she wrote. In mid-July, after a large militia of pots and pans had been marshaled to catch drips from leaks, the chimney and part of the roof of the guest room "fell in with a fearful crash," and three days later the corridor roof collapsed. That day Mrs. Sill wrote to her son, "Heat is no name, rain is no name, disagreeable is no name for the weather today." That same day a "big stoat" got into the house and could not be located. A month before these calamities, she had written that recent days had passed "about the same as usual—company, company, company." Between the roof collapses, she wrote, "Just the same program as usual today—packing, tired-out, and visitors." She "believed she was getting more homesick all the time."

If Korea had become more important during the Sill regime, with growing realization by Koreans that the very survival of their country necessitated that contacts with the outer world be sought, not avoided, the pattern of its politics had not changed much. In August, 1896, Mrs. Sill observed, "Plots are so thick that someone is coming almost hourly to see your Father and to consult with him . . . This Cabinet has been in power about as long as usual and it is time for ructions to take place." Four days later: "Seems to be quieting down; a number of arrests . . . but no murders." In December came another plot with the same concomitants, including the multitude of native and foreign "consultors" coming to the minister's office. (The isolationist secretaries of state in Washington did not have to meet the diplomatic problems at the grass roots where they sprouted and flourished.) In April, Mrs. Sill's sister, who had become an amateur photographer of local note, was officially asked by the individuals concerned to take photographs of all the Korean cabinet members; regarding these likenesses Mrs. Sill commented: "They should have historical value since unless things governmental have materially changed some of the sitters will be massacred before they are 'off with the old and on with the new.' "

There must have been a great strain in the relationship between the Sill and Allen families during the months following the mid-January day when Mrs. Sill wrote, "Dr. Allen is very anxious to secure the place here for himself and will leave no stone unturned to get it," until that other day exactly six months later when she recorded that Allen had received by cable notice of his appointment and "seems to be very much elated." But however tense the strain, no single bitter word appears in any of the collection of family letters. Mrs. Sill and Mrs. Allen were socially together every few days, with Mrs. Sill reporting pleasure in such meetings, and the families met at dinners which must have been matters of invitation between them. On July 25 Mrs. Sill wrote to her son, "You never saw anyone so delighted as the Allens are, and for their sakes I am glad he has the appointment." At the hour of the auction sale of their household goods, the Sills all went over to the Allens, a tactful thing to do from two points of view. If there was such a "quarrel" as Professor Harrington mentions on page 294 of his story about Allen, there is no trace of it in the Sill family correspondence recording the current relations of the two families during a six-month period. Even in the Harrington record of the "quarrel," Sill's part of it was dignified; Allen's was not. "Sill charged that Allen had gone back on his word after promising assistance. It was not so, shrieked Allen, Sill was 'small,' a 'liar,' a 'spoiled old man in his dotage.' "

In any event, John M. B. Sill's retreat from the glory of diplomacy was far more that of a well-poised, self-controlled man of the world than was that of Dr. Horace N. Allen eight years later. "Rich and ambitious," "pompous," "contemptible," "hypocritical character," were some of the terms in which, while still in Korea, Allen then referred to his own successor.

The Sills left Seoul on September 23, 1897, shortly after Sill had had a siege of malaria. Both of the "well" members of the family had been ill, and Mrs. Sill on the journey to Japan reported herself as "really the strongest of the family." But her own illness was to delay them two weeks in Los Angeles, where they arrived November 7. They reached Detroit on one of the last days of that month.

Mr. Sill's health was plainly not what it had been, but after his return, he still had in him one last public service which, like his first, was in the field of education. At that time election to the Detroit Board of Education was from the individual city wards. Membership in the Board of Education thus became the first step on the political ladder, with the result that the public schools were drawn inescapably into the area of local politics. Frederick L. Bliss, A.B. 1877, A.M. (*hon.*) 1901, long principal of the Detroit High School, and founder of the Detroit University School, on the invitation of a group of citizens outlined a new idea in public school administration which won their confidence and approval and led to the formation of a Citizens Committee on Education. The plan was two-fold: first it provided for a small board of education elected at large, and second, for assigning to a superintendent of schools the educational program and to a business manager the business functions of the school system.

The plan was submitted to leading educators of the country and won their hearty approval. It met, however, with immediate political opposition. Inasmuch as legislation, state as well as local, was necessary, its advocacy led to two years of public discussion involving many meetings, much newspaper debate, and numerous pamphlets, as well as exciting ward elections. In the end dominant political interests defeated the plan by a close vote in the legislature. But this "end" was only a beginning, for some fifteen years later the plan was adopted for Detroit after having won wide acceptance in hundreds of cities throughout the country, including many in Michigan.

As a member of the Citizens Committee on Education, Sill devoted almost the whole of his time to its work. He spoke, he wrote, and he labored indefatigably. He was one whose efforts were respected even by those who opposed him; his wit and humor softened many tense occasions; and the arguments he left for his successors to use contributed to the final victory for the plan years after he was gone.

He and his wife had only a few brief years with the children and grandchildren for whom they had yearned throughout their Korean days. Mr. Sill died in Detroit on April 6, 1901, and Mrs. Sill survived her husband only until February 23, 1903.

Henry Thomas Thurber

1853	*Born in Monroe, Michigan*
1874	*Graduated from the University of Michigan*
1877	*Admitted to the bar of Michigan*
	Began practice with Griffin and Dickinson in Detroit
1880	*Married Elizabeth Brady Croul*
1893	*Appointed private secretary to President Cleveland*
1897	*Resumed the practice of law in Detroit*
1898	*Mrs. Thurber died*
1904	*Died in Detroit, Michigan*

Henry T. Thurber

Henry T. Thurber

By Fred G. Dewey

ONE of Grover Cleveland's immediate tasks in 1892, after having been elected President for the second time, was to choose a private secretary. Daniel S. Lamont, who had ably served him in that capacity when he was governor of New York and during his first administration in Washington, was not available, for the President-elect had selected him for his secretary of war.

Lamont, who had been a newspaperman and a clerk in the New York Assembly, was so thoroughly conversant with New York politics that his advice had been invaluable to Cleveland as governor. In Washington, he quickly mastered the problems of the larger field and remained a favorite adviser of the President. Indeed, Lamont is said to have been "the first presidential secretary to give that position the importance it has held ever since." For him it became the steppingstone to a cabinet office, as it did also for George B. Cortelyou, who, entering the White House as a stenographer for Cleveland and remaining to serve both William McKinley and Theodore Roosevelt as private secretary, later became postmaster general and secretary of the treasury.

The position of private secretary to the President was one of responsibility. The secretary had to be affable, tactful, industrious, discreet, and loyal. Besides receiving the President's mail and answering a large part of it, he had to meet the daily throng of people who were determined to talk with the President. It was his task to turn away the great majority without hurting their feelings, usually by directing them to some other government official. The secretary also represented the President on many occasions when he himself could not be present, and he frequently served as a link between the chief executive and legislative leaders.

Don M. Dickinson, who helped Cleveland to select his Cabinet, suggested that one of his partners in Detroit, Henry T. Thurber, was just the man for the position of private secretary. The President-elect, who was acquainted with Thurber, gratefully accepted the recommendation and formally offered him the position.

Henry T. Thurber was born in Michigan. His father, Jefferson G. Thurber, a native of New Hampshire, had settled in Monroe when Michigan was still a territory. He had taught school, had studied law, and had begun to practice when he was twenty-six years old. Within six years he had served as prosecuting attorney, had married a girl from his native state, and had been elected judge of probate on the Democratic ticket. Subsequently he became state representative, speaker of the house, and state senator. In 1840 he was a delegate to the national convention of his party and later was presidential elector. Of his six children the youngest were twins, born April 23, 1853, and were named Mary Darrah and Henry Thomas Thurber.

Many years later a biographer asserted that Henry T. Thurber had been born with a silver spoon in his mouth. The evidence scarcely warrants the use of the phrase. His father died when the boy was three years old, leaving, it is true, a name honored in his community, and a widow who brought up her children in an atmosphere of culture and religion. Henry was graduated from high school as valedictorian of his class. But there seems to be no reason to suppose that he was favored beyond the average carefully reared small-town boy who lived in congenial surroundings and acquired an education.

At the age of seventeen the young man matriculated at the University of Michigan, enrolling in the classical course leading to the degree of Bachelor of Arts. The four years, 1870–74, that Thurber spent in Ann Arbor happened to be momentous ones for the University. Co-education had its beginning in 1870, and in this, his freshman year, eleven women enrolled in the Literary Department to join their pioneer sister co-ed, Miss Madelon L. Stockwell, who had been admitted the preceding February. The inauguration of James B. Angell as president of the University occurred on June 28, 1871. This marked the beginning of a new epoch in University history. On the same day, the cornerstone of University Hall was laid. On October 8, 1873, at the opening of Thurber's senior year, the building was dedicated.

Thurber took part in the student activities; he appeared in amateur theatricals, and was an editor of the *Palladium* in his senior year, in short, was an average, but not especially prominent, college student. He was sociable by nature, and men who were on the campus at the turn of the century recall his visits to his fraternity, Zeta Psi, and his inexhaustible store of interesting and delightful reminiscences. From the class history we are able to picture the young graduate in June, 1874, somewhat as follows: he was twenty-one years old, five feet eight inches tall, and weighed 140 pounds. He was fair, blue-eyed, and his coloring gave him what used to be called a sandy complexion. His manner was frank and pleasing, and a twinkle in his eye bespoke his enjoyment of a good story. His home was given as West Lebanon, New Hampshire, because his mother, who had remarried after her children were grown, was living there. The class historian records that Henry T. Thurber intended to become a lawyer.

When, shortly thereafter, he began to read law in the office of Griffin and Dickinson in Detroit, young Thurber was following the usual method of entering the legal profession. The qualifications of a lawyer in Michigan had always been determined by the courts. Any citizen of full age who had a good moral character and sufficient learning in the law to represent clients and to assist the courts in carrying on their business might be admitted to practice by the supreme court or by any circuit court on motion by a member of the bar. When such a candidate presented himself, the judge occasionally examined the prospective lawyer, but usually he appointed a committee of two or three lawyers to interrogate the would-be member of the bar and to make a report. The proceedings were highly informal, and there was no uniformity in the various circuits; the length of time which the young man must spend in his legal studies was not prescribed, and the examination covered only so much of the field of jurisprudence, procedure, and practice as the examiner at the time considered necessary.

An increasing number of young men who planned to become lawyers were turning to the law schools of the country to obtain the fundamentals of their profession. One might wonder why young Thurber, after obtaining his bachelor's degree, did not continue formal study at the University in the Law School. To take both a bachelor's degree and a law degree, however, was as yet an unusual procedure; the common alternatives for most who could afford university training were a bachelor's degree and law office training or simply a law school degree. Thurber chose the former alternative, perhaps because of his youth when he entered the University. The student personnel of the Law Department was made up largely of men considerably beyond college freshman age.

The Law Department had been established in 1859, with a course consisting of two terms of six months each. The first faculty numbered three, of whom Thomas M. Cooley was the only professor in residence. The other two lecturers were Justice James V. Campbell, of the State Supreme Court, and C. I. Walker, a prominent member of the bar in Detroit. Campbell was the only one of the three who could boast a degree.

Instruction was entirely by lectures, but students were urged to seek the advice of professors as to which textbooks to buy. The announcements emphasized the superiority of law school instruction over the training offered in a law office, and in 1884 featured the following excerpt from the American Bar Association committee's 1879 report:

> There is little, if any, dispute now as to the relative merit of education by means of law schools, and that to be got by mere practical training or apprenticeship as an attorney's clerk. Without disparagement of mere practical advantages, the verdict of the best informed is in favor of the schools.

The lecturers included prominent lawyers, chiefly from Detroit. Levi T. Griffin, the senior member of the firm with which Thurber was first associated, was one of those who spoke before the law students of the University, and for more than a generation leaders of the bar journeyed to Ann Arbor to lecture in the great law school of the West. It is probable, however, that fully half of the lawyers in Michigan who were Thurber's contemporaries had been admitted to practice without a degree and without classroom training.

In 1877, when Thurber was admitted to the practice of law, the bar of Wayne County consisted of about two hundred and fifty attorneys. At first the young lawyer remained in the office of Griffin and Dickinson, but before long he and George S. Hosmer were taken into partnership. The senior member withdrew after a time, and the firm was continued as Dickinson, Thurber, and Hosmer. When, in 1887, Hosmer began his career as circuit judge, his place was taken by Elliott G. Stevenson. This man was pre-eminently suited to the needs of the partnership. A year younger than Thurber, he was by nature not only a stronger advocate than Hosmer, but probably the equal of Dickinson himself, lacking only the prestige of the senior member. He was a prodigious worker and able to take over pending litigation when Dickinson shortly left active practice to become postmaster general.

In the estimate of the layman the successful lawyer is the trial lawyer. The drama of the courtroom, the handling of witnesses on cross-examination, the moving appeals to the jury, the occasional clashes with opposing counsel or with the court —these are the things which stir the imagination of newspaper reporters and the reading public. But the work of the office lawyer is behind the scenes. His brethren at the bar will recognize the importance of his legal acumen, his familiarity with statutes and decisions, his skill and judgment in drafting contracts, or his ability to marshal his material and write cogent briefs for appellate courts, but outside his profession little will be known of his abilities.

Whether or not Henry T. Thurber would have developed

forensic ability cannot be known. The senior partner at all times had other juniors to assist in the trial of cases. Thus, Thurber was destined for other work and for fifteen years was involved in a wide variety of legal problems. The foundation of the firm's business was commercial law. It not only represented the leading merchants of Detroit, but wholesalers from New York and other cities became clients, and Thurber frequently was called upon to handle doubtful accounts in Detroit and elsewhere. This led to cases involving mortgages, foreclosures, assignments for the benefit of creditors, attachments, and receiverships. The business of banks, insurance companies, and public utilities came in due course. The firm was drawn into litigation over such large estates as that in the Rivard will case and the estate of George H. Hammond. It represented R. G. Dun and Company in a libel action; it defended the Evening News Association on a like charge, and at one time or another was counsel for every Detroit newspaper with one exception. Briefs were filed in many jurisdictions; in Illinois (protection of the corporate lien on stock for a debt of the stockholder as against the claim of a pledgee), in New York (right of a corporation to be sued where domiciled), and in Tennessee (seeking habeas corpus for a farmer whose conviction for violation of the Sabbath by plowing his field had been upheld by the state Supreme Court). On several occasions Thurber crossed the Atlantic on legal business. The broad scope of his legal experience is amply apparent.

In 1880 Henry T. Thurber married Elizabeth Brady Croul. Her family was prominent in Detroit, and her grandfather was General Hugh Brady, a veteran of General Anthony Wayne's western campaign and the War of 1812. The bride not only enjoyed the best social standing, but was pretty, charming, and popular in her own right. Four children were born to the Thurbers in Detroit—Donald M. Dickinson, Marion, Henry Thomas, and Elizabeth, the last-named in 1893 after her father had assumed his duties in Washington.

Thurber received the offer of the position of private secretary to the President on February 24, 1893. In Detroit there was some doubt about the likelihood of his being willing to exchange his legal work, which was estimated to produce an annual income of $10,000 to $15,000, for a position with a salary of only $5,000. When newspaper reporters asked him if he could afford to go to Washington, he was quoted as replying:

> Afford to go? There is nothing to be considered except Mr. Cleveland's call. I hope he is not mistaken in his confidence in and judgment of me, but he thinks that I can serve him, and I shall go. I would rather leave my children the record that he summoned me, that I accepted, and, above all, that I in some measure, fulfilled in his service his expectations of me, than to leave them a great fortune.

Don M. Dickinson told newsmen:

> My boys [Stevenson, incidentally, was thirty-eight and Thurber thirty-nine years of age] are a part of my life, and I would not give up either of them on any other demand than that of the chief. Mr. Stevenson and I have agreed to buckle to it, and to do Mr. Thurber's work, as well as our own, and we will keep his office, his chair, and his desk ready for him. He has an extra sense—tact; and that temperament of his is a sure comfort to all about him in time of perplexity and trial.

The news of Thurber's appointment was hailed in Michigan as a compliment to the state. Editors of Democratic and Republican papers alike praised the President for his discernment in choosing the right man, and Thurber for his capability. The new secretary was described variously as bright, industrious, affable, discreet, tactful, tireless; he was lauded for his sound judgment, splendid business ability, and great intellectual force.

As soon as it was known that Thurber had accepted the appointment, more than a hundred leading citizens of Detroit, both Democrats and Republicans, invited him to attend a farewell banquet in his honor at the Detroit Club. Thurber, obviously pleased by the invitation, nevertheless declined with thanks because he had to leave at once for Washington. Upon his arrival at the capital, Major E. W. Halford, private secretary to President Harrison, took him to the White House and explained to him the duties of his office.

President-elect Cleveland, Dickinson, and Thurber stayed at the Arlington Hotel until the inauguration. Dickinson had secured Thurber's appointment, in part at least, for the purpose of protecting the "Chief" against inquisitive newspaper reporters and importunate office seekers. Thurber assumed this duty at once, much to the disappointment of the people who thronged the hotel insisting on seeing Mr. Cleveland.

On March 4, laying his hand upon his mother's Bible, the new private secretary took the oath of office. After the inaugural parade, he and Mr. and Mrs. Dickinson and a few other guests had dinner at the White House with the President and Mrs. Cleveland.

The retiring secretary in a newspaper interview expressed the opinion that four-fifths of the President's time was taken up with matters of appointment to office. Certain it is that Thurber found himself in a welter of confusion. Hordes of office seekers descended on the capital; assorted Democratic organizations from various cities were on hand to demonstrate their party loyalty and incidentally to urge appointments of deserving members, and a mountain of telegrams and letters was piled on every desk and table in the secretary's office.

A few days after the inauguration Thurber set rules for the purpose of regulating visiting hours and furnished copies of them to the press. These rules aided the secretary in systematizing his work, yet even so, a great deal of his time and energy throughout the term was consumed by callers, the majority of whom had to be persuaded that their business could be taken care of without a personal interview with the President of the United States. Three weeks after the inauguration letters and telegrams still numbered eight hundred in a single day.

In addition to letters, official documents of many kinds, including bills which had been passed by Congress, came to the secretary's desk. He read them through, made a digest of each, and laid them before the President. Together they discussed the most important papers, the President sometimes asking

Thurber's advice. When such a conference was over, Thurber retired to his office, called his secretary, and dictated to him the President's decisions. It was his rule to complete each day's work before going home. Frequently, he remained until midnight, and during the fortnight before Congress adjourned he was at his desk until three or four o'clock in the morning.

The newspapers in general reacted favorably to the new secretary. The correspondents described him as a man of medium height, compactly built, with iron gray hair and close-clipped "burnsides." His manner impressed them as courteous, dignified and pleasant. They compared him with Daniel Lamont, the new secretary of war, who had been private secretary in the first Cleveland administration, and speculated as to whether this young man of thirty-nine, unknown to the arena of politics, could carry on as well as had his predecessor. They noted with approval his tact and energy.

Of course, correspondents of opposition newspapers, on the alert for some new means to criticize the administration, did not overlook any of Thurber's foibles. His genuine admiration of Cleveland was pictured as exaggerated reverence and awe. His dignity and formality gave rise to observations that he was too serious and his language too stilted. A Washington reporter wrote a fourth of a column about the secretary's whiskers; a Philadelphia paper found space to record that he wore brown spats over morocco slippers, and in Louisville a cartoonist depicted him in livery, with knee breeches and silver-buckled shoes, brushing a Prince Albert coat of enormous girth.

It remained for an editorial writer on the *New York Tribune* to combine the acme of sarcasm with a new low in common sense. The depression of 1893 had thrown thousands out of work, and, as always, the administration was charged with the catastrophe. Dickinson wrote to his former partner to "look out for the Great Chief." Well aware that suffering makes men desperate, Thurber saw to it that additional sentries were stationed about the White House grounds. "These extra-ordinary precautions," sneered the editor, "which the ever-faithful

Thurber has taken to guard the sacred person of the Consecrated One from the rude contact of the common herd have provoked unfavorable criticism from old-fashioned Americans, who resent the idea of surrounding the chief executive with armed men." Six years later Cleveland's successor became the third president to fall under the bullets of an assassin.

Thurber had reason enough to resort to "extra-ordinary precautions." Dozens of disturbing letters came to his desk, some of them containing direct threats against the President, and others warned that dangerous men were plotting to assassinate him. One read: "I am an old man, but I can kill you if I am. You are a big thing to shoot at." A group calling themselves Populists wrote in red ink: "We write to you in letters of blood to show we are mad . . . your life is not safe . . ." A police chief, "an old democrat" of Shenandoah, Virginia, warned the President that he had overheard a gang of tramps planning to join Coxey's Army and go to Washington to destroy Cleveland and his Cabinet with a dynamite bomb. Another writer reported a plot to kidnap the Cleveland children.

Some of these letters bear the notation, in red pencil, "eccentric" or "crank," but others were turned over to the Treasury Department with a request for investigation by the secret service. Reports by operatives indicate that there was real concern about the danger to the President.

In August, 1894, after Coxey's Army had arrived and been dispersed, the detectives were dismissed, probably because of the continued editorial clamor, and the newspapers reported that only Secretary Thurber accompanied the President on his drives. Nevertheless, guards were retained at Gray Gables, the President's summer home, to protect Mrs. Cleveland and the children.

Many of Thurber's social duties were pleasant. He represented the President at the spring dinner of the Gridiron Club and acquitted himself handsomely in a brief and witty after-dinner speech; he arranged the entertainment of visitors from various foreign countries; on occasions, he attended church with Mrs. Cleveland. Mrs. Thurber came to Washington in

October of 1893, and congenial and lasting friendships promptly developed between the two households. Occasionally, when free from the exactions of office, the President and his secretary spent an evening at the theater with their wives. But the common bond between the two young matrons was the children. Ruth Cleveland was about the age of the third of the Thurber children, and invitations to junior social events have been preserved, some of them printed in capital letters with a pencil on the White House stationery, and others written (by the maternal amanuensis) and subscribed "Wuf."

Politically, the closing months of the Cleveland administration constituted a period of anxiety for conventional Democrats. The free-silver movement was steadfastly opposed by Cleveland, as well as by Don M. Dickinson and Henry Thurber. In 1896 when Bryan was nominated by the Democrats at Chicago, Dickinson left his party and threw himself into the campaign to swing Michigan to the side of the Republicans. Thurber though less active in campaigning was also an anti-Bryan man; the third partner, Elliott G. Stevenson, opposed the free-silver doctrine, but refused to break with his party, with the result that he withdrew from the firm and opened a law office of his own.

When Henry Thurber returned from Washington in the spring of 1897, he took an extended vacation and a much-needed rest. He seemed to have been somewhat undecided as to his future course. The pleadings in a few law cases were endorsed with the names of Dickinson and Thurber, but eventually Thurber withdrew and opened an office in the Peninsular Bank Building, where he devoted himself principally to business interests. He was one of the promoters of the Detroit, Ypsilanti, and Ann Arbor electric railway and spent considerable time in securing the necessary franchises. He was a director of the company and also of the Ward Lumber Company. The generally successful character of these and various other enterprises with which he was connected bespeaks his sound business judgment.

With his wife and his five children * comfortably settled on Jefferson Avenue, Henry Thurber faced a future which promised success and happiness. He was in the prime of life, and he moved in the best social circles and belonged to the leading clubs. Family ties between the Thurber brothers and sisters had always been close, and, although the eldest had for many years been pastor of the American church in Paris, the other brother and two of the sisters, Mrs. Talcott E. Wing and Mrs. Herbert Dunlap, were living in Detroit; the third sister, Miss Julia Thurber, divided her time between Paris and Detroit. But a cruel blow was impending. Mrs. Thurber was stricken and died on May 3, 1898. She was only thirty-eight years old.

Probably no other letters of Grover Cleveland mirror so closely the human side of the man as those written to his former secretary between 1897 and 1904. There is little of politics in them. Scattered through the pages are names of friends and cronies; Joe Jefferson, the actor, and other mutual friends figure in the whimsical accounts of past fishing and shooting trips and plans for future ones. Cleveland repeatedly urges Thurber to visit Gray Gables, reminding him at one time that the Clevelands do not consider their vacation a success "without more or less of Thurber in it." And in all the letters are affectionate references to his own children and inquiries and good wishes for the Thurber "chicks." Referring to a visit of Thurber and his daughter Marion,† which he says was all too short, he concludes, "How lucky you and I are in having such nice children!"

The career of Henry T. Thurber was cut short before he reached his fifty-first birth anniversary. Stricken by appendicitis he died at St. Mary's Hospital in Detroit on March 17, 1904, more than four years before the death of the "Chief," whom he had served so faithfully and well.

At the end of the third year of his second administration Cleveland wrote a letter to Don M. Dickinson in which he re-

* The youngest, born in Washington, was named Cleveland Thurber. He is now a leading member of the Detroit bar.

† Later the wife of Edwin Denby, LL.B. 1896, secretary of the navy, 1921–24.

corded his unhappiness because of "ingrates and traitors who wear the stolen livery of Democracy." But in this letter is a passage which may well stand as the epitome of the character of Henry T. Thurber:

> As to Mr. Thurber, I can honestly say that of all things you have done for me, I regard your suggestion of his selection as private secretary the most useful and fortunate. He has plenty of ability, good discretion, a pure heart and conscience, unquestioned honesty, sufficient tact, and is as loyal and devoted a helper as I ever had about me.

Edwin Fuller Uhl

1841	*Born in Rush Township, near Avon, New York*
1844	*Moved to "The Plains" near Ypsilanti, Michigan*
1862	*Graduated from the University of Michigan*
1864	*Admitted to the bar of Michigan*
1865	*Married Alice Follett*
1871	*Elected prosecuting attorney of Washtenaw County*
1876	*Moved to Grand Rapids*
1890	*Elected mayor of Grand Rapids*
1892	*Elected delegate-at-large from Michigan to the Democratic National Convention*
	Member of Whitney conference in New York City
	Placed the name of Allen B. Morse of Ionia in nomination for the vice-presidency
1893	*Appointed assistant secretary of state*
1894	*Nominated for the position of United States senator from Michigan*
1895	*Decided the Misiones boundary controversy between Brazil and Argentina*
	Brought about the settlement of the "Alliance" incident with Spain
	Made an official tour of Europe and recommended reform of the consular service
1896	*Appointed ambassador to Germany*
1899	*Retired from public life*
1901	*Died in Grand Rapids, Michigan*

Edwin F. Uhl

Edwin F. Uhl

By Earl D. Babst

THE first time I ever saw Mr. Uhl was in the Wagner murder trial at Ann Arbor. He was prosecuting attorney of Washtenaw County, and the murder had been committed in the store next to the one in which I was at that time at work. As a lad of fifteen years I took much interest in the trial of this case and attended court every day. Mr. Uhl appeared like an Apollo to me and in his treatment of the court and the witnesses and jurors, a veritable Lord Chesterfield. His manner during that trial made an impression upon my mind which I have carried ever since.

These are the words of George P. Wanty, LL.B. 1878, A.M. (*hon.*) 1903, long an outstanding lawyer and United States district judge of the Western District of Michigan.

The background of that courtroom scene of the early seventies in which Edwin Fuller Uhl, A.B. 1862, A.M. 1865, took part is to be found in the often repeated history of a Michigan pioneer family. When one reads or thinks of the country's frontier, one ordinarily visualizes a belt of travel or of settlement moving westward more or less uniformly. This is far from the fact. There are many variants. The state of Ohio, for example, had flourishing settlements on the Ohio River and later on Lake Erie, but the central part of the state, even after the Indian treaty of 1817 (personally negotiated by Lewis Cass) remained a frontier wilderness considered unfit for settlement. The contrast is even greater in the state of Michigan.

The belief that Brulé, the French lad whom Champlain sent into the wilderness in 1610, was the first white man to paddle the northern waters of Michigan may not be substantiated, but there is ample proof that Champlain's Récollet mission settled on the present Georgian Bay in 1615, and that Nicolet and his Huron paddlers entered the Straits of Mackinac in 1634 and crossed to Green Bay in present-day Wisconsin. Furthermore, there are those almost unbelievable dates of the early missions and settlements, 1641 marking the first attempt of the Jesuits at Sault Ste Marie, and 1668 that of Father Marquette on the present-day Michigan side of the Straits, soon to be followed by establishments at Michilimackinac and St. Ignatius.

The white man probably looked upon the northern waters of Michigan before the Pilgrims set foot on Plymouth Rock, and the settlements on their shores are older than the settlement of Charleston, South Carolina. In dramatic contrast, the southern part of Michigan, aside from Detroit, still in 1830 was on the country's frontier. Washtenaw County, including Ypsilanti and Ann Arbor, had a population of 4,042, and the entire state only 31,639, although it had doubled in a ten-year period. The change had come with the completion of the Erie Canal in 1825, and the resulting flow of pioneer settlers from New York and New England.

Lured from Germany, Holland, and France by the promising lands, the ancestors of that virile young Washtenaw prosecuting attorney had come two hundred years before into colonial America. On both sides of his family there are records and monuments of a long sojourn on the Hudson River, especially in Staatsburg, Rhinebeck, and Poughkeepsie. His father and mother, David Mulford Uhl and Katharine de Garmo, had been neighbors in Dutchess County, New York, and, following their marriage, they had responded to the restless urge of those pioneer days to journey westward in search of a new home. They became "settlers," a general term descriptive of those brave pioneers whose migrations are now treasured as part of the American Epic.

They settled first in Rush Township, near Avon, Livingston County, New York, a little south of Rochester, where their two sons were born, John Henry Uhl on October 6, 1839, and Edwin Fuller Uhl on August 14, 1841. A few years later, in answer to the irresistible call of the West, they "moved on" with their three- and five-year-old boys, by way of the Erie Canal and Lake Erie to the state of Michigan, which was then attracting numerous settlers. The three-year-old boy was Edwin F. Uhl, the Apollo and Lord Chesterfield of that courtroom scene at Ann Arbor, later mayor of Grand Rapids, then assistant secretary of state at Washington, and United States ambassador at Berlin.

Washtenaw County, with the settlements at Ypsilanti and Ann Arbor, had its beginnings in the early 1820's, and the Norris and Follett families, who influenced the early career of Edwin F. Uhl, had long been prominent in the community when the Uhl family arrived in the neighborhood. All three families were of early colonial origin: the Follett and Norris families reached New England about 1650; the Uhl family became residents of the original Livingston Manor in the province of New York about 1710. The three families had participated in the struggles and in the perils, as well as in the civic pioneering, of their period. They included members of the Susquehanna Company and of its committee which superintended the settlement of Wyoming Valley, survivors of the Wyoming Massacre, members of the Revolutionary forces, some of whom had been captured by the British forces and imprisoned in England, naval privateers in the War of 1812, and various civic and religious officers. Members of all three families later answered the call of the West, moved through northern New York, settled there for a time, then once more moved on through the Buffalo gateway and Lake Erie to Ypsilanti, Michigan, and founded there a joint branch of their families.

Mark Norris came in 1827, making the trip from Buffalo to Detroit in the schooner "Marie Antoinette" in a quick passage of seven days, and by stagecoach from Detroit to Ypsilanti in fifteen hours. Benjamin Follett arrived about ten years later and became cashier of a bank of which Mark Norris was one of the founders. Then followed, over the years, the marriages which brought these families together. Elvira Norris, daughter of the Mark Norrises, married Benjamin Follett, and Alice

Follett, daughter of the Benjamin Folletts, married Edwin F. Uhl.

Although he visited Ann Arbor, Mark Norris preferred Ypsilanti. This "huddle of log cabins in the Wilderness," had, at the suggestion of Judge Augustus B. Woodward, been named after Demetrius Ypsilanti, hero of the Greek Revolution. Mark's son, Lyman Decatur Norris, 1841–44, A.M. (*hon.*) 1869, was the first matriculate of the first class of the University of Michigan.* He was later a regent and for many years practiced law with his nephew by marriage, Edwin F. Uhl, in the firm of Norris and Uhl, at Ypsilanti and later at Grand Rapids.

The Uhl family arrived in Michigan in the spring of 1844 and settled on a farm on "The Plains," near Ypsilanti, called the "Banner Farm of Washtenaw County." Twenty-two years later they acquired and improved a larger tract of land on the famous Chicago Road,† and named the farm "Willow Run," from the willow-lined brook which ran through it. The same brook earlier gave its name to a rural settlement, and recently provided the name, now world famous, for the bomber plant erected in the immediate neighborhood.

David Mulford Uhl, the father of Edwin, was a broad-shouldered, sturdy pioneer, well to do and widely respected.

* "For a time he was lonely, as no other student appeared for three weeks, and Mr. Norris had the undivided attention of the entire faculty of four professors. In the spring of 1844, the faculty of the University desired to compare their curriculum with that of eastern colleges, and Mr. Norris was chosen by them to go east and enter Yale, which he did successfully, entering Yale with the same standing which he had at the University of Michigan. He was graduated from Yale in 1845, in time to return and attend the graduation exercises of his old class." Memorial Report—Kent County. *Michigan Pioneer and Historical Collections,* Vol. 26, p. 142. Lansing, 1896.

The respect of Michigan for Yale revealed in this incident was reciprocated 77 years later when Yale, for the first time departing from her tradition of always entrusting her presidency to a Yale man, selected for the position a distinguished alumnus of the University of Michigan—James Rowland Angell, A.B. 1890, A.M. 1891.

† "Originally an Indian trail it became the most notable highway in the Northwest. Settlers from the East thronged over it Westward, including the first stagecoach into Chicago in 1833." M. M. Quaife, ed., *The Bark Covered House, or Back in the Woods Again* (Chicago: Lakeside Press, R. R. Donnelley and Sons Co., 1937).

Katharine de Garmo Uhl, his mother, who was of French descent, was keenly alert to the opportunity for her sons in the establishment of a University at near-by Ann Arbor. The older son, John, followed in his father's footsteps as a hard-working farmer to his life's end. The younger son, Edwin, responded to his mother's thought in seeking a new field of activity. This did not mean, however, that Edwin F. Uhl was not a farmer boy. On the contrary, no one could look in later years on his broad shoulders without recognizing that in youth he too had taken his full share of work behind the plow and in the field.

As so often happens, even in his busy life, the memories of those boyhood years became a dominant note that "neither college walls nor court rooms, official life nor imperial function could dim, much less obliterate." Only near his life's end, however, did he carry out his cherished dream and build the beautiful country place outside Grand Rapids, called "Waldheim," beneath the spreading oaks, near the murmuring brook, and surrounded by broad acres of farmland. Unfortunately, this dream home was completely destroyed by fire a few years after his death. Included in the destruction were his files and papers, which, if available, would have contributed greatly to the history of the period. This loss made it essential to seek elsewhere the data necessary for this chapter.

District schools, churches, stores, hotel, flour mill, and bank were serving Ypsilanti when the Uhl family arrived. In all of these the Norris and Follett families were already playing a leading part. The Central Road—the present Michigan Central Railroad—had already passed on its western way through Ann Arbor, Dexter and Jackson. Ypsilanti was a thriving pioneer town. It was also unusually influential, by reason of the high type of its citizenship. Educational projects naturally flourished in such a community; the first "graded" school in Michigan eventually became the Ypsilanti Union Seminary, whose diploma was long considered to be second only to that of the University of Michigan. Later came the establishment of the famous State Normal School, with John M. B. Sill, A.M. (*hon.*) 1870, the subject of one of the chapters in this volume, its first male graduate, and, a little later, a member of its faculty.

Back of the American way of life, to use the current phrase, has been the capacity of the American people to develop shining achievements from pioneer conditions. Fortunately, in large measure such is still their privilege and opportunity. There are few instances of this progressive spirit more interesting and vivid than those recounted in the history of these early settlers in southern Michigan.

The farm, the district school, the thriving village were a part of the background of Edwin F. Uhl's boyhood and youth. When he was about thirteen years of age he entered the Ypsilanti Union Seminary, under Joseph Estabrook, later regent of the University and superintendent of public instruction, and was graduated at seventeen. "His work was characterized by faithful and diligent attention to his studies," said a schoolmate, "rather than especial brilliancy, although he was one of the most proficient students in the school. He was perhaps best known for his brilliant oratorical ability, in which regard he was easily the leader in his class." These were the words of General Byron M. Cutcheon, A.B. 1861, A.M. 1866, LL.B. 1866, an Ypsilanti boy, later a resident of Grand Rapids, and also a fraternity associate of Uhl in Alpha Delta Phi at the University of Michigan.

On the occasion of the memorial exercises of the Kent County bar for Uhl, General Cutcheon, a regent of the University and a representative from Michigan in the Forty-eighth Congress and the three succeeding congresses and Uhl's lifelong friend, gave an interesting glimpse of those Ypsilanti schooldays and of the undergraduate years at Ann Arbor:

> In April, 1855, when I entered the Ypsilanti Seminary to prepare for the University, I found Mr. Uhl already a pupil in that school. Of course, he was a lad, not quite fourteen, and during the time we were at Ypsilanti and at the University, I had the pleasure of being intimately associated with him, in some of those very close and kindly relations which grow up among students at college. That friendship then formed has always existed. It is said that the boy is father of the

man, and the same characteristics that we recognize in Edwin F. Uhl as a man, were recognized in him as a boy. I might say that he was one of the handsomest boys that I ever knew; was bright, keen-eyed, with heightened color upon his cheek, and with all the characteristics of healthy young manhood. At the close of our University course we drifted apart. He commenced the practice of law and I entered the army. To come together again when he was Assistant Secretary of State during President Cleveland's administration and I was occupying an executive position in the War Department as a member of the Board of Ordnance and Fortifications, was a matter of deep gratification to me.

Edwin Uhl entered the University of Michigan in October, 1858. The Literary Department had seventeen professors and 213 students, with special and graduate students bringing the grand total to 287. Not until the senior year were electives offered. Instances of unexcused absence, tardiness, or failure in recitation, if they amounted to five in number, meant probation; if ten, expulsion. No absence from town was allowed without permission of the president. Attendance was required daily at chapel and weekly at church. Including board, laundry, and books, the necessary expense for a year was estimated as varying from $125 to $150. Upon graduation in the Literary Class of 1862 Uhl received the degree of Bachelor of Arts and three years later the degree of Master of Arts in course. He was a member of the Alpha Delta Phi fraternity, and he has been followed in that organization by his son, Marshall M. Uhl, A.B. 1906, LL.B. 1908, of the law firm of Uhl, Bryant, Snow, and Slawson of Grand Rapids, and also by two grandsons, Commander John Howard Uhl, U.S.N.R., A.B. 1937, J.D. 1939, and Edwin Fuller Uhl 2d, A.B. 1943, J.D. 1948, both sons of Marshall M. Uhl and both veterans of World War II. According to tradition he was introduced into Alpha Delta Phi by William E. Quinby, who was later to be distinguished by his long service on the *Detroit Free Press* and by his ministry to the Netherlands.

Uhl's life, public and private, was greatly influenced by the friendships growing out of his seminary and university days.

Andrew D. White, LL.D. 1867, one of his University professors, was in after years, as minister to Russia, "instructed" by his former student, then assistant secretary of state. Later, White succeeded Uhl as ambassador to Germany. The exchange of letters between teacher and student on these occasions emphasizes the well-known devotion of White to the University of Michigan and to his students on its "benches."

In his *Autobiography*, White said his students at Michigan stimulated him greatly. He commented:

> Most of them were very near my own age; several were older. As a rule, they were bright, inquiring, zealous, and among them were some of the best minds I have ever known. From among them have since come senators, members of Congress, judges, professors, lawyers, heads of great business enterprises, and foreign ministers. One of them (Charles Kendall Adams, A.B. 1861, A.M. 1862) became my successor in the professorship in the University of Michigan and the presidency of Cornell, and, in one field, the leading American historian of his time. Another (Edwin F. Uhl) became my predecessor in the embassy to Germany. Though I had what might be fairly called "a good start" of these men, it was necessary to work hard to maintain my position; but such labor was then pleasure.*

Upon graduation Uhl read law in the office of Norris and Ninde of Ypsilanti, and eighteen months later he was admitted to the bar. Within a few months came his marriage to Alice Follett, eldest daughter of Benjamin Follett and Elvira Norris Follett, who was the daughter of Mark Norris and the sister of Lyman Decatur Norris, the University's first matriculate. Benjamin Follett, a leading citizen of Michigan, was, according to Colburn's *The Story of Ypsilanti*, "one of the real builders of Ypsilanti." † He was head of a bank, owner of a flour mill, builder of a hotel—the Follett House—choir leader, warden in St. Luke's Episcopal Church, member of the first city council, foreman of the first volunteer fire department, mayor, member of the National Democratic Committee, and

* Andrew D. White, *Autobiography . . .* (New York: Century Co., 1905), I, p. 264.

† Harvey C. Colburn, *The Story of Ypsilanti* (Ypsilanti, Mich., 1928), p. 134.

delegate to Democratic national conventions. His large residence had a parklike setting and was long the center of the social life of the community.

Alice Follett Uhl in her life and interests shared and complemented fully the endeavors of her husband and, in addition, had scarcely less notable a career of her own. The oldest of seven children, she had the advantages of a home of unusual culture as well as the prestige of the Follett and Norris families. In a social life of more than ordinary complexity, Mrs. Uhl was a conspicuous success at Washington and at Berlin. At the World's Fair of 1893 she initiated the suggestion of the National Federation of Music Clubs, and, as one of its founders, "she influenced the development of music locally and nationally." As its first president, she gave it life and purpose, aiding in its development until in present years it numbers more than four thousand clubs with over five hundred thousand members. Later, she was succeeded in its presidency by Mrs. Elmer J. Ottaway (Ruth Louise Haller, A.B. 1909), of Port Huron. This organization has often been acclaimed as probably the most influential factor in the development of music in this country.

The eleven years following Uhl's marriage were spent at Ypsilanti and typify the activities of a young lawyer feeling his way, testing his powers, enlarging his interests, and challenging attention. That Uhl gave early promise of a brilliant career as a lawyer and as a citizen is demonstrated by his admission in 1866 into the law firm of Lyman Decatur Norris under the title of Norris and Uhl, a relationship which continued until Norris moved to Grand Rapids in 1871. Meanwhile, Uhl became attorney for the Detroit, Hillsdale and Indiana Railroad Company and for the Detroit, Eel River and Illinois Railroad Company, both long since absorbed into the present New York Central system. As a young lawyer he won such repute as to cause his selection as prosecuting attorney of Washtenaw County for 1871 and 1872, but he declined a renomination which would have been equivalent to an election. In this period he also displayed marked business ability in the handling of various receiverships to which he was appointed. In 1873, after Norris had moved to Grand Rapids, Uhl formed a law partnership with Albert Crane under the firm name of Uhl and Crane.

The memory of earlier family migrations made this alert young lawyer fully cognizant of the changes in southern Michigan in that fateful period following the Civil War. Railroads were being built in all directions, the trend of population toward more promising areas was under way, and the outstanding progress already made at Grand Rapids was generally recognized. Although there was comparatively little "riding of the circuit" in Michigan at any time, lawyers practiced widely throughout the southern part of the state, and it was quite in keeping with the changes of the period that they should make their homes and establish their offices in these growing cities. Lyman D. Norris moved from Ypsilanti to Grand Rapids in 1871, the same year in which Thomas J. O'Brien, LL.B. 1865, LL.D. 1908, moved there from Marshall and began his career, distinguished not only at the bar, but in public life, as minister to Denmark, ambassador to Japan, and ambassador to Italy, a continuous period of eight years in the diplomatic service. In 1876 Uhl also moved from Ypsilanti to Grand Rapids and resumed his place in the firm of Norris and Uhl, a partnership which continued for eleven years until he was joined by his former Ypsilanti partner and the firm again became Uhl and Crane.

For a picture of Uhl during this period we have the words of Roger W. Butterfield, LL.B. 1868, a former regent and long a leader of the Michigan bar. Butterfield said:

> I remember his appearance when he tried the first jury case that he ever tried at this bar, in which I happened to be engaged. The lithe strong body seemed a fit habitation for an active and well-poised mind. He found on his coming a community that was quick to appreciate his merits and was glad to welcome him, and from the very commencement until he left the active practice of law, for seventeen years, the story of his life was a story of continued development in strength as a lawyer and in an increased reputation and popularity.

Mr. Uhl became known first as a rising lawyer, and afterwards, as one of the leaders of the bar of Western Michigan. I think he was probably the most finished speaker that ever came to this bar.

Two instances of a crowded law practice will serve to illustrate Uhl's ability as a trial lawyer and in the more complicated role of counselor. The first instance is condensed from an account in *Michigan Pioneer and Historical Collections*,* of the "Jockey Brown" will case. All advocates connected with the case were well-known: for the proponents were Major J. Dunham, E. A. Maher, *law* 1873–74, and Willard Kingsley, B.S. 1868, LL.B. 1870, of Grand Rapids, and Alfred Russell, of Detroit; for the contestants were C. H. Gleason, Ph.B. 1873, LL.B. 1875, M. J. Smiley, and Edwin F. Uhl. All the dry bones of family skeletons were thoroughly shaken and dusted. According to the account, Uhl and Smiley had long been considered among the leaders of the Kent County bar, had long been rivals, and were generally on opposite sides; now they were associated, and each was determined to surpass his own best efforts. Russell had a national reputation as a lawyer and advocate. For weeks during the trial the courtroom was filled, and at the time of the arguments, all available space in reach of the voices of the advocates was crowded. The jury did to "Jockey Brown" dead what no man had been able to do to him living: it broke his will, and the verdict was sustained by the Michigan Supreme Court, *Haines* v. *Hayden*, 95 *Mich.* 332.

We are indebted to John W. Blodgett of Grand Rapids for an account of the second instance, which related to riparian rights and the navigability of inland streams and rivers, a field then new in Michigan law. For many years Uhl was general counsel of the Muskegon Booming Company, organized under Act No. 16, Laws of 1864: "To authorize the formation of corporations for the running, booming and rafting of logs." Corporations organized under it had power to construct and maintain booms in the navigable waters of the state, provided the booms did not obstruct navigation. Penalties were provided should any person put logs into a stream and neglect to

* Vol. 35 (1907), 83-84.

make adequate provision for driving them and breaking their jams. The booming companies practically had a regulated monopoly—recognized by statutory law—of driving logs on the rivers on which they operated. The loggers, however, were protected from exorbitant rates, since the profit above necessary expenses was limited. The Muskegon Booming Company thus acted as a common carrier for all the logs in the territory drained by the Muskegon River down to Muskegon Lake, where they were sorted and delivered to their owners. The logging operations of the whole area and the welfare of Muskegon depended on the continuous operation of the company, which was driving three hundred million to five hundred million board feet a year. Uhl's problem was to see that this operation was not interrupted. Numerous suits were brought alleging damage to crops and to fields due to flooding, and also charging obstruction of navigation by log jams. Some were meritorious, but many merely sought to block the company. For the most part, Uhl acted through local counsel, but he directed the legal policy of the company through the years and thwarted all attempts to tie up its operations.

In the meantime he became president of the Grand Rapids National Bank, a post which he held for nearly twenty years. He also headed several other business enterprises, he was attorney for the Michigan Central Railroad Company, president of the bar association, first president of the Peninsular Club, and warden and vestryman of St. Mark's Episcopal Church. He was actively interested in the Democratic Party. For many years at both Ypsilanti and Grand Rapids he had been prominent in the councils and conventions of his party, and especially as an influential speaker in its campaigns. Those were the days of torchlight processions and large political gatherings attended by the whole countryside. Speakers came from other states to aid the local leaders, and the Grand Rapids speakers of both parties spent night after night at meetings and debates throughout western Michigan. Just as in frontier days the state was divided by events into northern and southern spheres of interest, so Michigan today is divided into eastern and western zones, primarily because of the growth of Grand Rapids and Detroit, with a natural division of political influence, and of judicial, religious, and economic affairs.

In eastern Michigan, Don M. Dickinson, LL.B. 1867, long had been an outstanding political personality and gradually had become a state and national figure in the Democratic Party. In western Michigan, Uhl was a prominent political factor throughout the Cleveland era, although, in spite of being frequently mentioned for the governorship, he never ran for state or national office. The background and career of these two men ran in close parallels—both were born in New York state, came to Michigan in early boyhood, were graduated from the University, entered upon the practice of law—one at Detroit and the other at Ypsilanti—and both took an active part in civic and political affairs. A personal friendship which extended also to their families complemented the parallel in their careers. Their co-operation was not only an important element in uniting the Democratic Party in Michigan before the Bryan interlude, but was also a significant factor in bringing into national prominence many Michigan citizens, most of whom were drawn from the staff and alumni of the University of Michigan.

In 1890, Grand Rapids had reached a critical stage in its development. In the matter of public improvements, even of streets and sidewalks, the city was far behind its growth. Many citizens felt that the time had come when its affairs needed the guidance and direction of men of outstanding capacity and experience. Although often urged to accept office, Uhl had continued to decline political preferment; however, his name again began to appear in the current newspaper discussion, and prominent citizens urged him privately to accept the mayoralty nomination of his party. His acceptance of the freely tendered nomination won wide acclaim from citizens and newspapers, and in the following election he received a large plurality, making him a Democratic mayor in a normally Republican city. A year later he was elected to a second term.

This two-term service as mayor was a gratifying experience

evidently to Grand Rapids and doubtless also to Uhl. It was a period of great community activity aimed directly at the correction of faulty municipal procedure and the advancement of public improvements. The council proceedings are full of his suggestions and also record some vetoes, indicating his very close supervision of all municipal matters, especially in accounting and legal phases and in expenditures. Noteworthy advances were made in building sewers, extending water mains, initiating the paving of streets and sidewalks, improving public lighting, safeguarding the banks of the Grand River, establishing a system of street numbering, erecting buildings for the fire and police departments, and developing the park system. All answered the particular needs of the period.

An exciting incident which attracted wide publicity was a city order to the Western Union to remove its poles from Canal Street in the heart of the business section. The company ignored the order, and Mayor Uhl accompanied the city's workmen, who forcibly removed the poles. There were threats of damage suits against the city; possibly, however, the legal acumen of Rush Taggart, LL.B. 1875, long counsel of Western Union, may have helped to induce the company to accept a community adjustment. As Democratic mayor of the second largest city in Republican Michigan, Uhl was drawn further into party councils and occasions and even shared the preliminary confusion over the free silver craze which visited the leaders of both parties in that period of uncertainty. When the crisis of 1896 brought a definite alignment, Uhl was emphatically in the "sound money" wing of his party.

Meanwhile, Cleveland, in retirement in New York after his first administration, was much in demand for public appearances. Late in 1889 he spoke at a public dinner in Boston, and again a year later at Columbus, Ohio, in celebration of the birthday of Allen G. Thurman, who had been the candidate for vice president in his 1888 campaign. The "Old Roman" banquet was organized and managed by John J. Lentz, A.B. 1882, then a rising young lawyer in Ohio and an active Michigan alumnus. United States Senator Calvin S. Brice, *law*

1865–66, was host to Cleveland, and Don M. Dickinson, postmaster general in Cleveland's first administration, was one of the speakers. Others attending, included Sidney D. Miller, A.B. 1848, A.M. 1854, William A. Moore, A.B. 1850, A.M. 1854, Edwin F. Uhl, Dr. Charles S. Hazeltine, *med.* 1865–66, Thomas A. E. Weadock, LL.B. 1873, Henry Russel, A.B. 1873, LL.B. 1875, and Peter White, A.M. (*hon.*) 1900, later a regent of the University.

At about the time that the call was sent out for the New York State Democratic Convention on February 22, 1892, afterward known as the "Snap Convention," Dickinson persuaded Cleveland to accept a long-standing invitation from the law students of the University of Michigan to deliver the Washington birthday address at Ann Arbor. This meant that Cleveland would be addressing the country on the very day that the convention of his own party in his own state possibly would be condemning him. Naturally, such a crossing of political currents immediately attracted national attention. On the platform at Ann Arbor were assembled a numerous group of alumni friends and supporters of Cleveland, giving to crowded University Hall the air of a great occasion. Cleveland's address was not only one of the most painstakingly prepared but one of the most fruitful of his career. It proved to be a turning point in his life, as well as in the careers of many of the individuals of that devoted alumni group, including the Democratic mayor of Grand Rapids.

At the Michigan State Democratic Convention held a few months later in Muskegon, Uhl was elected a delegate-at-large to the Democratic National Convention called to meet in Chicago in June. The political partnership between Dickinson and Uhl was now moving very actively toward consolidating the state's party strength behind Cleveland for nomination at Chicago. On the eve of the national convention came the famous "Whitney conference" in New York City, secretly attended by both Dickinson and Uhl.

Long a mystery in American political history, the "Whitney conference" was held on June 9, 1892, at the call, and in the

New York home, of William C. Whitney. Its secretary was George F. Parker, later a biographer of Mr. Cleveland, and author of one of the few accounts of the proceedings of the conference. Picked men from ten states not registered at their hotels, and all known to each other, reporting for their states and for others of which they had knowledge, effected a working program for the approaching Democratic National Convention.* Dickinson and Uhl attended its adjourned sessions at the Hotel Richelieu in Chicago. Here representatives from about twenty states foregathered and gradually enlarged their number until the nomination of Cleveland was assured.

It was the strategy of the conference to center its influence on the nomination of Cleveland and to avoid any commitment on the vice-presidency. In the convention Dickinson was the floor leader of the Cleveland forces and valiantly held them in line even under the final eloquent attack of W. Bourke Cockran of New York. Four years later, it may be interesting to recall, these two men struggled side by side at the memorable Grand Rapids meeting to hold back the free silver wave of western Michigan.

When the convention took up nominations for the vice-presidency, Uhl, in behalf of the Michigan delegation, presented the name of Allen B. Morse, of Ionia. Uhl's presence and eloquence brought him immediate acclaim at the convention and national recognition from the press, although Adlai E. Stevenson, rather than his candidate, won the nomination. These conference and convention activities were important steps in Uhl's political career, for they paved the way for his future honors in the Cleveland era.

Uhl declined the post of assistant secretary of war which Cleveland, upon his inauguration in March, 1893, offered him, giving as a reason his unfamiliarity with military affairs. Later, he was asked to accept a diplomatic post abroad, which he also declined. Upon the resignation of Josiah Quincy as

* "This body selected in advance the principal committees of the convention, those on credentials, resolutions, and organization, and decided upon the temporary and permanent chairmen." Allan Nevins, *Grover Cleveland, A Study in Courage* (New York: Dodd, Mead and Co., 1932), p. 489.

assistant secretary of state in October, 1893, the post was tendered to Uhl by President Cleveland, and he accepted. He continued in that office from November 1, 1893, until February 10, 1896, when he was commissioned ambassador to Germany. He held that assignment until April 5, 1897, remaining at his post, however, until the middle of June, when he was succeeded by Andrew D. White.

When it was announced in Grand Rapids that Uhl had been chosen assistant secretary of state under Judge Walter Q. Gresham, congratulations, according to the press, came from all sides. The Jefferson Club of Grand Rapids gave him a banquet at the New Livingston Hotel. The guests as well as the fifteen speakers came from all parts of the state. Justice John W. Champlin, LL.D. 1887, later a member of the faculty of the Law Department of the University of Michigan, was the toastmaster. Again, when Uhl was appointed ambassador to Germany, the news was first announced in Grand Rapids at Powers Opera House, and resolutions were adopted by the audience calling for a committee to arrange a public reception, which was held later in the city hall and attended by thousands of Grand Rapids citizens.

Judge Walter Q. Gresham was a Republican of Indiana and had been postmaster general under President Arthur. His selection as secretary of state by President Cleveland turned on their common advocacy of tariff reform and led to the close personal friendship of the two men. Uhl's relations with Secretary Gresham were also especially congenial and cordial. Because of the illness of the secretary, Uhl found his post one of unusual responsibility; he was acting secretary of state a considerable part of his more than two years in the State Department. This brought him into close relations with President Cleveland. The two men had much in common: both were physically impressive, both had "read law" and had become successful in its practice, both in early life had held county office at a time when the local political power was in opposition, both had entered politics through an unsought office, each had served his city as mayor, and each highly esteemed the other.

The President soon began designating Uhl for conspicuous individual service.

By treaty between the Argentine Republic and Brazil there was submitted to the arbitration of the President of the United States their claims to a tract of territory popularly known as *Misiones*. The controversy involved an area of 11,823 English square miles, about as large as Massachusetts and Connecticut combined. Both countries claimed to have possession of the area, which had considerable strategic value. The Jesuits had carried their exploration and settlement into the region, following the papal bulls of 1493 and the Treaty of Tordesillas of 1494, with express permission in later years to establish missions. The dispute arose between 1600 to 1650 when Mamelukes or Paulistas from Sao Paulo and San Vincente made raids on the missions of the Jesuits. The controversy involved the grants of both Spain and Portugal and their attempt to establish a boundary by a treaty in 1777. Under the treaty, however, doubts subsequently arose as to which of two systems of rivers constituted the designated boundary. These two rivers were a hundred miles apart. One river system was claimed by Brazil, and the other system by Argentina, to be the boundary. Both asserted their claims under joint commissions between Spain and Portugal, which by an early treaty had attempted to locate boundaries between Spanish and Portuguese possessions in South America.

It was a serious controversy of long standing, and of a highly complicated and technical character, involving the bulls, decrees, grants, and legislation of several centuries, and the evidence of scores of maps of explorers, surveyors, and geographers. The voluminous records and briefs were laid before the President on February 10, 1894, the award to be made within a year. Argentina was represented by Dr. Don Estanislo S. Zeballos, its former foreign minister, and at the time its minister at Washington, together with a large mission of experts, including the Honorable Josiah Quincy of Massachusetts, as counsel. Brazil was represented by a special mission of six members, headed by Baron de Rio Branco, afterward the eminent Brazilian minister of foreign affairs.

President Cleveland assigned to Uhl the task of recommending an award. Aside from hearing the evidence and arguments by the representatives of the two countries, Uhl devoted a large part of the summer of 1894 to studying the numerous and elaborate documents.* This work was performed so thoroughly and judicially that President Cleveland, after a painstaking review, signed the suggested award without the change of a word. Furthermore, to signify approval of his labors, President Cleveland graciously commissioned Uhl to deliver the award to the diplomatic representatives of the two countries. The ceremony took place in the State Department on February 6, 1895, and was followed by a reception at the White House. The award, favorable to Brazil, was accepted in good spirit by Argentina. Both countries made cordial statements of appreciation to the President for having "carefully and conscientiously exercised his functions as arbiter." The president of the Argentine Republic proclaimed:

> Both peoples have the honor of showing to the world a practical application of the principle of international arbitration, and the Argentine Nation, although not favored in the decision of the high judge to whom the solution of the ancient controversy was entrusted, congratulates itself on the disappearance of the only possible cause of dissension with its former ally.

Uhl was widely acclaimed in diplomatic and official circles as possessing one of the keenest legal minds in the State Department in his time. Cleveland, years later, in discussing the *Misiones* arbitration paid this high tribute to his former associate, "Mr. Uhl was one of the ablest men I ever knew in public life." It may be of interest to record that the *Misiones* arbitration led to a series of arbitrations resulting in a general settle-

* This is intimately and dramatically disclosed by the following long-hand, partly burned note to Edwin F. Uhl, of Grand Rapids, from Henry T. Thurber, A.B. 1874, of Detroit, secretary to the President: "The President has directed me to send over the arbitration papers, re Brazil-Argentina, to occupy your leisure moments. I understand you have a wagon attached to your Department, which we hear about. Can you send it over and we will load it up?"

ment of the boundary disputes which have constituted such a large part of the international problems of South America. In fact, arbitration became a sort of international religion with Brazil, whose brilliant interpreter was Baron de Rio Branco, the head of its special mission to Washington on the *Misiones* arbitration.

In the meantime the State Democratic Convention in Michigan in 1894 had unanimously nominated Uhl for the office of United States Senator. He withdrew his name, however, on the assembling of a Republican legislature, which subsequently elected James McMillan, of Detroit.

A few months after the *Misiones* award, Uhl again came to national attention by the part he played in the "*Alliance*" incident. On March 8, 1895, when six miles off the coast of Cuba, the United States mail steamship "*Alliance*," on her usual homeward course from Colon to New York, was fired upon repeatedly with solid shot by a Spanish gunboat. The shot, fortunately, fell short. Although a formal protest was promptly made, Spain parried and delayed. In early May, as acting secretary of state, Uhl by forthright firmness obtained from Spain a disavowal, "with full expression of regret and assurance of nonrecurrence of such just cause of complaint, while the offending officer was relieved of his command," to quote from President Cleveland's message to Congress. The incident came at a time of national apprehension over Spain's course in Cuba and proved to be one of the forerunners of the Spanish-American War. Uhl's firm and resolute handling of the incident was highly praised officially and by the press of the country.

Another important task in which President Cleveland called on Uhl was in connection with the reorganization and elevation of the consular service. In his message to Congress of December, 1893, the President had dealt with the subject, referring to recommendations in his former administration for "a recast of the laws relating to the consular service." Civil service reform, long in the foreground, was one of the dominant notes of the Cleveland era. In the summer of 1895, at the suggestion of the President, Uhl made an extensive tour of inspection of the consular service in Europe, visiting all the important posts except those in Russia.

Basing his action on Uhl's report and recommendations, and without further waiting for congressional action, President Cleveland issued an executive order on September 20, 1895, bringing appointments to the service, at least in part, under a system of examinations, and assigning to the secretary of state the task of presenting the subjects and mode of examination. This was the beginning of the very far-reaching reorganization of the consular service which was later extended by President Theodore Roosevelt, again by executive order, on November 10, 1905.

Upon the death, early in 1896, of Theodore Runyon, of New Jersey, ambassador to Germany, the President promptly appointed Uhl to the post. Just as promptly the Senate paid him its highest compliment by confirmation without the usual reference to a committee. The farm boy from "The Plains" near Ypsilanti became the fifth of his country's representatives to hold the rank of ambassador. Berlin had long been one of the country's great diplomatic assignments, and the post had been filled in recent years by Bayard Taylor, George H. Pendleton, William Walter Phelps, and Andrew D. White, who was later to reappear at Berlin as Uhl's successor.

Berlin itself was in a period of great court activity. Kaiser Wilhelm II and the royal family were in residence at both Berlin and Potsdam, moving through a daily round of public occasions and stimulating a social court life of great brilliance, which made demands upon the cultural resources of the various international diplomatic groups. The United States embassy was staffed by career men who later advanced to high diplomatic assignments. A glimpse of the period may be gathered from a press report, considerably condensed, of the pomp and circumstance surrounding the presentation of Uhl and his credentials to the emperor:

At three o'clock promptly, Baron Usedom, court chamberlain, called with gorgeous court equipages. In the first of these rode John B. Jackson, first secretary of the embassy, bearing the letter of credence for the new ambassador. In the second carriage rode Mr. Uhl himself and Baron Usedom, preceded by two outriders bearing the white and red Brandenburg colors, their uniforms being trimmed with heavy embroidery. All the officials wore elaborate uniforms and enormous lackies were in attendance in livery. The horses were gaily caparisoned.

The third carriage was occupied by the suite of the embassy, including Herbert G. Squiers, the second secretary, and Lieutenant Robert K. Evans, the military attaché. While driving up Unter den Linden, the military guards marched up to the carriages and presented arms to the roll of the drums. There were large crowds in the streets to witness the pageant.

Then follows a lengthy account of the ceremony at the Schloss, all of which, while exceedingly interesting, merely led the modest ambassador to caution the younger members of his family that these were necessary official incidents and of importance only for their memory books. Mrs. Uhl and their two daughters in their presentation at court were received in turn with similar ceremony. The Imperial German Court was probably the most brilliant the world has known in modern times.

As for the more serious implications of the new position, there was the usual flow of delicate questions of commercial importance to both nations, and it was recognized that Uhl maintained a most favorable atmosphere for the continuance of friendly relations. There was no crisis, so-called, during his ambassadorship.

The embassy residence on Tiergarten-strasse was the scene of brilliant social occasions, including the marriage of the older daughter, Lucy Follett Uhl, to Guy V. Thompson, of Grand Rapids, professor at Yale and the brother-in-law of William Wallace Campbell, B.S. (C.E.) 1886, M.S. (*hon.*) 1899, Sc.D. (*hon.*) 1905, also of Grand Rapids, the director of the Lick Observatory and later president of the University of California. The younger daughter, Alice Edwina Uhl, inherited her mother's musical talent and interest. She had long been a pupil of Hahn at Detroit, and at Berlin she studied and coached with Barth and at Weimar with Stavenhagen, in preparation for her many public appearances as an amateur concert pianist.

Because the family spoke fluently the language of the country and also because of their musical talent and interest, they enjoyed more than the ordinary contact with the German court itself and with the international groups. This, combined with the recognition accorded to the character and ability of the ambassador, gave the embassy a distinction which was acclaimed officially on Uhl's departure from Germany and again at the time of his death.

The four years, 1893 to 1897, during which Uhl was absent in government service, had brought great changes to Grand Rapids and to western Michigan as well as to Uhl's political alignment. In the 1896 free silver campaign he reversed completely his earlier endorsement of "free silver" and stated his "sound money" views with such vigor and forthrightness as to become a political target for the silverites among his political associates in western Michigan. The state meanwhile had returned to its Republican tradition; the Democratic party continued to suffer from its split over free silver.

Uhl returned to his banking post and entered into two law partnerships; in Grand Rapids, he joined the old law firm of Wesley W. Hyde and J. Edward Earle, which was now newly styled as Uhl, Hyde, and Earle, and in Chicago, a new law firm, which included his Washington associates, Frank H. Jones, formerly assistant postmaster general, and Kenesaw M. Landis, formerly secretary to Secretary of State Gresham, and which was styled Uhl, Jones, and Landis. It soon became apparent, however, that Uhl's health had become impaired, and he promptly withdrew from the Chicago firm. Gradually, he limited his activities and lived in semiretirement at his country home in Grand Rapids and at the family cottage at the Chicago Club of Charlevoix of which, in 1881, he had been one of the founders.

One of his few public appearances had been with Mrs. Uhl at the first dinner of the University of Michigan Club of Detroit, recently organized on October 21, 1895, under the presidency of Dickinson. A large delegation came from the University headed by President and Mrs. Angell, and alumni came from all parts of the state.* The distinguished gathering filled completely the large dining room of the old Russell House. It was the success of this outstanding occasion which soon led, largely under the guidance of Regent Levi L. Barbour, A.B. 1863, LL.B. 1865, A.M. 1876, to the organization, in 1897, of the present general Alumni Association, which has been such an important factor in the upbuilding of the University.

Toward the end of his life Uhl made his final appearance in the courts in Grand Rapids. As he sat day after day at the counsel table he may have cradled the thoughts of many occasions, even his early appearance as prosecuting attorney at the Wagner murder trial at Ann Arbor. His final appearance, however, was as the defendant in an equity action for a receiver and accounting in the conduct for the years 1879–99 of a lumber business, as assignee in a common-law assignment. The decisions of the courts, both in the Kent Circuit Court and on appeal in the Michigan Supreme Court, 130 *Mich.* 198, sustained his action.

Uhl's semiretirement was followed by semi-invalidism and then by a lingering illness which caused his death on May 17, 1901, in his sixtieth year. To quote a press comment:

> The death of Hon. Edwin F. Uhl has had a deep effect upon the community. Expressions of sincere sorrow are heard upon every hand and coupled with them are countless little stories illustrative of his sterling character. Incidents in his business career, his professional work in the courts, his administration as mayor, his experience as a diplomat, and his social side are being narrated wherever men group together, with tender reminiscent touches as a tribute to his worth as a citizen, an official, a worker and a man.

On the day of the funeral services, business and courts were suspended at Grand Rapids, and on the day of the burial, at Ypsilanti.

The material for this sketch has been taken largely from the news and editorial columns of the newspapers of the day, from the memorial addresses at the meetings of the Washtenaw

* Also in attendance; Adams, Palmer, Quinby, Sill and Thurber.

County bar, the Kent County bar, and the Michigan Supreme Court, and from the resolutions of the Michigan Legislature, Grand Rapids City Council, Grand Rapids National Bank, vestry of St. Mark's Church, and the Alpha Delta Phi fraternity at the University of Michigan.

His contribution to the America of his day may be summarized in the editorial appraisal of Uhl by the *Detroit Free Press:* "In all his relations of life he was one of Michigan's really great men."

Edwin Willits

1830	*Born in Otto, Cattaraugus County, New York*
1836	*Moved to Delhi Mills, Washtenaw County, Michigan*
1849–51	*Attended Lodi Plains Academy*
1855	*Graduated from the University of Michigan*
	Became assistant principal of Adrian High School
1856	*Married Jane Ingersoll*
	Read law with Isaac P. Christiancy, of Monroe
	Became assistant editor of the Monroe Commercial
1857	*Admitted to the bar of Michigan*
	Became editor of the Monroe Commercial
1860	*Elected prosecuting attorney of Monroe County*
	Elected member of the State Board of Education
1863	*Appointed postmaster of Monroe*
1873	*Chosen member of the State Constitutional Commission*
1876	*Elected member of the United States House of Representatives*
1883	*Appointed principal of the Michigan State Normal School, Ypsilanti*
1885	*Inaugurated president of Michigan Agricultural College, East Lansing*
1889	*Appointed assistant secretary of agriculture*
1893	*Placed in charge of government exhibits, World's Columbian Exposition*
1894	*Opened law office in Washington, D.C.*
1896	*Died in Washington, D.C.*

Edwin Willits

Edwin Willits

By F. Clever Bald

SECRETARY of Agriculture J. Sterling Morton in his annual report to President Cleveland for the year 1894 included the following paragraph:

> On January 1, 1894, the Hon. Edwin Willits retired from the office of Assistant Secretary of the Department of Agriculture. He remained by request, up to that date, so that he might complete satisfactorily his arduous duties in connection with the Government's exhibit at the World's Fair. The sense of obligation which the Secretary is pleased to cherish of Mr. Willits, because of his many good services to the Department, is hereby very frankly acknowledged, and a sincere admiration for his rugged honesty, industry, and vigilance, as an official and efficient friend of agriculture during his entire connection with this administration, is unconcealed.

This was high praise by a Democrat of his Republican assistant; but Morton had good reason to be gracious, for in the spring of 1893, Willits was almost an indispensable man. Appointed assistant secretary of agriculture by President Benjamin Harrison in 1889, he had served capably under Secretary Jeremiah M. Rusk. When the World's Columbian Exposition was planned, Congress appropriated money to erect a building in which the work of various government agencies would be displayed. Secretary Rusk, without relieving Willits of any of his regular work, put him in charge of preparing the department's exhibits. In addition, President Harrison named him chairman of the board which managed all of the national government's participation in the Chicago Fair. It was his responsibility to supervise expenditures from the $949,000 appropriated by Congress for exhibits and to sign warrants drawn against this fund.

These were, indeed, heavy burdens. If Willits had retired on March 4, 1893, President Cleveland could scarcely have found anyone to replace him; for the exposition was scheduled to open on May 1, and much yet remained to be done. Asked to remain in office, Willits acquiesced; and his capable performance of the manifold tasks won him the warm commendation of his chief.

Willits and Morton were not entirely strangers to each other. From 1852 to 1854 they had been fellow students at the University of Michigan. Afterward their paths had diverged. Morton went to Nebraska to seek his fortune, and Willits moved to Monroe, Michigan, which had formerly been Morton's home. Probably they had not seen each other again until they met in Washington.

Before he became assistant secretary of agriculture, Willits had had a long and varied career in public office. Born on April 24, 1830, in Otto, Cattaraugus County, New York, he had been brought to Michigan by his parents when he was six years old. They had settled in Delhi Mills, a village about five miles from Ann Arbor. Edwin's father, Elijah, worked in a grist mill. The boy attended the village school, and, as soon as he was able, worked at odd jobs to help support the family. This duty fell to him because he was the eldest son and the second born of nine children. Although he could expect no financial assistance from his parents, Edwin early decided that he would attend the University of Michigan.

At Lodi Plains, about ten miles south of Delhi, was a preparatory school called Lodi Academy. Founded in 1847, the Academy had already an established reputation as a leader of its type. Young Willits enrolled in the classical department and worked to pay his expenses. His daughter remembers hearing him tell about going away to school. He had earned some money during the summer before he entered the Academy. When he was ready to leave home, realizing his family's needs, he gave his father all but twenty-five cents. With only a quarter in his pocket and his extra clothing in a little bundle under his arm, he set out to acquire an education.

In the fall of 1852, Willits entered the University of Michigan as a sophomore and applied himself assiduously to his studies in the classical course. The minutes of faculty meetings during the years of his attendance contain no record of punishment for youthful escapades or even of demerits; failure to pass an examination in German was the only recorded slip in his University career. Willits was absent frequently, by permission, so that he could earn money to continue his education. During part of the time he taught school in Monroe. Nevertheless, he was able to keep up with his class, and in June, 1855, he received the Bachelor of Arts degree. During the ensuing fall and winter, Willits taught school in Adrian, then the second largest city in Michigan. He was assistant principal and had charge of the academic department of the high school. At the end of the spring term he resigned and went immediately to Marshall, Michigan, where on April 10, 1856, he married Jane Ingersoll, who had been a fellow student in Lodi Academy. The young couple set up housekeeping in Monroe, which was to be their home for many years. Three children were born to them—a daughter who lived only a short time, George S., who became a lawyer and practiced in Chicago, and Mary E., who married Walter Bordwell and now lives in Los Angeles.

Having decided to abandon teaching for the law, Willits entered the office of Isaac P. Christiancy, one of the leading lawyers of the state, and began reading under his guidance. He also taught evening classes in the Monroe Academy. Willits soon had an opportunity to engage also in newspaper work. With the purpose of furthering the presidential campaign of John C. Fremont, a group of Republicans purchased Edward G. Morton's Democratic newspaper, the Monroe *Commercial*, and made Christiancy editor.* Willits became his assistant. He wrote vigorously in support of the party candidate, taking special pains to deny the Democrats' charge that the Republicans were associated with Garrison's abolitionists. Undaunted by Fremont's defeat at the polls, the *Commercial* continued to

* Edward G. Morton was the uncle of J. Sterling Morton, the subject of one of the sketches in this volume.

carry his name at the masthead, urging his nomination again in 1860.

Upon his admission to the bar in 1857, Willits began to practice law, but continued working on the newspaper. After Christiancy was elected to the Michigan Supreme Court in the same year, Willits was sole editor until 1860, when he gave up the position. By this time he was a prominent citizen of Monroe. In 1858 he had received the Master of Arts degree from the University of Michigan. He was a successful lawyer, taught an adult Bible class in the Presbyterian Church, and was secretary of the county Sunday School Association.

Through his newspaper work, Willits had acquired considerable influence among Republicans—with both the local and the state organizations. In 1860 he was elected prosecuting attorney of Monroe County; in a state-wide election he was chosen a member of the State Board of Education. The first position he held for only two years, but after having served one six-year term on the board, he was re-elected and remained in office until 1873. From 1863 to 1866, Willits was postmaster of Monroe. In later years he was proud to record the fact that he had been appointed "by Abraham Lincoln," and apparently just as proud that he had held the position until he was "removed by Andrew Johnson."

The people of Michigan in the election of 1872 voted in favor of revising the state constitution. Governor John J. Bagley appointed Willits a member of the eighteen-man commission charged with the work of revision. Meeting in Lansing from August 27 to October 16, 1873, the commission labored industriously to shape the fundamental law to fit changing conditions. The records show that Willits favored woman suffrage and officeholding by women. He voted also for a clause prohibiting officeholders from accepting free passes from railroads and for another to give the legislature authority to fix "reasonable maximum rates of charges" for passenger and freight traffic. This was during the period in which the people of the western states were painfully conscious of the abuses practiced by the railroads and were attempting to redress their grievances by the so-called "granger laws." All the labors of the commission were in vain, however, for, when the revised constitution was submitted to the people in November, 1874, it was rejected by a vote of three to one.

Now that Willits had served his apprenticeship in local and state politics, his promotion to the national field was not long delayed. In 1876 he was elected representative of the second Michigan district to the Forty-fifth Congress. Since the district included Washtenaw County, his former Delhi Mills neighbors and the faculty of his University were to be counted among his constituents. When he took his seat, his mentor in the law, Isaac P. Christiancy, was a member of the Senate, to which he had been chosen in 1875, defeating Zachariah Chandler. Willits was re-elected in 1878 and again in 1880.

At first he took little part in legislative business or debate, preferring to get his bearings before launching out into the treacherous seas of parliamentary procedure. During the second session of the Forty-fifth Congress, however, he made a long speech against an amendment to a law requiring payments to southern mail contractors for their services during 1859, 1860, and part of 1861. The amendment would have extended the period to May 31, 1861.

Willits opposed the amendment on the ground that it would legalize payments to these men for three months or more after some of the states had seceded. He attacked especially the statements of Representative John H. Reagan of Texas, former postmaster general of the Confederacy and chief supporter of the measure. Quoting from Reagan's official reports to the Confederate government, Willits showed that as postmaster general Reagan had ordered postmasters in the South to keep all cash which they had collected. By research in the Confederate archives, Willits discovered that $800,000 had been appropriated to pay these claims, and that no further compensation was required; he offered as proof the discovery of a bundle of claims that had actually been paid. The amendment failed of adoption; it is fair to assume that Willits' conclusive arguments were determining factors in its fate. Because of its sound basis of fact, this maiden effort in the House won praise and support for Willits. His later speeches also were characterized by the same evidence of thorough investigation and straightforward presentation. He had short patience with members who spoke in generalities. Frequently, he would interrupt such a speaker and subject him to a veritable cross-examination, demanding that he give the "actual facts."

Polygamy in Utah at this time was a lively issue. Willits showed his interest in the subject by introducing several bills intended to abolish the practice. All of them died in committee, but in 1882 he voted for the Edmunds Bill that outlawed polygamy in the territories.

Although Willits was a Republican, he did not always follow party leadership. He was orthodox on protective tariffs, but he voted against two river and harbor bills, and he was strongly opposed to special privileges for corporations. On February 4 and 5, 1880, he spoke in favor of a bill which would have compelled a corporation doing business in a state to be considered a citizen of that state for purposes of jurisdiction. If this bill had passed, it would have prevented foreign corporations from suing in federal courts on the ground of diverse citizenship.

Speaking for this bill, Willits said:

> There seems to be no valid reason why a corporation that competes with local corporations, that goes into every hamlet and almost every household in the land, should not be the subject of State control in that business, and should have the right to remove its causes to a distant court . . .

He declared that corporation suits occupied too much time of the federal courts, and that corporations had unfair advantages over individuals because their greater financial resources permitted them to pay the higher costs of United States courts.

This argument was certainly not sound Republican doctrine, and Willits' conclusion might have been uttered by a Jeffersonian. He asserted:

> So it becomes a fact that the only party or entity which in the United States represents the old feudal system of property tenure, so

unanimously opposed by our forefathers, transmitted from generation to generation in increasing value and influence, has sought refuge behind the judicial system of a government that boasts it has no primogeniture and that large estates are divided up by the natural order of things in one or two generations.

Mention should also be made of a speech in which Willits urged that government funds be spent to give the Indians a practical agricultural or industrial education rather than to pay soldiers to kill them. Important bills on which he voted "yea" during the last Congress of which he was a member were for a protective tariff, for the exclusion of Chinese, and for a classified civil service.

In 1883, after Willits had completed his third term in Congress, the State Board of Education, of which he had formerly been a member, appointed him principal of the Michigan State Normal School at Ypsilanti. Apparently feeling obliged to justify their choice of a man outside the teaching profession, the board asserted that no one was better fitted for the position than Willits. As proof, they cited as the best possible qualifications his service on the Monroe Board of Education and on the State Board, his years in Congress, and his wide practical experience and acquaintance with men and affairs. The board pointed out that the law which provided for establishing the Normal School required that students be instructed "in the fundamental laws of the United States, and in what regards the rights and duties of its citizens."

In addition to performing executive and administrative duties as principal, Willits taught civil government, Constitutional law, and congressional procedure. In his teaching he emphasized the practical side of politics, and he stressed the idea that teachers are also citizens and should be actively concerned in public affairs.

The Normal School prospered under Willits' direction, but his tenure of office was too brief to permit any important changes in policy, for on November 24, 1884, the State Board of Agriculture elected him president of Michigan Agricultural College at East Lansing. He accepted the position, but remained at Ypsilanti until the end of the school year in the spring of 1885. On July 1, he entered upon his duties as president of the Agricultural College. A member of the faculty described Willits as "about six feet tall, straight, well proportioned, filling out his clothes well, having a full beard, heavy dark hair and eyebrows; in fact he was a handsome man with many winning ways."

One of his first official duties as college president was to attend a convention of representatives of agricultural colleges and experiment stations, which opened in Washington on July 8. He read a paper on industrial education, and he was appointed to a committee charged with reporting to the next Congress the need of agricultural colleges and experiment stations for funds to conduct and report their investigations.

Inaugural ceremonies for the new president were held at East Lansing on August 19, 1885. In his address on this occasion, Willits characterized Michigan Agricultural College as a college that can "educate the scholar yet save the artisan." After castigating those who believe that manual labor is degrading, he set forth his own educational creed:

> We believe that that institution is the best that not only teaches the law, but teaches a trade; that not only teaches a science, but what to do with it; that teaches the application with mind and heart and hand; that teaches that all labor is honorable; that trains the hand as well as the intellect.

Willits, however, did not intend, in seeking to provide a practical education, to neglect culture. In conclusion he declared:

> We cannot be oblivious to the fact that the man exists before the farmer or the mechanic, and that every system of education to be harmonious and complete must include that general culture that forms so important a function in life's work.

The new president found about 250 students in the college. He hoped to double that number, and in order to provide room for them, he asked the board to build more dormitories. During the spring of 1886, the total number enrolled was 295, of whom twelve were women. The latter were living with professors' families and in neighboring farmhouses. Willits declared that many more would enter the college if suitable quarters were provided for them. The following year the 323 students overcrowded the dormitories, and the legislature was induced to appropriate funds for a new building and for enlarging shops and laboratories.

President Willits was greatly interested in the recently established department of mechanic arts. He believed that young men should have college training for industrial as well as for agricultural pursuits, and he appealed to the owners of factories to send their young employees to the college. When industrialists expressed disapproval on the ground that workmen would be spoiled by too much theory, Willits won their support by demonstrating that the boys were taught practice as well. In attempting to build up the mechanical program, the president also had to meet adverse criticism from farmers who charged that their sons would be encouraged to become factory workers. He placated them by the assurance that no student would be permitted to enter the mechanical department "unless he has a special bent in that direction."

During 1886, Willits spent some time in Washington working for the passage of a bill to establish agricultural experiment stations. The following year the Hatch Act provided funds for such stations in every state in the Union. President Willits immediately set about making effective the opportunity this law furnished his college, and, before he resigned, he had the satisfaction of establishing the station at East Lansing on a sound basis.

Willits infused new spirit into the Michigan Agricultural College. One member of the faculty later declared that Willits found it only a school, but made it a college. He transmitted some of his own energy and zeal to members of the faculty, with whom he conferred frequently and helpfully about their problems.

It was upon the students, however, that Willits made the greatest impression. The historian of the college asserts that no other president was as popular with them. On Sunday mornings they attended his Bible talks. He visited them often in their rooms, took an interest in their work, and appealed to their pride to keep their rooms neat. A contemporary observer wrote: "Always trusting largely to the good sense and manliness of the students, his trust is rarely betrayed." His management of the college was described as "firm and paternal." He could be severe if occasion required, for he had a strong sense of responsibility for the welfare of his boys. His secretary recalled in later years that "he never slept without fearing that something might go wrong, and many a night when we were sound asleep, he was pacing the campus keeping watch and ward." The students were proud of their president and appreciated his interest in them. They displayed their affection for him when he returned, after his resignation in the spring of 1889, to deliver the commencement address: ". . . in a body [they] met him over the hill at the west entrance to the campus and greeted him with round after round of applause, and then marched to the central portion of the campus."

The reason for Willits' resignation was his appointment by President Benjamin Harrison to be assistant secretary of agriculture. Since 1862 there had been a Department of Agriculture under the direction of a commissioner. By an act of February 9, 1889, Congress had raised the department to executive status under a secretary of cabinet rank and provided for an assistant secretary. President Cleveland at once promoted Commissioner Norman J. Colman to secretary of agriculture. After less than a month in office, he was succeeded by Governor Jeremiah M. Rusk of Wisconsin, appointed by President Harrison. Willits became the first incumbent of the newly created position of assistant secretary.

Willits was named to the post on March 29 and took office on April 24, 1889. Secretary Rusk began at once to reorganize the department, dividing the work into two parts. For his own direct supervision he kept all the divisions involving particularly administrative and executive functions, and to his assistant he assigned all those engaged in scientific investigations.

Willits at first had under his direction the Pomological, the

Microscopical, the Chemical, the Botanical, the Ornithological, the Forestry, and the Entomological divisions, the Section of Vegetable Pathology, the Silk Section, and the Office of Experiment Stations. It was his duty to direct and control the scientific policy and operations of these divisions and sections. All correspondence on the scientific work of the department was submitted to him for his approval and signature. Only when questions of administrative policy were involved was it necessary for him to consult the secretary before he made a decision. Subsequently, in addition to the sections and divisions already mentioned, the assistant secretary was given charge of the library and the museum, artesian wells and irrigation, fiber investigation, rainfall experiments, and the exhibit of the department at the World's Fair.

Secretary Rusk liked Willits' work. In his first annual report to the President he wrote:

> Thanks to the wisdom of your choice in the selection for this position of a gentleman combining a large experience in public affairs with a thorough knowledge of scientific agriculture and trained executive ability, I have been enabled to meet a want that has long existed in the Department and to take one of the most important steps in its reorganization.

The assistant secretary had a broad view of the services which the department should provide. He stated:

> The Department of Agriculture should be so amply endowed with material, money, and men as should make it an authority on all agricultural questions, capable of assisting in every laudable way the experiment stations and colleges and all voluntary organizations, clubs and associations. It should be a mine of information to the press . . . and should always be able and ready to co-operate with every other agent, to the mutual advantage of all.

In order better to serve as a source of information for the farmers and the press, Willits organized an editorial division to help prepare for publication reports of the sections under his charge. This office made possible the issuing of a greater variety of pamphlets than had previously been possible, and the assistant secretary was pleased to notice that an increased demand required larger and larger editions.

Willits had almost a paternal interest in the Office of Experiment Stations. He had lobbied for the passage of the Hatch Act, he had established the station at Michigan Agricultural College, and now he was the first to have charge of the office provided for co-ordinating and fostering the activities of the various stations. His policy was to co-operate cordially with them, advising them, and doing for them what they could not do for themselves.

Some of the special activities under Willits' supervision were the investigation of artesian wells as sources of water for irrigating arid regions, experiments in the relative strength of timbers in the Division of Forestry, the importation by the Division of Entomology of an Australian parasite that exterminated a scale insect which was threatening the destruction of the orange groves of California, and investigation of the possibilities of growing and preparing for manufacture certain fibers such as flax, sisal hemp, and ramie. Another set of experiments that was placed in Willits' department had to do with the production of rain by means of explosives. No report on this subject by Willits has been found, but Secretary Rusk declared in 1892 that the results after two years' trials were not such as to please advocates of this means of rain making.

The assistant secretary recognized the importance to farmers of good roads as a means of easy access to markets, and he believed that the Department of Agriculture should help provide them. Consequently, he asked Congress to appropriate $10,000 for a study of road building and for the publication of bulletins on the subject.

In his report for 1892, written after the election of Grover Cleveland when Willits expected to retire from the Department within a few months, he stated that he would be sorry to give up his position because he had found the work very interesting. Continuing, and speaking of himself, he said:

> He knows more of this great country, of its possibilities, of the obstacles to agriculture, of the means to overcome them—vastly more

than he did when he entered upon his duties . . . such rapid progress is observable that he congratulates himself on the fact that in small part he has been connected therewith.

Contrary to his expectations, Willits was not permitted to resign at the end of President Harrison's administration. For two years he had been carrying the triple burden of assistant secretary, representative of the Department of Agriculture on the Board of Management of Government Exhibits for the World's Columbian Exposition in Chicago, and chairman of the board. He had planned the displays of the Department and was having them placed in the Government Building on the fairgrounds. No new appointee could have performed all these duties in a satisfactory manner, especially since the exposition was scheduled to open on May 1, 1893, only two months after the inauguration. President Cleveland and Secretary Morton needed him, and at their request he remained.

The World's Columbian Exposition grounds were principally in Jackson Park near the shore of Lake Michigan. Around the Great Basin and the Lagoon and beside the canals were placed the principal buildings—"The White City." The huge golden statue of the Republic, the Columbian fountain, and other statuary groups were considered artistic triumphs, and velvet-canopied gondolas propelled by gondoliers dressed in colorful costumes of the fourteenth century prompted writers to call it "the Venice of the West." The Fair provided both amusements and educational features. The former were on the Midway Plaisance, which extended westward from the lagoon to Washington Park. Here was the Ferris wheel, 264 feet high, with its thirty-six coaches, each capable of holding sixty passengers, from which one had a panoramic view of the exposition grounds and Chicago. There were also the South Sea Island village, Hagenbeck's trained animals, the captive balloon, the tower of Blarney Castle, the Street of Cairo, and other exotic attractions.

Among the educational features were the replicas of Columbus' three caravels which had been built in Spain and sailed across the Atlantic, an exact copy of a Viking ship which had crossed the ocean from Norway, and the great variety of exhibits in the buildings devoted to agriculture, manufactures, machinery, liberal arts, government and other activities. Six buildings housed government exhibits exclusively. Four of them showed the services provided respectively by the Naval Observatory, Army hospitals, the Weather Bureau, and the Indian Bureau. A fifth was unique. It was the battleship "Illinois" constructed just offshore in Lake Michigan, of brick covered with concrete. Complete in every detail from fighting mast to the latest model naval guns, the "Illinois" appeared to be riding at anchor, ready to sail at a moment's notice against her country's foes. Visitors were invited to inspect the "ship."

The principal government building was an imposing structure of modern Renaissance architecture surmounted by a central dome. In it were placed the exhibits of most of the departments and bureaus. For example, the Department of State displayed, among other things, the Declaration of Independence and the Constitution, the War Department showed weapons and battle flags, the Mint had a press in operation striking a commemorative medal, and the Patent Office exhibited models of inventions.

The exhibit of the Department of Agriculture had been planned with great care. Willits was determined that it should show the specific functions of the various divisions and sections and that it should have educational value. Although there were some displays that would interest the casual visitor, such as realistic wax models of fruits and flowers, and a section of a California redwood twenty-three feet in diameter, on the whole the idea of the assistant secretary was to illustrate what the government was doing to improve the quality and increase the quantity of farm products.

Willits took particular pride in his extensive collections of cereals, fibers, and tobaccos. On display were 2,500 samples of wheat, 1,600 of corn, 1,200 of oats, and smaller groups of rye, barley, buckwheat, and other grains. Besides, there were 1,500 samples of wool, more than 1,400 of cotton, and 1,500 of tobacco. These exhibits were intended not simply to attract the notice of the curious. Willits hoped that the collections would interest experts who would make exhaustive studies of the distribution, varieties, care, and culture of each, and write monographs based upon their findings.

The assistant secretary had overestimated the intellectual interest of his fellow countrymen at the Fair. No one was moved to write monographs on his samples of cereals and fibers, and the people who visited the building spent little time studying the displays. Most of them simply passed through, giving only casual attention to whatever caught their eyes. Willits reported that scarcely anyone took the trouble to climb the stairs to see the exhibits on the second floor. Perhaps the attraction of the Ferris wheel, the South Sea islanders, and the dancing girls of the Street of Cairo was too great. He admitted frankly that "my plan was too comprehensive, and from present appearances the result will not be adequate to the time, thought, and money engaged in its preparation."

Nevertheless, Willits believed that his work had not been in vain. In spite of mistakes which he had made, and which he candidly reported, he wrote:

> . . . I may be pardoned expressing a feeling of pride in the symmetry, the unity, and the completeness of the exhibit as a whole and in detail. It had a purpose running all through it. Its idea was educational, and had a significance that was highly appreciated by the intelligent visitor who stopped to study its scope. It has commanded the respect of experts in the line of the functions sought to be illustrated, and it has met the commendation of so many people competent to judge such matters in their several parts, that though my high standards were not attained and my purposes as to ultimate results have not been fully realized, I rejoice that I was considered worthy of projecting and carrying out an enterprise that so fully illustrated the functions of the Department which I have served to the best of my ability for nearly five years and from which my relations are soon to be sundered.

The exposition was officially closed on October 30, 1893. Willits and the other members of the board of management were busy afterward for a time supervising the packing of the exhibits for return to Washington. When he had completed his task, he tendered his resignation to Secretary J. Sterling Morton, who accepted it with the expression of sincere gratitude which has already been quoted. On January 1, 1894, Willits retired to private life. The former assistant secretary remained in Washington, where he opened an office and resumed the practice of law.

Throughout his life, Willits had retained a sincere affection for his alma mater. In 1866 the Society of the Alumni of the University of Michigan appointed him a member of a committee to draft a petition asking the state legislature to make an appropriation for the support of the University. The petition, which was presented in January, 1867, contained the suggestion that one-twentieth of a mill on each dollar of taxable property be allotted to the University. At the same time, the Board of Regents also petitioned the legislature for funds. As a result, a law was passed embodying the provision suggested by the alumni; this constituted the beginning of the "mill tax," which has ever since been the principal support of the University.

Thirty years later, Willits was still active in alumni affairs. In February, 1896, he wrote to his former chief, Morton, urging him to attend the annual reunion and dinner of the University of Michigan alumni at the Down Town Club in Washington. "For many reasons, among which prime is the fact that you are a good fellow and your presence adds interest to any such occasion, I hope you can make it possible to be present . . ."

This was the last annual alumni dinner that Willits attended. He died in Washington on October 23, 1896, and was buried in Monroe. After the death of her husband, Mrs. Willits returned to Monroe, which was her home until she died on May 16, 1906.

Cushman K. Davis

Alumni in the Congress

By Ira A. Campbell

THE Cleveland era spanned the Forty-ninth and Fiftieth Congresses of the United States, March 4, 1885, to March 3, 1889, and the Fifty-third and Fifty-fourth Congresses, March 4, 1893, to March 3, 1897. The membership of these four Congresses included forty-seven men who were alumni of the University of Michigan.

Of the seventy-six senators and 325 representatives in the Forty-ninth Congress, the University of Michigan was represented by one senator, Thomas Witherell Palmer from Michigan, and by ten representatives, Byron M. Cutcheon, Seth Crittenden Moffatt, William C. Maybury, and Timothy Edward Tarsney from Michigan; George Ford from Indiana; Adoniram Judson Holmes from Iowa; William Warner from Missouri; James Laird from Nebraska; Samuel Ritter Peters from Kansas; and Augustus Herman Pettibone from Tennessee. Senator Palmer and Representatives Cutcheon, Holmes, Laird, Moffatt, Peters, Pettibone, and Warner were Republicans, and Representatives Ford, Maybury, and Tarsney were Democrats.

In the Fiftieth Congress, one among the seventy-six senators and sixteen of the 337 representatives had received their education at the University of Michigan: Senator Cushman Kellogg Davis from Minnesota, and Representatives Edward Payson Allen, John Logan Chipman, Byron M. Cutcheon, Seth Crittenden Moffatt, Timothy Edward Tarsney, and Justin Rice Whiting from Michigan; William Warner from Missouri; Melvin Morella Boothman and Samuel Sampson Yoder from

Ohio; Nils Pedersen Haugen from Wisconsin; Walter Ingalls Hayes and Adoniram Judson Holmes from Iowa; James Laird from Nebraska; Samuel Ritter Peters from Kansas; John Henry O'Neall and Benjamin Franklin Shively from Indiana. Of these, Senator Davis and Representatives Allen, Boothman, Cutcheon, Haugen, Holmes, Laird, Moffatt, Peters, Warner and Whiting were Republicans, and Representatives Chipman, Hayes, O'Neall, Shively, Tarsney and Yoder were Democrats.

In the Fifty-third Congress, of eighty-eight senators and 381 representatives, eighteen were from the University of Michigan: two senators, Calvin Stewart Brice from Ohio and Cushman K. Davis from Minnesota, and sixteen representatives, John Logan Chipman, Levi Thomas Griffin, James Sedgwick Gorman, Henry Franklin Thomas, Thomas Addis Emmet Weadock, and Justin R. Whiting from Michigan; John James Gardner from New Jersey; Hamilton Kinkaid Wheeler from Illinois; Walter Ingalls Hayes from Iowa; Darius Dodge Hare from Ohio; Marriott Brosius from Pennsylvania; Nils Pedersen Haugen from Wisconsin; George de Rue Meiklejohn and David Henry Mercer from Nebraska; John Alfred Pickler from South Dakota; and John Charles Tarsney from Missouri. Senator Davis and Representatives Brosius, Gardner, Haugen, Meiklejohn, Mercer, Pickler, Thomas, Wheeler, and Whiting were Republicans, and Senator Brice and Representatives Chipman, Griffin, Gorman, Hare, Hayes, Tarsney, and Weadock were Democrats—ten Republicans and eight Democrats. The increase in the number of Democrats reflected the political sentiment which resulted in Cleveland's second election to the presidency.

In the Fifty-fourth Congress, the University's representation increased to four senators and eighteen representatives of a total membership of ninety senators and 376 representatives. In the Senate were Lucian Baker from Kansas, Arthur Brown, first senator from the newly admitted state of Utah, Calvin S. Brice from Ohio, and Cushman K. Davis from Minnesota; and in the House of Representatives, Roswell Peter Bishop, Horace Greeley Snover, and Henry Franklin Thomas from Michigan;

John Kissig Cowen from Maryland; John James Gardner from New Jersey; William Flavius Lester Hadley from Illinois; Joseph Morgan Kendall from Kentucky; Winfield Scott Kerr from Ohio; Marriott Brosius from Pennsylvania; Snyder Solomon Kirkpatrick from Kansas; George de Rue Meiklejohn and David Henry Mercer from Nebraska; Theobald Otjen from Wisconsin; John Alfred Pickler from South Dakota; John Franklin Shafroth from Colorado; John Charles Tarsney from Missouri; Charles Arnette Towne from Minnesota; and Edgar Wilson from Idaho—eighteen Republicans and four Democrats (Senator Brice and Representatives Cowen, Kennedy and Tarsney). This party ratio—typical of this 1894 election—forecast the eclipse of Democratic rule under President Cleveland.

From the time of President Lincoln's inauguration in 1861 to President Wilson's in 1913, a period of fifty-two years, the eight years of the Cleveland era alone intervened in the long stretch of Republican domination of national administrations. Since 1893 there have been eight years of Democratic administration, followed by twelve years of Republican, and by 1948, fifteen years of Democratic control, changes which evidence the virile and well-working democracy that is America.

Of the forty-seven members of the four Congresses of the Cleveland era who had received their training at the University of Michigan, eighteen had in their youth served with loyalty and distinction in the Civil War. It is an interesting fact that of these eighteen veterans, fifteen took up the study of law at the University of Michigan, just as so many G.I.s are now doing, but in those days not with the generous governmental aid being accorded the men of World War II. Only two of the veterans, Senator Cushman K. Davis and Representative William Warner, had begun their study of law at the University before the war. Another veteran, Representative Samuel S. Yoder, studied medicine at the University after the war.

By reason of the character of the work falling upon the members of Congress, it was to be expected that lawyers would predominate in its membership, and it is worthy of note that with the exception of Senator Palmer, Dr. Henry Franklin Thomas, Justin R. Whiting, and Samuel S. Yoder, the Michigan-trained members of the four Congresses were educated at the University as lawyers.

Nearly all of these lawyers followed the same general pattern of professional career: they were poor boys, starting humbly in the law, mostly in the smaller towns and cities, elected as county and state attorneys, going into state legislatures, steadily developing substantial practices, and then achieving election to Congress.

A number of the representatives served long terms in Congress, others came to the bench, and several were governors of their states before or after their terms in Congress.

These were the men of the University of Michigan, who, in the Cleveland era, were most outstanding in national affairs and leaders in their home communities. Their domiciles show that the greatest range of influence of the University of Michigan was throughout the Middle West, in a time when the vigorous expansion of the West and the rapid development of its industrial and agricultural resources offered careers to worthy and aspiring young men.

Of the forty-seven University of Michigan men in the four Congresses, fourteen were from Michigan; five from Ohio; three each from Indiana, Kansas, and Nebraska; two each from Iowa, Illinois, and Minnesota; and one each from New Jersey, Maryland, Kentucky, Tennessee, Pennsylvania, South Dakota, Colorado, Utah, and Idaho.

Among the representatives, the career of Byron M. Cutcheon, of Michigan, was most varied. He was born in Pembroke, New Hampshire, May 11, 1836, and, after attending the common schools and Pembroke Academy, taught in Pembroke several years. He then moved to Ypsilanti and became principal of Birmingham Academy, attended Ypsilanti Seminary, and finally graduated from the University of Michigan in 1861. Upon graduation he became a teacher of ancient languages in the Ypsilanti High School. In 1862 he enlisted in the Twentieth Regiment Michigan Infantry, attaining the rank of lieutenant colonel. In October, 1864, he was brevetted colonel of the United States Volunteers "for gallant service in the Battles of the Wilderness and Spottsylvania Court House, Va.," and on November 12 was commissioned colonel of the Twentieth Michigan Regiment. Owing to the death of his superior officer, he commanded the second brigade, Second Division, Ninth Army Corps, from October 16, 1864, until his resignation on March 6, 1865. Seven days later, on March 13, he was brevetted brigadier general of the United States Volunteers.

Cutcheon immediately entered the Law Department of the University of Michigan and graduated in 1866, at the age of thirty years. He was admitted to the bar, commenced practice in Ionia, and continued it later in Manistee. He immediately attained success in the profession. In 1866 he became president of the Michigan Soldiers' Home Commission and served as a member of the Board of Control of Railroads of Michigan from 1867 to 1883.

He was a presidential elector on the Republican ticket of Grant and Colfax in 1868; city attorney of Manistee and prosecuting attorney of Manistee County between 1870 and 1874; and from 1875 until 1881 served as a regent of the University. After that he became postmaster of Manistee for six years and was finally elected on the Republican ticket as representative to the Forty-eighth, Forty-ninth, Fiftieth, and Fifty-first Congresses. On June 29, 1891, he was awarded a medal of honor by Congress "for distinguished gallantry at the Battle of Horseshoe Bend, Ky., May 10, 1863." He had failed, however, of re-election to the Fifty-second Congress, in the Democratic victory in 1890 which presaged the return of President Cleveland.

In July, 1891, President Harrison appointed Cutcheon a civil member of the Board of Ordnance and Fortifications. He served on this Board until March 25, 1895, when he became an editorial writer for two years on the *Detroit Daily Tribune* and the *Detroit Journal*. He then resumed the practice of law in Grand Rapids, Michigan, where he remained until his death on April 12, 1908. He was a scholarly man and pursued a more continuously active and diversified life in public affairs than falls to the lot of most men. Authorship was among his more important pursuits. He was particularly active as a writer of history, producing a *History of the Twentieth Michigan Infantry,* two of the four volumes comprising the well-known work, *Michigan as a Province, Territory, and State,* and numerous articles on historical subjects.

Representative John Franklin Shafroth of Colorado, who was elected to the Senate in 1913, was especially devoted to the development of the West. He was born and brought up in Fayette, Missouri, and graduated from the University of Michigan in 1875. He studied law at Fayette, was admitted to the bar in 1876, and went to Denver in 1879, where he actively engaged in the practice of the law. After nine years of private practice he was elected city attorney of Denver, and then, in 1894, was elected to Congress on the Republican ticket. Two years later he bolted the Republican Convention and, with Senator Henry M. Teller, helped found the Silver Republican Party. He was endorsed by the Democratic Party and reelected in 1896 and 1898, but his election in 1902 was contested; the ballot boxes were taken to Washington, and Representative Shafroth asked permission to examine them. Finding evidence of fraud in some districts, he took the honorable course of immediately resigning from Congress (February 15, 1904), with the assertion that he would not hold a "tainted seat." He was generally praised for his action, for it constituted a course practically without precedent. Later that year he ran for Congress, but was defeated. In 1908 and 1910 he was elected governor of Colorado and took an active interest in the direct primary, initiative, and referendum reforms which were adopted by Colorado.

In 1913 Shafroth was elected to the United States Senate, where he served on the Banking and Currency Committee and helped frame the Federal Reserve Act. He was especially interested in all measures pertaining to the conservation of national resources and successfully fought for the Reclamation Act; but failed in his efforts for "free silver." Although he apparently broke with President Wilson on the subject of conservation, he supported him on the League of Nations. He was defeated for re-election in 1918, but served for two years as chairman of the War Minerals Relief Commission. He died in 1922.

Representative Benjamin Franklin Shively, from Indiana, was elected to the United States Senate in 1909 and served with great distinction until his death in 1916. Levi T. Griffin, who served in the Fifty-third Congress, from Detroit, was probably as well known to University of Michigan alumni as any of the forty-seven congressmen, for he taught during many years in the University Law School, where his lectures were highly rated. His eminent success at the bar made him especially respected by the embryonic lawyers. Representative John Kissig Cowen, a member of the Fifty-fourth Congress, was for twenty years, from 1876 to 1896, general counsel of the Baltimore and Ohio Railroad Company, and was president of the company from January, 1896, to June, 1901. Representative Roswell Peter Bishop from Michigan served in five successive Congresses, March 14, 1895, to March 3, 1907. He failed of reelection in 1906 and was subsequently appointed a member of the Spanish Treaty Claims Commission.

Representative Charles Arnette Towne had as eventful a political career as any of the forty-seven University of Michigan men. He graduated from the University in 1881, studied law and was admitted to the bar in 1886, and commenced practice in Lansing. In 1890 he removed to Duluth, Minnesota, and continued the practice of the law. He was elected as a Republican to the Fifty-fourth Congress, but was an unsuccessful Democratic candidate in 1896 for election to the Fifty-fifth Congress, and in 1898, to the Fifty-sixth Congress. He declined nomination for vice-president by the Populist and Silver Republican parties in 1900 and was unsuccessful as a Democratic candidate for election to the Senate in the same year. On the death of Senator Cushman K. Davis, Towne, as a Democrat, was appointed to the Senate to fill the vacancy and served from January 5, 1900, to January 28, 1901. Senator Towne moved to New York City in June, 1901, took up the practice of law, and in 1904 was elected to the Fifty-ninth Congress as a Democratic representative from New York. Towne was notable as a public speaker, and he died with his "political boots" on, while on a speaking tour on behalf of the Smith-Robinson ticket, on October 26, 1928. He was one of the most eloquent and picturesque men in the public life of his time.

In the Senate, Senator Thomas W. Palmer of Detroit was held in high esteem because of the eminence he had attained as a successful business man and a public-spirited citizen. His life and notable contributions to public welfare are reviewed in full detail elsewhere in this volume.

The figure of Senator Calvin Stewart Brice was stalwart among the men of his time. He was born in Ohio in 1845, his father being a Presbyterian minister and his mother a person of cultural attainments. He was educated in the common schools and entered Miami University, at Oxford, Ohio, but his studies were interrupted by the war. In 1861, although only fifteen, he enlisted, but was rejected because of his youth. The following year he re-enlisted and served three months, and then returned to Oxford to complete his college course. He graduated in June, 1863, and, after teaching three months, recruited Company E of the 180th Ohio Volunteer Infantry and became its captain, serving until July, 1865. A few days before the end of the war he was promoted to lieutenant colonel for meritorious service. Brice was just twenty-one years old when he left the Army. He immediately entered the Law Department of the University of Michigan, and in the spring of 1866 he was admitted to the bar.

In the course of his career Brice attained eminence as a business lawyer in connection with the development of railroads and coal properties in Ohio. He was responsible for the organization of the Lake Erie and Western Railroad, of which he became president in 1887; and he planned, built, and sold the road known as the "Nickel Plate." Altogether, he was connected with the development of some ten different railroads. His greatest project in railroading, however, was in China, where, under a concession from the Imperial Government, he undertook the building of a railroad between Canton and Hankow. His death intervened, however, before he completed it. These operations were carried on under an organization which became known as the "Brice Syndicate."

Brice was active in Democratic politics. He was a presidential elector for Tilden and Hendricks in 1876 and for Cleveland and Hendricks in 1884; in 1889 he became chairman of the Democratic National Committee. In 1890 he was elected senator from Ohio to succeed Senator Henry B. Payne for the term expiring March 4, 1897, and became a leading figure in the Senate at the zenith of the Cleveland era. He was made a member of the Steering Committee and of the Committee on Appropriations. He took little part in public discussions, but his quiet influence was generally recognized as very powerful. Significant tribute to his high principles as a public servant was paid in the following comment in the *Way Bill:*

> For all of Mr. Brice's official relations with various railroads and other corporate properties he never accepted a dollar of salary for his services. We do not know of another man in a similar position of whom the same can be said.

On retiring at the close of his term Senator Brice took up his residence in New York City and became prominent in financial circles. He died in 1898.

Of all the men from Michigan who graced the Cleveland era in Congress, beyond question the most distinguished was Senator Cushman Kellogg Davis from Minnesota. His most notable service to his country was rendered as chairman of the Foreign Relations Committee of the Senate during the period of the Spanish-American War and as one of the commissioners who negotiated the treaty in Paris at the close of the hostilities. Davis was born in Jefferson County, New York, June 16, 1838. When he was two months old, his parents moved to Wisconsin, where he grew up as a farmer boy. He was a highly gifted youth, and largely through his own efforts he obtained an education in the district schools, in Carroll College, and finally in the University of Michigan, from which he graduated in 1857, at the age of nineteen. He immediately took up the study of law and was admitted to practice in Wisconsin in 1859. In 1862 he enlisted in the Civil War as first lieutenant of Company B, Twenty-first Wisconsin Regiment, and served with distinction until 1864, when, on account of poor health, he was compelled to resign.

In 1865 Davis moved to St. Paul, Minnesota, and resumed the practice of law. Early in his career he gained recognition as one of the ablest and most eloquent members of the bar, with a large and lucrative practice. The qualities which distinguished Davis as a lawyer were described in the eulogy delivered in the Senate at the time of his death by his associate, Senator Knute Nelson. Nelson praised Davis, saying that he was:

> . . . a most profound lawyer who mastered the great fundamental principles of the law that govern human affairs and had the intuitive faculty to correctly apply these to the manifold transactions of an ever-expanding civilization. In practice he was always ready and always a complete master of the evidence, the facts, and the law of his case, and his eloquence was of a character to instruct, impress, and convince both court and jury, and he was equally at home and equally strong both in a nisi prius and in an appellate court.

Davis was an early supporter of the Granger movement, in connection with which he delivered an unusual speech entitled "Modern Feudalism," in which he attacked the railroads for their exactions and practices in the Northwest. The speech attracted such attention that it was repeated on numerous occasions and largely contributed to his election as governor, in 1874, at the age of thirty-six. After one term, he resumed his career at the bar, and his firm of Davis, Kellogg and Severance attained pre-eminence in the Northwest. From it later came Frank B. Kellogg, Secretary of State. Davis was elected to the Senate in 1887 and re-elected in 1893 and 1899. On entering the Senate he was assigned to the Committee on Pensions, of which he became chairman, and for many years he devoted himself largely to the interests of Civil War veterans. He was instrumental in pushing through the Dependent Pension Bill.

Senator Davis early became a member of the Committee on Foreign Relations and soon disclosed such unusual knowledge and aptitude for international affairs that he was accorded recognition as an outstanding authority. He became chairman of the committee and in that capacity drew up the declaration of war with Spain; he was the first-named of the senators on the commission that framed the treaty of peace in Paris. With Senator Davis on the commission was another of the University of Michigan's most distinguished sons, William R. Day, of the class of 1870. Day resigned as secretary of state to undertake the chairmanship of the commission. Thus, through her share in the personnel of the commission, Michigan may claim particular service in the negotiations ending the Spanish-American War.

In his relations with President Cleveland, Senator Davis was both with and against the President on important national and international matters. The principles which guided him were always stated with such clarity and courage and illumined by such great learning that they left no misunderstanding as to his position and the underlying reasons for his action. In connection with them he made pronouncements that were remarkably prophetic and apposite to conditions in recent times which have involved and threatened the fate of the country. Davis supported President Cleveland in sending federal troops to Chicago in 1894 to keep the mail trains running against strikers. A resolution was introduced in the Senate, the object of which was to allow strikers to stop all railway traffic, provided this did not interfere with the carriage of United States mails. A committee assuming to speak in the name of working men of Duluth wired Senator Davis requesting him to support the resolution. The message arrived after he had gone to bed. Without waiting to dress, and without seeming to have any anxiety but to do his duty, he wrote in pencil and sent back by the messenger an answer in which he unequivocally refused to support the resolution, saying:

I have received your telegram. I will not support the resolution. It is against your own real welfare. It is also a blow at the security, peace, and rights of millions of people who never harmed you or your associates. My duty to the Constitution and the laws forbids me to sustain a resolution to legalize lawlessness. The same duty rests upon you and your associates. The power to regulate commerce among the several States is vested by the Constitution in Congress. Your associates have usurped that power at Hammond and other places, and have destroyed commerce between the States in these particular instances. You are rapidly approaching the overt act of levying war against the United States, and you will find the definition of that in the Constitution. I trust that wiser thoughts will control. You might as well ask me to vote to dissolve the Government.

According to the word of one of his contemporaries, expressed in the eulogies pronounced in the House of Representatives on the occasion of his death, "This message, instinct with the courage of a patriot and the kindness of a father, was published in all the newspapers of the country, and was everywhere regarded as 'the word fitly spoken.'"

When President Cleveland became involved in controversy with Great Britain over the Venezuelan boundary dispute, Senator Davis brought before the Senate a joint resolution which reaffirmed adherence to the Monroe Doctrine. In support of it he laid down the following principle which has much pertinence in the world of today:

The President of the United States says "Great Britain's present proposition has never thus far been regarded as admissible by Venezuela, though any adjustment of the boundary which that country may demand for her advantage and may enter of her own free will can not of course be objected to by the United States." I undertake to say that the American people will never vindicate that statement. It is no part of the Monroe Doctrine and never was that any adjustment which a South American State might make of its own free will as to a cession of territory under any pretext whatever "could not, of course, be objected to by the United States." Mr. Calhoun is the only statesman in our history who ever asserted that the doctrine could not prevent a voluntary cession of her sovereignty by a South American State.

In the course of that remarkable address Senator Davis gave utterance to these words which correctly envisioned the future relations between Great Britain and the United States:

> Mr. President, there has been talk of war. To simply declare and define American policies and American rights has been attacked as tending to bring on war. There never has been the least danger of war throughout this controversy. Neither Government has ever threatened it or pressed it. The interests of Great Britain and the United States in the great and common cause of civilization are too enormous and too vital to each other to bring about such a consummation.

Differing with the policy of President Cleveland, Senator Davis supported the establishment of the Provisional Government of Hawaii, set up on January 17, 1893, and thoroughly castigated Blount, President Cleveland's special commissioner to Hawaii, for directing Rear Admiral Joseph S. Skerrett, commander of the Pacific Squadron, to haul down the United States ensign from the Government building and to embark the troops who were on shore. The Senator said in an address to the Senate:

> The history of this country may be hunted over and no other instance can be found where a civil officer or a citizen of our States ordered an admiral of the American Navy to haul down the flag of our Government.

In the course of the debates in the Senate on this controversy, the Senator showed his statesmanship and his vision of the future of his country, by this declaration:

> I am not in favor of a colonial system such as Great Britain has, and such as France is striving for, but I want to see my country well defended and her hold upon the enormous commerce of the future in the Pacific Ocean assured. That the Sandwich Islands were in time to be an indispensable element of the prosperity, protection, and defense of our country has been a cardinal theory with every statesman who ever sat in the chair of the Secretary of State from the beginning of the question down to the present time.

Thus, his imagination foresaw, nearly half a century before "Pearl Harbor," the "outpost of defense" which the Hawaiian

Islands were to become and the "vitalness of the commerce of the Pacific" to the well being and security of his country.

Senator Davis' standing as a statesman and the regard and affection in which he was held were best expressed by his contemporaries at the services held in the Senate on November 27, 1900. In the course of the services, Senator John C. Spooner, of Wisconsin, who had known Senator Davis from youth, said:

> He was a great constitutional lawyer, and he made of himself here a great international lawyer. I have not known one in public life who knew more accurately, in general and in detail, the great transactions of this Government, from the beginning in its international relations. . . .

Senator Henry Cabot Lodge added his encomium:

> That he was a statesman in the best acceptance of that term can not be gainsaid. He dealt with large questions in a large way. He looked before and after, not to sigh for what is not, but that he might deal successfully with the present and prepare wisely for the future. Like most men learned in the law his tendencies were conservative, but he did not shrink from innovation, nor was he the slave of precedent. The past, which he studied so faithfully, was to him a wise teacher, not an unbending tyrant. He was not one of those who hide dislike of the present and distrust of the future under the guise of loyalty to the past. Although a man of strong will and masterful temper, he was ever open to new ideas. Above all, he had the two attributes essential to the highest statesmanship—sentiment and imagination.

It was not alone in the mastery of the principles and precedents of international law that Senator Davis excelled; he was always the student and scholar. He was master of a fine literary style and had rare facility in the use of language. Every word he used fitted its place and was chosen to give precise expression to the thought he intended to convey. While his work at the bar and in public service absorbed most of his attention, he always devoted a share of his time to the study of literature and history. He was a profound Shakespearean scholar and was thoroughly familiar with the life and all the works of that great genius. He lectured on Hamlet and wrote a book entitled *The*

Law in Shakespeare, a valuable contribution to Shakespearean literature. He was a master of the French language, knew Italian well, and had a serviceable use of Spanish and German. One of the most valued sets of books in his collection was a complete and uniform edition of the Italian poets, through which, in leisure hours, "he wandered ever with senses alive to each peculiar beauty, from Dante and Petrarch to Leopardi."

In history he became attracted to Napoleon and was a thorough and profound student of his life, mission, and work. There was scarcely a book on Napoleon in English or French that he did not have in his library and had not read and mastered. "To him Napoleon was the spirit in that mighty whirlwind that crushed the feudalism of ages and paved the way to the democracy of modern time." His library was his most congenial habitat, and his love of the classics abided with him from his college days to the end of his life.

These alumni of the University of Michigan in the Congresses of the Cleveland era brought honor, distinction, and credit to their alma mater by work well done. They played a part in the enactment of measures that contributed to the upbuilding of the country in a period of growth that was the forerunner of its great industrial expansion; many of them were especially concerned with those matters of government which related to the natural resources of the great western areas of the country whence they came. They constituted the largest body of alumni in Congress from any one educational institution, and without doubt their influence was in proportion to their numbers.

Fine as were the public services rendered by the University of Michigan alumni in the Congresses of the Cleveland era, however, they were neither the beginning nor the end of the contributions of Michigan men to our national welfare. The University continues to play the role of great contributor to our national statesmanship in which, ever since her first alumni were old enough to participate in political leadership, she has so distinguished herself. For example, an alumnus, Arthur H. Vandenberg, a Senator of twenty years' experience, again occupies the highly important position which Cushman K. Davis held in the Cleveland era—the Chairmanship of the Foreign Relations Committee of the United States Senate—and like Davis attended a Paris peace conference as well as the organizations and conferences that followed.

The appended list of one hundred and eighty-two Michigan alumni who served in the Congresses over nearly a century, 1858 to 1947, is proof sufficient of the continued influence which the University of Michigan has had in the preservation of the United States and in its rise to its present position of leadership and responsibility in world affairs.

UNIVERSITY OF MICHIGAN ALUMNI IN THE UNITED STATES CONGRESS, 1858–1947 *

Adair, Jackson Leroy. Born February 23, 1888, Clayton, Illinois. LL.B., 1911. Representative from Illinois; served as a Democrat in Congress, 1933–37.

Allen, Edward Payson. Born October 28, 1839, Sharon, Michigan. LL.B., 1867. Representative from Michigan; served as a Republican in Congress, 1887–91.

Allen, John Beard. Born May 18, 1845, Crawfordsville, Indiana. Literary Department, 1866–67. Delegate to Congress for the Territory of Washington, March to November, 1889; as a Republican Senator from the state of Washington, 1889–93.

Allen, Leo Elwood. Born October 5, 1898, Elizabeth, Illinois. College of Literature, Science, and the Arts, 1919–21; Law School, 1921–22. Representative from Illinois; served as a Republican in Congress, 1933– .

Anderson, Clinton P. Born October 23, 1895, Centerville, South Dakota. College of Literature, Science, and the Arts, 1915–16. Representative from New Mexico; served as a Democrat in Congress, 1941–45.

Anthony, Daniel Read, Jr. Born August 22, 1870, Leavenworth, Kansas. LL.B., 1891. Representative from Kansas; served as a Republican in Congress, 1907–29.

Ashurst, Henry Fountain. Born September 13, 1874, Winnemucca, Nevada. Law School, 1903–04. Senator from Arizona; served as a Democrat in the Senate, 1912–40.

* Those serving in the Cleveland era are indicated by italics. This list is not complete.

Baker, Lucien. Born June 8, 1846, near Cleveland, Ohio. Law School, 1868–69. Senator from Kansas; served as a Republican in the Senate, 1895–1901.

Bannon, Henry Towne. Born June 5, 1867, near Portsmouth, Ohio. B.L., 1889. Representative from Ohio; served as a Republican in Congress, 1905–09.

Barclay, Charles Frederick. Born May 9, 1844, Owego, New York. Law School, 1866–67. Representative from Pennsylvania; served as a Republican in Congress, 1907–11.

Beakes, Samuel Willard. Born January 11, 1861, Burlingham, New York. LL.B., 1883. Representative from Michigan; served as a Democrat in Congress, 1913–19.

Bilbo, Theodore Gilmore. Born October 13, 1877, near Poplarville, Mississippi. Law School, 1909. Senator from Mississippi; served as a Democrat in the Senate, 1935–47.

Bishop, Roswell Peter. Born January 6, 1843, Sidney, New York. Literary Department, 1867–72. Representative from Michigan; served as a Republican in Congress, 1895–1907.

Blackney, William W. Born August 28, 1876, Clio, Michigan. LL.B., 1912. Representative from Michigan; served as a Republican in Congress, 1935– .

Boothman, Melvin Morella. Born October 16, 1846, Williams County, Ohio. LL.B., 1871. Representative from Ohio; served as a Republican in Congress, 1887–91.

Borland, William Patterson. Born October 14, 1867, Leavenworth, Kansas. LL.B., 1892. Representative from Missouri; served as a Democrat in Congress, 1909–19.

Brainerd, Samuel Myron. Born November 13, 1842, Albion, Pennsylvania. Literary Department, 1865–66. Representative from Pennsylvania; served as a Republican in Congress, 1883–85.

Brice, Calvin Stewart. Born September 17, 1845, Denmark, Ohio. Law School, 1865–66. Senator from Ohio; served as a Democrat in the Senate, 1891–97.

Brick, Abraham Lincoln. Born May 27, 1860, near South Bend, Indiana. LL.B., 1883. Representative from Indiana; served as a Republican in Congress, 1899–1908.

Brosius, Marriott. Born March 7, 1843, Colerain Township, Pennsylvania. LL.B., 1868. Representative from Pennsylvania; served as a Republican in Congress, 1889–1901.

Brown, Arthur. Born March 8, 1843, Prairie Ronde, Michigan. A.M.,

LL.B., 1864. Senator from Utah; served as a Republican in the Senate, 1896–97.

Brucker, Ferdinand. Born January 8, 1858, Bridgeport, Michigan. LL.B., 1881. Representative from Michigan; served as a Democrat in Congress, 1897–99.

Bulow, William John. Born January 13, 1869, Clermont County, Ohio. LL.B., 1893. Senator from South Dakota; served as a Democrat in the Senate, 1931–43.

Burke, James Francis. Born October 21, 1867, Petroleum Center, Pennsylvania. LL.B., 1892. Representative from Pennsylvania; served as a Republican in Congress, 1905–15.

Cable, Benjamin Taylor. Born August 11, 1853, Georgetown, Kentucky. B.S., 1876. Representative from Illinois; served as a Democrat in Congress, 1891–93.

Carpenter, William Randolph. Born April 24, 1894, Marion, Kansas. LL.B., 1917. Representative from Kansas; served as a Democrat in Congress, 1933–37.

Chalmers, William Wallace. Born November 1, 1861, Strathray, Ontario, Canada. A.B., 1887. Representative from Ohio; served as a Republican in Congress, 1921–23, 1925–27, 1929–31.

Chandler, Walter Marion. Born December 8, 1867, near Yazoo City, Mississippi. LL.B., 1897. Representative from New York; served as a Progressive in Congress, 1913–19, 1921–23.

Chipman, John Logan. Born June 5, 1830, Detroit, Michigan. Literary Department, 1843–45. Representative from Michigan; served as a Democrat in Congress, 1887–93.

Church, Ralph E. Born May 5, 1883, near Catlin, Illinois. A.B., 1907. Representative from Illinois; served as a Republican in Congress, 1935– .

Clancy, Robert Henry. Born March 14, 1882, Detroit, Michigan. A.B., 1907. Representative from Michigan; served as a Republican in Congress, 1923–25, 1927–33.

Codd, George Pierre. Born December 7, 1869, Detroit, Michigan. A.B., 1891. Representative from Michigan; served as a Republican in Congress, 1921–23.

Colton, Don B. Born September 15, 1876, near Mona, Utah. LL.B., 1905. Representative from Utah; served as a Republican in Congress, 1921–33.

Comstock, Solomon Gilman. Born May 9, 1842, Argyle, Maine. Law

School, 1868–69. Representative from Minnesota; served as a Republican in Congress, 1889–91.

Conry, Michael Francis. Born April 2, 1870, Shenandoah, Pennsylvania. LL.B., 1896. Representative from New York; served as a Democrat in Congress, 1909–17.

Cooper, Allen Foster. Born June 16, 1862, Franklin Township, Pennsylvania. LL.B., 1888. Representative from Pennsylvania; served as a Republican in Congress, 1903–11.

Copeland, Royal Samuel. Born November 7, 1868, Dexter, Michigan. M.D., 1889. Senator from New York; served as a Democrat in the Senate, 1923–38.

Cowen, John Kissig. Born October 28, 1844, near Millersburg, Ohio. Law School, 1867–68. Representative from Maryland; served as a Democrat in Congress, 1895–97.

Cox, William Elijah. Born September 6, 1861, Birdseye, Indiana. LL.B., 1889. Representative from Indiana; served as a Democrat in Congress, 1907–21.

Cramton, Louis Convers. Born December 2, 1875, Hadley Township, Michigan. LL.B., 1899. Representative from Michigan; served as a Republican in Congress, 1913–31.

Crumpacker, Maurice Edgar. Born December 19, 1896, Valparaiso, Indiana. A.B., 1909. Representative from Oregon; served as a Republican in Congress, 1925–29.

Cunningham, Paul. Born June 15, 1890, Indiana County, Pennsylvania. A.B., 1914, LL.B., 1915. Representative from Iowa; served as a Republican in Congress, 1941– .

Currie, Gilbert Archibald. Born September 19, 1882, Midland Township, Michigan. LL.B., 1905. Representative from Michigan; served as a Republican in Congress, 1917–21.

Cutcheon, Byron M. Born May 11, 1836, Pembroke, New Hampshire. A.B., 1861, A.M., 1866, LL.B., 1866. Representative from Michigan; served as a Republican in Congress, 1883–91.

Darragh, Archibald Bard. Born December 23, 1840, La Salle Township, Michigan. A.B., 1868. Representative from Michigan; served as a Republican in Congress, 1901–09.

Davis, Cushman Kellogg. Born June 16, 1838, Henderson, New York. A.B., 1857. Senator from Minnesota; served as a Republican in the Senate, 1887–1900.

Day, Stephen. Born July 13, 1882, Canton, Ohio. A.B., 1905. Representative from Illinois; served as a Republican in Congress, 1941–45.

Denby, Edwin. Born February 18, 1870, Evansville, Indiana. LL.B., 1896. Representative from Michigan; served as a Republican in Congress, 1905–11.

DeVries, Marion. Born August 15, 1865, near Woodbridge, California. LL.B., 1888. Representative from California; served as a Democrat in Congress, 1897–1901.

Diekema, Gerrit John. Born March 27, 1859, Holland, Michigan. LL.B., 1883. Representative from Michigan; served as a Republican in Congress, 1907–11.

Dodds, Francis Henry. Born June 9, 1858, Louisville, New York. LL.B., 1880. Representative from Michigan; served as a Republican in Congress, 1909–13.

Downey, Sheridan. Born March 11, 1884, Laramie, Wyoming. LL.B., 1907. Senator from California; served as a Democrat in the Senate, 1939– .

Duffey, Warren Joseph. Born January 24, 1886, Toledo, Ohio. LL.B., 1911. Representative from Ohio; served as a Democrat in Congress, 1933–37.

Evans, Robert Emory. Born July 15, 1856, Coalmont, Pennsylvania. LL.B., 1886. Representative from Nebraska; served as a Republican in Congress, 1919–23.

Ferguson, Homer. Born February 25, 1889, Harrison City, Pennsylvania. LL.B., 1913. Senator from Michigan; served as a Republican in the Senate, 1943– .

Ferris, Woodbridge Nathan. Born January 6, 1853, Spencer, New York. Medical School, 1873–74. Senator from Michigan; served as a Democrat in the Senate, 1923–29.

Ford, George. Born January 11, 1846, South Bend, Indiana. LL.B., 1869. Representative from Indiana; served as a Democrat in Congress, 1885–87.

Fowler, Hiram Robert. Born February 7, 1851, near Eddyville, Illinois. LL.B., 1885. Representative from Illinois; served as a Democrat in Congress, 1911–15.

Fulkerson, Frank Ballard. Born March 5, 1866, near Edinburg, Missouri. Law School, 1890–91. Representative from Missouri; served as a Republican in Congress, 1905–7.

Gahn, Harry Conrad. Born April 26, 1880, Elmore, Ohio. LL.B.,

1904. Representative from Ohio; served as a Republican in Congress, 1921–23.

Gardner, John James. Born October 17, 1845, Atlantic County, New Jersey. Law School, 1866–67. Representative from New York; served as a Republican in Congress, 1893–1913.

Gibson, Ernest Willard. Born December 29, 1871, Londonderry, Vermont. Law School, 1898–99. Representative from Vermont; served as a Republican in Congress, 1923–33. Senator from Vermont; served as a Democrat in the Senate, 1933–40.

Gill, Joseph John. Born September 21, 1846, Barnesville, Ohio. LL.B., 1868. Representative from Ohio; served as a Republican in Congress, 1899–1905.

Gittins, Robert Henry. Born December 14, 1869, Oswego, New York. LL.B., 1900. Representative from New York; served as a Democrat in Congress, 1913–15.

Good, James William. Born September 24, 1866, near Cedar Rapids, Iowa. LL.B., 1893. Representative from Iowa; served as a Republican in Congress, 1909–21.

Gordon, William. Born December 15, 1862, near Oak Harbor, Ohio. LL.B., 1893. Representative from Ohio; served as a Democrat in Congress, 1913–19.

Gorman, James Sedgwick. Born December 28, 1850, Lyndon Township, Michigan. LL.B., 1876. Representative from Michigan; served as a Democrat in Congress, 1891–95.

Griffin, Levi Thomas. Born May 23, 1837, Clinton, New York. A.B., 1857, A.M., 1860. Representative from Michigan; served as a Democrat in Congress, 1893–95.

Hadley, William Flavius. Born June 15, 1847, near Collensville, Illinois. LL.B., 1871, A.M., 1898. Representative from Illinois; served as a Republican in Congress, 1895–97.

Harding, John Eugene. Born June 27, 1877, Excello, Ohio. LL.B., 1900. Representative from Ohio; served as a Republican in Congress, 1907–9.

Hare, Darius Dodge. Born January 9, 1843, near Adrian, Ohio. Law School, 1866–68. Representative from Ohio; served as a Democrat in Congress, 1891–95.

Harlan, Byron Berry. Born 1886, Greenville, Ohio. LL.B., 1909. Representative from Ohio; served as a Democrat in Congress, 1931–39.

Harter, Dow Watters. Born January 2, 1885, Akron, Ohio. LL.B.,

1907. Representative from Ohio; served as a Democrat in Congress, 1933–43.

Haugen, Nils Pedersen. Born March 9, 1849, Modum, Norway. LL.B., 1874. Representative from Wisconsin; served as a Republican in Congress, 1887–95.

Hayes, Walter Ingalls. Born December 9, 1841, Marshall, Michigan. LL.B., 1863. Representative from Iowa; served as a Democrat in Congress, 1887–95.

Helvering, Guy Tresillian. Born January 10, 1878, Felicity, Ohio. LL.B., 1906. Representative from Kansas; served as a Democrat in Congress, 1913–19.

Henderson, Charles Belknap. Born June 8, 1873, San Jose, California. LL.B., 1895, LL.M., 1896. Senator from Nevada; served as a Democrat in the Senate, 1918–21.

Hill, Lister. Born December 29, 1894, Montgomery, Alabama. Law School, 1915. Representative from Alabama; served as a Democrat in Congress, 1923–38. Senator from Alabama; served as a Democrat in the Senate, 1938– .

Hinshaw, Carl. Born July 28, 1894, Chicago, Illinois. College of Literature, Science and the Arts, 1916–17. Representative from California; served as a Republican in Congress, 1939– .

Holmes, Adoniram Judson. Born March 2, 1842, Wooster, Ohio. LL.B., 1867. Representative from Iowa; served as a Republican in Congress, 1883–89.

Hubbell, Jay Abel. Born September 15, 1829, Avon, Michigan. A.B., 1853. Representative from Michigan; served as a Republican in Congress, 1873–83.

Jefferis, Albert Webb. Born December 7, 1868, near Embreeville, Pennsylvania. LL.B., 1893. Representative from Nebraska; served as a Republican in Congress, 1919–23.

Johnson, Adna Romulus. Born December 14, 1860, Sweet Springs, Missouri. LL.B., 1887. Representative from Ohio; served as a Republican in Congress, 1909–11.

Jonkman, Bartel John. Born April 28, 1884, Grand Rapids, Michigan. LL.B., 1914. Representative from Michigan; served as a Republican in Congress, 1940– .

Keefe, Frank Bateman. Born September 23, 1887, Winneconne, Wisconsin. LL.B., 1910. Representative from Wisconsin; served as a Republican in Congress, 1939– .

Keightley, Edwin William. Born August 7, 1843, near Scott, Indiana.

LL.B., 1865. Representative from Michigan; served as a Republican in Congress, 1877–79.

Kelley, Patrick Henry. Born October 7, 1867, near Dowagiac, Michigan. LL.B., 1900. Representative from Michigan; served as a Republican in Congress, 1913–23.

Kendall, Joseph Morgan. Born May 12, 1863, West Liberty, Kentucky. Law School, 1881–82. Representative from Kentucky; served as a Democrat in Congress, 1892–93, 1895–97.

Kern, John Worth. Born December 20, 1849, Alto, Indiana. LL.B., 1869. Senator from Indiana; served as a Democrat in the Senate, 1911–17.

Kerr, Winfield Scott. Born June 23, 1852, Monroe, Ohio. LL.B., 1879. Representative from Ohio; served as a Republican in Congress, 1895–1901.

Kimball, Harry Mahlon. Born August 27, 1878, Orland, Indiana. LL.B., 1904. Representative from Michigan; served as a Republican in Congress, 1935.

King, William Henry. Born June 3, 1863, Fillmore City, Utah. LL.B., 1887. Representative from Utah; served as a Democrat in Congress, 1897–1901. Senator from Utah; served as a Democrat in the Senate, 1917–41.

Kinkaid, Moses Pierce. Born January 24, 1856, near Morgantown, West Virginia. LL.B., 1876. Representative from Nebraska; served as a Republican in Congress, 1903–23.

Kirkpatrick, Snyder Solomon. Born February 21, 1848, near Mulkey, Illinois. Law School, 1866–67. Representative from Kansas; served as a Republican in Congress, 1895–97.

Kraus, Milton. Born June 26, 1866, Kokomo, Indiana. LL.B., 1886. Representative from Indiana; served as a Republican in Congress, 1917–23.

Laird, James. Born June 20, 1849, Fowlerville, New York, LL.B., 1871. Representative from Nebraska; served as a Republican in Congress, 1883–89.

Landis, Frederick. Born August 18, 1872, Sevenmile, Ohio. LL.B., 1895. Representative from Indiana; served as a Republican in Congress, 1903–7.

Larson, Oscar John. Born May 20, 1871, Uleaborg, Finland. LL.B., 1894. Representative from Minnesota; served as a Republican in Congress, 1921–25.

Leavitt, Scott. Born June 16, 1879, Elk Rapids, Michigan. Literary

Department, 1899–1900. Representative from Montana; served as a Republican in Congress, 1923–33.

Lehr, John Camillus. Born November 18, 1878, Monroe, Michigan. LL.B., 1900. Representative from Michigan; served as a Democrat in Congress, 1933–35.

Lentz, John Jacob. Born January 27, 1856, St. Clairsville, Ohio. A.B., 1882. Representative from Ohio; served as a Democrat in Congress, 1897–1901.

Lindbergh, Charles August. Born January 20, 1859, Stockholm, Sweden. LL.B., 1883. Representative from Minnesota; served as a Republican in Congress, 1907–17.

Lucking, Alfred. Born December 18, 1856, Ingersoll, Canada. LL.B., 1878. Representative from Michigan; served as a Democrat in Congress, 1903–5.

McCumber, Porter James. Born February 3, 1858, Crete, Illinois. LL.B., 1880. Senator from North Dakota; served as a Republican in the Senate, 1899–1923.

McGowan, Jonas Hartzell. Born April 2, 1837, Smithtown, Ohio. B.S., 1861, LL.B., 1868. Representative from Michigan; served as a Republican in Congress, 1877–81.

McLaughlin, James Campbell. Born January 26, 1858, Beardstown, Illinois. LL.B., 1883. Representative from Michigan; served as a Republican in Congress, 1907–31.

McMillen, Rolla C. Born October 5, 1880, Monticello, Illinois. LL.B., 1906. Representative from Illinois; served as a Republican in Congress, 1943– .

Main, Verner Wright. Born December 16, 1885, Ashley, Ohio. J.D., 1914. Representative from Michigan; served as a Republican in Congress, 1935–37.

Mapes, Carl Edgar. Born December 26, 1874, near Kalamo, Michigan. LL.B., 1899. Representative from Michigan; served as a Republican in Congress, 1913–31.

Marland, Ernest W. Born May 8, 1874, Pittsburgh, Pennsylvania. LL.B., 1893. Representative from Oklahoma; served as a Democrat in Congress, 1933–35.

Martin, Eben Wever. Born April 12, 1855, Maquoketa, Iowa. Law School, 1879–80. Representative from South Dakota; served as a Republican in Congress, 1901–13.

Maybury, William Cotter. Born November 20, 1848, Detroit, Michigan. A.M., 1870, LL.B., 1871. Representative from Michigan; served as a Democrat in Congress, 1883–87.

Mays, James Henry. Born June 29, 1868, Morristown, Tennessee. LL.B., 1895, LL.M., 1896. Representative from Utah; served as a Democrat in Congress, 1915–21.

Means, Rice W. Born November 16, 1877, St. Joseph, Missouri. LL.B., 1901. Senator from Colorado; served as a Republican in the Senate, 1924–27.

Meiklejohn, George de Rue. Born August 26, 1857, Weyauwega, Wisconsin. LL.B., 1880. Representative from Nebraska; served as a Republican in Congress, 1893–1903.

Mercer, David Henry. Born July 9, 1857, Benton County, Iowa. LL.B., 1882. Representative from Nebraska; served as a Republican in Congress, 1885–87.

Mesick, William Smith. Born August 26, 1856, Newark, New York. Law School, 1880–81. Representative from Michigan; served as a Republican in Congress, 1897–1901.

Michener, Earl Cory. Born November 30, 1876, Attica, Ohio. Law School, 1900–01. Representative from Michigan; served as a Republican in Congress, 1919– .

Moffatt, Seth Crittenden. Born August 10, 1841, Battle Creek, Michigan. LL.B., 1863. Representative from Michigan; served as a Republican in Congress, 1885–87.

Murphy, James William. Born April 17, 1858, Platteville, Wisconsin. LL.B., 1880. Representative from Wisconsin; served as a Democrat in Congress, 1907–09.

Needham, James Carson. Born September 17, 1864, Carson City, Nevada. LL.B., 1889. Representative from California; served as a Republican in Congress, 1899–1913.

Newberry, John Stoughton. Born November 18, 1826, Waterville, New York. A.B., 1847, A.M., 1854. Representative from Michigan; served as a Republican in Congress, 1879–81.

Noonan, Edward Thomas. Born October 23, 1861, Macomb, Illinois. LL.B., 1883. Representative from Illinois; served as a Democrat in Congress, 1899–1901.

O'Neall, John Henry. Born October 30, 1838, Newberry, South Carolina. LL.B., 1864. Representative from Indiana; served as a Democrat in Congress, 1887–91.

Otjen, Theobald. Born October 27, 1851, West China, Michigan. LL.B.,

1875. Representative from Wisconsin; served as a Republican in Congress, 1895–1907.

Owens, James W. Born October 24, 1837, Springfield Township, Indiana. Law School, 1864–65. Representative from Ohio; served as a Democrat in Congress, 1889–93.

Packard, Jasper. Born February 1, 1832, Austintown, Ohio. A.B., 1855. Representative from Indiana; served as a Republican in Congress, 1869–75.

Palmer, Thomas Witherell. Born January 25, 1830, Detroit, Michigan. A.B., 1849. Senator from Michigan; served as a Republican in the Senate, 1883–89.

Person, Seymour. Born February 2, 1879, Livingston County, Michigan. LL.B., 1901. Representative from Michigan; served as a Republican in Congress, 1931–33.

Peters, Samuel Ritter. Born August 16, 1842, Walnut Township, Ohio. LL.B., 1867. Representative from Kansas; served as a Republican in Congress, 1883–91.

Pettibone, Augustus Herman. Born January 21, 1835, Bedford, Ohio. A.B., 1859. Representative from Tennessee; served as a Republican in Congress, 1881–87.

Phelps, William Wallace. Born June 1, 1826, Oakland County, Michigan. A.B., 1846, A.M., 1854. Representative from Minnesota; served as a Democrat in Congress, 1858–59.

Pickler, John Alfred. Born January 24, 1844, near Salem, Indiana. LL.B., 1872. Representative from South Dakota; served as a Republican in Congress, 1889–97.

Plumley, Frank. Born December 17, 1844, Eden, Vermont. Law School, 1867–1868. Representative from Vermont; served as a Republican in Congress, 1909–15.

Quarles, Joseph Very. Born December 16, 1843, Kenosha, Wisconsin. A.B., 1866. Senator from Wisconsin; served as a Republican in the Senate, 1899–1905.

Reeves, Henry Augustus. Born December 7, 1832, Sag Harbor, New York. Literary Department, 1848–51. Representative from New York; served as a Democrat in Congress, 1869–71.

Rice, John Birchard. Born June 23, 1832, Fremont, Ohio. M.D., 1857. Representative from Ohio; served as a Republican in Congress, 1881–83.

Scott, Frank Douglas. Born August 25, 1875, Alpena, Michigan.

LL.B., 1901. Representative from Michigan; served as a Republican in Congress, 1915–27.

Shafroth, John Franklin. Born June 9, 1854, Fayette, Missouri. B.S., 1875. Representative from Colorado; served as a Republican in Congress, 1895–97, Silver Republican and Democrat in Congress, 1897–1905. Senator from Colorado; served as a Democrat in Senate, 1913–19.

Sharp, William Graves. Born March 14, 1859, Mount Gilead, Ohio. LL.B., 1881. Representative from Ohio; served as a Democrat in Congress, 1909–15.

Shively, Benjamin Franklin. Born March 20, 1857, Osceola, Indiana. LL.B., 1886. Representative from Indiana; served as a Democrat in Congress, 1887–93. Senator from Indiana; served as a Democrat in the Senate, 1909–16.

Smith, John McMunn. Born February 6, 1853, Belfast, Ireland. Literary Department, 1878–80. Representative from Michigan; served as a Republican in Congress, 1911–23.

Smith, Samuel William. Born August 23, 1852, Independence Township, Michigan. LL.B., 1878. Representative from Michigan; served as a Republican in Congress, 1897–1915.

Snover, Horace Greeley. Born September 21, 1847, Romeo, Michigan. A.B., 1869, LL.B., 1871. Representative from Michigan; served as a Republican in Congress, 1895–99.

Stearns, Ozora Pierson. Born January 15, 1831, DeKalb, New York. B.S., 1858, LL.B., 1860. Senator from Minnesota; served as a Republican in the Senate, January 23 to March 3, 1871.

Stout, Byron Gray. Born January 12, 1829, Richmond, New York. A.B., 1851, A.M., 1854. Representative from Michigan; served as a Democrat in Congress, 1891–93.

Sutherland, George. Born March 25, 1862, Buckinghamshire, England. LL.B., 1892. Representative from Utah; served as a Republican in Congress, 1901–03. Senator from Utah; served as a Republican in the Senate, 1905–17.

Sweet, Edwin Forrest. Born November 21, 1847, Dansville, New York. LL.B., 1874. Representative from Michigan; served as a Democrat in Congress, 1911–13.

Swift, Oscar William. Born April 11, 1869, Hollow, New York. Literary Department, 1888–90. Representative from New York; served as a Republican in Congress, 1915–19.

Tarsney, John Charles. Born November 7, 1845, Medina, Michigan.

LL.B., 1869. Representative from Missouri; served as a Democrat in Congress, 1889–96.

Tarsney, Timothy Edward. Born February 4, 1849, Ransom, Michigan. LL.B., 1872. Representative from Michigan; served as a Democrat in Congress, 1885–89.

Taylor, Edward Thomas. Born June 19, 1858, Metamora, Illinois. LL.B., 1884. Representative from Colorado; served as a Democrat in Congress, 1909–43.

Thomas, Charles Spalding. Born December 6, 1849, Darien, Georgia. LL.B., 1871. Senator from Colorado; served as a Democrat in the Senate, 1913–21.

Thomas, Henry Franklin. Born December 17, 1843, Tompkins, Michigan. M.D., 1868. Representative from Michigan; served as a Republican in Congress, 1893–97.

Towne, Charles Arnette. Born November 21, 1858, near Pontiac, Michigan. Ph.B., 1881. Representative from Minnesota; served as a Republican in Congress, 1895–97. Senator from Minnesota; served as a Democrat in the Senate, 1900–1901. Representative from New York; served as a Democrat in Congress, 1905–07.

Townsend, Charles Elroy. Born August 15, 1856, near Concord, Michigan. Literary Department, 1877–78. Representative from Michigan; served as a Republican in Congress, 1903–11. Senator from Michigan; served as a Republican in the Senate, 1911–23.

Vandenberg, Arthur H. Born March 22, 1884, Grand Rapids, Michigan. Law School, 1901–02. Senator from Michigan; served as a Republican in the Senate, 1928– .

Vincent, Bird J. Born March 6, 1880, near Clarkston, Michigan. LL.B., 1905. Representative from Michigan; served as a Republican in Congress, 1923–31.

Warner, William. Born June 11, 1840, Shullsburg, Wisconsin. Law School, 1861. Representative from Missouri; served as a Republican in Congress, 1885–89. Senator from Missouri; served as a Republican in the Senate, 1905–11.

Wasielewski, Thaddeus Francis. Born December 2, 1904, Milwaukee, Wisconsin. A.B., 1927. Representative from Wisconsin; served as a Democrat in Congress, 1941–47.

Waterman, Charles W. Born in Waitsfield, Vermont. LL.B., 1889. Senator from Colorado; served as a Republican in the Senate, 1927–33.

Weadock, Thomas Addis Emmet. Born January 1, 1850, Ballygarrett, Ireland. LL.B., 1873. Representative from Michigan; served as a Democrat in Congress, 1891–95.

Webster, John Stanley. Born February 22, 1877, Cynthiana, Kentucky. Law School, 1897–99. Representative from Washington; served as a Republican in Congress, 1919–23.

Wedemeyer, William Walter. Born March 22, 1873, near Lima Township, Michigan. B.L., 1894, LL.B., 1895. Representative from Michigan; served as a Republican in Congress, 1911–13.

Weichel, Alvin F. Born September 29, 1893, Cleveland, Ohio. A.B., 1922, LL.B., 1924. Representative from Ohio; served as a Republican in Congress, 1943– .

Weideman, Carl May. Born March 5, 1898, Detroit, Michigan. College of Literature, Science and the Arts, 1914–19. Representative from Michigan; served as a Democrat in Congress, 1933–35.

Welch, Adonijah Strong. Born April 12, 1821, East Hampton, Connecticut. A.B., 1846, A.M., 1850. Senator from Florida; served as a Republican in the Senate, 1868–69.

Welty, Benjamin Franklin. Born August 9, 1870, near Bluffton, Ohio. LL.B., 1896. Representative from Ohio; served as a Democrat in Congress, 1917–21.

Wharton, Charles Stuart. Born April 22, 1875, Aledo, Illinois. Law School, 1894–96. Representative from Illinois; served as a Republican in Congress, 1905–7.

Wheeler, Burton Kendall. Born February 27, 1882, Hudson, Massachusetts. LL.B., 1905. Senator from Montana; served as a Democrat in the Senate, 1923–47.

Wheeler, Hamilton Kinkaid. Born August 5, 1848, Ballston Township, New York. LL.B., 1872. Representative from Illinois; served as a Republican in Congress, 1893–95.

Whitacre, John Jefferson. Born December 28, 1860, Decatur, Nebraska. LL.B., 1887. Representative from Ohio; served as a Republican in Congress, 1911–15.

White, John Daugherty. Born January 16, 1849, near Manchester, Kentucky. LL.B., 1872. Representative from Kentucky; served as a Democrat in Congress, 1875–77, 1881–85.

Whitelaw, Robert Henry. Born January 30, 1854, Essex County, Virginia. Law School, 1872–73. Representative from Missouri; served as a Democrat in Congress, 1890–91.

Whiting, Justin Rice. Born February 18, 1847, Bath, New York. Literary Department, 1863–65. Representative from Michigan; served as a Democrat in Congress, 1887–95.

Wiley, Alexander. Born May 26, 1884, Chippewa Falls, Wisconsin. College of Literature, Science, and the Arts, 1904–6. Senator from Wisconsin; served as a Republican in the Senate, 1938– .

Willits, Edwin. Born April 24, 1830, Otto, New York. A.B., 1855, A.M., 1858. Representative from Michigan; served as a Republican in Congress, 1877–83.

Wilson, Edgar. Born February 25, 1861, Armstrong County, Pennsylvania. LL.B., 1884. Representative from Idaho; served as a Republican in Congress, 1895–97, 1899–1901.

Wilson, William Warfield. Born March 2, 1868, Ohio, Illinois. LL.B., 1928. Representative from Illinois; served as a Republican in Congress, 1903–13, 1915–21.

Wood, Thomas Jefferson. Born September 30, 1844, Athens County, Ohio. LL.B., 1867. Representative from Indiana; served as a Democrat in Congress, 1883–85.

Wood, William Robert. Born January 5, 1861, Oxford, Indiana. LL.B., 1882. Representative from Indiana; served as a Republican in Congress, 1915–33.

Yoder, Samuel Sampson. Born August 16, 1841, Berlin, Ohio. Medical Department, 1866–67. Representative from Ohio; served as a Democrat in Congress, 1887–91.

Thomas M. Cooley

Charles I. Walker

James V. Campbell

Alumni in the Judiciary

By Edward S. Rogers

As Thomas M. Cooley wrote in *To Wit*, the annual of the law class of 1894, "The Law Department of Michigan University has always been in a high sense what its founders meant it should be—a truly national school." He pointed out that students were then present from practically all the states and territories and from five foreign countries. "So they come and go," he wrote, "and as they go each of them, it is hoped and believed, carries with him respect for law and order, and gives important aid in distributing the blessings of good government throughout the globe."

The original faculty of 1859 was composed of James V. Campbell, LL.D. 1866, a justice of the Supreme Court of Michigan, Charles I. Walker, LL.D. 1874, a practicing lawyer of Detroit, and Thomas M. Cooley, LL.D. 1873, of Adrian. Later, Ashley Pond, A.B. 1854, and Charles A. Kent, LL.D. 1899, of Detroit, and still later William P. Wells, of Detroit, and Alpheus Felch, of Ann Arbor, were added—a distinguished group opening the way for their distinguished successors.

Justice William R. Day, B.S. 1870, *law* 1871–72, LL.D. 1898, observed in 1911 at the National Dinner in his honor in New York:

> How many thousands of lawyers of this country have carried with them a lasting influence from the character and conduct of that great constitutional lawyer, Thomas M. Cooley? How many careers have been shaped in the legal profession by the inspiration of his example? Who looks back over the upturned furrows of the years but will acknowledge how much he owes to the example as well as to the

instruction of such great lawyers and great men as Cooley and Campbell and Walker and Kent?

Those who knew Judge Cooley in the evening of his life always think of him as a frail and gentle old man with a high thin voice. I picture him in 1895 in a wing chair in the bay window of his house on State Street, where the Union Building now stands, sitting for the portrait bust which was to be the gift of the law class of 1895 to the University. Lorado Taft was busy with the modeling clay and a sculptor's queer-looking tools. The old judge was not well and was a little feeble. Taft wanted to get animation for his portrait, and it was a part of my job to induce the judge to talk about his experiences when he practiced law at Adrian, or Tecumseh and Toledo, the early days of the Law Department, his work on the Supreme Court of Michigan, and as chairman of the Interstate Commerce Commission to which he was appointed by President Cleveland in the spring of 1887. Then his face lighted up, and Taft worked furiously until the light grew dim again. It is hard for us who knew him in the evening of his life to realize that when he first came to the Law Department he was only thirty-five.

When the Law Department was established in 1859, Cooley was for a time secretary, and later he succeeded Judge Campbell as dean (1871). It was thought to be important to have a professor who was a resident of Ann Arbor, and Judge Cooley accordingly moved there from Adrian. Judge Campbell, as the first dean, delivered his inaugural address on October 8, 1859. The next morning, Professor Walker gave the first formal law lecture. The three men who composed the faculty seem to have been elected without any previous consultation, and they were left to their own devices in arranging a curriculum. The three worked together harmoniously until Walker's resignation in 1876.*

Constitutional law, with which the name of Professor Cooley was ultimately to be so intimately associated, was not included

* Walker returned to his professorship from 1879–81 and again from 1886–87.

in the instruction during the first year of the existence of the Law Department. The two-year curriculum arranged in advance, made provision, however, for its being offered the second year. There was considerable discussion among the three professors as to which man should give the course. Cooley thought that Judge Campbell was the best qualified to teach the subject. When Judge Campbell declined and Walker would have none of it either, Cooley reluctantly agreed to prepare the lectures for the course. Accordingly, in the fall of 1860, he started the lectures in constitutional law which later formed the basis for his famous work, *Constitutional Limitations*, first published in 1868.

The course of instruction embraced two terms of six months each, and this was increased in 1884 to two terms of nine months. All instruction was by lectures. There were six series of lectures—three each term. The lecture period was two hours. Two distinct lectures were given in each period, with a short interval between them to let the students get the kinks out of their fingers, which must have been cramped from note-taking. To the lawyers trained during the twentieth century, the nineteenth-century practice of taking notes of slowly elaborated and enunciated lectures appears antiquated indeed. Each course must have seemed labored and tedious. At the end of the term as conditions to graduation there were an oral examination and a thesis. That the early graduates of the department have attained eminence is a tribute to the men who taught them and to the endurance of those they taught. It required a sturdy and persistent student to bear the punishment one had to take. If a man could endure so much to become a lawyer, the hardships of practice held no terrors.

Andrew C. McLaughlin, A.B. 1882; LL.B. 1885; LL.D. 1912, says of Judge Cooley:

> His lectures were characteristically clear, thoroughly organized, and so straightforward and even apparently simple, that the art and drudgery involved in preparation were concealed from the listener. They were commonly written and read to his classes. They were con-

densed, terse and telling; but, doubtless because of their very merits, the students often failed to realize that they were being led unerringly by a master.

We are fortunate in having among the student lecture notes preserved in the Michigan Historical Collections of the University a particularly complete notebook kept by an early student, Walter O. Balch, *law* 1866, of Kalamazoo, Michigan. His account of his first classroom experience as a law student is uniquely interesting:

The members of the Law Department assembled in their room on Monday morning October 3d 1864, and were called to order by Professor Thomas M. Cooley, who urged in the strongest terms, strict attention to the lectures to be delivered during the term, and he also said that this Law School was founded for the purpose of inculcating a thorough knowledge of the principles of Law, as well as to give forth a plan for the practice of these principles, when the student should go forth to mingle in the active duties of life.

He said there was no better illustration of the honor that the profession brought with it than to enter our courts, and there could be seen evidences of its workings, there could be seen honorable counsel engaged upon either side of a cause, striving for the interests of their clients, and what was more an upright judge presiding over the whole, each too, striving for truth and justice. As to the students manner of conduct, he thought it would not be necessary to speak, for he had this to remark that the law students as a class conducted themselves as gentlemen should do. He said: Statute Laws consist in the enactments of the State Legislature, and that the great body of the Law in this country is the English Common Law; it has means of determining, how real estate should be transferred, and also the manner of the passing of personal estate. Common Law was derived from the customs of the English, but the customs of nations change and therefore the laws change. The advancement of the nation caused a change in the Laws, but Common Law adapts itself to the uses of the people. Roads used by the people were governed by the law of corporations. Rules were changed in regard to the control of Rail Roads. Statute Law steps in and changes the Common Law. There were different varieties of Courts, Common Law Courts, Chancery and Admiralty Courts. Statutes not easily used on account of their construction, a code of rules has sprung up for the regulation of the Common Law.

The use of the Law School is to inculcate investigation. The course adopted is the same as used in all the Law Schools of the United States. He said there would be a Moot Court held once a week for the purpose of discussing such questions as should be given out by the professors, these were to be conducted by Seniors, one upon a side. A day or two after the discussion the Professor would decide the cause. It was customary to appoint a reporter from among their numbers, to write down the case and its decision and to have it placed in the library for after-reference. Papers were to be prepared, and read before the class, and the aid of any of the professors would be freely given in correcting all errors, and pointing out benefits. Finally he would say that the course before us was a difficult one, and if from the mass of indigestible lectures that were to be given, we could derive benefit he was truly certain, that he for one would certainly be made happy. He then dismissed the class asking us to be prompt in coming in, and to make our appearance to-morrow at half past ten o'clock A.M.

According to Burke A. Hinsdale's *History of the University of Michigan,** the first class, graduating in 1860, numbered twenty-four. Growth was rapid, however; the enrollment was 260 in 1865, 308 in 1870, 345 in 1880, 262 in 1885, and 533 in 1890.

At first there was no building for the Law Department. The lectures were delivered in the old chapel in the north wing and the law books were in the University Library. A new building to serve the entire needs of the Law Department was dedicated in October, 1863, with an address by Judge Cooley.

The ideal of the school was never essentially changed. The first announcement stated that its purpose was "to give a course of instruction that would fit young gentlemen for practice of the law in any part of the country." It was originally and still is a national school.

Apart from the many eminent practitioners who did not become judges, it is significant that at times a tenth of the members of the federal judiciary received their education at

* Edited by Isaac N. Demmon, A.B. 1868, A.M. 1871, (Ann Arbor, Michigan: Published by the University, 1906).

the University of Michigan, and the list of graduates who have sat in the upper courts of the various states is an impressive one. The record of seventy-two Michigan alumni * who served in the federal judiciary is as follows:

Achi, William Charles. Born July 1, 1889, Honolulu, Hawaii. Attended St. Louis College (Honolulu), 1904; Oahu College (Honolulu), 1908; Stanford, 1909–11; Yale, 1911–12; University of Chicago, 1912–13; University of Michigan, A.B. 1914, LL.B. 1917. United States Circuit Judge for the Fifth Circuit of Hawaii, 1919–34.

Adair, Jackson LeRoy. Born February 23, 1877, Clayton, Illinois. Attended Illinois State College; University of Michigan, LL.B., 1911. United States District Judge for the Southern District of Illinois, 1938– .

Aldrich, Edgar. Born February 5, 1848, Pittsburg, New Hampshire. University of Michigan, LL.B. 1868, LL.D. 1907, Dartmouth, A.M. 1891 (*hon.*), LL.D. 1901. United States District Judge for New Hampshire, 1891–1921.

Angell, Alexis Caswell. Born April 26, 1857, Providence, Rhode Island. University of Michigan, A.B. 1878, LL.B. 1880. Professor of Law, University of Michigan, 1893–98. United States District Judge for the Eastern District of Michigan, 1911–12.

Baker, Francis Elisha. Born October 20, 1860, Goshen, Indiana. Attended the University of Indiana; University of Michigan, A.B. 1882, LL.D. 1914; University of Colorado, LL.D. United States Circuit Judge for the Seventh Circuit, 1902–24; presiding judge, 1911–24.

Barnard, Job. Born June 8, 1844, Porter County, Indiana. Attended Valparaiso University; University of Michigan, LL.B. 1867, LL.D. 1907. Associate Justice of the Supreme Court of the District of Columbia, 1901–14.

Barnes, John Peter. Born March 15, 1881, Beaver County, Pennsylvania. Attended Geneva College, B.S. 1904, LL.D. 1936; University of Michigan, LL.B. 1907, LL.M. 1933 (*hon.*). United States District Judge for the Northern District of Illinois, 1931– .

* Owing to the difficulties in obtaining biographical data, this list is not complete. Those serving in the Cleveland era are indicated by italics.

Barnes, William H. Born 1843, Hampton, Connecticut. Attended Illinois College; University of Michigan, A.B. 1865. United States Associate Justice for the Supreme Court of the Territory of Arizona, 1885–93.

Bethea, Solomon Hicks. Born Lee County, Illinois. University of Michigan, B.S. 1872. United States District Judge for the Northern District of Illinois, 1905–09.

Booth, Fenton Whitlock. Born May 12, 1869, Marshall, Illinois. Attended DePauw University; University of Michigan, LL.B. 1892; Howard University, LL.D. 1923. Justice for the United States Court of Claims, 1905–39; Chief Justice, 1928–39.

Boynton, Charles Albert. Born November 26, 1867, East Hatley, Compton County, P.Q., Canada. Attended Glasgow Normal University (Kentucky), B.S. 1888; University of Michigan, LL.B. 1891. United States District Judge for the Western District of Texas, 1924– .

Brown, Henry Billings. Born March 2, 1836, Lee, Massachusetts. Attended Yale University, A.B. 1856; Harvard University; University of Michigan, LL.D. 1887. Lecturer, Admiralty Law, 1887–93. United States District Judge for the Eastern District of Michigan, 1875–90. Associate Justice of the Supreme Court of the United States, 1890–1906.

Burke, Thomas. Born December 22, 1849, Clinton County, New York. Attended University of Michigan, 1870–71, Law Department, 1871–72; Whitman College, LL.D. 1902. Chief Justice, Supreme Court of Washington Territory, 1888–89.

Burrows, Warren Booth. Born September 14, 1877, Groton, Connecticut. University of Michigan, LL.B. 1904. United States District Judge of Connecticut, 1928–30.

Cant, William Alexander. Born December 23, 1863, Westfield, Wisconsin. Attended Minnesota State Normal School; University of Michigan, LL.B. 1885. United States District Judge for Minnesota, 1923–33.

Carland, John Emmet. Born December 11, 1853, Oswego County, New York. University of Michigan, 1874–75. Associate Justice of the Supreme Court, 1888–89. United States District Judge for the District of South Dakota, 1896–1910. United States Circuit Judge, serving on the United States Commerce Court, 1910–12. United States Circuit Judge for the Eighth Circuit, 1913–22.

Clark, Chase A. Born August 21, 1883, Hadley, Indiana. University of Michigan, Law Department, 1903–4. United States District Judge of Idaho, 1943– .

Cotteral, John Hazelton. Born September 26, 1864, Middletown, Indiana. University of Michigan, 1883–84; Oklahoma City University, LL.D. 1924. United States District Judge for the Western District of Oklahoma, 1907–28. United States Circuit Judge for the Eighth Circuit, 1928–33.

Crumpacker, Jonathan Williams. Born 1856. Medical Department, 1871–72. Justice, Supreme Court of the Territory of New Mexico, 1898–1904.

Day, William Louis. Born August 13, 1876, Canton, Ohio. Attended Williston Seminar, 1896; University of Michigan, LL.B. 1900. United States District Judge for the Northern District of Ohio, 1911–14.

Day, William Rufus. Born April 17, 1849, Ravenna, Ohio. University of Michigan, B.S. 1870, Law Department, 1871–72, LL.D. 1898; New York University, LL.D. 1899. United States Circuit Judge for the Sixth Circuit, 1899–1903. Associate Justice of the Supreme Court of the United States, 1903–23.

Denison, Arthur Carter. Born November 10, 1861, Grand Rapids, Michigan. University of Michigan, LL.B. 1883, LL.D. 1916. United States District Judge for the Western District of Michigan, 1910–11. United States Circuit Judge for the Sixth Circuit, 1911–32. Presiding Judge, United States Court of Appeals, 1925–32.

DeVries, Marion. Born August 15, 1865, near Woodbridge, California. Attended San Joaquin Valley College, Ph.B. 1886; University of Michigan, LL.B. 1888. Associate Justice of the United States Court of Customs Appeals, 1910–22; Presiding Judge, 1921–22.

Donovan, Dennis Francis. Born April 9, 1889, Champion, Michigan. University of Michigan, LL.B. 1913. United States District Judge of Minnesota, 1945– .

Galbraith, Clinton Alexander. Born March 6, 1860, Hartsville, Indiana. Attended Hartsville College, A.B. 1883; University of Michigan, Law Department, 1883–84; Huntington College, LL.D. 1917. Associate Justice of the Supreme Court of the Territory of Hawaii, 1900–04.

Gilbert, William Ball. Born July 4, 1847, near Lewinsville, Virginia. Attended Williams College, A.B. 1868, LL.D. 1898; University of Michigan, LL.B. 1872. United States Circuit Judge for the Ninth Circuit, 1892–1931.

Hainer, Bayard Taylor. Born May 31, 1866, Columbia, Missouri. Attended Iowa State College, B.S. 1884; University of Michigan, LL.B. 1887. United States Judge for the Supreme Court of the Territory of Oklahoma, 1898–1907.

Harding, Justin Woodward. Born December 19, 1888, Franklin, Ohio. University of Michigan, LL.B. 1914. United States District Judge for the First Division of Alaska, 1929–33.

Hellenthal, Simon. Born July 18, 1877, Holland, Michigan. University of Michigan, LL.B. 1909. United States District Judge for the Third Division of Alaska, 1934–45.

Helvering, Guy Tresillian. Born January 10, 1878, Felicity, Ohio. Attended the University of Kansas; University of Michigan, LL.B. 1906. United States District Judge for Kansas, 1943– .

Holzheimer, William Andrew. Born September 29, 1870, Saginaw, Michigan. University of Michigan, LL.B. 1898. United States District Judge for the Second Division of Alaska, 1917–21.

Howe, Harland B. Born February 19, 1873, St. Johnsbury, Vermont. University of Michigan, LL.B. 1894. United States District Judge for Vermont, 1915–40.

Jenney, Ralph E. Born February 20, 1883, Detroit, Michigan. University of Michigan, A.B. 1904, LL.B. 1906. United States District Judge for the Southern District of California, 1937–45.

Johnson, Elias Finley. Born June 24, 1861, Van Wert, Ohio. University of Michigan, LL.B. 1890, LL.M. 1891. Assistant and Instructor, Law Department, 1890–96, Assistant Professor, 1896–97, Professor of Law, 1897–1901, University of Michigan. Associate Justice of the Supreme Court of the Philippine Islands, 1901–33.

Jones, Paul. Born November 4, 1880, Youngstown, Ohio. University of Michigan, LL.B. 1905, LL.M. 1932 (*hon.*). United States District Judge for the Northern District of Ohio, 1923– .

Joyce, Matthew M. Born April 29, 1877, Emmetsburg, Iowa. University of Michigan, 1895–97, Law Department, 1898–1900. United States District Judge for Minneapolis District, 1932– .

King, William Henry. Born June 3, 1863, Fillmore City, Utah. Attended Brigham Young Academy; University of Utah; University of Michigan, LL.B. 1887. Associate Justice of the Supreme Court of the Territory of Utah, 1894–97.

Knappen, Loyal Edwin. Born January 27, 1854, Hastings, Michigan. University of Michigan, A.B. 1873, A.M. 1876, LL.D. 1913. Regent, University of Michigan, 1904–11. United States District Judge for the Western District of Michigan, 1906–10. United States Circuit Judge for the Sixth Circuit, 1910–24.

Koscinski, Arthur A. Born April 1, 1887, Poland. University of Michigan, LL.B. 1910. United States District Judge for the Eastern District of Michigan, 1945– .

Lindsay (Junior), Alexander. Born October 29, 1871, Scotland. University of Michigan, LL.B. 1902. United States Circuit Judge for the Territory of Hawaii, 1905–10. Associate Justice of the Supreme Court of the Territory of Hawaii, 1922–26.

Lyons, Thomas Richard. Born March 19, 1867, Bendigo, Australia. Attended Whitmore College (Washington); Ottawa College (Canada); University of Michigan, 1888–90, LL.B. 1892. United States District Judge for the Territory of Alaska, 1909–13.

McAllister, Thomas Francis. Born March 4, 1896, Grand Rapids, Michigan. University of Michigan, A.B. 1918, LL.B. 1921. Member, Alumni Council, University of Michigan, 1940. Justice, United States Emergency Court of Appeals, 1945. United States Circuit Judge for the Sixth Circuit, 1941–45.

McVicar, Nelson. Born January 25, 1871, Chatham, Ontario, Canada. University of Michigan, Law Department, 1894–96. United States District Judge for the Western District of Pennsylvania, 1928– .

Malcolm, George Arthur. Born November 5, 1881, Concord, Michigan. University of Michigan, A.B. 1904, LL.B. 1906, J.D. 1921, (*hon.*); Hogaku Hakushi, Imperial University of Tokyo, Japan, LL.D. 1922. Associate Justice of the Supreme Court of the Philippine Islands, 1917–36.

Moinet, Edward Julien. Born July 14, 1873, Louisville, Ohio. University of Michigan, LL.B. 1895. United States District Judge for the Eastern District of Michigan, 1927– .

Murphy, Frank. Born April 13, 1893, Harbor Beach, Michigan. University of Michigan, LL.B. 1914, LL.D. 1939; postgraduate work, Lincoln's Inn, London, and Trinity College, Dublin. Associate Justice of the Supreme Court of the United States, 1940– .

Northcott, Elliot. Born April 26, 1869, Clarksburg, West Virginia. Attended Northwestern Academy (Clarksburg); McCabe's University School (Petersburg, Virginia); University of Michigan,

Law Department (special course), 1890–91. United States Circuit Judge for Fourth Circuit, 1927–39.

Parker, Frank Wilson. Born October 16, 1860, Sturgis, Michigan. University of Michigan, LL.B. 1880. Associate Justice for the Supreme Court of the Territory of New Mexico, 1898–1912.

Parsons, Charles Francis. Born January 18, 1872, Manakato, Minnesota. University of Michigan, LL.B. 1893. United States Circuit Judge for the Fourth Circuit of the Territory of Hawaii, 1904–16. Judge, Second Division, First Circuit Court of the Territory of Hawaii, February-October, 1926. Associate Justice, Supreme Court of the Territory of Hawaii, 1926–35.

Phillips, Orie Leon. Born November 20, 1885, near Viola, Illinois. Attended Knox College, 1903–4; University of Michigan, J.D. 1908, LL.D. 1935. Associate Justice of the Supreme Court of the Territory of New Mexico, 1912. United States District Judge of New Mexico, 1923–29. United States Circuit Judge for the Tenth Circuit, 1929– .

Picard, Frank A. Born October 19, 1889, Saginaw, Michigan. University of Michigan, LL.B. 1912. United States District Judge for the Eastern District of Michigan, 1939– .

Powers, Orlando Woodworth. Born June 16, 1851, Pultneyville, New York. Attended Sodus Academy; Marion Collegiate Institute; University of Michigan, LL.B. 1871. Associate Justice of the Supreme Court of the Territory of Utah, 1885–86.

Quarles, Joseph Very. Born December 16, 1843, Southport (now Kenosha), Wisconsin. University of Michigan, 1862–64, A.B. 1866, LL.B. 1867, LL.D. 1903. United States District Judge for the Eastern District of Wisconsin, 1905–11.

Raymond, Fred Morton. Born March 22, 1876, Berlin (now Marne), Michigan. University of Michigan, LL.B. 1899. United States District Judge for the Western District of Michigan, 1925–46.

Riner, John A. Born 1850, Preblo County, Ohio. University of Michigan, LL.B. 1879. United States District Judge for Wyoming, 1890–1925.

Rogers, Henry Wade. Born October 10, 1853, Holland Patent, New York. University of Michigan, A.B. 1874, A.M. 1877, Law Department, 1876–77; Wesleyan University, LL.D. 1890; Yale, A.M. 1907 (*hon.*); Northwestern University, LL.D. 1915. University of Michigan, Tappan Professor of Law, 1882–90; Dean, Department of Law, 1885–90; Professor of Roman Law, 1885–

90; Lecturer on Domestic Relations and Criminal Law, 1890–91. United States Circuit Judge for the Second Circuit, 1913–26.

Sessions, Clarence William. Born February 8, 1859, Ionia County, Michigan. University of Michigan, 1877–80. United States District Judge for the Western District of Michigan, 1911–31.

Shaw, Elwyn Riley. Born October 19, 1888, Lyndon, Illinois. University of Michigan, LL.B. 1910. United States District Judge for the Northern District of Illinois, 1944– .

Silliman, Reuben Daniel. Born May 17, 1871, Hudson, Wisconsin. University of Michigan, LL.B. 1894. United States Circuit Judge for the First Circuit of the Territory of Hawaii, 1900–01.

Simons, Charles C. Born May 21, 1876, Detroit, Michigan. University of Michigan, B.L. 1898, LL.B. 1900. United States District Judge for the Eastern District of Michigan, 1923–32. United States Circuit Judge for the Sixth Circuit, 1932– .

Slick, Thomas Whitten. Born July 5, 1869, South Bend, Indiana. University of Michigan, LL.B. 1893. United States District Judge for the Northern District of Indiana, 1925–43.

Starr, Raymond Wesley. Born August 24, 1888, Harbor Springs, Michigan. University of Michigan, LL.B. 1910; Detroit College of Law, J.D. (*hon.*) 1938; Ferris Institute, LL.D. 1945. District Judge for the Western District of Michigan, 1941– .

Sutherland, George. Born March 25, 1862, Stony Stratford, Buckinghamshire, England. Attended Brigham Young University, A.B. 1881; University of Michigan, 1882–83, LL.D. 1917; Columbia University, LL.D. 1913; George Washington University, LL.D. 1921. Associate Justice of the Supreme Court of the United States, 1922–38.

Swan, Henry Harrison. Born October 2, 1840, Detroit, Michigan. University of Michigan, 1858–62, A.M. 1891 (*hon.*), LL.D. 1902; Lecturer on Admiralty Law, 1893–1909. United States District Judge for the Eastern District of Michigan, 1891–1911.

Tarsney, John C. Born November 7, 1845, Medina, Michigan. University of Michigan, LL.B. 1869. Judge of the Supreme Court of the Territory of Oklahoma, 1897–1900.

Thayer, Rufus Hildreth. Born June 29, 1849, Plymouth, Michigan. University of Michigan, A.B. 1870, A.M. 1874, LL.D. 1911; Columbian University (now George Washington University), LL.B. 1873. Assistant Librarian, University of Michigan, 1870–71. Judge Advocate General of the National Guard of the District of

Columbia, 1894–1902. Judge, United States Court for China, 1909–13.

Thomas, Seth. Born May 18, 1873, Morgan County, Ohio. Attended Central Normal College (Indiana), 1896–97; University of West Virginia, 1898–1900; University of Iowa, Ph.B. 1904, A.M. 1906, LL.B. 1910; University of Michigan, summer sessions, 1907–08. United States Judge for the Eighth Circuit, 1935– .

Tuttle, Arthur J. Born November 8, 1868, Leslie, Michigan. University of Michigan, Ph.B. 1892, LL.B. 1895, LL.M. 1930 (*hon.*). United States District Judge for the Eastern District of Michigan, 1912–44.

Van Valkenburgh, Arba Seymour. Born August 22, 1862, Syracuse, New York. University of Michigan, A.B. 1884, LL.D. 1938; University of Missouri, LL.D. 1935. United States District Judge for the Western District of Missouri, 1910–25. United States Circuit Judge for the Eighth Circuit, 1925–44.

Waite, Byron Sylvester. Born September 27, 1852, Penfield, New York. University of Michigan, B.L. 1880. Judge, United States Customs Court, 1902–30.

Wanty, George Proctor. Born March 12, 1856, Ann Arbor, Michigan. University of Michigan, LL.B. 1878. United States District Judge for the Western District of Michigan, 1900–06.

Webster, John Stanley. Born February 22, 1877, Cynthiana, Kentucky. University of Michigan, 1897–99; Gonzaga University, LL.D. 1916. United States District Judge for the Eastern District of Washington, 1923–39.

The following list of one hundred and one men who have had training at Michigan and who have served their states in courts of last resort is only approximately complete. As in the list of federal judges, the names of those serving in the Cleveland era are printed in italics.

Anders, Thomas Jefferson. Born April 4, 1838, Bloomville, Ohio. University of Michigan, LL.B. 1861. Justice, Supreme Court of Washington, 1889–1904. Chief Justice, 1889–93.

Baker, Francis Elisha. Born October 20, 1860, Goshen, Indiana. University of Michigan, A.B. 1882, LL.D. 1914. Justice, Supreme Court of Indiana, 1895–1902.

Black, Charles Clarke. Born July 29, 1858, Mt. Holly, New Jersey. Princeton University, A.B. 1878, A.M. 1881; University of Michigan, Law Department, 1879–80. Justice, Supreme Court of New Jersey, 1914–30.

Blair, Charles Austin. Born April 10, 1854, Jackson, Michigan. University of Michigan, A.B. 1876, LL.D. 1909. Justice, Supreme Court of Michigan, 1905–12; Chief Justice, 1909.

Boggs, Carroll Curtis. Born October 19, 1843, Fairfield, Illinois. University of Michigan, 1862–63, Law Department, 1863–64. Justice, Supreme Court of Illinois, 1897–1906; Chief Justice, 1900–01.

Boyles, Emerson Richard. Born June 29, 1881, Chester, Michigan. University of Michigan, LL.B. 1903. Justice, Supreme Court of Michigan, 1940– .

Budge, Alfred. Born February 24, 1868, Providence, Utah. University of Michigan, LL.B. 1892, A.M. (*hon.*) 1919. Justice, Supreme Court of Idaho, 1914–41; Chief Justice, 1917–18, 1923, 1929, 1933–35, 1940–41.

Burch, Rousseau Angelus. Born August 4, 1862, Williamsport, Indiana. University of Michigan, LL.B. 1885, LL.D. 1924; Washburn College, LL.D. 1929. Justice, Supreme Court of Kansas, 1902–36; Chief Justice, 1935–36.

Burr, Alexander George. Born February 25, 1871, Pitrodie, Scotland. University of Michigan, LL.B. 1894, LL.M. (*hon.*) 1934; University of North Dakota, LL.D. 1938. Justice, Supreme Court of North Dakota, 1926–34; Chief Justice, 1934– .

Butler, Charles Cicero. Born February 6, 1865, Milwaukee, Wisconsin. University of Michigan, LL.B. 1891. Justice, Supreme Court of Colorado, 1927–37.

Butzel, Henry Magnus. Born May 24, 1871, Detroit, Michigan. University of Michigan, Ph.B. 1891, LL.B. 1892, LL.D. 1942. Justice, Supreme Court of Michigan, 1929– ; Chief Justice, 1939.

Callaway, Llewellyn Link. Born December 15, 1868, Tuscola, Illinois. University of Michigan, 1886–87, LL.B. 1891. Chief Justice, Supreme Court of Montana, 1922–35.

Campbell, James Valentine. Born February 25, 1823, Buffalo, New York. University of Michigan, LL.D. 1866; Marshall Professor of Law, 1859–85; Justice, Supreme Court of Michigan, 1858–90.

Carpenter, William L. Born November 9, 1854, Orion, Michigan. Michigan Agricultural College, B.S. 1875; University of Michi-

WHY MICHIGAN AND THE CLEVELAND ERA WAS WRITTEN

This copy of **Michigan and the Cleveland Era** comes to you through the University of Michigan Press with the compliments of the Michigan Historical Collections, 156-168 Rackham Building, University of Michigan, Ann Arbor, Michigan.

Our country has for more than three hundred years been engaged in developing an educational system, culminating in the colleges and universities, public and private. The success of such a program is properly measured by the degree to which it contributes enlightened leadership to the communities, large or small, which provide its support. In the present volume a group of alumni of the University of Michigan have collaborated to show how one institution, at one period in American history, provided from among its graduates and faculty members a generous measure of leadership in a variety of important public functions. The collected result will, we trust, provide further evidence that American higher education justifies by its output the effort which has gone into its establishment and continued support.

MICHIGAN HISTORICAL COLLECTIONS
UNIVERSITY OF MICHIGAN

gan, LL.B. 1878, LL.D. 1913. Justice, Supreme Court of Michigan, 1902–08.

Carr, Leland W. Born September 29, 1883, Livingston County, Michigan. University of Michigan, LL.B. 1906. Circuit Court of Ingham County, 1921–45. Justice, Supreme Court of Michigan, 1945– .

Carter, Joseph Newton. Born March 12, 1843, Hardin County, Kentucky. Illinois College, B.S. 1866, LL.D. 1894; University of Michigan, LL.B. 1868. Justice, Supreme Court of Illinois, 1894–1903; Chief Justice, 1898–99.

Cartwright, James Henry. Born December 1, 1842, Maquoketa, Iowa Territory. University of Michigan, LL.B. 1867. Justice, Supreme Court of Illinois, 1895–1924.

Cassoday, John Bolivar. Born July 7, 1830, Herkimer County, New York. University of Michigan, 1855–57; Beloit College, LL.D. 1881; University of Wisconsin, LL.D. 1905. Justice, Supreme Court of Wisconsin, 1880–1907; Chief Justice, 1895–1907.

Champlin, John Wayne. Born February 17, 1831, Kensington, New York. University of Michigan, LL.D. 1887; Professor of Law, 1891–96. Justice, Supreme Court of Michigan, 1884–91.

Clark, George Maitland. Born April 6, 1874, Nicholsville, Ohio. University of Michigan, LL.B. 1903. Justice, Supreme Court of Michigan, 1919–25.

Cochrane, John McDowell. Born 1850, Franklin County, Pennsylvania. University of Michigan, LL.B. 1881. Justice, Supreme Court of North Dakota, 1902–04.

Conrey, Nathaniel Parrish. Born June 30, 1860, Franklin County, Indiana. University of Michigan, LL.B. 1883; DePauw University, A.B. 1881, A.M. 1884. Justice, Supreme Court of California, 1935–36.

Cooley, Thomas McIntyre. Born January 6, 1824, Attica, New York. University of Michigan, LL.D. 1873; Harvard University, LL.D. 1886. University of Michigan, Jay Professor of Law, 1859–84; Professor of Constitutional Law and Medical Jurisprudence, 1861–65; Professor of American History and Constitutional Law, 1885–98. Justice, Supreme Court of Michigan, 1864–85.

Corfman, Elmer Ellsworth. Born March 2, 1865, Toledo, Iowa. University of Michigan, LL.B. 1890. Justice, Supreme Court of Utah, 1917–23.

Day, Robert Henry. Born July 8, 1867, Ravenna, Ohio. University of Michigan, 1885–88, Law Department, 1888–89; University of Cincinnati, LL.B. 1891. Justice, Supreme Court of Ohio, 1923–33.

Dean, James Renwick. Born September 15, 1862, St. Louis, Missouri. University of Michigan, LL.B. 1885. Justice, Supreme Court of Nebraska, 1908–10, 1917–35.

Dethmers, John R. Born October 15, 1903, Plesis, Iowa. University of Michigan, LL.B. 1927. Chief Assistant Attorney General, 1943–44. Attorney General, 1944. Justice, Supreme Court of Michigan, 1946– .

Drew, James Byron. Born April 27, 1877, Pittsburgh, Pennsylvania. University of Michigan, Law Department, 1896–97; Columbia University, LL.B. 1900, A.M. 1900; DuQuesne University, LL.D. 1917. Justice, Supreme Court of Pennsylvania, 1931– .

Eberly, George Agler. Born February 9, 1871, Fort Wayne, Indiana. University of Michigan, LL.B. 1892, LL.M. 1893. Justice, Supreme Court of Nebraska, 1925–43.

Elkin, John Pratt. Born January 11, 1860, West Mahoning Township, Pennsylvania. Indiana Normal School of Pennsylvania, M.E. 1880; Lafayette College, A.M. 1892; University of Michigan, LL.B. 1884. Justice, Supreme Court of Pennsylvania, 1904–15.

Elliott, Victor Alanson. University of Michigan, Law Department, 1860–61. Justice, Supreme Court of Colorado, 1889–95.

Eschweiler, Franz Chadbourne. Born September 6, 1863, Houghton, Michigan. University of Michigan, 1885–86; Marquette University, LL.D. 1918. Justice, Supreme Court of Wisconsin, 1916–29.

Evans, Robert Emory. Born July 15, 1856, Coalmont, Pennsylvania. University of Michigan, LL.B. 1886. Justice, Supreme Court of Nebraska, 1925.

Fead, Louis Henry. Born May 2, 1877, Lexington, Michigan. University of Michigan, LL.B. 1900, LL.D. 1934; Olivet College, LL.D. 1928. Justice, Supreme Court of Michigan, 1928–37.

Galen, Albert John. Born January 16, 1876, Three Forks, Montana. University of Michigan, LL.B. 1897; University of Notre Dame, LL.B. 1896. Justice, Supreme Court of Montana, 1921–33.

Goss, Evan Benson. Born December 8, 1872, Rockford, Michigan. University of Michigan, LL.B. 1894, LL.M. 1895. Justice, Supreme Court of North Dakota, 1910–16.

Grant, Claudius B. Born October 25, 1835, Lebanon, Maine. University of Michigan, A.B. 1859, A.M. 1862, Law Department, 1865–

66, LL.D. 1891. Justice, Supreme Court of Michigan, 1890–1909.

Hanson, Ephraim. Born March 10, 1872, Ephraim City, Utah. University of Michigan, LL.B. 1898. Justice, Supreme Court of Utah, 1929–38.

Harris, Lawrence Thomas. Born September 13, 1873, Albany, Oregon. University of Oregon, A.B. 1893; University of Michigan, LL.B. 1896. Justice, Supreme Court of Oregon, 1915–25.

Hart, William Lincoln. Born February 5, 1867, Salinerville, Ohio. Mount Union College, A.B. 1895, LL.D. 1929; University of Michigan, LL.B. 1897. Justice, Supreme Court of Ohio, 1934, 1939– .

Haselton, Seneca. Born 1848, Westford, Vermont. University of Vermont, A.B. 1871, A.M. 1874, LL.D. 1909; University of Michigan, LL.B. 1875, Instructor in Mathematics, 1873–74. Justice, Supreme Court of Vermont, 1910–21.

Herrick, Lott Russell. Born December 8, 1871, Farmer City, Illinois. University of Illinois, B.L. 1892; University of Michigan, LL.B. 1894. Justice, Supreme Court of Illinois, 1933–37.

Holland, Eldridge Vanleer. Born November 10, 1880, Jefferson County, Kansas. University of Michigan, Law Department, 1903–04. Justice, Supreme Court of Colorado, 1933–39.

Holloway, William Lawson. Born November 8, 1867, Kirksville, Missouri. University of Michigan, LL.B. 1892. Justice, Supreme Court of Montana, 1902–26.

Hooker, Frank Arthur. Born January 16, 1844, Hartford, Connecticut. University of Michigan, LL.B. 1865. Justice, Supreme Court of Michigan, 1893–1911.

Horton, Albert Howell. Born March 12, 1837, Brookfield, New York. University of Michigan, 1856–58, LL.D. 1889. Chief Justice, Supreme Court of Kansas, 1877–95.

Howard, Timothy Edward. Born January 27, 1837, Northfield, Michigan. University of Michigan, 1855–56; University of Notre Dame, A.B. 1862, A.M. 1864, LL.D. 1893. Justice, Supreme Court of Indiana, 1893–99.

Kinne, La Vega George. University of Michigan, LL.B. 1868; Western College (Iowa), LL.D. Justice, Supreme Court of Iowa, 1894–98.

Knauf, John. Born April 5, 1868, Waterloo, Michigan. University of Michigan, LL.B. 1892. Justice, Supreme Court of North Dakota, 1906.

Lairy, Moses Barnett. Born August 13, 1859, Cass County, Indiana.

University of Michigan, LL.B. 1889. Justice, Supreme Court of Indiana, 1915–20.

Lawrence, Edwin Apollo. Born May, 1827, Monroe, Michigan. University of Michigan, A.B. 1845. Justice, Supreme Court of Michigan, 1857.

Main, John Fleming. Born September 10, 1864, Mercer County, Illinois. Princeton University, A.B. 1891, LL.D. 1926; University of Michigan, 1895–97, LL.D. 1937. Justice, Supreme Court of Washington, 1912–25; Chief Justice, 1923–25.

Marston, Isaac. University of Michigan, LL.B. 1864. Justice, Supreme Court of Michigan, 1875–89.

Martin, Clarence Reuben. Born December 10, 1886, near Aberdeen, Ohio. University of Indiana, LL.B. 1906; University of Michigan, LL.B. 1907. Justice, Supreme Court of Indiana, 1927–32; Chief Justice, 1928–31.

Matthews, John Aaron. University of Michigan, LL.B. 1899. Justice, Supreme Court of Montana, 1919–20, 1925–37.

Maxey, George Wendell. Born February 14, 1878, Forest City, Pennsylvania. University of Michigan, A.B. 1902; University of Pennsylvania, LL.B. 1906. Justice, Supreme Court of Pennsylvania, 1931– ; Chief Justice, 1943– .

McAllister, Thomas Francis. Born March 4, 1896, Grand Rapids, Michigan. University of Michigan, A.B. 1918, LL.B. 1921. Justice, Supreme Court of Michigan, 1938–41.

McAlvay, Aaron Vance. Born July 19, 1847, Ann Arbor, Michigan. University of Michigan, A.B. 1868, LL.B. 1869, LL.D. 1910; Professor of Law, 1897–1903. Justice, Supreme Court of Michigan, 1904–15.

McDonald, John Samuel. Born February 8, 1865, Ontario, Canada. University of Michigan, LL.B. 1891. Justice, Supreme Court of Michigan, 1922–33.

McGrath, John Wesley. Born 1842, Philadelphia, Pennsylvania. University of Michigan, LL.B. 1868. Justice, Supreme Court of Michigan, 1891–95.

Moore, Joseph B. Born November 3, 1845, Commerce, Michigan. University of Michigan, Law Department, 1868–69; Hillsdale College, A.M. 1879, LL.D. 1903. Justice, Supreme Court of Michigan, 1896–1925.

Murphy, Loren Edgar. Born July 23, 1882, Cuba, Illinois. University of Michigan, LL.B. 1906. Justice, Supreme Court of Illinois, 1939– .

North, Walter Harper. Born November 1, 1871, Somerset, Michigan. Hillsdale College, A.B. 1896, A.M. 1899, LL.D. 1929; University of Michigan, LL.B. 1899, LL.D. 1942. Justice, Supreme Court of Michigan, 1927–45.

Ostrander, Russell Cowles. Born September 1, 1851, Ypsilanti, Michigan. University of Michigan, LL.B. 1876. Justice, Supreme Court of Michigan, 1905–19.

Parker, Frank Wilson. Born October 16, 1860, Sturgis, Michigan. University of Michigan, LL.B. 1880. Justice, Supreme Court of New Mexico, 1912–32; Chief Justice, 1919–20, 1923–29.

Person, Rollin Harlow. Born October 15, 1850, Livingston County, Michigan. University of Michigan, Law Department, 1872–73. Justice, Supreme Court of Michigan, 1915–16.

Potter, Charles Nelson. Born October 31, 1852, Cooperstown, New York. University of Michigan, LL.B. 1873. Justice, Supreme Court of Wyoming, 1895–1927; Chief Justice, 1897–1903, 1905–11, 1915–19.

Potter, William W. Born August 1, 1869, Barry County, Michigan. University of Michigan, LL.B. 1895; University of Detroit, LL.D. 1920. Justice, Supreme Court of Michigan, 1928–40; Chief Justice, 1935– .

Remick, James Waldron. Born October 30, 1860, Hardwick, Vermont. University of Michigan, LL.B. 1882; Dartmouth University, A.M. 1901 (*hon.*). Justice, Supreme Court of New Hampshire, 1901–04.

Reynolds, Frank Bernard. Born January 20, 1874, Quincy, Michigan. University of Michigan, 1891–93, LL.B. 1895. Justice, Supreme Court of Montana, 1921–22.

Rice, John Campbell. Born January 27, 1864, Cass County, Illinois. Illinois College, A.B. 1885, A.M. 1888, LL.D. 1935; University of Michigan, Law Department, 1888–89; Cornell University, LL.B. 1890. Justice, Supreme Court of Idaho, 1917–22; Chief Justice, 1921–22.

Richards, John Evan. Born July 7, 1856, San Jose, California. University of the Pacific, A.B. 1877; University of Michigan, LL.B. 1879, LL.D. 1927. Justice, Supreme Court of California, 1924–32.

Riddick, James Edward. Born August 29, 1849. Macon College, A.B.

1868; University of Michigan, LL.B. 1872. Justice, Supreme Court of Arkansas, 1894–1906.

Riner, William Addison. Born June 26, 1878, Greene, Iowa. University of Southern California, A.B. 1899; University of Michigan, LL.B. 1902. Justice, Supreme Court of Wyoming, 1928– .

Robinson, James E. University of Michigan, LL.B. 1868. Justice, Supreme Court of North Dakota, 1917–22.

Robinson, John Sherman. Born December 17, 1880, Mansfield, Ohio. University of Michigan, A.B. 1903; Columbia University, LL.B. 1910. Justice, Supreme Court of Washington, 1936– ; Chief Justice, 1941–43.

Rosenberry, Marvin Bristol. Born February 12, 1868, River Styx, Ohio. University of Michigan, LL.B. 1893, LL.D. 1926; Michigan State Normal College, A.M. 1941 (*hon.*); University of Wisconsin, LL.D. 1930; Marquette University, LL.D. 1938; Nashotah House, LL.D. 1942. Justice, Supreme Court of Wisconsin, 1916–22; Chief Justice, 1929– .

Rudolph, Herbert Blaine. Born May 22, 1894, Canton, South Dakota. University of South Dakota, A.B. 1916; University of Michigan, LL.B. 1918. Justice, Supreme Court of South Dakota, 1931– .

Sedgwick, Samuel Hopkins. Born March 12, 1848, Bloomingdale, Illinois. University of Michigan, Law Department, 1871–72. Justice, Supreme Court of Nebraska, 1902–07, 1910–20; Chief Justice, 1903–05.

Sharpe, Edward MacGlen. Born December 18, 1887, Bay County, Michigan. University of Michigan, LL.B. 1914. Justice, Supreme Court of Michigan, 1933– .

Shauck, John Allen. Born March 26, 1841, Richland County, Ohio. Otterbein College, A.B. 1866, A.M. 1869, LL.D. 1900; University of Michigan, LL.B. 1867. Justice, Supreme Court of Ohio, 1895–1914; Chief Justice, 1901– .

Shaw, Elwyn Riley. Born October 19, 1888, Lyndon, Illinois. University of Michigan, LL.B. 1910. Justice, Supreme Court of Illinois, 1933–42.

Shenk, John Wesley, Jr. Born February 7, 1875, Shelborne, Vermont. University of Michigan, J.D. 1903; Ohio Wesleyan University, A.B. 1900, LL.D. 1930. Justice, Supreme Court of California, 1924– .

Shields, John Calhoun. Born 1848. University of Michigan, LL.B.

1872. Chief Justice of the Supreme Court of the Territory of Arizona, 1886–87.

Smith, William Redwood. Born January 19, 1851, Peru, Illinois. University of Michigan, LL.B. 1872. Justice, Supreme Court of Kansas, 1899–1905.

Snow, Ernest Albert. Born April 15, 1875, Jackson County, Michigan. University of Michigan, LL.B. 1896. Justice, Supreme Court of Michigan, 1926–27.

Starr, Raymond W. Born August 24, 1888, Harbor Springs, Michigan. University of Michigan, LL.B. 1910; Detroit College of Law, J.D. 1938 (*hon.*); Ferris Institute, LL.D. 1945. Justice, Supreme Court of Michigan, 1941–46.

Steere, Joseph Hall. Born May 19, 1852, Addison, Michigan. University of Michigan, A.B. 1876, LL.D. 1920. Justice, Supreme Court of Michigan, 1911–27.

Steinert, William Joseph. Born March 7, 1880, Versailles, Kentucky. Central University of Kentucky, A.B. 1900; University of Michigan, LL.B. 1905. Justice, Supreme Court of Washington, 1932– ; Chief Justice, 1937–39.

Thurman, Samuel Richard. University of Michigan, 1879–80. Justice, Supreme Court of Utah, 1916–28; Chief Justice, 1927–28.

Travis, Julius Curtis. Born July 31, 1868, Pleasant Township, Indiana. University of Michigan, 1888–92, LL.B. 1894. Justice, Supreme Court of Indiana, 1921–33; Chief Justice, 1922–30.

Varian, Bertram Stetson. Born May 12, 1872, Unionville, Nevada. University of Michigan, 1891–94. Justice, Supreme Court of Idaho, 1929–32.

Vermilion, Charles William. Born November 6, 1866, Centerville, Iowa. University of Michigan, LL.B. 1889. Justice, Supreme Court of Iowa, 1923–27.

Watson, John Clinton. Born January 28, 1878, Alma, Michigan. University of Michigan, Ph.B. 1898, Law Department, 1899–1900. Supreme Court of New Mexico, 1924–34; Chief Justice, 1933–34.

Weadock, Thomas Addis Emmet. Born January 1, 1850, County Wexford, Ireland. University of Michigan, LL.B. 1873. Justice, Supreme Court of Michigan, 1933.

Webster, John Stanley. Born February 22, 1877, Cynthiana, Kentucky. University of Michigan, 1897–99; Gonzaga University,

LL.D. 1916. Justice, Supreme Court of Washington, 1916–18.

Wernette, Nicodemus. May 5, 1885, Remus, Michigan. University of Michigan, LL.B. 1907. Justice, Supreme Court of Idaho, 1933–35.

Whiting, Charles Sumner. Born May 25, 1863, Rochester, Minnesota. University of Michigan, 1887–88; University of Minnesota, LL.B. 1889. Justice, Supreme Court of South Dakota, 1908–22.

Williams, Roy Hughes. University of Michigan, LL.B. 1897. Justice, Supreme Court of Ohio, 1934– .

Young, John Elsworth. University of Michigan, 1886–87. Justice, Supreme Court of New Hampshire, 1898–1901, 1904–25.

Zollars, Allen. Denison University, A.B. 1863, A.M. 1867, LL.D. 1888; University of Michigan, LL.B. 1866. Justice, Supreme Court of Indiana, 1883–89.

By their decisions and public service, these men, trained in the University of Michigan, applied the law they had been taught by Judge Cooley and his colleagues and followed the example they had set. More important still, there had been impressed upon their still plastic minds the ideals so well expressed by Grover Cleveland in his address to the students at Ann Arbor on February 22, 1892:

"*You may be chosen to public office. Do not shrink from it, for holding office is also a duty of citizenship. But do not leave your faith behind you. Every public office, small or great, is held in trust for your fellow-citizens.*"

The Authors

ALEXANDER GRANT RUTHVEN, *Ph.D. 1906, LL.D., Sc.D., though a native of Iowa and a resident of that state until the completion of his college training at Morningside College, in 1903, has been a resident of Michigan ever since. He came immediately to the University of Michigan for graduate work in Zoology under Professor Jacob Reighard, and his career as a member of the staff began immediately after he obtained the doctorate. For more than twenty years he carried the dual role of teacher and museum administrator, becoming director of the University Museums in 1922 and chairman of the Department of Zoology in 1927. In 1928 he was made dean of administration of the University, and in 1929 became its president. Through his long association with the University, and particularly through his many years as its president, he has acquired an enviable record of acquaintance with Michigan graduates and is uniquely qualified to introduce to the public a book written by Michigan alumni about Michigan alumni.*

James Rowland Angell, A.B. 1890, A.M. 1891, LL.D. 1931, though he was born in Vermont and spent his entire professional career outside of Michigan, is nevertheless pre-eminently a Michigan man. From the age of two until he was twenty-two he lived in the President's house on the University campus, witnessing at closest range the first half of the enormously successful career of his father, President James Burrill Angell. Throughout his career as a University teacher, administrator, and counselor—at the University of Minnesota in 1893, at the University of Chicago from 1894 to 1919 (where he served as Dean from 1911 to 1919 and as acting president from 1918 to 1919), as president of the Carnegie Corporation from 1920 to 1921, and of Yale University from 1921 to 1937; as educational counselor of the National Broadcasting Company since 1937—his loyalty to his alma mater has been outstanding. His filial interest in his father's career has naturally been enhanced by his own experiences as the head of a great University. As an eleven-year-old-boy, he accompanied his parents to China during the mission described in the sketch of James Burrill Angell in this volume. This experience left with him a lasting impression of the importance of his father's diplomatic services and enabled him to contribute first-hand information about James Burrill Angell, diplomat.

EARL D. BABST, *Ph.B. 1893, LL.B. 1894, A.M. (hon.) 1911, began his college education at Kenyon College, in his native state of Ohio. Transferring to the University of Michigan in 1891, he soon found opportunity to indulge his interest in writing. He was correspondent of the* Chicago Inter-Ocean, *editor of the 1893* Palladium, *managing editor of the 1894* To Wit; *and editor of the western department of the* University Magazine, *of New York. He practiced law in Detroit and Chicago; in New York he was general counsel of the National Biscuit Company. In business, he was, from 1915 to 1925, president, and, has been since 1925, chairman of the American Sugar Refining Company. Always active in alumni affairs, he served as an officer of his city associations, and for many years on the executive committee of the Alumni Advisory Council of the general association and now as a director-at-large. In New York he was chief sponsor of the famous National Dinner of 1911, and has long been chairman of the Senior Advisory Council. In June, 1947, when the S. Spencer Scott Medal for Distinguished Alumni Service was first awarded, Mr. Babst was one of six singled out for this honor. In 1903, he married Alice Edwina Uhl, daughter of Edwin F. Uhl. Mrs. Babst died in 1945. Mr. Babst knew personally all except one of the subjects of the individual sketches of this volume, and hence was peculiarly well qualified to make suggestions as to authorship of the sketches, as well as to supply material for their content.*

F. Clever Bald, *A.B. 1920, Ph.D. 1943, transferred to the University of Michigan, following his service with the Twenty-eighth Division during the First World War; previously he had attended Mercersburg Academy and Franklin and Marshall College. After graduation from the University, he served for seven years as teacher, and then for three years as headmaster, of a private school for boys in Detroit. From 1932 to 1943 he was Professor of History and Government in the Detroit Institute of Technology. Meanwhile he pursued graduate study in history, and received the Ph.D. degree from the University in 1943. In that year he became Instructor in History; since early in 1945 he has, as University War Historian, been preparing a comprehensive account of the University's multiplicity of activities in World War II; in 1947 he was made Assistant Director of the Michigan Historical Collections. He is the author of a large number of articles on early Michigan history; a book,* Detroit's First American Decade 1796–1805, *is shortly to be published by the University Press. As a teacher and a scholar in Michigan history, he naturally found particular interest in the career of a Michigan educator, Edwin Willits, who essayed a role in political history.*

HENRY MOORE BATES, *Ph.B. 1890, LL.D. 1941, after coming to the University from his native Chicago, took his law training in Northwestern University, receiving the LL.B. degree in 1892. After practicing law in Chicago for eleven years, he became Tappan Professor of Law at the University of Michigan in 1903, and Dean of the Department of Law (now the Law School) from 1910 to his retirement in 1939. In 1917–18 he was Professor of Law in the Harvard Law School. Member and one-time officer of various legal associations, he was president of the Association of American Law Schools in 1912–13. Former students in the Law School remember him for his high standards of scholarship and of teaching and for his vigorous professional ideals; Michigan men of the first two decades of the present century, particularly, remember him for the great leadership he exercised in the movement leading to the establishment of the Michigan Union. Since Lawrence Maxwell, the subject of the sketch he has written for this volume, was a fellow-member of the Union Building committee, as well as a nonresident lecturer in the Law School, Dean Bates was the logical choice to write the sketch about him.*

HENRY EDWARD BODMAN, *Ph.B. 1896, began the practice of law in his native Toledo, a year after his graduation from the University. Moving to Detroit, he was from 1902 to 1919 a member of the firm of Angell, Bodman and Turner. Loyally attached to the University and active in Detroit alumni circles, he served on a committee for the Union Building campaign. Now a member of Bodman, Longley, Bogle, Middleton and Armstrong, he is also Vice President and General Counsel of the Packard Motor Car Company, director of the National Bank of Detroit, and of the Pennsylvania, Ohio and Detroit Railroad Company; general counsel of the Automotive Council of War Production and of the Automobile Manufacturers Association. His long residence in Detroit and his business and professional career there have given him an intimate knowledge of Detroit history, and a wide acquaintance with its leading citizens. Senator Thomas W. Palmer, the subject of the sketch he has written for this volume, was for almost the whole of his long life an important integral part of that history.*

BREWSTER P. CAMPBELL, *A.B. 1922, who came to the University from Detroit, was associated with* Chimes *and with the* Michigan Daily *throughout his campus career; as a senior he was managing editor of the* Daily. *He belonged to Sphinx, and to Michigamua. His career as a newspaperman began with the* Baltimore Evening Sun, *from which he went to the General Electric Company's* Schenectady Works News *as associate editor. After moving successively to Baton Rouge, Atlanta, and Mobile, he joined the staff of the* Detroit Free Press *in 1933 and now is its city editor. Since he is a native of Detroit and already a veteran on the* Free Press, *the life story of that newspaper's long-time owner and editor, William E. Quinby, has a strong attraction for him. With Edgar Guest, Jr., he has written the Quinby sketch for this volume.*

IRA A. CAMPBELL, *B.L. 1900, LL.B. 1902, was active in student publications, having been editor of the* University of Michigan Daily, *managing editor of the* Oracle, *University correspondent for the* Detroit Tribune *and occasionally for the Cleveland* Plain Dealer *and the* Chicago Inter-Ocean. *He was a member of the Athletic Association Board and treasurer of the Association. He was one of the organizers of the Triangle Club. Following his graduation from the law school he practiced law for sixteen years in Seattle and San Francisco, being a member of the firm of Page, McCutchen, Knight & Olney in San Francisco. He specialized in admiralty law. In 1918 and 1919 he was admiralty counsel to the United States Shipping Board and special assistant to the attorney general in admiralty. Washington, D.C. Since 1919 he has been in New York, where he is senior member of the firm of Kirlin, Campbell, Hickox & Keating. He is also an officer and director in several commercial and industrial firms, and an active member of the University of Michigan Club of New York.*

Fred Gray Dewey, *A.B. 1902, took a lively interest in campus affairs throughout his four years in the University. He was on the editorial board of the* Inlander, *held various offices in Adelphi, was vice-president of the Good Government Club, class president his senior year, a member of Toastmaster Club and Quadrangle, and was the first sachem of Michigamua. His entire post-university career has been spent in Detroit, where, following receipt of the LL.B. degree in 1905 from the Detroit College of Law, he has conducted a general law practice. He is an active member and a past secretary of the University of Michigan Club of Detroit. For twenty-three years following 1915 he was Professor of Evidence, first in the Detroit College of Law and then in Wayne University Law School. He has been active in Bar organizations, and is a past president of both the Detroit Bar Association and the State Bar of Michigan. Mr. Dewey's career as a Detroit lawyer did not begin until a year after the life of Henry T. Thurber, the subject of his sketch, came to a close. Nevertheless, similarity of environmental conditions and of professional interests has been a helpful factor in his presentation of an understanding portrayal of the career of his subject.*

EDGAR A. GUEST, JR., *A.B. 1934, returned to Detroit upon graduation from the University, and, starting as a reporter on the city news staff of the* Detroit Free Press, *remained with the paper for nearly ten years. During World War II he rose to the rank of Lieutenant in the Navy, and served for a time overseas. After the war he devoted his time to radio. He initiated the "In Our Opinion" program on WJR, and directs that station's special events broadcasting. From his father, Edgar Guest, one of the few remaining staff members of the* Free Press *who was on the paper during the regime of William E. Quinby, he has obtained information which has been particularly useful to him and to Mr. Brewster Campbell in the preparation of the sketch of the former owner-editor of the* Free Press.

PAUL ALLEN LEIDY, *A.B. 1909, A.M. 1911, J.D. 1924, had several years of experience as secretary of the Chamber of Commerce of Pontiac and as business manager of the* Michigan Alumnus, *before taking his legal training. Following graduation from the Law School, he practiced law in his native Toledo as a member of the firm of Miller, Brady, Yager, and Leidy, before returning to the University in 1926 to become a member of the faculty of the Law School, and its secretary until 1945. From 1943 until 1945, while on leave of absence from the University, he was associated in Chicago with William D. McKenzie, general counsel and vice-president of the Quaker Oats Company, with whom he has collaborated in writing the sketch of J. Sterling Morton. He returned to the University in September, 1945, to resume his duties as Professor of Law and to become placement director of the Law School, a position for which he is peculiarly well qualified by reason of the broad acquaintance with the personnel of the Bar acquired during his long period of service as secretary of the Law School.*

WILLIAM DEXTER MCKENZIE, *A.B. 1896, A.M. (hon.) 1936, was one of the earliest Michigan men to be able to claim a University background for both of his parents, his father, Judge James Wheeler McKenzie having received his law degree here in 1868, and his mother, Ruth Delia (Hemingway) McKenzie, having attended the University for a year. Following graduation from the University, where his distinctions had included playing first base on the University baseball team, and winning the University tennis championship, he spent five years teaching in a Chicago high school. In 1901, he became a member of the Chicago Bar; from 1928 to 1946 he was general counsel for the Quaker Oats Company; since 1934 he has been a vice-president of the company. He has been active in the life of his home community, having served as president of the New Trier Township High School Board and as President of the Village of Winnetka, Illinois. He has been for over thirty-five years a director of the University of Michigan Club of Chicago, and is a past director of the Alumni Association.*

ARTHUR POUND, *A.B. 1907, coming to the University from Pontiac, was throughout his campus career interested in student publications, reaching in his senior year the post of managing editor of the* Michigan Daily; *he was also managing editor of the* Inlander. *Following graduation, he worked on newspapers in Akron, Grand Rapids, and New York. In 1924–25 he was editor of the Atlantic Monthly Press; from 1924 to 1927, associate editor of* The Independent. *From 1935 to 1936 he was research professor of American history in the University of Pittsburgh. Active in various historical societies and historical projects, and for some years New York State historian, he has published a number of volumes with historical themes; in several instances he has concerned himself with Michigan subjects; one of his most recent volumes is* Lake Ontario *in the Great Lakes series. In 1937, at the celebration of the one hundredth anniversary of the University in Ann Arbor, he led a round table discussion on "Should the University Encourage Creative Art?"*

MARVIN B. ROSENBERRY, *LL.B. 1893, LL.D. 1926, a native of Ohio, attended the State Normal School at Ypsilanti (now Michigan State Normal College) for three years before entering the University. Obtaining his law degree, he began practicing at Wausau, Wisconsin. From 1902 to 1908 he served as city attorney. In 1916 he was appointed Justice of the Supreme Court of Wisconsin; in 1929 he was elected for a ten-year term, and was re-elected in 1939. He became Chief Justice in 1929. As one of the Law School's most distinguished alumni, he was invited to deliver an address at the dedication of the Law Quadrangle in 1934; in 1937 at the celebration of the one hundredth anniversary of the University in Ann Arbor, he participated in a program devoted to the theme "Higher Education in the World of Tomorrow," speaking on the subject "Higher Education in Government."*

Henry E. Riggs, *C.E. 1910, Eng.D. 1937, though born in Kansas and receiving his first degree from Kansas State University, A.B. 1886, has been identified with Michigan and the University of Michigan throughout most of his career. Six years (1890 to 1896) as chief engineer of the Toledo, Ann Arbor and North Michigan Railway and fifteen years of consulting practice preceded his long term (1912 to 1930) as Professor and Head of the Department of Civil Engineering in the University of Michigan. Retirement from this position by no means brought an end to his career as a Civil Engineer. He has remained an active member of the various national organizations representing his professional interest, serving as director, vice-president, and president of the American Society of Civil Engineers from 1932 to 1938. Though now residing in Evanston, Illinois, he maintains active interest in the University and its alumni. This distinguished leader among Michigan's Civil Engineers was obviously the logical alumnus to write the sketch of Alfred Noble.*

Edward Sidney Rogers, *LL.B. 1895, LL.M. (hon.) 1910, LL.D. 1930, who was born in Maine, came to the University from the Michigan Military Academy at Orchard Lake. Since graduation he has been practicing law in Chicago and New York, specializing in the law of unfair competition, trade-marks, and copyright. In 1947 he was elected chairman of the Board of the Brand Names Foundation, Inc. He is also chairman of the Board of Sterling Drug, Inc. As nonresident lecturer on the law of trademarks and copyright at the University, he is a regular visitor to the campus. He has held various offices in alumni associations and has been president of the Lawyers Club. As his sketch of "Michigan Men in the Judiciary" shows, he is much interested in the history of the Law School, which he has known at firsthand through more than half of the period of its existence.*

WILFRED BYRON SHAW, *A.B. 1904, came to the University from near-by Adrian. His graduation was followed by a brief experience as a newspaper reporter in Chicago; he then returned to the University as general secretary of the Alumni Association and editor of the* Michigan Alumnus. *This position he held for twenty-five years; since 1929 he has been director of the Bureau of Alumni Relations. He has also, since the establishment of the* Michigan Alumnus Quarterly Review *in 1934, served as its editor, and as its uniquely effective illustrator. He has published two books on the history of the University, and is editor of* The University of Michigan—an Encyclopedic Survey, *which is now in process of publication. He has been especially interested in that important one-third of the University's history which was spanned by the presidency of James Burrill Angell. His sketch of President Angell as a diplomat, written with the co-operation of Dr. James Rowland Angell, will be of particular interest to the many alumni who as students sat at the feet of President Angell in his courses in International Law.*

SHIRLEY WHEELER SMITH, *B.L. 1897, A.M. 1900, LL.D. 1945, began his long career as a University staff member in 1898, serving first as Instructor in English for three years, and then until 1904 as secretary of the University of Michigan General Alumni Association and editor of the* Michigan Alumnus. *Following four years in executive work with an insurance company, he returned to the University in 1908 to become its secretary until 1927, when his position was changed to that of secretary and business manager. In 1930 he became vice-president and secretary of the University, and held this position until his retirement in 1946. His loyal service to the University was formally recognized at Commencement in June, 1947, when he was one of the first six to be awarded the S. Spencer Scott Medal for Distinguished Alumni Service. His retirement from University duties has been followed by very active participation, as a member of the City Council, in the solution of the increasingly complex problems of Ann Arbor's government. The son of a Michigan alumnus (Judge Clement MacDonald Smith, LL.B. 1867), his loyalty to alumni interests is of long standing, and he has been a particularly interested contributor to this series of sketches about Michigan men of his father's generation.*

LEWIS GEORGE VANDER VELDE, *A.B. 1913, A.M. 1921, who began his undergraduate work at Hope College, and received his doctoral training at Harvard, became an instructor in the History Department of the University in 1928, and is now professor of history. He is at present engaged in the preparation of a biography of Thomas M. Cooley, about whom he has written a sketch for this volume. Since 1938 he has been director of the Michigan Historical Collections, which, established by the Regents in that year as a depository for manuscript and printed materials pertaining to the history of Michigan, naturally serves as the guardian unit of the records of the state's most important nonpolitical institution—the University itself. Among the University records on deposit in the Michigan Historical Collections—including faculty minutes, collections of the papers of individual members of the staff, records of student organizations, student lecture notes, files of the various student and University publications, pictures, programs of University events, letters and diaries of students and professors—are many sources which proved of great use in the preparation of the sketches comprising this volume on* Michigan and the Cleveland Era.